RECLAIMING
PUBLIC HOUSING

RECLAIMING PUBLIC HOUSING

A HALF CENTURY OF STRUGGLE IN
THREE PUBLIC NEIGHBORHOODS

Lawrence J. Vale

HARVARD UNIVERSITY PRESS

Cambridge, Massachusetts

London, England

2002

Copyright © 2002 by the President and Fellows of Harvard College

ALL RIGHTS RESERVED

Printed in the United States of America

Publication of this book was generously assisted by a grant from the Graham Foundation.

Library of Congress Cataloging-in-Publication Data

Vale, Lawrence J., 1959–
Reclaiming public housing : a half century of struggle in three public neighborhoods /
Lawrence J. Vale.
p. cm.
"This book is intended as a companion volume to
From the Puritans to the projects : public housing and public neighbors"—Pref.
Includes bibliographical references and index.
ISBN 0-674-00898-7 (alk. paper)
1. Public housing—Massachusetts—Boston—History.
2. Low-income housing—Massachusetts—Boston—History.
3. Housing policy—Massachusetts—Boston—History.
4. Poor—Massachusetts—Boston—History.
5. Urban renewal—Massachusetts—Boston—History.
6. Neighborhood—Massachusetts—Boston—History.
I. Title.

HD7288.78.U52 M483 2002
363.5′85′0974461—dc21
2002068598

CONTENTS

PREFACE

AYN RAND'S 1943 BESTSELLER, *The Fountainhead,* is not often characterized as a novel about public housing. Yet Rand's paean to the egoist-architect Howard Roark is singularly revealing about issues of high design and low-income people. When Roark is told that Cortlandt Homes—a fifteen-story public housing tower that he had designed—will represent a "noble deed" and a "humanitarian undertaking," he scoffs, saying: "Whatever we do don't let's talk about the poor people in the slums. They have nothing to do with it, though I wouldn't envy anyone the job of trying to explain that to fools. You see, I'm never concerned with my clients, only with their architectural requirements." Rand's anticollectivist diatribe reaches its climax when Roark, in righteous anger, dynamites Cortlandt because its architectural "integrity" had been compromised in the final execution by the alterations of other designers ("second-handers" who added such "incomprehensible features" as a gymnasium, individual balconies, extra doors at ground level, color, and bas-relief sculpture).

Roark goes on trial for his act of destruction and delivers his own defense: "I designed Cortlandt. I gave it to you. I destroyed it. I destroyed it because I did not choose to let it exist. It was a double monster. In form and implication. I had to blast both." The jury comes back with a verdict even before the courtroom has emptied—a resounding "not guilty."

Rand's novel prefigures the conservative backlash against all manner of government-subsidized social welfare programs. Rand captures the resentment of middle-class Americans who are "not incompetent enough" to warrant government aid, but find themselves squeezed between the rich who can afford good housing and the poor who are given subsidized gifts. Roark and Rand's rejection of public housing is made complete by the fact that Cortlandt, in its rebuilt and finished form, is turned over to a private development company.

My own book also examines the fate of American public housing since the 1940s, but does so principally from the perspective of the people whom Howard Roark so memorably disdained. It is a story of the struggles—by tenants, by designers and planners, and by housing authority staff—to sustain public housing projects as desirable living places and to *avoid* destroying them.

This book is intended as a companion volume to *From the Puritans to the Projects: Public Housing and Public Neighbors.* That book set out a broad institutional and intellectual history of public housing, whereas this one takes a more "bottom-up" perspective centered on public housing residents—emphasizing their activism, their coping mechanisms, and their partnerships with outside professionals.

This book is rooted in slowly nurtured relationships with tenant organizations at three housing developments. Although many past and present staff at the Boston Housing Authority (BHA) cooperated fully with requests for interviews and documents, the BHA was in no way a client or sponsor for this work. Rather, the book was financially supported entirely by a Guggenheim Fellowship, a grant from the Graham Foundation (which also provided a substantial publication subvention), and other seed funds from the Massachusetts Institute of Technology. I am most grateful for the full intellectual freedom provided by such support. To guarantee candor in the interviews with residents, especially, the research had to be perceived as entirely independent of the BHA.

I have followed each of the three housing developments since 1986, and have endeavored to reconstruct the broader social history of each place in the decades that preceded my own direct involvement. I particularly appreciate the efforts of three public housing residents—Bart McDonough, Sister Margaret Lanen, and Thelma Smith—who served as my principal points of entry into their communities, and who provided the sustained support necessary to gain the trust of the hundreds of other residents who agreed to be interviewed (see Note on Literature and Methods). I am also enormously grateful to the late Donald Rapp, a gifted tenant organizer who graciously lent me his voluminous files.

This book would have been impossible without the support of principal research assistants Sharon Greenberger, Kristen Harol, and Dan Serda, and additional help from Anne Beamish, Regina Blair, Charles Bradley, Carolyn Brown, Lisa Cole, David Fernandes, Alissa Herbst, Jamie Jencks, Anne Kinsella, Paul Lambert, Susan Lilly, Josephine Louie, Lisa Makuku, Noah Maslan, Carla Morelli Francazio, Tony Petropulos, Lisa Picard, Lisa Rosan, Warren Ross, Liz Shaw, Judy Su, George Samuels, Jeff Shumaker, Genevieve Vachon, and Andrew Weaver.

Rachel Bratt, Karen Franck, and Sam Bass Warner, Jr., provided detailed and invaluable comments on the full draft of this manuscript, and numerous other colleagues have provided salient advice over many years, including Phil Clay, Lois Craig, John Davis, John de Monchaux, Margaret dePopolo, Gayle Epp, Roberta Feldman, Bob Fogelson, Dennis Frenchman, Bernard Frieden, Gary Hack, Steve Hornburg, Langley Keyes, Jeff Lines, Peter Marcuse, Oscar Newman, Ellen Pader, Martin Rein, Ruth Rae, Bill Rohe, the late Lloyd Rodwin, Bish Sanyal, Amy Schectman, Wayne Sherwood, David Varady, and Dan Wuenschel.

At Harvard University Press, I am particularly grateful to former editor Jeff Kehoe, who steered *From the Puritans to the Projects* to publication and was an early champion of this volume, as well. Michael Aronson sustained enthusiasm for the project and coordinated the invaluable contributions made by three outside reviewers of the manuscript. I also greatly appreciate the editing skills of Christine Thorsteinsson.

Finally, for a project that dates all the way back to my first semester as a Master's student, I am grateful for the patience of the five new family members who have joined me in the intervening years: Julie Dobrow, my wife, and our children, Mira, Aaron, Jeremy, and Jonathan.

FIGURES AND TABLES

TABLES

O N E

Introduction: Reclaiming Public Housing

ACROSS THE UNITED STATES, local city officials have authorized the demolition of well over 100,000 units of public housing since 1993. They stage implosions and bulldozings with a level of gusto and ceremony curiously reminiscent of the ardor that once marked public housing construction a half-century before. Most Americans now view "the projects" as the country's least desirable domestic environments, and so welcome the spectacle of their demise.[1] Moreover, even those who defend continued government housing subsidies increasingly see large projects as a political liability. The Department of Housing and Urban Development (HUD) issues repeated proclamations touting its dramatic overhaul of public housing under its HOPE VI program.[2] Each document shows similar pairs of starkly juxtaposed images: a bleak and dilapidated flat-roofed, poverty-stricken project labeled "Before" and its companion set piece—a colorful pitched-roof, picket-fenced, mixed-income slice of Americana, labeled "After" (Figs. 1.1–1.2). On the basis of HUD data, researchers estimate that 11,000 units of public housing are being demolished each year, most of these previously occupied by residents earning less than 30 percent of the area's median income. When replacing these apartments with "mixed-income communities," housing authorities are mixing in only about 4,000 public housing units— and most of these are targeted to households with higher incomes than those of current housing residents.[3] In recent years, despite ongoing shortages of "afford-

FIGURE 1.1 Public housing implosions: a new national sport?

able housing" in many cities, frustrated policymakers of both major parties have stopped talking about how to expand public housing. Instead, they debate how best to eliminate it.

Before the dust settles, however, it is worth pausing to ask whether public housing can be salvaged.

Despite all the attention given to most egregious failures of the system, public housing has not faltered everywhere equally. This book resists the usual blanket judgments of failure by looking closely at three attempts to reclaim devastated public housing projects for continued occupancy by extremely low income households. Reclamation entails more than the process of staving off destruction and loss. It is also a forward-looking process premised on the desirability of re-use. So, too, it is a backward-looking exercise intended to reveal the underlying causes of decline. We cannot plan the future of public housing unless we know its past. Most public housing projects opened as places of hope. Even if this hope has been followed by a half-century of struggle, we cannot fully judge the future viability of public housing communities until we examine the full trajectory of their development. Reclaiming low-income public housing is much more difficult than eliminating it.

It is not enough to ask whether public housing projects can be salvaged; the

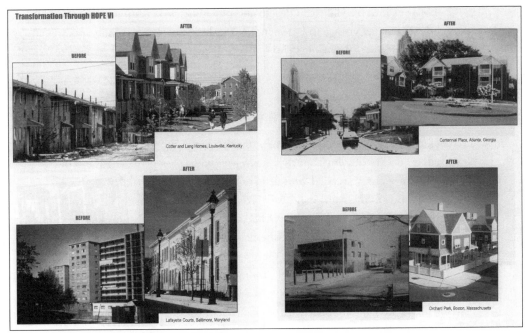

Transformation Through HOPE VI

Cotter and Lang Homes, Louisville, Kentucky

Centennial Place, Atlanta, Georgia

Lafayette Courts, Baltimore, Maryland

Orchard Park, Boston, Massachusetts

FIGURE 1.2 Public housing transformations under HUD's HOPE VI program

more pressing public policy question is whether they should be reclaimed for continued occupancy by extremely low income households. This is not something that can properly be answered in the abstract or the aggregate. Individual places matter. So do the particular residential communities that inhabit them. By examining the actions and reactions of residents who have worked with architects, planners, and housing authority officials to destigmatize public housing environments, this book investigates public housing in a neighborhood-specific and multifaceted way. A positive future for public housing and its residents will emerge only if the personal and institutional perspectives of all participants are examined together, and only if these are understood both as individual community struggles and as manifestations of deeply rooted societal ambivalence about the place of the poor in American cities.[4]

This book looks at public housing through the lens of neighborhood development, a commitment that necessarily entails bridging the individual disciplines from which public housing is usually observed. In the search to explain the often troubled but sometimes ennobling histories of specific housing projects, I examine the complex interplay between design and policy, between institutional structures and resident activism, and between historically grounded antagonisms and future prospects. If we are truly to "end public housing as we know it," we need to know it intimately.

PUBLIC HOUSING: CRITICS AND APOLOGISTS

Even before the disillusioned pioneer of public housing Catherine Bauer publicly lamented its "dreary deadlock" in 1957, there was widespread concern about the future of the program she called "not dead but never more than half alive."[5] Since 1957, painful postmortems of half-dead projects have proliferated. Nationwide, there are well over 3,000 separate local housing authorities—most of them very small and relatively untroubled—but the national media focus has understandably been on the largest 5 percent of these authorities, which collectively house two-thirds of the country's 1.3 million public housing households.[6] It is here, in some (but not all) of the large family projects of center-city America, that the most extreme public housing problems are concentrated, and this book is about these kinds of places. For decades, the American media have graphically conveyed the desperation of those who inhabit such projects; the dominant images have long been of crime, physical collapse, financial and managerial corruption, and economic decay. Almost always, public housing makes headlines for its deaths rather than for its lives. To all but those who live in public housing or who have made it the subject of their professional practice, the coping mechanisms of residents remain invisible. Their infrequent victories, whether large or small, go largely undocumented. This has begun to change as more attempts are made to analyze and report on the activism of residents; nonetheless, one scholarly review article that surveyed ninety-three pieces of writing about public housing was subtitled "The Dreadful Saga of a Durable Policy" and found almost no signs of life, notwithstanding the optimism of the earliest public housing reformers.[7] This book, too, deals metaphorically with questions about the "life" and "death" of public housing. Entering the anguished wards of the public policy intensive care unit, it is a search for evidence of project resuscitations. At least in some cases, it is still too soon for an autopsy.

Defending the projects is hardly a growth industry, unless one is in the home-security business. Still, many advocates of low-income housing continue to support conventional public housing (that is, public housing developed and owned by local public housing authorities), stressing its vital importance as a source of guaranteed long-term affordable housing in cities where such housing is at a premium. Some have gone so far as to suggest that the worst public housing problems are still quite narrowly concentrated in a subset of "problem projects," many of which could be revitalized by specially targeted redevelopment funds. As recently as 1992, the *Final Report of the National Commission on Severely Distressed Public Housing* (NCSDPH) concluded that only about 86,000 of the country's public housing units should be designated "severely distressed." This figure— constituting only about 6 percent of the total stock—certainly understated the case since it was based on a study that chiefly measured the physical distress of buildings and did not attempt to take account of the socioeconomic "severe distress" of residents.[8] The bricks-and-mortar problems of many public housing developments had become increasingly acute, but the National Commission and others were also rightly alarmed by the broader pattern of inadequate management and deepening resident poverty.

Those who championed the construction of public housing during the 1930s and 1940s would be startled and chagrined by what has transpired. These early "housers" saw the projects as the modern alternative to slums—enclaves of sturdy construction and carefully vetted households. Instead of cold-water flats and dark alleyways, public housing promised central heating, modern appliances, and wide-open spaces. Congress premised the whole system on the ability of tenant rents to cover operating expenses, and local authorities dutifully stocked the new projects with families who could afford to pay for this privilege. City officials built public housing to reward the worthiest among the temporarily poor, those who passed muster as good citizens and good investments. During the 1960s, however, public housing authorities shifted their mission.

Pressured by civil rights reforms that limited the capacity of local officials to maintain segregated projects or to reject single-parent households, public housing authorities increasingly accepted those deemed neediest among the permanently destitute. Meanwhile, the Housing Act of 1949 gave priority for admission to those displaced by urban-renewal actions, which disproportionately uprooted the poor and nonwhite. Gradually, public housing became viewed as a kind of coping mechanism rather than as a form of reward. Many upwardly mobile white families who once would have applied for public housing enjoyed new opportunities for federally guaranteed mortgages in the suburbs and no longer needed to rely on the increasingly stigmatized resource of "the projects." Low-income families with viable alternatives to project-based family public housing began abandoning it soon after they moved in or avoided applying for it altogether. In 1969 Congress acted to protect low-income tenants by capping public housing rents at 25 percent of income, but this well-intentioned act (known as the first Brooke Amendment) only further squeezed the fiscal viability of housing authorities, especially given that additional legislation needed to subsidize operating costs was slow to gain passage. The original financial premise of public housing proved completely unworkable during this era of diminished tenant rent-paying ability, rampant inflation, and deteriorating building systems. Partly as a result of the entrenched patronage machines that staffed big-city housing agencies, standards for project management and maintenance frequently plummeted. By the 1970s residents of most large American cities viewed public housing as housing of last resort. And then matters got even worse.

Between 1979 and 1984, the federal government accelerated this trend toward concentrated impoverishment by passing legislation that skewed public housing admissions to favor the least advantaged applicants. In 1979 Congress expanded federal preferences to include those who were living in "substandard housing" (a definition that later came to include the homeless), and, in 1981, legislators severely constrained the number of public housing units that could go to those earning more than half of the median income. Congress also increased the percentage of income that participant families would have to pay for rent from 25 to 30 percent, thereby undercutting the incentives for higher-earning families to remain in public housing. By 1984 Congress gave explicit preference to a broad array of disadvantaged applicants, encompassing the homeless, the disabled (including the mentally ill), and those paying more than 50 percent of their income in rent. The Reagan administration defended these federal preferences as a necessary recognition of the broader societal trends toward greater impoverishment and multiple problems among low-income persons needing housing assistance.[9] In the 1990s, however, such policies came under bipartisan criticism for having ghettoized the most vulnerable.

A half-century before, public housing had valiantly serviced the working poor, but now it struggled to house America's most desperate urban residents. As the 1990s ended, only about one in five public housing households reported earned wages as its primary source of income, and more than three-quarters of households were headed by a single female. Moreover, since the majority of public housing residents were black or Latino, the program as a whole faced increased political marginality, especially at a time when affirmative action programs were under sustained attack. The result of all this has been a convergence of increasing economic distress among residents, managerial incapacity, design failures, and budgetary contraction, all at a time of persistent violence, struggling public education, lingering racism, and inadequate job opportunities in inner cities. As a symbol and a symptom of these broader societal problems, public housing has been blamed for contributing to them. When public housing is viewed together with the bipartisan frontal assault on the welfare programs that had helped sustain a large proportion of its tenants, it is easy to see why this housing has so frequently been seen as a national failure.

Public Neighborhoods

A public housing project is more than a system of subsidized homes; it is a *public neighborhood.* In a society that still thinks of residential areas as bastions of compartmentalized privacy where community engagement is a valued but deliberate choice, a neighborhood that is meant to be *public* creates special strains. Most city neighborhoods are public in the sense that they are made accessible to outsiders without being gated or privately maintained, yet housing projects are public neighborhoods in two additional respects. Their public ownership and management imposes an unparalleled level of centralized control over both (1) the socioeconomic make-up of the community, and (2) the design of the neighborhood and its amenities (or lack thereof). Some of this centralized control is inherent in any kind of designed community—including "private housing projects" such as condominium complexes and gated suburban subdivisions targeted to particular market niches. However, public housing projects stand out precisely because they are located in central cities—places that are otherwise characterized by the ever-changing diversity of building forms, land uses, and people that emerges from the interplay of market forces and the richness of individual choices. Moreover, because such projects are public entities subject to a variety of local, state, and federal laws, these neighborhoods are uniquely sensitive to the vagaries of public policymaking.

Tenanting Public Neighborhoods

In all neighborhoods except those owned and managed by the public sector, residents rely on judgments of private landlords or bankers to confer legitimacy on newcomers, hoping that any outsider allowed in will have been vetted at least in terms of financial stability, if not for social acceptability. Those who live in neighborhoods of single-family, owner-occupied homes, in particular, often assume that a similarity of housing form and price will confer a similar commonality of income, lifestyle, and life-cycle stage—and ideally will yield a convergence of interests. When public housing began, public authorities were also able to deliver stable and reputable communities, fostered in large part by the intensity of their tenant-selection process and the enormity of their applicant pool. Once this selectivity was lost, however, public neighborhoods became uniquely vulnerable.

Slowly but inexorably, the publicly owned and centrally managed neighborhoods of large inner-city public housing projects abandoned the parallel institutional frameworks that once controlled access and mimicked private vetting mechanisms. Instead of a staff of housing authority "inspectors" armed with intimate reports on each potential tenant, public housing admissions fell prey to the machinations of an unseen bureaucracy that held little individualized knowledge about whom it housed. Instead of the patronage-driven networks of local politicians assisting constituents to find subsidized refuge in the project closest to their neighborhood of choice, the power to allocate public housing and to distribute public housing residents became increasingly vested in the mixed-messages of distant legislative acts aimed at racial desegregation, vacancy elimination, and reduction of homelessness. In the push to meet diverse (and often contradictory) public policy goals, the process for selection and assignment of tenants became dangerously attenuated. Tenants received placement in a project not because they wished to live in that particular place but because it was the only development where the Authority made their subsidy tenable. In choosing to follow a subsidy, tenants increasingly forfeited their choice of neighborhood. Once public housing became reconceptualized as a publicly funded resource for coping with the needs of the most desperate city-dwellers, public neighborhoods inevitably became treated as storage facilities rather than as communities.

Designing Public Neighborhoods

Public housing projects are also public neighborhoods in another sense. They are public not just in terms of their bureaucratic structure but also in terms of their urban form. Right from the start, public housing proponents explicitly sought to distinguish the projects as much as possible from surrounding areas. They strove to create independent enclaves that would be socioeconomically stronger and morally purer than the slums they replaced. The resultant places filtered out the temptations of bars, the dangers of cars, and the entire realm of commercial activity. Public housing designers, following government guidelines and ample European precedent, reconfigured the chaotic complexity of the urban world into architecturally homogeneous superblocks. Housing officials helped define each project as a separate neighborhood by assigning it a distinct name. Sometimes these names drew upon the existing names of adjacent areas, but even in such cases the project quickly gained its own informal moniker.

To some extent, these earliest public housing communities might better be described as *enclaves* rather than as neighborhoods, since their driving impulse was so pointedly antineighborhood. Still, given that these projects certainly represented an attempt to rethink the nature of neighborhoods (and drew upon aspects of Clarence Perry's influential thinking about the "neighborhood unit"), the term *public neighborhood* still seems useful. At the very least, it highlights the extent to which the construction of such distinct government-run residential areas carried spatial—as well as social—consequences. Precisely because so few privately constructed residential communities chose to imitate the urban design of the projects, this form quickly gained its persistent association with government-sponsored design. Even today, nearly every urban public housing project built between 1935 and 1970—whether high-rise or low-rise—remains instantly recognizable as a distinct type. The combination of flat roofs and streetless superblocks distanced public housing from the more desirable models of American domestic life, both urban and suburban. As the modernist conception of "towers in a park" gave way in recent decades to a rediscovery of the value of streets and street life as sources of both vitality and security, public housing projects became seen not as progressive enclaves of slum reform, but as discredited visions that carried many of the worst aspects of slum conditions to a new degree of degradation and isolation. Initially intended to highlight the superiority of a new kind of neighborhood, the same spatial distinctiveness would soon, less generously, be used to stigmatize both the projects and their inhabitants.

Unlike traditional urban and suburban streetscapes that clearly signaled the boundary between public streets and realms meant to be under private control, the public neighborhoods of the projects—especially those built after WW II—were increasingly left wide open to public access. As the federal manual *Public Housing Design* put it in 1945, "there is a current tendency to avoid what had heretofore been customary, namely to face the dwelling upon the street so as to present its pleasant aspects to public view and to screen what generally have been its less tidy and more unattractive elements." Abandoning their early preference for semi-enclosed courtyard schemes, the urban designers of public neighborhoods resolutely followed European precedents and postwar federal "Minimum Physical Standards" that stipulated certain minimum distances between buildings. These standards were intended to maximize the penetration of sunlight and prevailing summer breezes, an orientation that often overrode all other considerations, to the extent that project buildings were deliberately set at an angle to the pattern of streets in surrounding areas. Federal officials also explained this openness by noting that public neighborhoods were laid out "to afford the widest scope of view," ostensibly for the benefit of residents.[10] Yet the ability to look out also meant that others could look in, a factor duly appreciated by police departments at the time, who saw the projects as much more conducive to surveillance than were the narrow warrens of the slums they replaced.

In many cases, designers abandoned even vestigial efforts to present a street edge and deliberately sited their long buildings perpendicular to their perimeter streets. Even though this afforded "an unrestricted public view" into the project, it gave tenants "the largest degree of freedom from traffic noise and dangers." Such freedom, however, was not to last. Built as superblocks to keep automobile and truck through-traffic out of a residential environment, the open sites over time encouraged penetration by cars as well as by outside persons. Increasingly, as maintenance declined, many projects lost all semblance of sociospatial mediating devices like sidewalks, shrubbery, pathways, and front yards. Eventually, many public housing developments became virtually undifferentiated landscapes of asphalt that seemed to extend the public realm of the perimeter streets all the way through the project. In short, as public housing declined, its admissions procedures increasingly let in many less desirable persons as tenants, while the openness of its urban design seemed to invite in everyone else. Both bureaucratically and spatially, these projects became open to all comers. And, unlike other kinds of public places where the public is drawn by the presence of amenities (such as parks or beaches or museums or libraries), these public neighborhoods offered few opportunities for productive engagement. Instead, these spaces of physical neglect communicated the extent to which both residents and public officials had ceded control over all common areas, making them easy targets for vandalism. For residents, the very publicness of their neighborhoods detracted from both their privacy and their community, making many of them feel that their home life was undesirably influenced by outsiders.

Public Housing as Constructed Communities

Even as the notion of neighborhood becomes increasingly collaged and etherialized, every major American metropolis still markets itself as a "city of neighborhoods." In some places, this may be no more than a publicity tool intended to attract tourists and capture an ever-present nostalgia for smaller communities; but in other places, the vestiges of neighborhood distinction remain wholly salient and partially viable, in terms of topography and architecture, as well as ethnicity, race, and class. Faced with an urbanized world of multiple overlapping identities, residents and promoters of many neighborhoods seek ways to assert their uniqueness, emphasizing local amenities. In this regard, the form and social meaning of public housing projects still stand out and apart, but often for wholly negative reasons that are beyond the control of residents.

The sociologist Gerald Suttles has observed that "identities in general are often proposed to us rather than being self-produced."[11] For those who find themselves "public housing residents" living inside "a public housing project," this certainly seems to be the case. To a large extent, public housing communities were originally the products of architects, planners, and the staffs of housing authorities, but the phenomenon of "the projects" is also constructed by other means, and not only by the more obvious daily presence and actions of residents. First of all, the initial form of the projects was a cultural product not only of design professionals but of economists, lawyers, real estate developers, slumlords, and politicians. Second, these diverse professionals operated both centrally out of Washington and locally out of each jurisdiction concerned with the perpetuation or alteration of its own identity. Third, the subsequent perception of such places is shaped not only by these groups and by those who live in the projects, but also by a variety of other neighborhood-based groups and institutions who work to shape public commentary and thereby affect residents' self-identity.

Public neighborhoods—like other neighborhoods—are defined, at least in part, by what—and who—they are *not*. As Suttles puts it, "Neighborhoods seem to acquire their identity through an ongoing commentary between themselves and outsiders. This commentary includes the imputations and allegations of adjacent residential groups as well as the coverage given by the mass media. It includes also the claims of boosters, of developers, of realtors, and of city officials."[12] As with many other named communities, the history of public housing projects shows that the terms that identify them were almost always coined by some outsider (many projects—such as Boston's Orchard Park—were named either out of wishful allusion to more rural charms or in ironic memory of the landscape feature or ecosystem that was bulldozed away to build them).

Outsiders help construct the identity of a community not only through naming and commenting upon it, but also through the nature and extent of their contact with community residents. In neighborhoods where members are well integrated into groups and institutions that transcend neighborhood boundaries, sustained social contact provides ample opportunity to lessen the production of negative stereotypes associated with the name or the newspaper coverage. In the case of public housing residents, whose contacts in the wider world are often disproportionately limited, such perceptions become harder to challenge. Many observers, following the lead of the political scientist Robert Putnam, see neighborhood social transformation in terms of lost *social capital,* noting the unfortunate consequences of declines in the network of local institutions, memberships, and affiliations, points of contact that seem to be quite differentially present in American urban neighborhoods.[13] Early public housing projects, when first built, were bastions of such social capital. In 1940, Boston's Old Harbor Village project, for instance, boasted twelve softball teams, an eight-team bowling league, two Girl Scout and three Boy Scout troops, a newspaper, a credit union, and a symphony orchestra—as well as numerous other clubs and societies that provided financial assistance, health care, and even programs for children living outside the project. In today's public neighborhoods, by contrast, the potential for social networking can be especially bleak. Often, the only project-based group is a tenants' association whose membership, by definition, is coterminous with the development. Workplace contact is limited to the minority who have jobs. Churches and supermarkets are likely to be located beyond walking distance, and few other amenities and institutions are convenient, since the projects were intended as single-use residential enclaves. In all these ways, public housing projects are constricted as well as constructed.

If public housing residents are to transcend the constraints of their public neighborhoods, they must be better understood by the broader society that judges them. As the cultural psychologist Jerome Bruner has argued, if we wish to understand the processes by which meanings are created and negotiated within a community, we must examine "acts of meaning" as well as more easily measured behaviors: "A culturally sensitive psychology . . . is and must be based not only upon what people actually *do,* but what they *say* they do and what they *say* caused them to do what they did. It is also concerned with what people *say* others did and why. And above all, it is concerned with what people *say* their worlds are like."[14] It is a central aim of this book to probe deeply into what public housing residents say their worlds are like, in order to understand how they assess what they (and others) have been able to do to make things better. At the same time, it is necessary to find ways to assess the meanings of the worlds themselves, for environments carry meanings too.

THE STIGMA OF THE PROJECTS

Nearly forty years ago, Erving Goffman's groundbreaking book *Stigma: Notes on the Management of Spoiled Identity* examined a range of ways that people become dehumanized in the eyes of others because they are seen to possess some kind of deeply discrediting attribute.[15] This concept of stigma, however, dates back at least to ancient Greece, when it referred to bodily signs that called attention to some moral failing on the part of the person bearing them. This earlier form of stigma involved the deliberate marking of persons through such acts as cutting or burning, which were intended to identify those who should be shunned, such as criminals. In 1994, the national furor in the United States over the decision by a court in Singapore to punish an American found guilty of vandalism by caning him (in a manner expected to leave permanent scars) is indicative of the lingering power of this brand of stigma and makes clear its ties to highly variable cultural and social norms. Today, though most societies do not engage in bodily disfigurement for these kind of reasons, stigma persists in other ways that still communicate this sense of moral disdain.[16] In the case of American public housing, the visible scars include not just psychically injured humans but also the disfigured landscapes of the projects; the stigma of person and the stigma of place have become linked in the most dispiriting of ways.

No place in the contemporary United States, with the possible exceptions of prisons and certain hospitals, stigmatizes people in as many debilitating ways as a distressed inner-city public housing project. As public housing resources became increasingly targeted to those with the fewest alternatives, the admissions pipeline served to consolidate and channel the victims of all the nation's most virulent prejudices into a single program. As more and more of the unemployed poor gravitated toward public housing, the societal prejudices that are rooted in racial, ethnic, class, and gender biases were augmented by the further concentrated presence of other stigmatized attributes and conditions, including mental illness, out-of-wedlock births, single parenthood, AIDS, physical disabilities, and drug and alcohol addiction. This very concentration, in turn, carried an added danger. As inner-city public housing projects became seen as a repository for the nation's "problem people," even the individual problems of a relatively small percentage of residents became treated as typical of all. A composite stereotype developed as the layers of stigmas blended and merged into a single image of the *undeserving poor*. Beyond this, however, the process of stigmatization operates on a geo-political level, as it is not merely person-based but place-based.

These stigmatized individuals have accumulated in environments that themselves have only added to the stigma. Built under pressure to economize and subjected to the lobbying efforts of a real estate industry that wished to make certain that nothing about public housing could be seen as a competitive threat to the private market, most housing projects were constructed to maximize the distinctiveness of a place beneath private-sector housing. While, to be sure, a major cause of the "dreary deadlock" of public housing has been the ever-greater levels of poverty faced by those forced to live in projects, the problems of these residents have been exacerbated by the disjunction of public housing's physical forms from any reference to preferred modes of domestic dwelling. In the course of a single generation, the people and the places that were once touted as the unblemished alternative to the slum-dweller and the slum, themselves became the most publicly vilified objects of disdain. The stigma of the good-project/bad-slum relationship underwent a wholesale figure-ground inversion, or, in the most dismal cases, all sanguine hopes of "figure" disappeared back into the broader expanse of asphalt-covered ground.

The most devastating consequence of stigma, as Goffman makes clear, is that its marks become internalized; stigma is more than a measure of societal distrust, it is a deeply destructive cause of self-doubt. In 1963 sociologist Lee Rainwater's article entitled "Fear and the House-as-Haven in the Lower Class" noted the internalized connection between social and physical forms of stigma in public housing. Writing about the Pruitt-Igoe project in St. Louis, Rainwater concluded:

> Their physical world is telling them they are inferior and bad just
> as effectively perhaps as do their human interactions. Their inability to control the depredation of rats, hot steam pipes, balky stoves,
> and poorly fused electrical circuits tells them that they are failures

as autonomous individuals. The physical and social disorder of their world presents a constant temptation to give up or retaliate in kind. And when lower class people do try to do something about some of these dangers, they are generally exposed in their interactions with caretakers and outsiders to further moral punitiveness by being told that their troubles are their own fault.[17]

The stigma that operates at an individual level through negative associations with a particular person's race, ethnicity, gender, health status, or behavior is reinforced in public housing by powerful group-based and place-based messages. Public housing forces stigmatized people to experience a bounded and stigmatized environment in two mutually reinforcive ways: as a group of buildings and as a system of rules and preferences. The end result of all this is that the physical environment of public housing often reinforces social stigmas by inducing yet another unwelcome form of group identity: that of project resident.

Public housing projects link geography to group identity at the level of both building and neighborhood. People are said to live "in" a public housing project rather than simply "at" it, as an American would describe a street address. The emphasis is on the enclosure. When asked to describe the neighborhoods where they live, many of the public housing residents interviewed for this book did not name (or draw) anything outside the boundaries of the housing development; some regard their "neighborhood" as no wider than a single building. For others, the neighborhood is completely interiorized, extending no further than the locked door of their apartment. In many cities, especially in the American West, housing authorities are moving toward reinforcing this sense of enclosure with impregnable fencing. Although the rhetoric is about "securing the perimeter" against the depredations of outsiders, the reality for residents is more ambiguous; fencing out is also fencing in.

The geopolitics of housing project identity goes still further. Beyond living in one particular project, residents often refer to themselves as living in "the projects." In so doing, they self-identify not simply with a specific neighborhood but with a type of place, one presumed to house a specific type of person. Such a characterization is probably even more prevalent among nonresidents. In some cities, where whole sections have been turned over to public housing, it may make sense to speak of the plural category of "projects." Here, the cityscape—as in parts of Chicago's South Side—is characterized by public housing that is concentrated, contiguous, and almost continuous. Living in "the projects," then, may connote a discrete zone of the city as well as a type of building or type of urban design.

But the geographical resonance of "the projects" as a term is more than this. "Projects" suggests not only a bounded place, like the original meaning of the word "ghetto," but a category of place whose image to outsiders is perpetually degraded by media portraits of the disasters that lurk within it, both actual and latent. The cognitive link in the minds of many people between persons and the public housing projects where they live reflects negatively on both the resident and the place of residence, even when such links are not actual. The power of the media to dwell on the most egregious failures (such as the decline and demolition of Pruitt-Igoe), and thereby to consolidate negative images of public housing and its residents, is immense. One recent poll intended to measure general societal attitudes toward public housing residents, commissioned by a large public housing authority, yielded such alarming results that its findings were never even released. For residents, living with such a barrage of press reports, while residing in neighborhoods that have frequently experienced disinvestment by private businesses and inadequate service from public agencies such as the police, stigma is an almost inevitable result.

The stigma of the project reinforces the stigma of those who are forced to live there for economic reasons, just as the composite socioeconomic desperation of the residents reinforces the stigma of the project as an environment. As one public housing resident revealingly phrased it, "Public housing is 'public' because they'll let anyone in here." From this insider's viewpoint, public housing is constructed by one alien form of "They" in order to be able to "let in anyone" (another kind of "They"). In this way, it becomes possible for those who live near public housing, but not in it, to regard public housing residents as suspicious, publicly dependent persons, at the same time that the residents themselves view newcomers to the project with much the same mistrust. In short, both insiders and outsiders can concur that there is a problem when one's neighbors become seen as "the public" rather than as a specific set of individuals and families of known qualities.

As I have argued in *From the Puritans to the Projects*, the stigma attached to residence in contemporary public housing projects is but one recent example in a long American tradition of sociospatial disdain.[18] Well before there was such a thing as a public housing project, other institutions served as "public houses."

Whether termed an almshouse, a workhouse, a Bridewell, a House of Correction, or a House of Industry, such places served to segregate—socially and spatially—those whose problems could not be relieved by the combined home-based efforts of family and kin, private charities, and public funds. They separated out community members who were socioeconomically unable or unwilling to meet the community's standards of industry or behavior. The stigmatized denizens of these early public houses constitute what I have termed *public neighbors:* needy people whom community leaders felt an obligation to assist or, since the early nineteenth century, to reform.[19] Public housing was not initially built to house such public neighbors; it was intended for a much more economically independent sort of tenant. By the mid-1960s, however, pressures from civil rights groups to open all projects to all races, regardless of family structure or source of income, irreversibly turned public housing into the last, desperate haven for precisely the sort of tenants the early housers had sought to keep out. The stormy history of public housing may therefore be seen as the confluence between the old tradition of the *public neighbor* and the new practice of the *public neighborhood.* With stigmatized persons and stigmatized places conjoined, insecurity necessarily predominated, preventing the enjoyment of either privacy or community.

Public Housing Transformations: Public and Private

Since at least the 1960s, housing authorities and political leaders have sought many ways to reduce the stigma associated with the projects and their inhabitants. Most dramatically, they simply stopped building large projects for low-income families, concentrating instead on new facilities to serve the elderly. Public officials saw the elderly as more easily managed, more amenable to life in high-rise elevator buildings, and more likely to include white tenants at a time when whites who were income-eligible for family public housing increasingly shunned it. Because elderly tenants were considered less objectionable than other populations, it was sometimes possible to build new housing for seniors in neighborhoods that would not have tolerated an influx of younger public housing families.[20]

At the same time that housing authorities sought out a less troublesome constituency, they also tried to disperse public housing, both through construction of much smaller, scattered site projects and, more fundamentally, through introduction of a voucher-based system. Section 8 of the Housing and Community Development Act of 1974 introduced two key programs, one that subsidized rent in specified new or substantially renovated buildings owned by either for-profit developers or non-profit organizations, and another that provided certificates carrying a similar subsidy to households for use in renting dwellings owned by private landlords. The use of these certificates and vouchers as a portable subsidy has been widely touted as both cost-effective and conducive to the individual well-being of participant families. As of 2002, more than 1.5 million households received Section 8 support, making what is now called the Housing Choice Voucher Program larger than the conventional public housing program itself.[21]

Still, these new programs and approaches did not obviate the need for housing authorities to work directly with the tenants who remained in the large projects. Ongoing efforts to increase the opportunities available to public housing residents include thirty-five years of experience with management reforms (including resident management initiatives) and homeownership experiments in a few developments, as well as a wide variety of counseling and job training strategies. Taken together, these programs do grapple with the basic issues of powerlessness and internalized stigma, though few would suggest that progress has been anything but slow and frustrating.[22]

The most dramatic changes in public housing have been architectural ones, in large measure because this is where the vast majority of the limited funding has been targeted. The decline in the maintenance and security of the built environment has long been the most visible measure of public housing's failure—the sensory evidence of deteriorated conditions has been foreground or backdrop in all media coverage—so it is hardly surprising that public housing redevelopment efforts have been focused on matters of physical "modernization." Since the 1980s, many large housing authorities have experimented with ways to turn around some of their most distressed projects. This commitment gained nationwide prominence in the 1990s with the cumulative decisions to allocate more than four billion dollars to the HOPE VI program—under implementation in most major U.S. cities—an approach that provides for an unprecedented orientation of redevelopment funds to social and economic programs as well as to architectural and urban change.

Everyone involved with public housing reform acknowledges that success must at some level be measured in socioeconomic terms, and that bricks-and-mortar reconfiguration of the projects is never sufficient. Yet the two are hardly independent: it may well be that the most encouraging evidence of public housing transformation inheres in the *socioeconomic* effects of physical redevelopment initiatives. Many authors have explored the links between public housing design and social behavior, but it was Jane Jacobs who first sounded the clarion call for change.

In *The Death and Life of Great American Cities,* the seminal treatise that helped shape a fundamental reorientation of the urban-planning profession, Jacobs saved some of her harshest criticism for public housing, but also reserved some of her highest hopes for its future. For Jacobs, writing in 1961, public housing was perhaps the most dangerous manifestation of the broader tendency to create large, single-function land-use projects that killed off the more fine-grained diversity of older city streets and neighborhoods. She viewed projectmaking as a practice that not only destroyed the architectural and urban form of the city but also limited social interaction and undermined the small entrepreneurial capitalism that forms the basis of its economic resilience. In a chapter called "Salvaging Projects," Jacobs contended that "unslumming" public housing projects depended on a mixture of physical and economic interventions to make the projects "safe and otherwise workable for city life," and thereby "capable of holding their populations through *choice.*" For Jacobs, this entailed a return to city streets and sidewalks that would deliver "casual public characters, lively, well-watched, continuously used public spaces, easier and more natural supervision of children and normal city cross-use of their territory by people from outside it." This, in turn, would require encouraging nonresidential uses, "because lack of enough mixed uses is precisely one of the causes of deadness, danger, and plain inconvenience." Ultimately, according to Jacobs, full physical, social, and economic reintegration of projects into cities would entail "gradual unslumming and self-diversification in the project population."[23] Although it is far from clear how "self-diversification" would occur in a system where admissions is controlled by a public authority, Jacobs' notion of "unslumming" nicely encapsulates the way that transformations of public housing ultimately involve more than issues of architecture. The most successful redevelopment processes are those that embrace this broader agenda. Destigmatizing public housing is about more than making its forms disappear into the landscape; it is also about bringing the best qualities of its residents into the foreground. Perhaps this is what Jacobs meant by self-diversification.

The effort to salvage public housing entails a fundamental transformation of power and identity. Oscar Newman's seminal treatise *Defensible Space* (published in 1972) set out a range of ways that redesign of public housing projects could enhance the security and self-expression of residents. By showing how architectural and urban design changes could introduce a sense of personal control and responsibility over dangerous public areas previously lacking in surveillance, Newman hoped to enhance the level of privacy possible in public housing. At the same time, he argued, once crime and fear were reduced, that defensible space could support a more satisfying community life. Despite some initial skepticism, many of Newman's ideas eventually entered both the lexicon and the standard practice of housing authorities nationwide, culminating in 1995 when HUD officially endorsed the approach in a booklet entitled *Defensible Space: Deterring Crime and Building Community*. Clearly, any discussion about reclaiming public housing must contend with Newman's propositions.[24]

PUBLIC HOUSING IN BOSTON

While it is certainly my aim to speak generally about the past, present, and future of public housing, I take the viewpoint that much of the diversity of experience with large-scale urban public housing can be found within the public neighborhoods of a single city, such as Boston. In Boston, as in many other American cities, the earliest incarnations of public housing enjoyed widespread support from City Hall and qualified support from neighborhood residents: those who gained new apartments were delighted, while those who were displaced from their homes by slum clearance but were not subsequently selected for occupancy in the new project harbored great resentment. Property owners objected to clearance of their businesses, but most others welcomed the arrival of construction jobs and housing opportunities for those temporarily experiencing hard times.

The Boston Housing Authority (BHA), established in 1935, constructed all of Boston's largest twenty-five public neighborhoods in two short bursts of activity, between 1938 and 1942, and between 1949 and 1954. In those years, public housing projects could still be regarded as political plums to be sought by city councilors seeking to serve the constituents of their particular ward (Figs. 1.3 and 1.4). Compared with other cities in the United States where massive project construction continued through the 1960s and even into the early 1970s, Boston's program stands out as both precocious and disproportionately large.

The first wave of eight projects emphasized slum clearance and job creation in the construction industries. In Boston, as elsewhere, these projects were touted as a way to eliminate the "cost of slums" (seen as a disproportionate drain on city

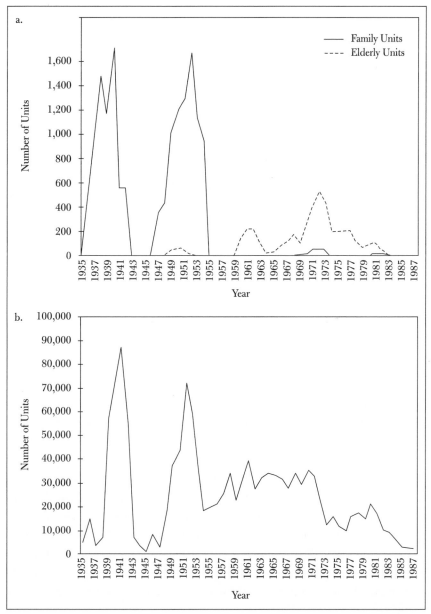

FIGURE 1.3 Public housing project construction in Boston, and in the United States, since 1935. In Boston, virtually all the city's family public housing constructed by the BHA was completed in two waves between 1938 and 1942 and between 1949 and 1954. A modest amount of public housing for the elderly was completed later, but the heyday of public neighborhood construction ended in 1954. Boston's pattern is similar to the peaks of public housing construction nationwide, although much more was built in other cities after 1955.

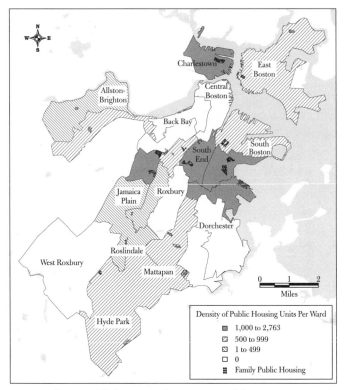

FIGURE 1.4 Boston public housing in almost every ward. In contrast to many cities where public housing was concentrated in a few areas, Boston's family projects found favor with local politicians and were built in all but a few of the city's wards.

services that yielded minimal municipal revenue). At the same time, the BHA treated the projects as a reward for good citizens; the new housing developments served as a spatial and formal means to distinguish these "deserving poor" from the less-worthy denizens of the surrounding slums. The advent of public housing allowed the displacement of "less-desirable" low-income tenants (often noncitizen immigrants who lived in rooming houses and other non-nuclear family households) and their replacement by native-born, "standard" two-parent families.

The second wave of public neighborhood construction in Boston involved the creation of seventeen more projects for families. In this phase, seven new federally financed projects were erected contemporaneously with ten state-sponsored projects for Massachusetts veterans. In Boston, most of these postwar projects were built on city-owned vacant land, an arrangement that both expedited construction (since the BHA did not have to worry about rehousing displaced persons in a tight housing market) and enabled the Boston Housing Authority to distribute its projects across most of the wards in the city. In a city that was still 91 percent white as late as 1960, the BHA built twenty-two of the twenty-five projects in white-majority neighborhoods and constructed only two in areas of highly concentrated poverty (Figs. 1.5–1.6). Public housing, as built, helped to sustain or

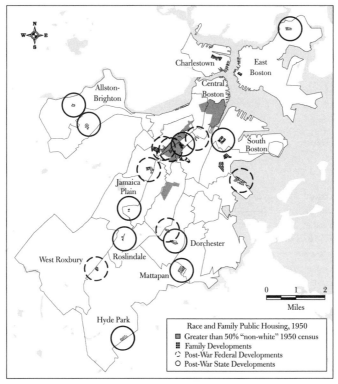

FIGURE 1.5 Sites of Boston's postwar family public housing developments. Many of Boston's ten state-sponsored postwar housing projects (shown with circles) were located in peripheral areas, as were some of the seven postwar federal developments (shown with dotted circles). Of the twenty-five family projects completed by 1954, all but the Lenox Street, Camden Street, and Whittier Street projects (intended for black occupancy) were located in majority-white neighborhoods.

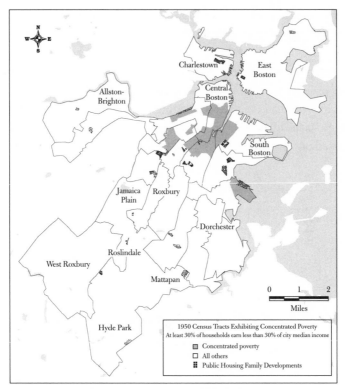

FIGURE 1.6 Boston public housing, built outside high-poverty areas. When Boston's family public housing projects were built, only two, Cathedral–South End and Columbia Point, were built in areas of concentrated poverty, and the latter was situated well away from population of any kind. Concentrated-poverty census tracts are defined as those in which at least 30 percent of households had incomes below 30 percent of the city median.

increase the neighborhood homogenization. As with the prewar projects, postwar public housing served as a reward for those judged worthy.

In all, these projects provided more than fourteen thousand new apartments for low-income families—selected for occupancy not only on the basis of need but also according to highly moralistic judgments about merit. The "investigators" of the "Authority" not only assessed the income and housing conditions of BHA applicants but also assembled an entire dossier on them. Those who gained admission to the BHA developments between 1938 and 1954 either had superior political connections or could demonstrate excellent landlord references, a stable track record of earned wages, a two-parent family structure, U.S. citizenship, and—in the second incarnation at least—evidence of service to the country during wartime. In the early 1950s, the BHA applicant pool was dominated by the families of working-class veterans; fully 90 percent of all who sought entry had engaged in military service, and 95 percent were employed. Thus, even before the BHA applied its own extensive selection criteria, the applicants were already a highly self-selected lot. Beyond this, until the challenges of civil rights activists compelled a formal change of policy during the mid-1960s, BHA tenant-selection staff could reject an applicant for any one of fifteen different listed reasons. These social prohibitions included "excessive" use of alcohol, use of drugs, cohabitation without marriage, out-of-wedlock children (except under certain specified conditions), "unsanitary housekeeping," and "obnoxious conduct or behavior in connection with processing of [an] application."[25]

Soon after the BHA completed its second round of project construction, however, the tenant composition and institutional standing of these public neighborhoods began to change. New public housing construction for families ceased completely, and the existing projects remained secondary to broader urban-renewal efforts premised on the pursuit of urban fiscal stability. Public housing had little role to play in the construction of what was touted as the New Boston, and its image became tarnished by its use as a repository for less desirable kinds of public neighbors displaced by other forms of public action (even though—in Boston, at least—relatively few people were brought into public housing for this reason).

The economic decline of public housing in Boston occurred not just because of urban renewal but because of a much broader widening of housing opportunities for white working-class people in the 1950s and 1960s, occasioned both by greater prosperity and by the increased availability of mortgage financing. By the mid-1950s, as many of the preferred sort of tenants gained the economic mobility to leave the projects, the moral standing of the remainder—as viewed by the Authority—entered into protracted decline.

Although the economic transformation of the public housing population in Boston paralleled that of many other older cities with well-established public housing stocks, Boston's public housing experience was distinctively influenced by the city's racial politics. This gets at the heart of what makes Boston public housing different from that of most other cities where this subject has been so extensively mined, such as Chicago, St. Louis, and Philadelphia. Whereas most cities with large public housing programs constructed their projects (at least the later ones) as a means to isolate nonwhites in their own neighborhoods, Boston's leaders built nearly all of the city's public housing to upgrade the neighborhoods of the white working class. By ceasing to build large, family public housing projects in 1954 (well ahead of most other large cities, and before some cities had even *started* such construction), the Boston Housing Authority completed its portfolio of public neighborhoods before the largest influx of nonwhites had occurred. In this way, the stories of public housing in Boston are, at least in part, stories of the ongoing neighborhood racial and ethnic tensions that emerged when the demographics of the housing waiting list changed sooner than the demographics of the neighborhoods that surrounded each project.

The struggle to cope with racial change and its concomitant neighborhood strains was only one part of the BHA's growing array of problems. Throughout the 1960s and 1970s, the financial and managerial difficulties of the Authority mounted, and project maintenance declined. The result was both physical degeneration of projects and social incapacity to stop either the depredations of "problem families" within the projects or the destructive incursions of outsiders who saw public property as an appropriate place to vent their frustrations. Increasingly, whatever reputation public housing once claimed as a source of neighborhood stability was lost. Now, the public-ness of the projects became a source of stigma and insecurity, landscapes that could be controlled neither by their managers nor by most of their residents. Especially where the racial and ethnic composition of the project differed sharply from that of the surrounding neighborhoods, those who lived in the private housing beyond the project bounds frequently regarded their public housing neighbors with suspicion and blamed the housing authority for sending them there. Within the projects themselves, residents chastised the management about the laxity of admission standards and the inability to evict problem families.

By the end of the 1970s, the BHA and its tenants suffered from the highest vacancy rate of any major housing authority in the country; many family developments were between one-third and one-half empty, and their vacant apartments were quickly vandalized. In many developments, major building systems collapsed and residents felt fearful, angry, and abandoned. Successful prosecution of a tenant-initiated class action lawsuit, *Perez v. Boston Housing Authority,* resulted in 1975 in the court-appointed position of master to oversee the Authority. Despite the master's best efforts, the egregious management problems at the Authority continued, and the presiding judge placed the agency in receivership, beginning in 1980.

Rather than dismantle the BHA, Receiver Lewis H. (Harry) Spence tried to redeem it, ushering in five years of sweeping organizational reforms and championing several ambitious redevelopment efforts. Spence recognized that the BHA's collapse had not played itself out equally in every neighborhood. Some places had suffered more than others; some places still had strong residents and neighbors with whom the Authority could work. To understand how the BHA's actions and inactions affected the course of life in the public neighborhoods the Authority managed, one must examine each place individually—not only during the receivership but during the turbulent decades that preceded it. Especially under conditions of the intense racial hypersensitivity that prevailed in Boston, public housing policy was carried out differentially from neighborhood to neighborhood, project to project. All of these decentralized political and design activities are both parochial and crucial. It is therefore essential to look locally, to see how the various programs that emerged under the shared name of "public housing" have played out over time in very different neighborhood contexts, subject to very different local political pressures.

PRESSURES ON PUBLIC HOUSING

Each public housing project—however architecturally anomalous it may be—is also one piece of a larger city, subject to broad currents of social and economic neighborhood change. As such, it cannot be usefully conceptualized as an independent enclave. Public housing residents often are very isolated, but it does them no service to perpetuate the stereotype that housing projects are independent outposts, subject only to the will of housing management or the wavering generosity of public subsidy. Instead, part of looking locally means that projects must be viewed as wholly interlinked to all other forms of regional transformation. In the 1970s, Boston suffered from more than just failed public housing. The city as a whole ranked "at the very bottom of urban America" in terms of its unemployment rate, incidence of violent crime, per capita income, poverty rate, and government indebtedness, and these indicators were worsening. What followed between 1980 and 2000, however, has been termed "The Boston Renaissance," a region-wide economic recovery marked by rapid and diverse urban immigration, industrial restructuring in favor of high technology and service-sector employment, and massive decentralization of residential location and business activity. Needless to say, this overall regional prosperity reached Boston's neighborhoods unevenly at best, yet it dramatically altered the nature and location of job opportunities for low-income Bostonians. It also meant that efforts to reclaim public housing in Boston have gone forward in a tight housing market, characterized by high rents and lingering racial segregation.[26]

The future of public housing policy is inseparable from other aspects of housing needs. Public housing residents currently pay about 30 percent of their income for rent, yet many others without the benefit of government subsidy are squeezed to find affordable housing. In 1998 nearly one-quarter of all renters in Greater Boston spent more than *half* of their income on housing. Boston's gap in housing affordability has affected not only those with the lowest incomes, but also working-class and lower-middle-class households. Still, a region-wide study showed that nearly half of the unmet affordable housing need was for units requiring "deep" subsidies, sufficient to reach families (like most of those in public housing) who earn less than 30 percent of the area median income.

The situation for renters in Boston itself became particularly dire. Between 1980 and 2000, the city gained 17,000 ownership units (through new construction and condo conversions) but lost about 4,500 rental units. Meanwhile, the rate of multifamily housing construction declined dramatically during the 1990s, reflecting a nationwide trend. Buoyed by the strong regional economy that further reduced vacancy rates, and spurred by the end of rent control that followed passage of a ballot initiative in 1994, market rents were bid up each year at a rate far surpassing the increase in family incomes. Between 1991 and 1999 the median advertised rent for a two-bedroom apartment in Boston increased by 77 percent, from $875 to $1,550. Public housing remained one of the last affordable options, but as of 2000, 14,000 households remained on the waiting list for BHA apartments.[27]

Neighborhood-based public housing has been buffeted by more than just regional economic trends; it has also suffered and benefited from a wide array of specific public policies. Indeed, every major effort at directing or restraining urban change in the second half of the twentieth century has affected public housing. From urban renewal to racially discriminatory redlining; from efforts to desegregate schools to attempts to stem the rise of drugs and violent crime; from the pressures of encroaching gentrification to the scourge of long-term neighborhood disinvestment—in all these ways and more, the fates of large urban public housing projects have been inextricably tied to larger currents of urban development in America's inner cities.

Yet public housing is more than a product or a victim of structural economic change or a succession of politically charged national policy directives. Its impacts and its character also depend on how federal policies have been received, implemented, and augmented by state and local authorities, and on how these policies are received and acted upon by the denizens of each public neighborhood and its surrounds.

Despite the external forces and institutional structures acting on public projects, it is clear when looking at specific housing developments that individual human agency plays a great role in the construction and constriction of project communities. The next three chapters of this book examine the history of three public housing developments in Boston, not just to examine the dynamics of their rise and fall, but also to take seriously the explicit roles played by public housing residents in the transformations of their communities, both in terms of physical alterations and in terms of less tangible conceptual shifts. By examining the origins of these three public neighborhoods, by identifying the sources of their declines, and by probing the dynamics of their attempted revitalizations, this book attempts to document and interpret three different neighborhood trajectories. Through giving voice to the experiences of those people who were most affected by social and environmental changes in public housing projects, it becomes possible to examine such concepts as *privacy, security, stigma,* and *community* in diverse, highly disadvantaged environments. Each case reveals aspects of the changing ways that public neighborhoods and their residents have been perceived by their nonproject neighbors, who so often resent their presence. At the same time, these stories emphasize the internal tensions within the projects themselves. They reveal how even the residents—who collectively came to be seen as undesirable public neighbors by outsiders—resented the unwanted intrusions of publicly assigned undesirables. As the empirical centerpiece of the book, the three case studies of public neighborhoods are in service of a broader interpretive goal: explicating the relationship between changes in the physical environment and changes in the social, psychological, and economic circumstances of those who live in such places.

THREE BOSTON PUBLIC NEIGHBORHOODS

Boston embarked on four major transformations of distressed public housing projects during the early 1980s. This put the city a full decade ahead of most American municipalities, where such ambitious reconstructions did not typically take place until the HOPE VI program emerged to provide both the incentive and the funding. In Boston, by contrast, public housing redevelopment now has a track record that is long enough to be measured and broad enough to be judged comparatively.

Of the four major attempts to transform public housing, the most widely discussed effort has been the redevelopment of the notorious 1,500-unit Columbia Point project into the mixed-income, privately developed, and privately managed community now known as Harbor Point.[28] This wholesale makeover razed most of the old project, introduced a street grid and more traditional architecture, stocked the new development with amenities such as tennis courts and swimming pools, and duly delivered more than two-thirds of the prime oceanfront site to market-rate housing. It preserved some semblance of affordable housing given that 400 units were subsidized to serve low-income households in perpetuity, but it cannot really be said to have *reclaimed* public housing. Rather, this model is premised on *eliminating* as much public housing as politically possible, while permitting market forces (aided by a massive public subsidy) to lay claim to a choice location. Today, despite its labyrinthine financing, Harbor Point is widely regarded as a national paragon for public housing redevelopment, but it is hardly the only way to move forward.

This book focuses not on Columbia Point, however, but on Boston's three other precocious redevelopment efforts. At these three places—unlike Harbor Point—the BHA truly did try to reclaim public housing as a resource for low-income households. The efforts to do so entailed long struggles, each one a continuation of the struggles faced by residents during the preceding decades. These three half-century sagas reveal both the promise and the pitfalls of salvaging public housing in this way.

Each of the three Boston public housing projects discussed here was built in the aftermath of World War II during a period of lingering municipal enthusiasm for public housing. Constructed under the 1948 Massachusetts Veterans Housing Program, each was intended to house chiefly white male veterans returning from war and their families. Despite initial optimism and considerable local political support, each project eventually suffered through an accelerating period of extreme decline characterized by physical decay, managerial corruption, and social disorder. These three Boston cases, however, add an important additional chapter to the usual failure story and raise the possibility of a very different denouement. Emerging from this nadir, each place received tens of millions of dollars for redevelopment during the 1980s, intended to revitalize these projects into desirable living environments. These wholesale transformations, initiated during the BHA receivership, entailed a shift from crowded apartments where large families had no single place to dine together, where as many as fifty children might share a single common hallway or entry stair, and where the entire outdoor realm was an undifferentiated asphalt wasteland, to an environment where apartments were enlarged, buildings were reconfigured into two-story or three-story townhouses with private entrances and private yards, and every portion of a project site was landscaped and subdivided in ways intended to promote resident control over space outside the apartments. In short, by de-institutionalizing and destigmatizing the appearance of public neighborhoods, the promoters of redevelopment efforts (both residents and nonresidents) sought to turn these projects into environments that mimicked the privacy, security, and sense of community expected of more desirable private residential neighborhoods. These efforts may thus be seen as early and especially well funded attempts to apply Newman's defensible space theories, and the case studies offer a triple opportunity to observe and assess the power and the limitations of such changes in diverse neighborhood settings over an extended period of time. At each place, these physical changes were accompanied by tenants' organizing efforts, by attempts to expand the range of educational, social, and economic alternatives available to residents, and by a willingness on the part of the housing authority to give residents a greater role in management.

These prodigious efforts at rebirth and revival have not, however, yielded uniformly happy results for all the developments and their residents. Although all three projects house very low income multiracial and multiethnic populations who suffer extremely high rates of unemployment, one is nationally touted as a triumphant "turnaround" of a devastated housing project, one seems a mixed success, and the third has fared quite poorly (Figs. 1.7–1.8). This book attempts to explain the sources and meanings of such disparities.

Chapter 2 tells the story of the West Broadway development, a 972-unit project completed in 1949 on slum-clearance land in what was then all-white South Boston. The chapter investigates the social and physical collapse of the project during the 1970s, after it became a hotbed of racial conflict during the crisis over forced busing; it also relates the way the well-connected South Boston political leadership secured funding for redevelopment, an effort that stressed the physical reintegration of the project into its neighborhood and eventually also entailed a controversial racial reintegration of the project population.

Chapter 3 takes up the saga of Franklin Field, a 504-unit project completed in

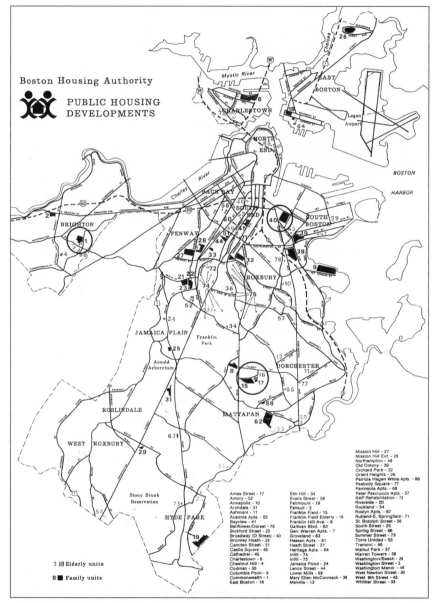

Boston Housing Authority

PUBLIC HOUSING DEVELOPMENTS

BOSTON HARBOR

Mission Hill - 27
Mission Hill Ext. - 28
Northampton - 48
Old Colony - 39
Orchard Park - 32
Orient Heights - 26
Patricia Hagen White Apts. - 68
Peabody Square - 77
Peninsula Apts. - 69
Peter Pasciucco Apts. - 57
RAP Rehabilitation - 72
Riverside - 20
Rockland - 54
Roslyn Apts. - 67
Rutland-E. Springfield - 71
St. Botolph Street - 56
South Street - 25
Spring Street - 66
Summer Street - 73
Torre Unidad - 53
Tremont - 48
Walnut Park - 37
Warren Towers - 36
Washington/Beech - 3
Washington Street - 3
Washington Manor - 48
West Newton Street - 60
West 9th Street - 43
Whittier Street - 33

Ames Street - 17
Amory - 52
Annapolis - 10
Archdale - 31
Ashmont - 11
Ausonia Apts. - 65
Bayview - 41
Bellflower/Dorset - 76
Bickford Street - 23
Broadway (D Street) - 40
Bromley Heath - 22
Camden Street - 51
Castle Square - 45
Cathedral - 45
Charlestown - 6
Chestnut Hill - 4
Codman - 55
Columbia Point - 9
Commonwealth - 1
East Boston - 18

Elm Hill - 34
Evans Street - 58
Fairmount - 19
Faneuil - 2
Franklin Field - 15
Franklin Field Elderly - 16
Franklin Hill Ave. - 8
Gallivan Blvd. - 62
Gen. Warren Apts. - 7
Groveland - 63
Hassan Apts. - 61
Heath Street - 21
Heritage Apts. - 64
Infill - 74
Infill - 75
Jamaica Pond - 24
Lenox Street - 14
Lower Mills - 59
Mary Ellen McCormack - 38
Melville - 13

3 ▦ Elderly units

8 ■ Family units

FIGURE 1.7 Location of public housing built by the Boston Housing Authority. Boston's public neighborhoods are scattered across the city. The three public housing developments highlighted in this book are Commonwealth, in Brighton; West Broadway, in South Boston; and Franklin Field, adjacent to Blue Hill Avenue in Dorchester.

FIGURE 1.8 Racial character of three Boston public neighborhoods. West Broadway, Franklin Field, and Commonwealth were all constructed in white neighborhoods, but as of 1990, only West Broadway still stood in an overwhelmingly white part of the city. Franklin Field's neighborhood was almost entirely black and Latino, and Commonwealth's neighbors were more racially and ethnically diverse.

1954 on the site of temporary postwar housing in Dorchester. Here the focus is on the long history of problems at the project occasioned both by its architectural deficiencies and by the enormity of the neighborhood transformation that occurred in and around it. The trouble began in the late 1960s, when the population of both project and neighborhood changed from predominantly Jewish to overwhelmingly black and Latino, during a period of redlining and blockbusting that, in turn, contributed to a legacy of mortgage foreclosures and disinvestment. In this case, the redevelopment of the housing project emerged, not out of tenant demand for remedial action, but out of an act of financial appeasement to Boston's black community, a fact that helps explain why this particular redevelopment effort proved disheartening to all involved, despite an investment of resources similar to that at West Broadway.

Chapter 4 narrates the story of Commonwealth development, a 648-unit project that opened in 1951 on the site of the last farm in Allston-Brighton. Here, the emphasis is on the ways this development became the scourge of an otherwise prosperous neighborhood. It details how strong mixed-race resident leadership emerged to help thwart the loss of the project to gentrification pressures; discusses how Commonwealth was chosen by the BHA for redevelopment through a careful planning process aimed at identifying the place where investment was most likely to succeed; and examines the successful components of this redevelopment, which included a shift to private management.

Each of these three public housing sagas charts a double redevelopment effort—two successive attempts to transform a neighborhood through public action. In each case the first public intervention consisted of the initial construction of public housing under the Massachusetts Veterans Housing Program between 1949 and 1954, and the second was the reconceptualization and reconstruction of that housing thirty years later. These two social and architectural experiments—both called public housing—were based on very different assumptions about who should be served and what form this service should take. The first redevelopment experiment was premised on the desirability of building a collective of mostly white male, working-class, upwardly mobile veterans and their families, while the second redevelopment experiment assumed that the housing project residents were themselves society's neediest families, characterized by single-parent households with high rates of unemployment and little prospect for socioeconomic advancement. Built initially as a public demonstration that public neighbors could be displaced or filtered out by construction of a more socially and morally auspicious environment, each of the three housing projects became instead a containment vehicle for those that private markets could not house—with the project itself regarded as an unwanted public neighbor by many residents who dwelled beyond its boundaries. The ambitious redevelopment efforts, in turn, aimed to rid the projects of their problem families, while nonetheless continuing to serve the neediest.

The history of these three places thus far is both general and generalizable, as it typifies the ambivalent struggle by the institutions of American society to come to terms with public neighbors. The reason for looking at specific neighborhoods, however, is to emphasize that all generalizations about American public housing have limitations. The experience with public housing varies not simply between city and suburb, or between one city and another, but also from one neighborhood to the next. Whatever the level of problems with public housing as a system, its impacts—both its successes and its failures—are experienced differentially. The next three chapters not only provide details about the struggles of three specific public housing projects but show how these struggles have been colored by three different neighborhood *contexts:* a working-class white-ethnic neighborhood resisting social change, an economically declining neighborhood responding to major ethnic and racial shifts and large-scale disinvestment, and an economically mixed multiracial and multiethnic neighborhood coping with the pressures of gentrification. It is possible to reclaim public housing under each of these scenarios, but the challenges—socially, economically, and urbanistically— are not entirely the same.

Despite such variations in neighborhood context, the three chapters are structured according to a common trajectory, one that views the course of public housing change not primarily from the top-down perspective of a downtown housing authority office, but from the bottom-up, highly individualized perspectives of those who reside in and around specific public housing neighborhoods. First comes a discussion of the neighborhood before the introduction of public housing, followed by a description of the project-enclave and its surrounds during the 1950s. Next is an account of the neighborhood-centered struggles that followed in the wake of urban renewal and the civil rights movement during the 1960s and 1970s, struggles that contributed to the BHA's own institutional decline. After this, each chapter details the revitalization process at each development during the 1980s, focusing on what happened to each project, but placing this in the context of adjacent neighborhood change. Finally, each chapter concludes with some assessment of the impact of the revitalization attempt, emphasizing the views of residents and other key players in the redevelopment process.

By way of conclusion, Chapter 5 steps back to compare the broader neighborhood trajectories of West Broadway, Commonwealth, and Franklin Field between 1950 and 2000, emphasizing similarities and differences in the overall project-neighborhood dynamic. It looks at how and why the projects declined, and then assesses the comparative "success" of the three redevelopment initiatives according to seven criteria: (1) smooth implementation, (2) recognized design quality, (3) improved tenant-organization capacity, (4) enhanced maintenance and management performance, (5) improved security, (6) progress on economic development, and (7) resident satisfaction. The chapter stresses the interlinked nature of efforts at public housing transformation, discusses the strengths and limitations of design-centered approaches, emphasizes the desirability of public-private-tenant partnerships, and attempts to identify the conditions under which successful redevelopment is most likely to occur. Finally, this chapter situates the Boston experiences with public housing in the current context of housing design and policy initiatives, both in Boston and elsewhere in the United States, under the HOPE VI program, a new round of efforts intended to strip public housing of its "project" stigma. Ultimately, the goal is to nurture the recovery of stable communities, regardless of their particular mix of incomes.

In short, through historically grounded critical examination of some of the country's earliest and most innovative efforts to reclaim public housing, this book seeks to reconsider the overwhelming pessimism that has pervaded most scholarly attention given to the topic. It challenges the over-simplistic assumption that we must always raze the projects and start over with neotraditional buildings housing a more affluent mixed-income constituency. At the same time, however, close study of three public housing neighborhoods reveals at least as much about the intractability of urban struggles as it does about the prospects for transcending them.

T W O

West Broadway: Public Housing for "Lower-End" Whites

THE BOSTON HOUSING AUTHORITY built South Boston's West Broadway public housing development in 1949 as the first and largest of the Massachusetts Veterans Housing projects (Fig. 2.1). Constructed on a slum-clearance site in the district's so-called Lower End, this public neighborhood was envisaged by its planners as the bulwark of neighborhood regeneration in one of the city's most blighted areas. At the same time, as the third public housing project to come to all-white South Boston in little more than a decade, it demonstrated the district's extraordinary political connectedness. This level of engagement by local politicians did not, however, prevent the project from experiencing a succession of social crises. At base, these crises stemmed from a working-class Irish-Catholic neighborhood's struggle to serve its own most impoverished residents while faced with a public housing program increasingly attuned to another kind of public purpose: racial integration. Initial attempts to sustain more than token integration at "D Street" (as the project was locally known) struggled throughout the late 1960s and foundered in the wake of the controversies over court-ordered busing of schoolchildren during the 1970s, a turning point that coincided with the accelerating institutional collapse of the Boston Housing Authority itself. At the end of the 1970s, owing to the strength of an exceptionally active group of resident leaders, South Boston's political clout reasserted itself in the scramble to obtain public housing redevelopment funds. This enabled the commencement of an ambi-

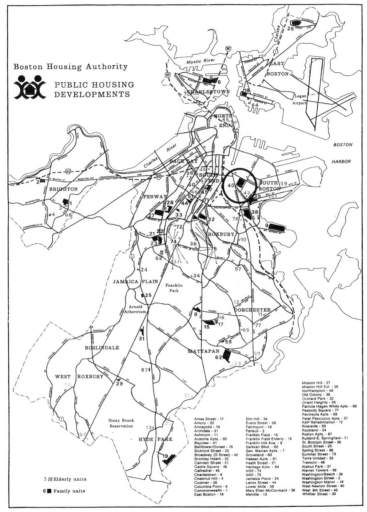

FIGURE 2.1 South Boston's West Broadway housing development. The BHA built the West Broadway development along its namesake street in South Boston.

tious, multiphase physical reconfiguration of the project, an intervention followed immediately by the extreme controversy of a renewed and far more concerted effort to integrate the newly redeveloped project.

To understand the fate of a public housing project in South Boston, then, one must understand something about this district's topographical history and its ethnic politics. These, in turn, affected where the West Broadway project was located, whom it housed, why its decline was so socially disruptive, and how it came to be selected as a priority for redevelopment.

South Boston's Lower End before Public Housing

South Boston is a district with a fascinating and contentious historiography, at once championed for its intimacy and generosity toward its members and vilified for its racist and lawless intolerance of outsiders. On the one hand, as the historian Thomas O'Connor observes, its story has been frequently told by "friendly local writers" in the form of loosely documented anecdotes and reminiscences, emphasizing religiosity, commitment to family, and service to country. On the other hand, nineteenth-century interpreters treated the "South Boston Irish" as synonymous with the broader problem of immigrant paupers, emphasizing their drunkenness, and early-twentieth-century chroniclers considered "Southie" a fount of political corruption, full of the antidemocratic tendencies that flourished in a slum district of ramshackle triple-decker homes, barrooms, and pool halls. And, most damaging of all, the neighborhood gained national infamy during the 1970s when television cameras captured the intensity of local resistance to forced interracial busing.[1]

Topography, History, and Invented Traditions

In this district, as in many others, topography encodes a politics. Before its annexation to Boston, the peninsula was known as Dorchester Neck, but its geographical distinction lay not only in its tenuous connection to the land but also in the advantages of its harborside high-ground for military strategy. "Dorchester Heights" gained lasting fame during the early months of the American Revolution as the site of George Washington's fortified redoubt. From there, the colonists' cannon-fire forced the British armed forces to evacuate Boston in March 1776, and on March 17, Washington's troops triumphantly entered the plundered city to survey the damage and contemplate reconstruction.

With the Irish political ascendancy in the late nineteenth century, March 17 became a city holiday in Boston formally known as "Evacuation Day" but celebrated in predominantly Irish South Boston as an excuse to mark St. Patrick's Day. As a prime example of what the historian Eric Hobsbawm has called an "invented tradition," the storied triumph of Yankee Dorchester came to serve the political purposes of twentieth-century Irish South Boston, celebrating not the defeat of the British but the triumph of the Irish, replete with an annual St. Patrick's Day Parade, first sanctioned by the city in 1901.[2] Thus the holiday and the parade not only symbolize the more recent Irish dominion, but serve retroactively to give the South Boston Irish deeper patriotic roots than they would otherwise be able to claim. This particular invented tradition is but one manifestation of a larger and ongoing concern to guard and to promote South Boston's symbolic development, a process that has always been linked to more conventional efforts to develop the peninsula in urban and architectural terms.

South Boston's Early Development: Insularity, Industrialism, and Immigration

After the prolonged turmoil of the Revolution, Boston resumed its growth, and, anticipating urban expansion, wealthy investors purchased land on Dorchester Neck. They soon successfully petitioned for the 600-acre peninsula's annexation to Boston, despite the objections of citizens in neighboring Dorchester who wished to retain their own claim to the land. With annexation, land values quickly increased tenfold, even in advance of the bridge construction that inevitably followed.[3] In 1805, the landholders and investors laid out two major thoroughfares—Broadway, which ran the east-west length of the peninsula and which eventually would be connected by bridge to Boston proper, and Dorchester Street, which ran north-south from Broadway to mainland Dorchester. Intersecting these at regular intervals would be new interior streets, marked with nothing more than numbers and letters for names (just as had been done to help facilitate lot sales in the nation's capital only a few years earlier). In this way, South Boston emerged through the collaboration of city officials and wealthy landowners, an early example of Boston's many public-private development partnerships.

South Boston, once a virtual island topographically, remained insular long after the peninsula's legal annexation and bridge-building. At first this insularity expressed itself through construction of a district of substantial homes for Bostonians eager to take advantage of the district's open spaces and short commute to the city center. Soon afterward, both private organizations and city officials found the salt air and peripheral location of the far end of the peninsula to be conducive to a wide variety of charitable and correctional institutions that would be grouped together in a way that allowed them to sort out and attempt to reform various types of dependency.[4] Local resentment to the consolidated presence of these public neighbors mounted, exacerbated by the corresponding failure of Boston

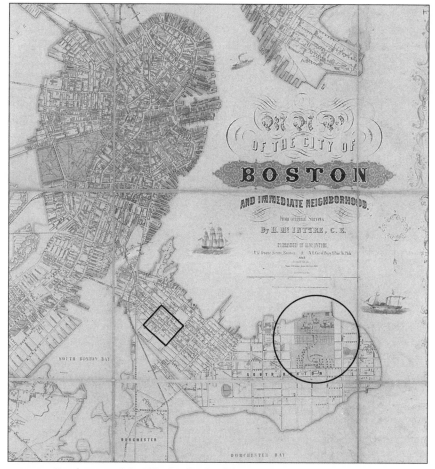

FIGURE 2.2 Development of the "City Lands," South Boston. This 1852 map shows South Boston's high concentration of facilities for public neighbors, then located in the zone known as the "City Lands" (see circle). The future site of the West Broadway housing development, on the peninsula's Lower End, is also visible (see square).

city officials to provide funds to support the maintenance of schools in the annexed district.

By the 1840s, the area of South Boston known as the "City Lands" contained not only the city's almshouse (renamed the House of Industry in order to make clear the need for able-bodied paupers to work), but a whole village of reformatories and treatment centers for institutionalized individuals (Fig. 2.2). Immediately adjacent to the House of Industry was a House of Correction, and the neighborhood also included the House of Reformation (for juvenile offenders), the City Lunatic Asylum, the School for the Feeble-Minded, a Small-Pox Hospital, and, nearby, the Perkins Institute for the Blind. Many South Boston citizens resented the perception that their community should be the dumping ground for the city's least wanted residents.

By 1838, South Boston's population had grown sufficiently to enable the district to constitute its own city ward, with four representatives to the forty-eight-member Boston common council. This newfound political voice soon made itself heard. In 1847, an appointed committee of Ward 12 inhabitants sent a harshly worded "Memorial" to Boston's mayor, aldermen, and common council members complaining that their district was being "treated as the Botany Bay of the city," a reference to the infamous British penal colony in Australia.

From the perspective of their South Boston hosts, the massed public institutions constituted a dubious prospect. "Some may have supposed at first sight that they were a benefit to South Boston," the citizens commented, "but this is a great mistake." "These institutions are among us but not of us. They give no business to South Boston. They employ none of our people. No one can enter the iron gate without a permit from the City Hall. Everything consumed in them comes from the City. They give us nothing but an undesirable name and an unpleasant association." The South Bostonians distrusted an entire system that uprooted dependent people from their families and neighborhoods and turned them into a mass of strangers concentrated just beyond their own doorsteps. "Nature meant that men should live in families," they argued, "and it is unwise and injurious to herd hundreds and thousands of them together in vast buildings, especially if they are all (or a great majority) of a low grade of intellect, and are broken down and hopeless." In an argument that prefigured in sentiment, if not in phraseology, some of the concerns expressed about public housing projects 150 years later, the South Bostonians worried about the sheer concentration of poverty and misery. "Mixed up in the great mass of society, such persons may be of use; but selected out and congregated together, they act unfavorably upon each other; they create about them a moral atmosphere in which the spirit of true life is wanting, and which is injurious to all who breathe it."[5]

In recounting the "undesirable notoriety" that had accompanied the arrival of the new institutions, South Bostonians wished to make clear that their own upstanding character should not be confused with that of the public neighbors sent to dwell among them. South Boston's own citizens were "not the scum thrown out from purer material." Nor did they comprise "men alone who lived from hand to mouth, and wanted only a temporary lodging place." Instead, they considered themselves "a class of intelligent and respectable persons of narrow means, but independent spirits, who wished to dwell in their own houses, and have elbow room about them, and pure air to breathe, and a wide prospect to enjoy." In sum, they declared, "South Boston has been sought as a residence by a very respectable class of persons, rather in spite of the policy which the City government has pursued with regard to the place, than in consequence of it." Whatever the future juxtaposition of the various institutions, these South Bostonians wanted the city's public neighbors out of South Boston.

Spurred in part by these protests and in part by the prospect of lucrative development alternatives on that peninsula, city officials soon agreed to start relocating many of the locally unwanted institutions to Deer Island in Boston Harbor, safely distant from all complaining neighbors and competing real estate interests. Despite what would seem to have been a successful resolution from the point of view of South Bostonians, the entire protracted controversy foreshadowed the recurrent antagonism between the citizens of South Boston and the leadership of "Boston proper," long blamed for having foisted upon Southie such unwelcome persons. As O'Connor puts it, "This notion of independent action in the face of municipal neglect, this resentful spirit of 'us against them,' was a theme that would continue on through the long history of the community and help explain episodes in that history when residents of South Boston would fail to cooperate with city authorities or withhold their support from municipal projects."[6]

Other factors combined with the controversies over the forced location of unwanted institutional housing in South Boston to increase greatly the antagonistic isolation of the district. Between 1820 and 1860, the northern and western sections of the peninsula gained a reputation as a major locus of industrial labor opportunities for immigrants, and class and ethnic conflicts quickly followed. From the early introduction of a chemical company, an iron works, and several glass manufacturers, the district grew to encompass major ship-building facilities and a variety of other heavy industries and smaller factories. At first, the labor force for these ventures commuted by water from the in-town tenement districts, but with the construction of the North Free Bridge in the early 1830s, the commute was made easier. At the same time, this encouraged further expansion of industries in South Boston and invited the construction of inexpensive housing adjacent to the factories. A peninsula that had once seemed a promising retreat for wealthy

Boston Yankees gradually became overrun not only by industry but by an Irish-Catholic immigrant labor force. As the western lowlands of the peninsula consolidated their industrial character, the wealthier settlers contented themselves with homes in Dorchester Heights and the beachside City Point section.[7]

As vacant lands and once-opulent country mansions were overtaken by industrial development, the western end of the peninsula gradually became a dense zone of two- and three-story tenement houses. With industry impinging from the west and unwelcome city institutions proliferating to the north, the group of Yankee citizens who delivered their Memorial to Boston city officials seemed relieved to be able to claim that at least their district still contained "not a single colored family." Yet this claim of racial exclusivity discounted the black presence in the district's institutions. When Charles Dickens visited these places in 1842, he discovered "many boys of colour" making palm-leaf hats in the House of Reformation but found no blacks in the adjacent (nonpenal) Boylston School, a jointly managed private and municipal refuge for "worthy" homeless boys.[8] In other words, South Boston's citizens could say that their district contained no black "families" only because under the reform practices of the day household members were institutionalized separately. Or, more likely, their boast about the absence of blacks—coming in the context of the wish to remove the correctional institutions to Deer Island—was a wishful affirmation of the fact that, but for the unfair presence of such institutions, the district would be more racially pure. Either way, it was clear that South Boston's leaders chose not to think of their district's public neighbors as part of the area's population profile. If blacks were present, this was the result of outside interference, not community choice. In all these ways, the 1847 claim to racial exclusivity painfully prefigured the language and the attitudes of South Boston's public housing segregationists more than a century later.

South Boston's Lower End

By the time of the Civil War, the industrialized western half of the South Boston peninsula was regularly described as the "Lower End," in contrast to the more desirable City Point side to the east, made much more attractive by the removal of most public institutions from the "City Lands." While the Lower End was certainly downhill from Dorchester Heights, the term carried a deprecatory tone ill-explained by resort to an altimeter.

Seeking alternatives to the congested quarters of the North End and Fort Hill districts, and drawn by the burgeoning employment opportunities in South Boston, the Irish working class moved onto the peninsula in increasing numbers at mid-century. Especially following the completion of the Dorchester railroad line in 1857 and the Broadway line a few years later, a South Boston residence afforded an easy commute to job opportunities elsewhere. By the 1880s however, the half-century of industrial growth began to reverse itself, as many of South Boston's heavy industries shut down in the face of technological obsolescence, or relocated their operations to other regions of the country. Although the Lower End retained many of its smaller factories, South Boston as a whole became more of a self-contained residential neighborhood, overwhelmingly Irish and Catholic. By the turn of the century, South Boston had 80,000 residents, and the Lower End now constituted its own ward, home not only to most of the district's industry, but also to its largest number of inhabitants, its highest proportion of immigrants, and its most dense population. Not surprisingly, this also meant that it contained the highest concentration of low incomes. The parishes of the Lower End were so poor that they could not even manage to support the system of parochial schools that rapidly took hold in other parts of the district, where such institutions taught not only religious education but also Irish ethnic history and culture. Unlike the more middle-class families of the City Point region, the parents living in the tenements and small wooden houses of the Lower End could not afford the nominal tuition and school supplies, and so they reluctantly continued to send their children to the "Protestant" schools.[9]

There were significant numbers of non-Irish—mostly Germans, Poles, Italians, and Lithuanians—living in the district, but the Irish dominated the politics of the local Democratic party so thoroughly that only about 10 percent of these other nationalities even bothered to become registered voters. Although the Brahmin leadership of Boston as a whole had managed to temporarily delay the citywide Irish political ascendancy by ensuring that the early Irish mayors (elected in 1884 and 1901) were compliant and acceptable to Yankee business interests, by the early decades of the twentieth century the South Boston Irish were well on their way toward a significant political voice.[10] At the same time, however, Boston's American-born Protestant leadership was more than content to let the Irish consolidate themselves in their own ethnic neighborhoods. As O'Connor comments, "Native Brahmins looked upon the exodus of the Irish, and of later ethnic groups, into the outlying neighborhoods as nothing less than a godsend." South Boston and other peripheral neighborhoods formed an ideal "safety valve" to keep the overflow of public neighbors from inner-city tenement districts from moving "into the heart of old Boston." The result, O'Connor concludes, was that "the neighborhoods siphoned newcomers off from the inner city at regular intervals and provided places where different nationalities could hold their church services, sing their rowdy songs, play their outlandish games and practice their ethnic customs without disturbing the peace and quiet of Beacon Hill." Moreover, far from feeling pushed aside, South Boston's ethnic neighbors fully embraced the positive opportunities that separate neighborhoods could provide, epitomized by the famous anthem "Southie Is My Home Town," first performed during World War I.[11]

In 1911, Eleanor Woods (the daughter of an Episcopal minister and the wife of Boston's famed settlement house leader Robert Woods) echoed the description of many earlier commentators who found South Boston to have the "atmosphere of a small separate city." "The ordinary citizen on some unusual errand" that took him across a bridge to South Boston, she wrote, "will think himself in another city although behind him scarcely five minutes away lies the South Station, a part of his daily coming and going." It was not just the predominance of factories that would startle an outsider, but also the tenement conditions of "lower South Boston." The South Boston district, she wrote, "naturally divides itself into two general parts," a congested "lower section" and an "upper section . . . which gives to South Boston its unusual advantages."[12]

Writing three decades before a large chunk of this lower section would be demolished to make way for the West Broadway public housing project, Woods complained about its "unexampled unattractiveness" and "the monotony of its numbered and lettered streets," noting that "the hand of man has indeed dealt unkindly with the promised grandeur of the first speculators." She described a neighborhood where "industry so far encroached as to almost wholly wipe out the gains to population from natural causes and immigration, without mitigating the prevalence of disease," noting that the infant mortality rate for Ward 13 was twice that of "more favored districts" and that the neighborhood housed "more victims of consumption than in any other quarter of Boston." In terms of housing conditions, Woods decried the absence of "proper sustenance and care," claiming that much of the stock was "insufficiently equipped with sanitary conveniences" and "stale with the dirt of the past." Such tenements, "forlorn in appearance," were "no longer suitable" for dwelling, since they "invite careless, unwholesome living." Woods singled out the slumlords for special disdain: "We are in the habit of assuming that a house once erected must remain indefinitely a monument to its builder . . . however well or ill constructed," since "the march of business [is] almost a sacred thing." "In these haunts of disease," she charged, "human life is sacrificed to the fetish of property." She took solace only in the scattered "small houses and cottages which have been kindly cared for and allowed to bear the insignia of family dignity"; elsewhere, she contended, "the ruthless usage of its houses by both landlord and tenant have combined to present to our observation the most menacing conditions which are to be found for human beings in city life." Such conditions, she concluded, should make South Boston's Lower End "a shining mark for housing reform."[13]

Woods was not content to document the scourge of the Lower End; she also sought to demonstrate the possibilities for elevation. As she walked further up Broadway toward Dorchester Heights, her tone changed completely: "As one reaches the higher level, prosperous looking stores suggestive of an independent city mitigate the earlier impression. With the ascent of the first hill the spirits rise and when the Avenue has topped the second the visitor feels he has discovered a part of Boston not hitherto known and deserving greater fame." By the time she reached the beachfront end of the peninsula, she was totally entranced: "when at last at Q Street the alphabet is finally vanquished by the sea one remembers its beginning at A and B Streets like an unpleasant dream." In the "upper section," she was free from the parts "most open to immigration and least desirable for residence," and looked approvingly upon the "high proportion of resident owners" found in the district's upper reaches. These places, she contended, were the homes "of those who know themselves citizens."

As for the Lower End, Woods emphasized the need to enforce tenement legislation and observed that this district's "best friends" were hoping that "industrial changes, since no other agency seems available, might wipe out the shame attached to the housing conditions." She urged others to enjoin this "veritable battle of the slums," arguing that "South Boston as a whole should have pride enough to insist upon radical action." The problem of the Lower End was more than a problem of health and housing; it was an *image* problem for those neighbors who, literally and figuratively, looked down upon it. Woods's call for "radical action" was pitched less as a humanitarian gesture to relieve suffering than as an economic development opportunity and, at base, a way to shame more privileged groups into taking steps to preserve their own elevated status. As the settlement leader Albert Kennedy put it, "Neighborhoods like individuals carry stigmata which tell their story plainer than statistical accounting could possibly do."[14] For those forced to pass the Lower End tenements on their streetcar ride down and across to Boston proper, housing reform was a way to improve their views, soothe their conscience, and import neighbors who were worthy of public support.

PUBLIC HOUSING AND SOUTH BOSTON'S LOWER END, 1935–1965

As South Boston's industries declined and suburban alternatives beckoned, the district began a long, slow contraction in population, losing fully half of its eighty thousand residents in the five decades following World War I.[15] During the 1920s and then the Great Depression, the growing inadequacy of housing conditions in South Boston's Lower End—derided in both absolute and comparative terms—gained increased attention among housing reformers. As a result, South Boston featured prominently on the map of Boston and Cambridge prepared in 1934 by the newly established Massachusetts State Housing Board highlighting "Blighted Areas that may be Considered for Rehousing Projects." Acknowledging the special urgency of the South Boston case, the State Board in its annual report for 1936 highlighted a twenty-seven-acre section of Southie's Lower End to illustrate the need for slum clearance and new housing (Figs. 2.3–2.4).

This site—known at the time as census tract M-3—had already been targeted for clearance under a plan put forward in 1934 by the South Boston Housing Corporation, a limited-dividend company. When the corporation failed to get financial assistance under Public Works Administration (PWA) guidelines, however, the plan became just one in a series of abortive early housing ventures during this era. Eventually, though, the site would become home to the West Broadway public housing project. The State Housing Board stressed the importance of developing this sort of site and justified action on the basis of a kind of cost-benefit analysis which revealed that the M-3 tract brought $27,000 of income to the city while absorbing $275,000 of city expenses: this slum, the bottom line showed, cost the city $248,000 a year to maintain.[16] To city officials, a quarter of a million dollars annually "dumped into this one small Section" was wholly unacceptable. As the State Housing Board put it, in terms that would have been utterly incomprehensible to the residents of the neighborhood, "Sub-standard areas of this character are indeed a luxury for the City to maintain."

rate of juvenile delinquency triple that of City Point and Telegraph Hill kids. In 1940 South Boston's Lower End suffered from one of the highest unemployment rates in the city, with nearly 40 percent of the labor force either seeking work or on work relief, a figure exceeded only by the North End and two neighborhoods in East Boston.[19]

REIMAGING THE LOWER END

Given such conditions, when discussion of a West Broadway public housing project revived in 1939, it initially received highly laudatory local press coverage. The *South Boston Gazette* gave the idea page-one coverage, and its headline for May 19, 1939, proclaimed: "Business Men Back Plan for New Low Rental Project Here." The *Gazette* credited local clergymen and business leaders with launching the idea of a "new rental project for the lower end" and insisted that the plan was "meeting with general approval in all parts of this section." All of South Boston's business community, the paper maintained, felt that "placing of a new village at the entrance to the district will be the first step in the right direction," leading to a "new South Boston."[20]

The economic justification previously provided by the State Housing Board for demolishing census tract M-3 was a strong motivator for change, but South Bostonians remained primarily concerned about their district's image to outsiders. Perhaps by more than mere coincidence, the *South Boston Gazette* paired the announcement of its approval of the new public housing initiative with an editorial letter, reprinted from the *Boston American,* explaining that "South Boston residents are engaged in a campaign to wipe out wrong impressions of that community, caused by unfair stories, cheap 'Southie' songs, slurs by public speakers and politicians, cheap jokes in theaters or in any other manner," concluding that "we are using postal cards and the press to make protests." In this context, the call to place a "new village" at the community's "entrance" was yet another mode of protest, a proactive attempt to rebuild the neighborhood's image in the eyes of dismissive outsiders.

At the same time, the *Gazette* clearly regarded public housing as a direct benefit to the residents of South Boston. One writer lauded the "fine arrangements" at the recently occupied Old Harbor Village project, observing that skeptics "are now fully convinced that the project surpasses in every way even their fondest ideals." The Lower End project, too, promised new opportunities for families "privileged to enjoy first class homes at a small rental." For the writers and editors of the *South Boston Gazette,* whose masthead motto read "Published to Protect the People," public housing portended the last, best hope for a declining portion of the neighborhood.

Throughout the preceding decade of depression the district had declined, with many houses "formerly occupied by local residents" torn down, and others in grave disrepair. "Unless a housing project is located there," the paper warned, "there is very little hope to bring that section back to the normal it was years back." Observing that many of the still-occupied houses were "far from being the type of homes people should live in today," the *Gazette* called for "the Government [to] take over this area and build a village." "Many persons living in that section will have the first chance to get tenements and they will be given an opportunity of having first class homes at a small cost per month."[21] Lost in this neat logic, of course, was the fact that such slum-dwellers would be displaced from even their inadequate housing for the eight years that it would take between demolition and inauguration of a new project. Moreover, the rent structure of public housing was set well beyond the means of most of those who would be displaced, a matter that should have already been well apparent to South Bostonians from the experience of renting-up Old Harbor Village during the preceding year.

Rehousing "Slum-Dwellers"

At Old Harbor, as a result of concerted tenant-selection efforts (10,000 applicants for 1,016 apartments), Boston's first public neighborhood quickly became one of South Boston's best-off areas. Its monthly median rent of $25.52 was the highest in that district, nearly double that of its least expensive areas, and only about three dollars below the median *citywide.* In 1940, a time when nearly 30 percent of South Boston's labor force was either seeking work or on work relief, this was true for only 8.8 percent of those living in Old Harbor Village. Amazing as it now seems, only five neighborhoods in the entire city of Boston had a lower proportion of unemployed than Old Harbor Village.

Even though the BHA promised that rents in subsequent projects would be less than those charged under the terms of this initial PWA venture, the Authority's tenant-selection system worked against the prospects for rehousing most "slum-dwellers." Despite the promise of "first chance" alluded to by the *South Boston Gazette*'s reporter, the panoply of BHA requirements meant that for hundreds of those displaced, first chance was no chance. To begin with, the Authority was bound by the terms of federal law and its agreements with the United States Housing Authority (USHA), as well as by the terms of the Massachusetts Housing Law, which in some aspects was even more stringent. Taken together, these stipulated four major requirements for eligibility: 1. The family income could not exceed five times the rent (or six times the rent for a family with three or more minor dependents); 2. The family had to be living under substandard conditions that were detrimental to health, safety, and morals, for the period of six months immediately prior to the filing of the application; 3. The family had to have resided in the city of Boston for at least one year immediately prior to the filing of the application; and 4. The head of the family had to be a U.S. citizen. This last requirement alone rendered hundreds of persons in South Boston's Lower End ineligible. Similarly, the income requirement—while it did not explicitly specify a minimum—was interpreted by the BHA to mean that admitted households should have a well-established track record of earned wages. Public housing in Boston was not for those who were unemployed, on work relief, or temporarily employed by some New Deal program. So too, with apartments designated for families of between two and nine persons, single individuals and very large families were also rendered ineligible. On top of all this, the BHA used its arsenal of home visits, credit checks, and landlord references to shoot down the applications of all but the most desirable. Those whose domestic struggle was hardest would not always make the best impression.

In this context, the BHA's commitment to giving preference to former site tenants whose homes were demolished to make way for the new projects, *as long as they were otherwise eligible,* generally meant that these individuals would never live in public housing. Analysis of City Directory and Police List data for Boston's first four slum-clearance public housing projects—comparing lists of those persons present on the site shortly before clearance with those who subsequently tenanted the projects—reveals that only between 2 and 12 percent of those who lost their homes were provided with apartments in the housing project that replaced them, even though, BHA records suggest, between 50 and 80 percent of displaced families submitted applications.[22] In the case of the project for South Boston's Lower End, the situation turned out to be even more extreme. Owing to the long delay between clearance in early 1942 and project occupancy in late 1949—and exacerbated by the fact that the development was designated as housing for veterans—residency records suggest that not a single family displaced

FIGURE 2.5 South Boston's Lower End before redevelopment. This photo, taken in 1940, shows a faint line drawn around B Street, West Broadway, D Street, and West Seventh Street, revealing the BHA's plans for clearance.

from the site gained a home in the West Broadway project (though a small percentage did secure places in other projects elsewhere in the city during the early 1940s).

LOCAL PRESSURES FOR AND AGAINST PUBLIC HOUSING

Despite simmering neighborhood protests over the proposed Old Colony site and comparable controversies in other city neighborhoods once BHA slum-clearance efforts went into high gear in 1939, the Lower End's most visible civic spokesmen pushed the Authority toward another round of demolition in South Boston. From 1938 to 1941, following the initial charge of Southie's Robert E. Lee—the pastor of Saints Peter and Paul Church—a variety of local clubs and

FIGURE 2.6 BHA documentation of deteriorating housing. Before commencing demolition, the BHA commissioned photo surveys to document poor conditions. The BHA's caption for this photo, showing a three-family house built in 1840, reads: "The owner, unable to keep the entire property in repair, has given up one side in the hopes of saving the other." The BHA destroyed both sides.

civic associations in South Boston met to promote plans for redeveloping the Lower End and creating "a decent entrance" to the district. Working both separately and in groups, they documented the dire housing conditions in letters sent to Housing Authority Board Chairman John Breen, circulated petitions, and collaborated with priests from other Lower End parishes, including the clergyman destined to lose both his church and his parishioners. One group, headed by John Flaherty—who soon won election as a state representative—commissioned a survey of the site, including extensive photography and film footage of "some of the wrecked and dilapidated houses," to be "used as convincing arguments before members of the Housing Authority" (Figs. 2.5–2.9).[23] These studies showed that many houses lacked bathtubs and central heating, and revealed the presence of multiple fire hazards, including many large tenements that lacked even a single fire wall. In early February 1941, following months of pressure from South Boston's two city councilors, Mayor James Tobin announced that plans to build a

FIGURE 2.7 Substandard basement, 164 D Street.

FIGURE 2.8 Substandard kitchen, 161 West Broadway.

FIGURE 2.9 Hallway toilet, 147 Silver Street.

new housing project in the Lower End would go forward, a statement timed to appease South Boston residents who had just learned that the federal government planned to take over the nearly completed Old Colony project for its own war-time use.[24]

Despite the promise of movement on a new project to be located in South Boston's most vilified area, the coming of the war brought a long and painful halt to the plans. Unfortunately for the residents of the Lower End, however, the decision to delay construction came only after the area had been razed. Within days of the mayor's announcement, the *South Boston Gazette* printed the first of several warnings to local residents, informing them of unscrupulous real estate practices and heavy-handed pressure tactics employed by the BHA in other ongoing clearance efforts. One piece, carrying the byline "The Critic," gave several examples from the South End where homeowners were offered less money than a city appraisal had stipulated, and other cases where obtaining more reasonable appraisals depended on the owner's prior agreement to seek new housing using only the listings of one particular real estate agent. In general, the South End displacees charged, those who had kept up their property to "modern standards" were financially penalized, "while those who let their homes decay through the years gained by the deal." The *Gazette*'s critic urged the residents of South Boston's Lower End to "stand by their constitutional rights" and "not stand for this type of bookkeeping." The piece closed with the promise of future investigative journalism: "The Housing Authority may be warned too that the *South Boston Gazette* will look into the deals as they start to come to light in this section and will publish the facts before the harm has been done."[25]

Even before individual residents were pressured to sell, the area's merchants expressed their own outrage. A week after the mayor's announcement, thirty-five business owners who operated along West Broadway in the proposed project-clearance area gathered together to try to save the West Broadway frontage (Fig 2.10). They pointed out that some stores had been in business in that locality for as long as fifty years; in fact, the *average* longevity of those businesses whose owners attended the meeting was more than twenty-five years. State Representative John E. Powers, City Councilor Joseph Scannell, and South Boston Citizens' Association President William M. Flannagan all addressed the group to pledge their cooperation and to help arrange meetings with BHA Board Chairman Breen and Mayor Tobin.[26]

Six weeks later, with no relief in sight for the merchants, the *South Boston Tribune* scooped the *Gazette* by reporting that mistreatment by the BHA had local residents "up in arms." Several residents complained that housing authority investigators simply walked into their homes unannounced, without so much as a knock, and "demanded information." Residents who declined to provide personal information were told that "they had better talk," and those who complained to the housing authority about the "untactful manner" and "type of questions asked" were dismissively reassured that the investigation was "routine." Councilor Scannell, who himself had received numerous complaints about this matter from his constituents, told them he would "demand that investigators be made to show more courtesy" and be told to "inform families that it was not compulsory for them to answer any questions."[27]

FIGURE 2.10 Buildings to be cleared at the corner of D Street and West Broadway.

Counting Rosaries and Census Tracts

Despite the pleas and promises of local officials, nothing stopped the wholesale demolition of the district. The very same week that the Japanese attacked Pearl Harbor, the BHA announced plans to take all the land for the project by eminent domain, a "sudden decision" occasioned by Breen's realization that "there is a critical need for homes for families of enlisted personnel." In exchange for the housing authority's agreement to "allocate a number of dwelling units in its proposed program and to give reasonable preference to families of servicemen and defense workers," the federal government agreed to help the BHA "secure priorities needed to procure critical materials to complete the projects."[28] Despite such assurance, however, the project stalled, leaving South Boston's Lower End with twenty-seven leveled acres for most of the next eight years. Some locals came to call this area "no man's land" while others referred to it as "the prairie"; others commented on its resemblance to areas of war-torn European cities. South Boston's politicians still preferred to term it "blight."

For others, however, the destruction seemed nothing short of a tragedy. City officials thought they had torn down census tract M-3, but many of its Irish Catholic residents felt as though the entire Holy Rosary Parish had been destroyed, including the small church that gave it its name. The *South Boston Gazette,* though more supportive of public housing than was the rival *South Boston Tribune,* struck a melancholy tone when it chronicled the old neighborhood's last Mass; after February 6, 1942, its writer lamented, "there will be no parish of the Church of Our Lady of the Rosary." One parishioner, Jack Reid, forced to depart his home in advance of the demolition crews, later recalled that his family moved "with our bathtub in a horse and wagon," and even took along their newly purchased front door, since his "mother was very proud of it." Fully sixty years after the neighborhood razing, some South Boston Irish still harbor resentment. As one elderly woman commented recently, "I used to live right where they built that jungle. It was nice and I was happy. We had three-decker homes, three families each. We all had grass and flowers in our yards. They got rid of the Rosary Church and the nice homes all in the name of the public domain and built that living hell. They thought they were helping people, but they ain't helped nobody. That project cost me my childhood."[29]

Neither the *Gazette* nor the *Tribune* carried news of the other major ethnic and ecclesiastical disruption: the wholesale destruction of South Boston's Lithuanian community. In this case, the BHA spared the Lithuanian church (St. Peter's) and built the project literally all around it, while demolishing the homes of many of its parishioners (Fig. 2.11). To read the South Boston papers, one would think that the Lower End slum-clearance effort had been directed at Irish Catholics, yet closer analysis of the ethnic demographics of the district shows that the public housing site instead disproportionately displaced a predominantly Lithuanian and Polish neighborhood, most of whose residents were forced to move at least ten to fifteen blocks away, where they continued to harbor "bitter feelings toward the project."[30] Laura Dapkiewicz's experience seems typical: "In 1941, when I was residing on Fourth St., South Boston, I was told by the City of Boston officials that I would have first preference into one of the Projects because we were forced out of our flats to make room for the D St. Project. We were put out, but I never got an apartment in the project." For the next twenty years, Dapkiewicz continued to try to get into "any local project," but to no avail. "I have always lived a respectable life and am a decent, good-living person," she asserted in a letter to Boston's mayor. "I am a Catholic and am a regular church attendant . . . but, because I am divorced, I have been told I cannot get in."[31]

FIGURE 2.11 South Boston's Lower End after construction of the West Broadway project. The completed twenty-seven-acre project retained the complex of Lithuanian church buildings (seen in bottom quadrant) and two schools (in top quadrant); all else was leveled in 1941–1942 to make way for the new public neighborhood.

The South Boston papers ignored the resentment caused by the Polish and Lithuanian displacement for forty years. Only in 1981, when the *Tribune* published a Letter to the Editor from Reverend Albert J. Contons of St. Peter's, did the issue enter into print. Contons, who watched the construction of the project in 1948–1949, and subsequently moved into the project-surrounded rectory, told how "the heart of the Lithuanian community"—some three hundred families— was displaced to make way for the housing project. When it was built, he charged, "the needs of the Lithuanian community were totally disregarded. Our people were victimized in the planning of the project and in the manner of its management."[32] Of all the dilapidated areas of the Lower End, housing officials and church leaders selected the one that caused the least amount of disruption to locally powerful Irish interests. Even within this least favored area of the district, some people were thought more worthy of subsidizing than others.

NEW NEIGHBORS FOR THE LOWER END

Within hours after the second atomic blast compelled Japanese surrender in August 1945, South Boston City Councilor Scannell took to the floor of the chamber to demand renewed action on the Broadway front. He decried the fact that his community faced a housing shortage because of the influx of "ridge runners" holding defense-related jobs while living in the housing projects, claiming that this displacement forced "former South Boston residents . . . to commute 20 or 30 miles from home to work." With "tens of thousands" on BHA waiting lists and minimal apartment turnover, he foresaw major problems when "the men came home" to find doubled-up families. He urged the mayor to "immediately contact" Washington to obtain the necessary preferences to launch the West Broadway project.[33]

Nothing happened, of course, since action depended on congressional funding of highly controversial housing legislation. A year after Scannell's call to action, all that South Boston's other city councilor, Bob Linehan, could do was get the Council to pass a resolution to record itself as in favor of the pending Senate legislation.[34] After another year passed, State Representative John B. Wenzler sent an equally out-of-jurisdiction plea directly to President Truman, informing him of the "blight" on his district occasioned by the failure to follow through with construction on the West Broadway site. He stressed the disruption that had been caused to local families, first by the order to vacate, and then by the broken promise to build "immediately" a low-income project on that site. He concluded by emphasizing the desperate need for housing for worthy veterans.[35] By the end of 1947, the *Gazette*'s page-one headline was "Residents Are Shouting for Housing Project." The paper described the stalled project as "the main topic of discussion in this village" and later amended its choice of the word "discussion" to say "it is a constant wailing . . . even by those who already have homes, so it is easy to visualize how those badly in need of a place to live feel about it." The *Gazette* cajoled its readers once again to send postcards "to those in authority" instead of "complaining to a neighbor." Committed to its "crusade against anything unfair to South Boston," the paper praised the exploits of its hero Linehan, who had "been fighting like a real warrior." Linehan, for his part, told the *Gazette*'s readers of his belief that "there are some members of the Boston Housing Authority who haven't a friendly feeling for a South Boston project." And so the call for postcards was launched again.[36]

MASSACHUSETTS VETERANS ON BROADWAY

Since 1941 all parties had assumed that the "Third South Boston Project" would be built with federal funds, using the usual contractual arrangements among the

BHA, the city of Boston, and the Federal Public Housing Authority. The postwar construction bids came in "far in excess" of the prevailing federal maximum cost standards for low-rent projects, however, and housing officials in Washington refused to allow any building to commence. The Wagner-Ellender-Taft Bill would have raised the federal ceiling for per unit construction costs, but this legislation was still delayed in Congress. Desperate to see construction get under way—especially since they were paying interest on the loans secured to obtain and clear the site—local housing officials turned instead to the Massachusetts legislature for sponsorship. This, in turn, entailed much legal wrangling over the question of whether land taken by eminent domain for one public purpose (federal low-rent housing) could be used for another (state-aided veterans housing).[37] Only in late 1948, when the push for the West Broadway project was channeled into the Commonwealth's new Veterans' Housing Program (known as Chapter 200), did construction finally seem "a certainty." Councilor Linehan, along with John Wenzler, made certain that the State Housing Board moved the South Boston project to the top of its priority list, and made equally certain that the South Boston newspapers were aware of the extent of their own successful lobbying. It would not be long, Wenzler promised, before "thousands of real South Bostonians" ("our displaced persons") could return. Mayor John Michael Curley pledged rapid construction to put an end to the "open eyesore and blight on the city." When actual construction finally did begin, the *Gazette* itself took credit for doing "its share" through "agitation for the project in its news columns," and its anonymous columnist looked forward to the repatriation of those who had "been forced to live outside of South Boston for eight years" (Fig. 2.12).[38] The long quest for the West Broadway development in South Boston was finally over. Despite its delays, the struggle revealed a community well-armed with political connections and determined that the new housing would be used to bring its own involuntary exiles back home to Southie.

SOUTH BOSTON FOR SOUTH BOSTONIANS

For many in South Boston, the challenge was not how to house the low-income families already in the Lower End, but how to retain or regain desirable South Boston families of all income levels. At the same time that South Bostonians editorially debated the merits of existing and proposed public housing for the low-income people of the district, they also worried about the exodus of the district's more affluent. Even before the war, the *South Boston Gazette* described the "cru-

FIGURE 2.12 Housing for veterans. The West Broadway development was long delayed in construction, and Mayor Curley and the BHA made sure that all who passed by the site in 1949 would know whom it was intended to house.

sade" under way to try to build large modern apartments in the district to encourage "hundreds of former residents" to return. These unwilling emigrants, the author claimed, truly lamented their decision to leave; they termed South Boston "the greatest place in America—at least morally"—and wished to return to "the finest living people in the United States."[39] The search for "men of affluence" to invest in "high priced apartments" in South Boston progressed, but the exodus continued.

Postwar public housing came to South Boston at a time when the private housing market was changing rapidly. As veterans returned to Southie, they found that their search for upward mobility increasingly took them beyond the bounds of their own neighborhood, since Boston banks refused to grant mortgages or assign home-improvement loans to "blighted" or "depressed" neighborhoods such as South Boston. Faced with such redlining, most of South Boston's young families who sought to own a home headed for the suburbs, where mortgage rates were lower and bankers were much happier to help out. The impact of this exodus on South Boston, O'Connor observes, was quite direct and perpetuated a cycle of decline: "In a short time, older parts of the neighborhood began to show signs of the blight and decay predicted by the banks. Maintenance and repairs became prohibitive, homes fell into serious disrepair, streets were no longer cleaned, parks and playgrounds were soon neglected, and vandalism became commonplace." Whether they were leaving by choice or by default, these departing families added one more dimension to South Boston's long-term population decline. With the postwar G.I. Bill of Rights providing housing loans, professional training, and college education, South Boston lost many of its upwardly mobile veterans directly to outlying areas; for many, however, the new public housing project served as a welcome first stop—at least for those who could afford it.

Low-Rent Housing?

Even before it formally opened in 1949, some veterans raised a furor over the project's rent structure. Writing under the headline "Veterans Roar over Housing Project Rents," one *Gazette* journalist noted that "when hundreds of homes were torn down a few years ago to erect these up-to-date apartments, it was generally believed that those who would move into them would be given them at prices they would easily be able to pay." Instead, it now became apparent, "only those with fancy salaries or incomes will be able to occupy them." Impoverished veterans living in other parts of South Boston complained that moving to the housing project would actually cost them more money. At a meeting with a BHA Board member called by the South Boston Allied Veterans Council in August 1949, distressed veterans pointed out that newspaper stories from 1940 had assured everyone that this housing would be for "the low income group," and that preference would be given to those displaced from the site. Instead, BHA Board Member Joseph Benkert now said, no such priority existed. Worse still, he claimed that any veteran who had lived three years anywhere in Boston was eligible to apply—there was not even to be an official priority for South Bostonians. The one priority would be for veterans whose excessive income threatened to displace them from federally funded projects, which had lower income ceilings than those proposed for the state program.

The veterans asked other embarrassing questions for which no satisfactory answers were forthcoming: Why did the BHA's internally circulated rent schedule show rents ranging from $36 to $72 for the project, whereas the rent schedule circulated to the Boston press showed rents capping out at $45? Was there a cover-up? Why was it that one veteran's application, long-delayed in consideration, was returned to him with the recommendation that it needed "a politician's name on

FIGURE 2.13 West Broadway in 1949. The new public neighborhood offered easy public transit into the heart of Boston.

it"? "Why," a veteran asked, "must one know a politician to get into the Housing project?"

Councilor Linehan, the much-praised "warrior" for veterans housing, probably wished he had not decided to attend this meeting. He complained that he had been responsible for enacting the law and had never received any help from the veterans themselves; only two veterans posts had even bothered to send him a letter of thanks. The reason the rents were so high, he explained, was that labor costs had soared since 1940, when the project had been first contemplated. Under present circumstances, he admitted to the veterans, "homes cannot be built for veterans with low income."[40] All in all, hardly an auspicious start for a housing project that had not yet opened.

Despite the intensity of criticism in some quarters about who would be able to live in the project, the development still garnered good press. The *Gazette* described it as "the talk of the town," and its columnist claimed that it "added greatly to the beauty of South Boston" (Fig. 2.13).[41] It also added markedly to the median income of South Boston's Lower End: in 1940, the preproject neighbor-

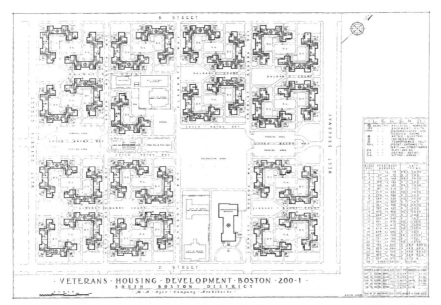

FIGURE 2.14 Site plan of the West Broadway "Veterans Housing Development," 1949. The superblock featured twenty-seven nearly identical L-shaped buildings, provided for great amounts of "open space," and completely eliminated all through streets. St. Peter's Lithuanian Church stands buried in the northwest quadrant of the project.

hood had a lower median income than any adjacent census tract; ten years later, the income of project residents was the area's highest. The predominantly Irish project residents of the new veterans project held three times as many professional and managerial jobs as the predominantly Lithuanian and Polish slum-dwellers they replaced. No other nearby area could boast such dramatic gains.

THE FORM OF THE NEW PUBLIC NEIGHBORHOOD

The West Broadway project (already sometimes referred to as "D Street") reached full occupancy in 1950. The BHA wished to emphasize its distinction from the rest of the Lower End in as many ways as possible. On a site that once held many hundreds of structures, each extending out to its sidewalk, the new project (together with three remaining schools, the Lithuanian church, and its rectory) offered up only thirty-four buildings, arranged to maximize the amount of the ground plane left open (Figs. 2.14–2.16). The repetitive pattern of equally spaced L-shaped apartment buildings varied only enough to accommodate the existing nonresidential structures, but the designers made no effort to highlight their presence. Instead, for example, the Lithuanian complex appears in the site

BOSTON   HOUSING AUTHORITY
PLAY   AREA
PROJECT MASS 2 10   M·A·DYER CO ARCHTS
BOSTON MASS

FIGURE 2.15 A play area planned for West Broadway. In an early sketch for the development, the architect Michael Dyer envisioned expansive play areas.

plan as little more than a missing piece left out of a puzzle. As Reverend Contons from St. Peter's later complained, displaced Lithuanian parishioners had "at least hoped that the new project . . . would provide a better setting for their parish church." Instead, however, the new superblock "made access to their church difficult," and the "apartment buildings, as if in spite, crowded in the church and rectory."[42] While there is no direct evidence that the site plan was also intended as a "spite" plan, the architect Michael A. Dyer made no effort to use the major remaining vestige of Lithuanian cultural life as a symbolic focus for the new community. St. Peter's was an urbanistic irrelevance.

Within the superblock site plan, Dyer focused on the housing itself. Except where existing institutions made it impossible, he grouped the L-shaped buildings into pairs, with each pair providing a semi-enclosed area for "drying yards," "sitting areas," and "playing areas," a contiguous expanse of open space intended to be differentiated by pathways. At the very center of the block Dyer placed a 200-foot square "recreation area," but there were also no fewer than 336 other

FIGURE 2.16 West Broadway girls at play, early 1950s.

unlabeled outdoor areas, each neatly boxed in the drawing but apparently without any sense of intended function.

The new public neighborhood completely disregarded the old neighborhood's existing pattern of gridded streets; not one road traveled straight through the project. It was impossible, in fact, to drive anywhere on the West Broadway side of the project from anywhere on the West Seventh Street side, except by first exiting the project completely. Roads that did penetrate the superblock perimeter were renamed after South Boston veterans who had died in the Second World War, including some who had once lived on the actual site of the project, with no regard for the names of intersecting neighborhood streets. The superblock lingo referred to these interior passages not as "streets" but as "ways." Their primary purpose was to afford automobile access to the project's two large central-parking areas, and so they were more like city-scaled driveways than streets. With each "way" a discontinuous series of several different road segments, visitors faced considerable disorientation. Dalessio Court, intended entirely for pedestrians, appeared in three different places, while Joyce-Hayes Way stuttered noncontinuously through the development in four pieces, two of which were really median strips between parking lots rather than traversable paths. The "Flaherty Way" that connected to B Street had no connection to the "Flaherty Way" that connected to D Street, a quirk that made partial sense only because the road was named in memory of two different veterans named Flaherty. Wholly undaunted by this particular complexity, the BHA subsequently named the asphalt "Recreation Area" between the two Flaherty Ways in memory of a *third* Flaherty—Father Patrick X. Flaherty, a chaplain who had died in a Texas plane crash. The resultant triple-Flaherty substituted linguistic continuity for actual automobile access. Also lost on the veterans groups of the day was the irony that the recreation area honored the man who just a decade before had celebrated his first Mass in the Church of the Holy Rosary, demolished to make way for the cleared ground that now bore his name.[43] In any case, the logic behind the names and positions of the "ways" seems fathomable only in plan, where it remains possible to see them as the vestigial memories of the premodern grid. On the ground, however, the circulation pattern relied on its own internal dynamic, intended to maximize separation of vehicles and pedestrians.

With its flat roofs, wide-open spaces, and modern kitchen appliances, the internally focused world of the West Broadway project stood as a manifest symbol of progress. For new arrivals as well as for old-timers, the quality of life in public housing must have seemed a remarkable contrast to the conditions prevailing elsewhere in the Lower End. With the exception of other public housing, fully 98 percent of the neighborhood housing stock was more than thirty years old, most much older. More than a third of these houses and apartments had no running water; the majority were without mechanical refrigeration; and three-quarters lacked a functioning private bath. Project residents needed do no more than cross the street to find such conditions.

WEST BROADWAY'S FIRST RESIDENTS

To play up the contrast between prevailing slum conditions and the brave new world of Massachusetts Veterans public housing is not, however, to suggest that the creation of public housing actually allowed many families to make the transition from one set of circumstances to the other. Despite the large public subsidy, the many amenities of public housing carried significant costs, and in most cases those costs were so great as to prohibit the possibility of a move. With median rents of $43 per month in the project compared with $17 per month in surrounding neighborhoods, the two tenant groups clearly had little overlap.[44] When the Broadway project opened, its residents boasted one of the highest median incomes of any neighborhood in South Boston, equaled or surpassed only by other public housing projects. Ninety-seven percent of the households had both spouses present, and 92 percent of the women listed their occupation as "housewife." About a third of their husbands held jobs as clerks and salesmen, while nearly all the rest were employed in a variety of semi-skilled or skilled occupations.[45] The veterans and their families enjoyed one of the lowest unemployment rates in the area (7 percent), a rate half that of immediately adjoining districts. Moreover, these publicly introduced neighbors had the highest median education in all of South Boston (12.3 years) and included 150 people who had completed some or all of college. And with citizenship a prerequisite for housing eligibility, only 2 percent of the new residents were foreign-born, compared with 20 percent of those in the immediately adjacent census tracts.[46] With public housing, the quality of the building stock improved. At the same time, public policy dictated a correspondingly "improved" sort of tenant, suitably employed and wholly Americanized.

With intense competition for apartments and ample opportunity for screening, the BHA also tried to control the social structure of project families. The overwhelming majority of initial tenants were two-parent households with children; the 1950 census reported 941 married males living at West Broadway, and the ratio of children-to-adults was almost exactly 1:1—about two thousand of each. And, just as many in the neighborhood had feared, only about one in five of these original households came from South Boston.[47]

Throughout the 1950s and into the early 1960s, the D Street project seems to have caused no great controversy for either its residents or its South Boston neighbors, aside from the still-simmering resentments of the displaced Lithuanians. Long-term residents who moved in during the 1950s still remember the early days quite fondly, stressing both the quality of the project's physical upkeep and the friendliness and neighborliness of fellow tenants. They speak of a place without language barriers or racial tensions, where "everyone got along" and "everyone watched out for each other." As one early arrival put it, "We were all a family then." Although still subjected to some criticism for its lack of adequate recreation facilities (complaints that began even before it opened), this project—like many others—boasted a full complement of social clubs and sports teams. One man who moved to D Street in 1952 recalled West Broadway as "saturated with children to such an extent that baby carriages and strollers seemed to outnumber automobiles." Eager to take advantage of the presence of more-affluent residents of the new public neighborhood, a Stop and Shop supermarket opened up directly across the street, and the *Gazette* reported that "South Boston's face lifting would surprise ex-residents."[48]

The Lower End of South Boston retained its stigma for some South Bostonians, but in 1960 as in 1950, the housing project residents could still be regarded as the best off in that neighborhood. The comparative health of public housing became all the more clear as the dismal residential living conditions on all sides of the project continued to decline. By 1960 the U.S. Census Bureau considered only 10 percent of these dwellings to be "sound," while 52 percent were deteriorating, and the other 38 percent were already deemed "dilapidated."

At the same time, however, the residents of these substandard private neighborhoods also paid "substandard" rents, about half of the median then prevailing in the more commodious public neighborhood of the housing project. In 1960, as in 1950, the project still charged the highest median rents in the area. Yet the median income of D Street residents was no longer one of the area's highest. With the outflow of the most prosperous families, the housing project's incomes now ranked behind those of several other neighborhoods; by 1970, D Street's median income would be far and away the lowest in its area (Fig. 2.17).

Many changes were already apparent by 1960, as the most upwardly mobile of the original tenants departed and were replaced by those with fewer resources. When the project opened, 921 project residents had jobs; by 1960, that number had already dropped to 743, the beginning of a long and continual decline that would only worsen in the decades ahead. In 1950, 58 residents had worked in professional and technical jobs; by 1960, there were only 15 with such high-end employment. From 150 college-educated residents in 1950, only 89 had completed some college a decade later.

All together, almost half of the original project population managed to move out in three years or less; two-thirds had departed by 1955, and 85 percent were gone by 1960 (Fig. 2.18). Those who entered West Broadway with clerical jobs

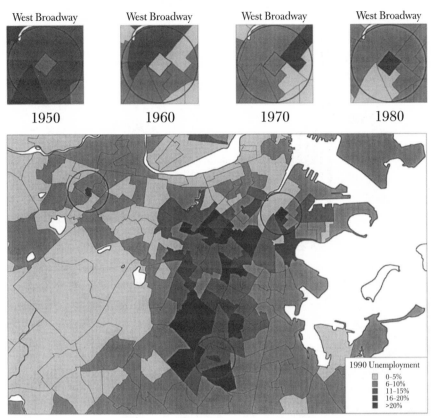

FIGURE 2.17 Project and neighborhood employment changes, 1950–1990. Data mapped from the U.S. Census for 1950, 1960, 1970, 1980, and 1990 show the changing pattern of unemployment between the West Broadway project and the areas within a half-mile radius of its center. In 1950 project unemployment was the lowest in the neighborhood; by 1970 project unemployment had surpassed some surrounding areas; and in 1980 and 1990 the project had the highest unemployment rate in the neighborhood. The 1990 data are shown on a citywide map, in which West Broadway appears circled at top right, along with Commonwealth (top left) and Franklin Field (bottom).

(and who presumably also had the highest educations and incomes) stayed on in the project only about three years on average, whereas those with semi-skilled or unskilled jobs lingered for an average of six years. The vast majority—regardless of their job classification—managed to find alternative private accommodation after a few years. As one woman who moved into the project soon after it opened recalls, "The project was occupied by a lot of WW II veterans and their families.

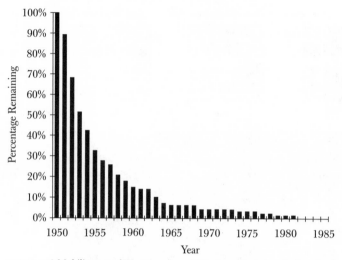

FIGURE 2.18 Mobility out of West Broadway. This chart, depicting the length of stay of West Broadway's original households, shows that most left very quickly. Two-thirds had moved on within five years, and 85 percent were gone by 1960.

Most of the neighbors had small children and everyone got along pretty well. However, after a few years, my husband advanced in his career and we were able to move back up to 'The Point,' a section of South Boston where I grew up." This family, like many others, used D Street as a waystation, just as the BHA's careful tenant-selection process had intended. Many of those who remained, however— like those new recruits who came to join them—were increasingly those with the fewest economic alternatives. When it was built the D Street public neighborhood brought sweeping socioeconomic change to a depressed area; by the end of its first decade of operation, however, there were already signs of renewed economic decline.[49]

Many of those who stayed on at D Street or who newly came to dwell there experienced the first effects of what would become a massive social shift away from the two-parent families that dominated the original cohort of households. In 1950, the number of adult males and females living in the project was about equal; a decade later the rest of the surrounding neighborhood still showed the same ratio, but at D Street there were 50 percent more adult females than adult males. By 1960, with 229 women listed as widowed, 33 divorced, and 66 separated, about one-third of all households were now without adult male heads. For the moment, however, this transformation seemed concentrated among older households because, in 1960, 84 percent of project children under eighteen still lived with both parents, and, in 1962, only 7 percent of D Street households relied on AFDC (Aid to Families with Dependent Children) as their primary source of income.[50]

In the early 1960s many D Street project residents still claimed South Boston roots and relations and, by their very numbers, remained an important part of its local politics. Leaders of South Boston's dense network of clubs and service agencies worked hard to ensure that the public neighborhood of the project remained a public resource for nearby residents, while also urging D Street tenants to make full use of the resources of the broader South Boston community. With a dense array of active parishes, a supportive local press, a solicitous corps of Southie politicians, a still-busy neighborhood settlement house, and an active strip of retail shops rising along West Broadway from the development up the hill, few communities in the city were better suited to incorporate the presence of public housing than South Boston. At the same time, however, it already seemed clear that special initiatives were needed to nurture the social connections between project and neighborhood.

In the early 1960s, South Boston's Olivia James House (founded in 1902) worked to emphasize social links between project residents and their South Boston neighbors. In late spring 1964, this settlement house (renamed the South Boston Neighborhood House) collaborated with D Street management to sponsor "Public Housing Week," seven days of athletic, recreational, and social events. Organizers brought together softball and basketball teams from both inside and outside the development, making clear that the athletic facilities of the housing project were a broader community resource. To gain more publicity for the event, Massachusetts Governor Endicott Peabody and Boston Mayor John Collins each presented the D Street manager with a trophy for "Outstanding Athlete in the D Street Development Athletic Tournament."[51] Teams from all over South Boston registered to play, many with church or ethnic affiliations, including the St. Vincent's Club, the Lithuanian Athletic Association, and Snuffy Dillion's Shamrock Club. The *South Boston Tribune* touted the "Athletic Tourney at D St. Project" with a banner headline, indicating that the project could still make local headlines for its positive contributions rather than for its tensions.[52] In addition to recreational activities, a variety of local service agencies also used D Street facilities as a way to reach out to the entire Lower End.[53]

Yet because of its location, even when D Street served as a social center it attracted primarily the denizens of South Boston's least favored realm. The West

Broadway development had never fully enjoyed the cachet of its waterfront South Boston alternatives, and in the early 1960s D Street was already losing its reputation as the domicile of carefully screened veterans. Already in 1961 and 1962, some tenants registered complaints about "noisy children who are out screeching and hollering until all hours at night." Another resident felt forced into isolation by "the belligerence of the youngsters in the neighborhood" who caused her to "keep her windows closed, and shades down, to avoid being molested." This tenant's doctor suggested that she be "transferred to an apartment over Broadway," where "she would feel rather more secure by the patrolling of the street, and the closer contact with the outside environment."[54] Despite such emerging concerns, D Street still seemed remarkably peaceable, and its neighborhood and neighbors continued to be seen as an asset to the district.

Urban Renewal and South Boston

For more than a century, South Boston's residents obsessively protected their district from outside control; for decades, they struggled to make sure that any government-subsidized public housing would chiefly serve local residents. For the most part, the BHA proved an acquiescent partner in the early years of this endeavor, but many worried about future entanglements with state and federal programs. After the outcry over urban renewal in Boston's West End (where an entire neighborhood was flattened in the late 1950s), South Boston leaders stood determined to forestall any such federal intervention in Southie. In 1962 the Boston Redevelopment Authority (BRA) prepared a "General Neighborhood Renewal Plan" for South Boston, a $30 million program to upgrade the district's housing, schools, and infrastructure. The BRA considered nearly half of the district's housing stock to be in need of major repairs or outright demolition. The plan proposed razing 22 percent of the most substandard units, rehabilitating other parts, and constructing limited amounts of new housing. Wholly unconvinced of the merit of such a venture, South Boston's citizens feared that "these ambitious plans would disrupt their old neighborhood, destroy the traditional family character of their community, and displace old-time residents," just as had happened in the West End. They envisioned the Lower End overrun by industrial operations and the beachfront side lost to high-income housing. Two South Boston based city councilors, Bill Foley and Johnny Kerrigan, were especially suspicious, viewing urban renewal as a kind of class legislation. Foley complained to the *New York Times* that BRA Development Director Ed Logue "interferes in the lives of people and tells them to fix up their homes. He says people shouldn't be allowed to live in lower-class neighborhoods. He wants to make poor people middle class, just like him." Ultimately, Logue conceded the fight, saying that the BRA would do nothing "until a broadly-based group of South Bostonians takes the initiative and comes to the development authority or the mayor and asks for urban renewal."

South Boston's citizens and their representatives valued self-determination and local control, and they saw outside intervention in housing as an attack on a way of life still centered on family, church, and neighborhood. Viewed this way, federal largesse carried unacceptable costs. Worse, just like the false promises that neighborhood public housing would serve primarily residents of South Boston, the BRA plan offered inadequate guarantees that the new South Boston would honor this crucial demand.[55] With urban renewal, mistrust between the neighborhood and the city still reigned, and the fear about new neighbors took novel forms. Public housing originally promised only to exchange one group of low-income people for another, whereas urban renewal was premised on the desirability of enticing middle-class professionals back to the city. Longtime Southie residents feared more than gentrification; they also worried that the civil rights movement would extend desegregation efforts into the realm of neighborhood housing.

THE D STREET WARS

Beginning in 1965, the peaceful coexistence between the Lower End's public neighborhood and its privately housed neighbors faced the first of a series of painful challenges, and a fifteen-year cycle of social unrest and physical decline soon gained momentum. South Boston residents blamed their difficulties on the outsiders who forced them to integrate their public housing and their public schools—and race is indeed at the heart of this story—yet at many points racial tension seemed more catalyst than cause. As the economic fortunes of D Street's residents declined and their skintones grew more diverse, four trends converged:

· The project erupted in a succession of racially motivated attacks that contributed to a pervasive climate of fear and contention;
· Residents and nonresidents alike extended their attacks onto the physical environment of the project itself, and the BHA grew increasingly powerless to stop them;
· The media increasingly portrayed D Street in wholly disparaging terms,

and many residents internalized these negative perceptions, contributing to further anger and withdrawal; and

A core group of dedicated residents reached out to other individuals and community institutions to initiate a new battle—not one against D Street and its residents—but a fight for full recovery.

What follows is an attempt to examine these four intersecting trends. Although the goal is to stress the interconnectivity among economic insecurity, racial and ethnic tensions, environmental and institutional collapse, socially constructed self-doubt, and indigenous efforts at reform, I approach this task by highlighting one factor at a time and exploring its links to the others.

Civil Rights and Civic Wrongs

In 1962 the National Association for the Advancement of Colored People (NAACP) and the Congress of Racial Equality (CORE) registered a complaint with the Massachusetts Commission against Discrimination (MCAD), charging that the BHA willfully restricted several of its public housing developments to white occupancy only. Led by a new reform-minded administrator, Ellis Ash, the BHA ambivalently embarked on its desegregation effort in 1963.[56] Initially the BHA and civil rights groups paid little specific attention to West Broadway, as it had long housed a dozen or so black families. In 1966, however, the Authority launched efforts to improve D Street's racial balance, and the number of non-white families rapidly tripled, from twenty to more than sixty by early 1967. The BHA referred to these carefully selected families as "pioneers," and they were overwhelmingly composed of two-parent households, usually with at least one employed adult member.[57]

Thus, there was nothing about the socioeconomic standing or family structure of these new residents that should have raised concerns. Instead, antagonism arose because of their race and because the public sector, using a public neighborhood as its tool, had encouraged them to become neighbors to South Boston whites.

Black Pioneers in the West Broadway Wilderness

The individual and collective presence of the new black residents in an otherwise all-white South Boston quickly proved destabilizing. To a community that regularly tolerated integrated beaches during daylight hours, the black incursion into public housing seemed somehow different. Even as residents recognized that beaches were indisputably public property, they resisted the parallel notion that public housing was a citywide resource. To these South Bostonians, residence implied full membership in a community. They continued to see Southie's public housing as South Boston property, just as had been claimed when it was first built. As one disgruntled South Bostonian told the *Boston Globe* in 1967, the social transformation of the D Street project symbolized the destruction of South Boston. Someone should "clean out the whole lower end," this resident urged. "We didn't want them. Broken Homes. ADC Cases. That darned old project has ruined it all. They have no loyalty here."[58] Another, older white South Boston resident who lived in private housing described Southie's public neighborhoods as a "disaster" owing to the influx of outsiders who were uneducated, unclean, incapable of cooking a meal, and unable to manage even their welfare money: "I'm not down on all welfare people—don't misunderstand me," she hastened to add, "but this is what you see in those public housing places. It all goes down the tubes and we end up with D Street."[59] For many of Southie's residents, the term "D Street" was no longer an address but a form of derision for the kind of welfare housing that their community deplored.[60]

Increasingly, as Gerald Taube pointed out in 1969, D Street's neighbors regarded project residents "as spiritual illegitimates in the South Boston family."[61] One neighborhood resident wrote to BHA Administrator Ash to complain that his office was sending "an undesirable element" to D Street, implying in racially coded terms that this was done chiefly to harass the manager. The director of the project's own Multi-Service Center noted that "there appears to be an indifference to the people, their problems and the place, by the rest of the community," adding that "the people in the D Street project are looked at as foreigners, newcomers, and/or 'problem people'—if you live in the West Broadway Project, you still aren't part of psychological South Boston."[62] In the late 1960s, Sister Louise Kearns moved into D Street with two other nuns to "form a community" in what she described as "the most deprived project in the area." She was shocked less by the "war zone" of a project "dissembled by graffiti" than by the reaction of fellow white South Bostonians who greeted her decision to move there with angry incredulity. When she informed her local Parish Mothers' Group about her plan, she expected "Christian support for the ministry" but instead, Sister Louise explained, "they talked about blacks and whites: 'How dare you go to them, and leave us! These people are not part of South Boston, so why should you put in the energy? You're here for *us*.' It was horrifying. I will never forget it."[63]

Some of this neighborhood denigration was already directed at D Street whites, who were seen as lacking the initiative and self-reliance of other working-class South Bostonians, but the situation came to a head with the influx of black tenants. Even though many of the most virulent white segregationists shared the poverty of their new neighbors, they regarded project-based poverty as a different and inferior kind. Historian Thomas O'Connor explains the mentality of his home town by contending that "natives of South Boston always considered themselves blue-collar—indeed, this was a proud part of their rough-and-ready exteriors. But they had always protested vehemently against the tendency of outsiders to categorize them as 'poor,' 'disreputable' or 'disadvantaged.'" They instinctively feared that these newcomers would burden the old neighborhood with just such labels.[64] The influx of nonwhites symbolized a further loss of reputability, but it also had a more tangible effect. Each space the BHA held vacant to await a nonwhite tenant, and each apartment thereby filled, seemed a direct affront to those South Bostonians whose names now never seemed to reach the top of the waiting list.[65] Even D Street—clearly the third-ranked choice for South Boston families—could not be so easily sacrificed. Yet precisely because of its lower prestige among South Bostonians and its correspondingly higher turnover of apartments, the BHA singled out D Street to bear the brunt of the integration push. By March 1967, the Authority had moved 111 black families into the three South Boston projects, with nearly two-thirds of them housed at D Street, even though this development contained little more than one-third of the district's total family public housing units.

In response to mounting anecdotal reports of racial incidents in South Boston during 1966 and early 1967, an independent Advisory Committee on Minority Housing asked the Authority to undertake a thorough investigation. In spring 1967, Roland Peters of the BHA's Intergroup Relations staff spent three weeks interviewing fifty of the sixty-one black families then residing at D Street. Two-thirds of these families said they had experienced "some form of harassment" during the preceding several months, and six additional families had already moved out because of this mistreatment.[66] These interviews may actually understate the problem; indeed, another BHA annotated list of all nonwhite D Street residents as of April 1967 indicated that more than three-quarters had registered one or more complaints.

The incidents reported ranged from name-calling to physical assaults, even death threats, often while the tenants were in transit to and from schools, transportation centers, and shopping areas. Within the development itself, black residents reported damaged cars, severed clotheslines, vandalized mailboxes, smashed hallway lights, and stolen front doorknobs. Some faced even worse threats: ignited papers thrust under their front doors; teens who urinated in their hallways and deposited fecal material at the entrance to their apartments; and doors smeared with racial epithets like "niggers live here," "black heaven," "Nigger, go home, KKK," and "niggers stay out." The families often cited instances of rocks, bricks, bottles, and other debris being hurled through their windows by unknown assailants—windows that subsequently remained unrepaired throughout the winter. One couple described their terror the time seven intoxicated youths banged on their door after midnight, shouting, "The nigger is in there!" and then tried to remove their window screens.

Other black respondents documented how white neighbors who had been helpful to them later found "Nigger lover" graffiti on their doors. One black woman told how a white repairman had been beaten to the point of hospitalization in the hallway outside her apartment, while his assailants scolded him for "fixing T.V.s for Niggers." A Georgia-raised resident, repeatedly taunted with references to the KKK, described the racial climate at D Street as far worse than that of her home state. Another woman said that she and her family "felt like prisoners," and that the "degradation and humiliation" was such that her children felt "as though they were being punished by having to stay at D Street."

Many of these reports contained unsubstantiated allegations or detailed incidents that had no corroborating witness, yet the overall pattern of reported harassment is wholly consistent and convincing; whether or not each event actually occurred as described, the net result was a demoralizing climate of fear and intimidation. Equally troubling, when the black families sought redress, they met with resistance. Many black tenants, Peters observed, said they felt like "they were the 'football' in a game": if they took a racial complaint to management the response was, "It's a police matter"; if they brought the matter to the police, the usual reply was, "Take it to your manager." Reflecting back after more than thirty years, Ellis Ash still found it "rather remarkable" that these pioneer families would knowingly and willingly move to a place where they would be "subject to a great deal of discrimination and hostility."[67]

As the number of incidents escalated during the summer of 1966, BHA Intergroup Relations Officer Thomas Francis obtained a special nighttime patrol at D Street, but this failed to stem the tide of harassment. In 1967 the BHA hired special paid police details in plain clothes to investigate any reported incident in an attempt to "apprehend the guilty" and to "determine whether the suspects were residents of this Project." Despite such measures, BHA staff acknowledged that few perpetrators were caught and prosecuted. Even in cases where suspicions against white project residents were well documented, BHA management preferred simply to hold meetings with parents and their children, inform them of the charges, and warn them that they would face immediate eviction notice if further complaints were registered. Francis reported that the white parents "have been most cooperative" and that "all are quick to explain that they are without prejudice." In fact, he added, there was "no evidence of any organized adult opposition to Negro occupancy," a comment that left wholly ambiguous the question of whether white D Street adults were unopposed to blacks or had just neglected to "organize" their opposition. In any case, the BHA's worst fear had not yet been realized, for there was ultimately "very little evidence . . . that white families are moving out because of Negro occupancy."[68]

Most white families who could afford to leave had already done so, and those who remained faced increased frustration with the declining social and physical condition of the project, quite apart from its racial tensions. Many women from D Street wrote directly to Mayor Collins to request transfers. One claimed that the "noise and aggravation" of life on the ground floor of the project had given her two heart attacks. "I've had my windows broken," she added, "and have had to call the Police at least once a week." Another commented, "I doubt if I have to tell you what type of project this has become . . . I love children but so many mothers here do not even care what their sons do to the project. There is no cooperation from other tenants in hall cleaning. It is the first time in my life that I have to apologize for my house entrance." A third begged the mayor for a transfer to a vacancy in Old Harbor, where she had "always wanted to live." "I know there are vacancies," she insisted. "Why firemen and policemen are living there and I can't is beyond me."[69] For D Street's nonwhite families, however, other South Boston projects offered no such hope for safe refuge.

The complaints of D Street's minority families required repeated visits from Francis and Peters. More than a third of those thirty black families who reported harassment told Peters that they had already applied for a transfer to other areas of the city. They found little fault with the residents of their own building, claiming that most attacks came from "outsiders," consisting of former teenage residents, those in other buildings, and people living on the perimeter of the development. In general, Peters pointed out, black residents blamed "95 percent of the harassment" on white South Bostonians from outside the development. He concluded that, "in the main, white residents of the D Street Development have afforded non-whites the respect and courtesy to which they are entitled." Thomas Francis, to whom Peters reported, felt differently, and he refused to exonerate the white teens from the project.

Francis agreed with Peters that intrabuilding relations remained generally stable, but remarked that there was "very little evidence" of "any social interaction between the races at this development." Instead, he observed, the racial climate was poisoned by the actions of "several groups of teenagers"—both male and female, both residents and abutters—who were "determined to make Negro residents as uncomfortable as possible in the hope that these tenants will move out." He did not speculate about whether the harassers were project residents, but he emphasized that large numbers of teenagers were "loitering about the development during school hours," observing that "the truant officer assigned to this district is either non-existent, overworked, or unconcerned." Whatever their home address, the invidious actions of white teens at D Street may well have been occasioned by the presence of nearly fifty black teens in the project; the other two, more nominally integrated South Boston projects housed no black families with teenagers, and complaints there were far fewer than at D Street.

In response to the situation, the BHA Intergroup Relations staff recommended several courses of action. Senior BHA officials agreed to improve security procedures and community outreach efforts but declined to take a consistent hard line with tenants. Peters, who had conducted the interviews with black residents, recommended that "special surveillance by the Authority and the Police Department" be undertaken at sixteen black-occupied residences "to ensure safe and sanitary housing for both white and non-white" residents. This was not done systematically, however, and many complaints by nonwhite residents were not taken seriously. Intergroup Relations officer Francis asked that "a strong letter of warning be sent to all tenants informing them that the Authority will deal firmly and rapidly with families involved in the harassment of non-white residents," but this never happened. Nor were nonwhite families living in especially vulnerable ground-floor units routinely transferred to higher floors, as the Intergroup Relations staff had also suggested. In the end, the BHA remained ambivalently committed to its integration policy, resisting efforts by nonwhite families to transfer out of D Street, except under the most egregious circumstances, while refusing to make a concerted effort to punish those whites accused of harassment. They also rejected the Intergroup Relations Officer's request that "the number of Negro residents be increased" at D Street in order to establish a less token presence.[70] Revealingly, perhaps, the BHA filed the entire sheaf of interviews with terrorized black residents in a folder labeled "Problem Family Data," thereby implicitly blaming the "problem" on its victims. Although BHA staff remained concerned about the welfare of its black pioneers, confusion still reigned about why these families were problematic. Were they really "problem families," or were they more accurately described as "families with problems" that the BHA itself had helped to inflict? Whatever the level of problems faced by the families individually, their collective, publicly sponsored neighborhood presence constituted a problem for the Authority that had actively encouraged them to make their homes at D Street in the first place.

Torn by a commitment to the integration program and a commitment to the safety of families, BHA officials reconciled themselves to an uneasy compromise. Richard Scobie, the BHA director of tenant and community relations, warned Administrator Ash about "the ample evidence of serious harassment, racially caused" at D Street, and concluded that it affected "the majority of the Negro residents" at the development. He stressed that ongoing BHA efforts to work with neighborhood groups were wholly insufficient, describing the prevailing atmosphere as one in which "terrorizing non-whites is tacitly condoned, if not encouraged."[71] The South Boston police, whom Francis considered the "most helpful in the city" in alerting him to instances of harassment, were the same folks who regularly announced their arrival in the development "with screaming sirens," thereby casting considerable doubt on the sincerity of "their intention to apprehend teenage drinkers, tormentors, and harassers."[72] The role of the police nicely illustrates the social complexity of the situation; like many of those who deplored the community violence, the police were also members of that community and wished to uphold what solidarity still remained. In so doing, they necessarily mixed cooperation with complicity. Similarly, Tenant Aide Roland Peters's frontline account of racial harassment lost much of its shocking urgency as his message was filtered and diluted—memo-by-abstracted-memo—all along its path back up to the highest echelons of the Authority, from Francis to Scobie to Ash. Although all these men regarded themselves as reformers committed to improving the quality of life in BHA developments, they were also committed to the integration policy, and the two aims did not exactly dovetail.

To some extent, BHA leaders recognized their own complicity in the problem and sought many novel ways to defuse hostilities. In addition to more police, occasional tenant transfers, and better interior courtyard lighting within the development itself, the Authority attempted to enforce truancy laws and to obtain assistance from the Cardinal's Human Rights Commission, efforts clearly targeted at white teens. Scobie also called for posting "No Trespassing" signs throughout the development and in the hallways, and the BHA gave police written encouragement to enter hallways and apprehend trespassers. Beyond this, Scobie wanted a broader, proactive community-based effort. He proposed that the BHA Advisory Committee assist in the identification of "responsible community leaders who might be moved to begin presenting a counter-force in the neighborhood."[73] Boston's Catholic leaders, however, rebuffed the efforts of housing reformers. According to a BHA staff member, "Cardinal Cushing was unwilling to issue a statement asking his pastors to back integration, claiming privately that he might lose one-half of his parishioners by such an action." Even without such a directive, though, one monsignor did visit the D Street neighborhood to try to reduce tensions.[74]

Following the spring 1967 study, BHA Administrator Ash actively sought the cooperation of the South Boston Area Planning Action Council (APAC), urging them to assist with mobilizing neighborhood groups "to approach this problem on a unified basis."[75] The racial problems continued, however, and a year later, it was the South Boston community organizations themselves who wrote to Ash seeking further help. As the summer of 1968 heated up, D Street residents coped with a renewed upsurge of violent episodes, "involving the throwing of molotov cocktails, arson, and shootings" as well as ongoing harassment, vandalism, and assaults. In mid-July, the director of the South Boston Action Center and a legal aid attorney wrote jointly to Ash to warn the BHA of "a potentially explosive problem in and around the West Broadway Housing Development," describing a climate of "constant fear."[76] Although most of Boston's racial unrest in 1968 remained concentrated in predominantly black neighborhoods, incidents continued at D Street. In October 1969 a black tenant who had lived in her third-floor apartment for three years without any overt discrimination was awakened after midnight by the shattering of glass in her kitchen. On the floor she found half a red building brick with a chilling message taped on one side: "No Nigger in Southie calls one of my friends a white trash and gets away with it. This is a warning—next time it will be a maltove [sic] cocktail bomb. P.S.—This is your eviction notice, move while you still live."[77]

While this particular instance was surely more blatant than most, it must be seen as part of a pervasive pattern of violence and violent threats. A "victimization survey" conducted in 1972 convincingly demonstrated that D Street residents experienced crime in a highly differentiated manner, with 41 percent reporting no victimization at all, and another 41 percent claiming that they had been victimized more than once. In every category of crime, D Street's blacks and Puerto Ricans (who also began moving into the project in small numbers during the late 1960s) reported the highest proportion of multiple victimizations, especially in categories of crime where the object seemed to be intimidation rather than economic gain to the offender. In those cases where respondents identified offenders, two-thirds pointed to project residents, especially teens and pre-teens.[78]

Despite the plethora of reported complaints that gained press coverage or aroused BHA concern during this time period, residents interviewed for the 1972 survey acknowledged that most crimes were not even reported. It is commonly assumed that fear of reprisals from offenders deters victims from filing reports, but most respondents explained that their decision not to report crimes was based on their belief that "the police couldn't do anything." In other words, inaction stemmed not from fear but from a heightened sense of futility. Similarly, the report found, police were reluctant even to record crimes that they felt they could not solve. In this climate, reporting a crime yielded the worst of all possible situations: police inaction *and* reprisals from the accused.

For many at D Street, even the threat of crime exacted a heavy toll. Numerous residents—whites as well as nonwhites—added extra locks to their doors or bars to their windows, or obtained watchdogs. Some tenants placed chairs or sofas against their doors at night and left a radio on. Others said they kept their windows nailed shut year-round and talked loudly to themselves to disguise the fact that they were home alone. Nearly one in five said that, in the past year, they had "frequently" or "very often" been unable to sleep because of fear of being victimized. In many cases, respondents reported that such "chronic nervousness and inability to sleep" persisted throughout the summer months, owing to "youths and adults drinking outside the building and in the halls or racing cars through the Project." In sum, the author of the victimization report concluded, the "volume of damage or destruction and the disfiguration of the physical environment which accompanies it [are] difficult for the middle-class resident to imagine. It would be comforting to think that people can get 'accustomed' to living in a turbulent setting . . . but unfortunately many, many tenants do not." Instead, the usual response seemed one of resignation. Some expressed gratitude that they still lived in the "good" parts of the project, while others acknowledged that things could be even worse—they could have been sent to Boston's least desirable development, Columbia Point.[79]

Murder and the First Exodus

For some tenants of D Street, matters did get even worse as the severity of crimes escalated. There were four homicides in the D Street project as early as 1970, and many injuries from gunshot wounds inflicted by neighborhood snipers in 1971 and 1972, but the racially charged killings in 1973 caused the greatest upheaval of all.[80] In March of that year, two Puerto Rican residents killed a white D Street youth, and the white friends of the victim went on a four-day rampage, firebombing and stoning Puerto Rican stores and apartments and forcing the "mass evacuation" of most of the fifty-five Puerto Rican families from the project. Remarkably, what one reporter later characterized as "a genuine all out race riot" received no press coverage until a week after it ended. A few weeks before the trouble began, Cardinal Humberto Medeiros had asked two priests to move into D Street to form the "Catholic Center" in order to "serve all the people in the project in any way that they can."[81] They spoke Spanish, and had only just succeeded in establishing Los Bravos, a Puerto Rican boys club in the project, when the need for exodus intervened. The priests took it upon themselves to relocate most of the Puerto Rican families temporarily into vacant archdiocese-owned housing elsewhere in the city. Many left with only the clothes on their backs, later reporting the theft of everything from living room furniture to socks. One seventeen-year-old later commented that he would never go back to South Boston "unless they give me license to kill." A mother who evacuated South Boston with her children said she hoped her family would suffer less abuse in another neighborhood, commenting that "the problem is because we are Puerto Ricans. I think that this is because the Irish think that South Boston is theirs." White D Street teens interviewed at the time repeatedly made comments deriding "all project residents who aren't Americans," meaning white, like themselves. As one commented, "You see them walking across here and they're not even talking American. You can't understand what they're saying. They might even be talking about you." Another added, "We've got to get rowdy. There's nothing else to do around here." Someone else pointed out that "[getting rid of] the 'Ricans was the most excitement that's happened around here in months."[82]

As the scramble to relocate desperate Puerto Rican families continued, the D Street priests worked to keep the race riot story unreported, on the grounds that "publicity would only egg on the white kids." They agreed to hold a press confer-ence to discuss what had occurred only after Joe Klein, a reporter for Boston's *Real Paper* (a progressive "alternative" weekly), refused to abide by the news blackout agreed to by other newspapers and television stations.[83]

That June, only weeks after angry white teens succeeded in undoing years of integration efforts with Puerto Ricans, two nineteen-year-old white residents at-tacked and killed George Pratt, a seventeen-year-old black fellow resident. This time there was no shortage of press coverage. Pratt, a high school junior who had lived at D Street with his parents and five siblings for nearly six years, was de-scribed in all accounts as a "quiet" person who spent most of his spare time with friends across town. His eighteen-year-old sister stressed that "we never talked to anybody at the project. We knew what they felt about us. We'd never go hang around outside—that'd be asking for trouble." Even without such provocation, "trouble" found her brother George when he returned home from Roxbury by taxi shortly after midnight. As he approached the door to his building, one of the white teens—both of whom were ex-marines—called out from a nearby hallway, "Here comes the nigger," and they both hurled bottles at him. The two assailants then raced up the stairwell and onto the roof, where one of them fired down at Pratt in the courtyard, killing him with a rifle shot to the forehead. Several wit-nesses to the crime recanted their initial finger-pointing once they realized they would never be able to return to the project if they testified against their friends. One key witness—a fourteen-year-old white boy who was sent to live with a po-liceman's family on Cape Cod until commencement of the trial—ran away the day before the case began, delaying the proceedings. In the end, however, he convinc-ingly told the court what he saw, and an all-white jury found both young men guilty of manslaughter. With the killers sentenced to eighteen to twenty years in prison, the case was over, but—from the perspective of the BHA's integration pol-icy—the problem was far from resolved.[84]

For three years before their son's murder, the Pratt family had unsuccessfully sought a transfer away from D Street, after failing to find private housing they could afford or a landlord who would accept so many children. A pediatrician's letter detailing the negative health and safety situation faced by the Pratt children (three of whom had asthma and all of whom faced "a constant barrage of bricks" thrown through their windows) had earned the family a "Number 1" priority for transfer, but in BHA parlance this was one short of the classification necessary to become an "emergency" priority. One BHA official stated that the letter gave insufficient evidence of an emergency, noting that "we get thousands of these things across our desk. We get letters from every bleeding-heart social worker in the city who is a bigger expert on housing conditions than we are." With a thousand apartments already empty but in nonrentable disrepair, the BHA claimed that not a single four-bedroom apartment could be found in the whole system. However, the BHA director of management services conceded, "If I had fully understood that Mrs. Pratt felt her [family's] life was in danger, that would have been different." Within days after the murder, the BHA found the Pratts a new apartment, a task made much easier by the fact that they did not now require as many bedrooms.

All the local papers covered the murder and subsequent trial assiduously, but only Joe Klein's four articles in the *Real Paper* attempted to probe the meaning of these events in a sustained way. After Pratt's death, Klein visited D Street to speak with residents, especially project teens, and tried to portray the culture of the place. He wrote of a "tall kid with acne" who described the accused killers as "good people [who] used to hang right here." "Look," he told Klein, "just because the cops picked them up for shooting that nigger, that doesn't mean they were guilty." Another teen, looking around at his circle of friends replied, "You won't catch any of us saying anything against Ritchie or Benjie. They were our people." When Klein asked what reason anyone could have had for killing George Pratt, another kid answered matter of factly: "You can't mix niggers with spics with whites. Everyone knows that." In the months that followed, during and after the trial, Klein openly chronicled his own personal disgust over the murder and over the apparent willingness of so many of D Street's youths to defend the perpetrators. He struggled to explain this solidarity from the perspective of those he met: "If you grow up at D Street, in the lower end of South Boston, the battle cries are 'Lower End Forever' and 'Keep Southie White' . . . you don't side with the niggers, you don't work with the cops and, perhaps, you don't leave, either."

Klein described how he had been "rooting for a conviction" during the trial, and he acknowledged the contempt he held for the "animals" who could, without provocation, commit such a crime. He described the two accused ex-Marines as "tough guys . . . housing project punks," but—once the reality of their conviction and sentencing to a particularly "brutal" state prison sunk in—he more reflectively concluded that "revenge is sour." Uncomfortable with the "abstract socio-economics" of an explanation that blamed "society" for the "well-defined pattern of whites who've been screwed by the system taking out their frustrations on blacks," he also was uneasy with the decision to send the youths to a place that would indeed treat them like "animals."

Klein's final article inspired a barrage of replies, most of which apparently came from fourteen-year-olds at the Gavin Junior High School in South Boston.[85] The eight published letters, individually and collectively, painted a revealing community portrait. Most respondents completely missed the subtlety of Klein's own professed ambivalence and saw his interpretation as a wholly unjustified attack. In a climate of extreme hypersensitivity about matters of race and class, even the straightforward description of two convicted killers as "animals" seemed to cast broader aspersions. One girl wrote that Klein was "very wrong for saying the Citizens of South Boston are animals"; another thundered, "What gives you the right to classify all the people in Southie as animals?" adding, "I'd like to see you live in Roxbury for a week and then tell us who the animals are." Someone else suggested that "if you think Black people are so civilized and it's us who start the trouble, try living in Roxbury and if you come out alive tell me how nice they are. Come down to South Boston. We are not animals. We won't bite you." A former D Street resident attacked Klein more personally:

> I think all you people that live in nice areas, nice houses are spoiled
> . . . You have no right to indict people from D Street or any other
> project because you are probably a nice little Jewish boy who grew
> up with meat on the table every night and other things people from
> D Street probably couldn't afford. Try living in a project, then I'll
> listen and probably you'll grow up and learn what it's all about. You
> know you remind me of Nixon—he's all for the rich, you're all for
> the blacks.

Again and again, the respondents condemned Klein for downplaying black-on-white violence: "You don't talk about a white person being shot do you, you prejudiced bum. You don't talk about the poor white cop that got shot that had four children, or the poor cab driver with ten children. You don't go and ask their wives questions do you? Why don't you and you'll see the saddest people you ever saw." Another added, "You made it sound like the whites are always picking on the blacks." One writer even insisted that the convicted killers were "probably innocent anyway," while another intimated that she was "sure the person who killed George Pratt had more of a reason than his color." At the same time that the youths defended the honor of Southie, however, their own words further acknowledged the depth of self-doubt and insecurity among D Street residents. "These people are poor and you go making them feeling down," one young commentator protested. "The people wouldn't be living in the district if they were not poor . . . I know a few families there and they were very down feeling about [your article]." As Southie's internal hierarchy of white poverty meshed with wider hierarchies rooted in race, even some who professed to sympathize with the plight of their D Street brethren did so in terms that damned them with faint praise. One conceded that "maybe D Street *is* a slum but the people in South Boston didn't like the way you said it," noting that "if D Street are animals there are some nice people there too."

Among those whose replies were published there was only a single dissenting voice, that of a Puerto Rican girl whose family had been one of those forced out of D Street the previous spring, after six years of residence ("a Spanish man killed a white kid . . . [and] they took it out on every Spanish family in the project"). She continued to commute to school in South Boston from her new home across the city, and she told how her teacher had disparagingly read Klein's article aloud to her class. She reported that the other kids in her class agreed with the teacher ("because they are all white"), whereas only she and a girlfriend felt differently "because we are Puerto Ricans [and] to them we are blacks." She went on to say that she knew the "trouble didn't start with the killing of the black kid," because "it never started, it always was." She pleaded with Klein to come to her class to "straighten out" her teacher and fellow classmates, and she closed with the hope that her letter would reach him ahead of the others she knew would follow. Klein did go to the Gavin School "to clarify the story for them," and he felt that "some understood" what he was getting at. Still, he observed, the letters themselves seemed the most telling "indication of the mood in a community which often claims to be misunderstood."

Amid all the rancor and miscommunication that followed George Pratt's murder, the words of George's own mother somehow seem the most disturbing. She did not rant about how the BHA had failed to get her family out of the project or neglected to secure the doorways to the roofs of its buildings. Nor did she choose to bemoan the fact that whites in the project had forced her children into social isolation. Instead, Mrs. Pratt chose to blame herself for the killing: "I feel in a way it's my fault," she lamented. "If I hadn't been living out here, my son would be alive today . . . The guilt I have for myself, I'll always have that."[86]

In the search to find someone or something to blame, some tried to destroy the public neighborhood while others sought to attack the public neighbor. For those who, like Minnie Pratt, turned inward, destruction just took a different form.

Busing and the Second Exodus

George Pratt's murder enabled his family to leave D Street in 1973, but even without this tragic impetus, it is unlikely they would have remained at the project much longer. Like the Puerto Ricans before them, the remaining Pratts joined in the first mass exodus from the dubious promise of a hostile public neighborhood. Not long after this rash of racially motivated crimes subsided, however, the need for a second exodus commenced. This time it was precipitated not by the exchange of gunfire but by the passing of school buses.

The controversy over school desegregation simmered throughout the 1960s and threatened to boil over following passage of the state's Racial Imbalance Act in August 1965. The act defined any school that was more than 50 percent black as "imbalanced," a definition that effectively exonerated the suburbs yet called attention to the fact that more than 60 percent of Boston's black students attended schools that were more than 70 percent black, whereas fully 84 percent of white pupils were enrolled in schools that were at least 80 percent white. South Boston citizens resented the haughty finger-wagging of more liberal suburbanites, whom they viewed as both hypercritical and hypocritical. School Committee Chairwoman Louise Day Hicks, a South Boston native, framed the issue as a matter of housing, not schools, emphasizing the desirability of sending children to local neighborhood schools and contending that segregation resulted from the wish of each racial group to live with its own kind. In 1967 Hicks took her neighborhood-schools message citywide, campaigning for mayor with the refrain "You Know Where I Stand." She carried the South Boston wards in overwhelming numbers but still narrowly lost the election to Kevin White. Even without Hicks in the mayor's office, the school desegregation battle raged on; each year the State Board of Education called on the Boston School Committee to enact a desegregation plan, and each year the School Committee demurred. Instead of insisting on forced transfers, the Committee relied on the availability of "open enrollment" in any school that had a vacancy, and preferred to work on upgrading predominantly black schools.

Throughout the early 1970s, open hostility to the concept of busing grew steadily in South Boston. As D Street residents urged construction of a new community-based school—seen as a hedge against the need for busing—attitudes hardened. Even in January 1972—before any court action had occurred—the *Tribune* described local feeling in foreboding terms: "parents are ready to do battle on many fronts to prevent any alteration in the concept of the neighborhood school as it applies to South Boston."[87] Later that year, the NAACP initiated a class-action suit against the School Committee, and on the last day of the 1974 school year, Federal Judge Arthur Garrity ruled in favor of the plaintiffs. Calling "the entire school system" of Boston "unconstitutionally segregated," he ordered a plan of cross-busing to begin that September. With a plan pairing white South Boston and predominantly black Roxbury, including students from six highly segregated public housing projects, the result was explosive. As the Boston journalist Alan Lupo later described it, "To mix Southie and Roxbury, to bus students from each into the other, was not to ask for war, for war was inevitable, but it was to insure that the war would be bloody."[88]

The general story of the Boston busing crisis has been well told elsewhere (and from a variety of perspectives); what is important to emphasize here is the extent to which the busing crisis exacerbated the housing crisis at D Street by making it once again impossible for nonwhites to live there in peace. South Boston's most vocal busing opponents phrased their major objection as a security issue—they feared sending their children into dangerous neighborhoods and provided crime statistics to substantiate their claims—but it was clear that they also resisted the influx of large numbers of blacks into South Boston. South Boston–based State Senator William Bulger, along with State Representative Michael Flaherty and Louise Day Hicks (by then a city councilor), jointly issued "A Declaration of Clarification" to the media in which they defended Southie's resistance and made the wholly unsubstantiated charge that there were "at least one hundred black people walking around in the black community who have killed white people during the past two years." "Any well informed white suburban woman does not pass through that community alone even by automobile," they continued. "Repairmen, utilities workers, taxi drivers, doctors, firemen have refused at one time or another to do what Judge Garrity demands of our children on an everyday basis."[89] As Bulger later put it, busing advocates "did not, or would not, understand that local schools, like libraries and churches, were institutions essential to a neighborhood. It was not bringing children *into* communities such as South

Boston, but taking them *out* that endangered our diverse identity . . . The issue
was not race. *The issue was misuse of the state's power, and forced busing was its
icon.*[90]

No matter how often or how loudly South Boston's leaders spoke about the
safety and welfare of their children, the outside world dismissed their protests
and viewed the whole affair as a cover story for racism. Staffers from the South
Boston Information Center (SBIC), created "to counter the official information
center at City Hall" by promulgating the local point of view, played a leading role
in defending the community. Each week, the *South Boston Tribune* published a
column written by South Boston Information Center staff that repeatedly condemned the ways that "the NAACP, using Judge Garrity, the liberals and big media, have created racial hatred and tensions in Boston and throughout the nation"
by seeking "preferential civil rights for blacks and forced integration of society."
From October 1974 on, the Information Center became the self-appointed "organized resistance to forced busing in Southie," claiming "roots in almost every
home and on every street corner." With a system of "block captains" and phone
lists in place throughout the district, the center's leaders claimed they could as-
semble "a couple of hundred mothers" in ten minutes to protest any new situation. To the twelve thousand students who had boycotted classes citywide, they
said, "Bless You All." They also commended the ten thousand South Boston residents who had taken to the streets to protest. Nonetheless, they pointed out that
the crisis carried many costs: South Boston residents were "subjected to crimes
of violence, loss of jobs, loss of education, loss of scholarship programs, loss of
athletic programs, lowering of real estate values, increased burdens of taxation
and the imposition of fear and intimidation by certain Federal, State and local
agencies." As the center spokesman Dan Yotts put it, the "yellow bus . . . symbol-
izes the destruction of our neighborhood." "You've got to remember," he told
readers, "you're fighting for your life. They want Southie. If they get Southie, under the guise of Racism, it's all over. Boston's gone, joining the list right behind
Detroit."[91] Billy Bulger later gave the matter a more literary interpretation: "It
seemed to be that our Neighborhood had become Judge Garrity's white whale,
and that only its destruction would bring him peace."[92]

The Information Center's Jim Kelly—who would later become the president of
the Boston City Council—argued that South Boston's whites were perfectly capable of judging people on the basis of their character rather than their race. Contending that black extremists deliberately provoked some of the neighborhood vi-

FIGURE 2.19 Shamrocks and leprechauns. The South Boston Irish had long staked their claim to Southie's projects.

olence, Kelly affirmed that "we've always welcomed good colored people to South Boston but we will not tolerate radical blacks or communists." Bulger railed against the "unremitting, calculated, unconscionable portrayal of each [South Bostonian], in local and national press, radio and television, as unreconstructed racists." He insisted that upholding "the natural right of parents to safeguard the education of children in their traditional local schools does not mean . . . that we bear any ill will to black children or children of other racial strains."[93] Yet the racial strains persisted, bringing newfound unity to the shouts of "Green Power" among many South Boston Irish, and re-enforcing a siege mentality among the proud denizens of the peninsula. D Street's tenants expressed their fierce loyalties through green leprechauns and shamrocks sprayed prominently on the project's red brick walls, a turf-marking symbol at least as potent as any gang's tag (Fig. 2.19).

O'Connor explains the vehemence of his home town's decade-long war against forced busing by emphasizing that it was symbolic of much larger concerns: local residents deeply believed that forced busing was part of a conspiracy "formulated by out-of-town liberals, irresponsible black militants and radical social engineers to redesign social boundaries, introduce new moral values and create a new modern and sophisticated society on the ashes of the old-fashioned and outmoded ethnic neighborhood."[94] They had already defeated the city's urban-renewal efforts, and, led by the 1,500-member South Boston Neighborhood Revival Group, they had rebuffed other attempts by big-time outside developers to gentrify the highly desirable waterfront side of the district in any way that detracted from its continued affordability to South Boston families.[95] Yet busing presented a different kind of threat. As the Information Center's Yotts envisioned it, the NAACP's lawsuit was the opening wedge of an invading horde: "What they're after is our property and our neighborhood and they're using the busing issue to accomplish it." Infiltration of the local schools, the center's John Ciccone charged, was a means "to cram minority culture down the throats" of South Boston's children. He quoted a teacher who observed, "No wonder the kids can't read or write properly. Too much of their school week is being devoted to this type of multi-racial brainwashing."[96] The people of South Boston quite logically feared that outside government agencies would launch their next attack on the beachheads of South Boston's public housing, including the still-beloved Old Harbor Village, now renamed Mary Ellen McCormack to honor House Speaker John McCormack's mother.

As tensions over busing mounted, South Boston's nonwhite residents found it impossible to remain in the district. Because their presence was almost exclusively concentrated in public housing, project communities faced the brunt of the changes. For the blacks of D Street, the antibusing backlash pushed the integration roller coaster into its steepest decline—a downhill run straight out of Southie. At the beginning of 1974, after surviving the first harrowing dip during the forced flight of Puerto Ricans and the Pratt murder in 1973, fifty-five nonwhite families still rode it out at D Street. By the end of the year, only fourteen persevered.

Moreover, there were only two black school-aged children among those who outlasted the first season of busing. For the two, who were siblings, continued residence at D Street meant harassment both at school and in the streets. Their mother, initially reluctant to send them to school at all, relented under an arrangement allowing them to leave class twenty-five minutes before the rest of their peers. As a group, a 1976 BHA report concluded, these fourteen "minority" families (who included not only blacks and Latinos but also Filipinos and three white families with nonwhite children) faced "no serious problems" and were "relatively satisfied with their security in D Street." In the same paragraph, however, the report noted that "many of the families, particularly the blacks, seldom venture outside of their apartments." That a situation characterized by frequent harassment and widespread entrapment could be described as essentially problem-free seems a mark of just how far the BHA bureaucracy had become inured to the effects of its integration policy. Compared with the barrage of crises during the preceding decade, however, this situation was indeed "relatively peaceful."[97]

Even with most of the nonwhite families gone from the development, the legacy of the school-integration effort continued to inflame passions. In February 1977 the intolerance surfaced again, this time in the form of a chilling hand-scrawled flyer distributed in the D Street development by the self-styled "South Boston Liberation Army" (Fig. 2.20).

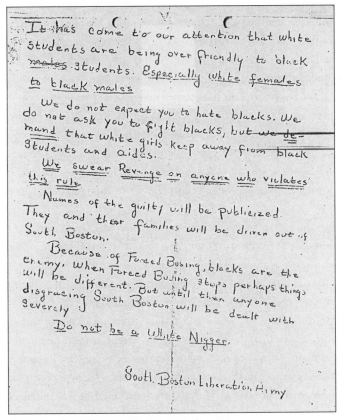

FIGURE 2.20 South Boston Liberation Army flyer, 1977.

As the flyer shows, in the harsh hierarchy of the public neighborhood, sexual contact was the worst form of illicit proximity, and the threat of excommunication still carried weight.

The Socioeconomics of Racial Tension

Although the day-to-day story of D Street seems characterized by divisions—black and white, Roxbury and Southie, Lower End and City Point—the schisms paradoxically resulted from self-doubts shared by all those involved. Despite the disproportionate level of crisis management attending the integration of D Street's nonwhite families, the bulk of the ongoing socioeconomic transformation in the community had little to do with the publicly sponsored arrival of blacks and Puerto Ricans. With nearly 90 percent of its population composed of non-Latino whites even at the peak of integration—and no indication that the balance would ever be allowed to tip further—the growing socioeconomic problems of D Street could never be very convincingly blamed on the arrival of "outsiders." Instead, the racial and ethnic transformation seems often to have been interpreted in symbolic terms: to many South Boston whites, racial transformation delivered a negative message about class. Long-term D Street residents interviewed in 1969 regarded the BHA integration initiatives as "an indication that the project is 'getting worse,'" not necessarily because of anything the new arrivals actually did, but simply because their presence signaled that the BHA now considered D Street to be in decline and no longer sought to protect what remained of its "good" reputation.[98]

Whatever the race or ethnicity of its residents, the fact remained that the public neighborhood built to reward South Boston's most fortunate poor had become, in less than twenty years, a place of last resort for whites as well as for nonwhites, for South Bostonians as well as for "outsiders." A comparison of the project and the surrounding neighborhood in 1970 reveals that almost every major socioeconomic descriptor from 1950 now showed its inverse. Instead of the highest median income in the area, the D Street public neighborhood now had by far the lowest, less than half that of some neighboring census tracts. Intended as an enclave of stability in a slum, the project had by 1970 the highest percentage of families living below the poverty level in the area. Although it was initially characterized by its absence of welfare-dependent families, twenty years later an absolute majority of families relied on AFDC and other public assistance programs—meager support yielding incomes that averaged only about one-third as much as that earned by D Street families whose principal source of funds came from employment. Once the best-educated among neighborhoods, D Street twenty years later had the lowest percentage of adult high school graduates in the area. Once a place where residents had friends, relatives, and civic ties scattered throughout South Boston, D Street had grown isolated, with ever-weakening institutional ties to the broader community. And, indicative of the overall socioeconomic decline, instead of the highest rents in the area, as had been the case in 1950, by 1970 D Street had the lowest.

D Street's decline was all the more devastating because it occurred relative to a surrounding area that was also in decline, physically as well as economically. As Taube's report put it in 1969, the project and its surrounding areas "negatively reinforced each other": the BHA "abandoned" D Street "like a carcass to rot in an industrial wasteland."[99] Despite its large superblock presence, the D Street project had done little to slow the decline of the rest of the Lower End's alphabet. Gradually, the decaying residential fabric on the B Street and Seventh Street sides of the project gave way to commercial and industrial interests, with truck-dominated roadways serving as further disincentive for project residents to seek out whatever community facilities remained beyond these barriers. As dilapidated houses of the Lower End gave way to empty lots and spreading industries, the D Street project gradually lost its residential neighbors on three sides. And, at the same time that its private neighbors struggled, the well-intentioned reformers in the public housing bureaucracy increasingly came to view D Street as a place for social experimentation among mutually hostile groups of the least advantaged.

The downward economic trends that began in the 1960s only intensified thereafter. A comparison of the D Street community in 1969 (near the peak of the integration effort) and 1975 (shortly after its collapse) reveals that poverty intensified among D Street's whites during the same years that their nonwhite neighbors were forced to leave. In 1969, 46 percent of D Street's nonelderly families were headed by single parents; in 1975, this was true for 71 percent. Already by 1969, two-thirds of families had no employed workers, but six years later, this number had jumped to 82 percent. Racial integration in America is difficult under the best of circumstances, but at D Street it coincided with a period of increasingly profound social and economic insecurity, conditions that integration only helped to exacerbate.

ASSAULTS ON THE PROJECT

Given its origins as a development of small apartments, limited recreation facilities, and two thousand children, the D Street environment was probably destined for abuse. When it was built, however, the ratio of children to adults was almost exactly one-to-one. Twenty-five years later, children outnumbered adults by 50 percent. In 1950, there was one adult male for every two youths; in 1975 the ratio was one-to-six. This is not to suggest that males are generically more effective disciplinarians than women; it merely illustrates the fact that the child-supervision burdens falling on women were made that much greater by the growing absence of men.

At the same time, the local public schools increasingly lost their hold on D Street's kids. In 1950, the majority of D Street's adults had graduated from high school, suggesting that this would also be an expected norm for their children. In 1975, however, the median education level of D Street adults was only tenth grade, and their children now had the turmoil over "forced busing" to use as a reason to evade school. In fact, though their reluctance to travel on buses across town was wholly understandable, most accounts at the time suggested that the South Boston school boycott was simply the latest "excuse" for students to skip school; BHA officials and neighborhood service agencies had assailed the high levels of D Street truancy for more than a decade.[100] Without the school to help structure young people's days, weeks, and years, the project environment became an even greater focus of attention, much of it hostile.

The physical decline of the development occurred in many ways, for many reasons, and over many years; it is not the result of a single concerted campaign but the sum total of tens of thousands of petty acts of protest and resentment—sometimes directed in very personal ways at those seen as unwanted public neighbors but sometimes, more anonymously, directed at the brick-and-asphalt outposts of the system responsible for sending them there. In the sincere effort to safeguard civil rights, the tenant-selection and assignment system shifted to a mechanism whereby neighborhood choice remained largely in the hands of a downtown bureaucracy. A parent could make the choice to seek accommodation in public housing, but to a large and increasing degree it was the public housing bureaucracy and not the parent (and certainly not the child) that controlled where a tenant would be "assigned." In every other form of American housing (except perhaps the prison system), the applicant chooses the neighborhood, answers the ad, meets the landlord or realtor, and inspects the premises. In the case of the public housing project, however, the applicant merely chooses the subsidy, and the system chooses the place where that subsidy may be utilized. Thus, the same assignment system that imported "them" may also be resented for having channeled "us" there, too. When long-term neighborhood residents complained that new D Street tenants lacked "loyalty" to Southie, it is not difficult to imagine how this could have come about. For many who launched attacks on their own project home, the message inside the broken bottle may well have been a question: Why did the system send me here?

In this interpretation, the growing devastation of the D Street landscape is more than the extrapolation of demographic ratios: it is a fundamental assertion of disrespect. Not every broken bottle is the shattered residue of a missile that failed to hit its intended human target, but there surely seems some archaeological connection between the project's material culture and its social unrest, futility, and isolation.

In addition to his devastating accounts of the racial harassment heaped upon black "pioneers" during early 1967, Roland Peters portrayed the growing signs of an all-out assault on parts of the project itself. As he moved from building to building to interview residents (the sixty-one black families were scattered into thirty-eight different entryways), Peters found "appalling" physical evidence of all the shattered window-glass and beer bottles that remained from the angry incursions and countless acts of narrow-minded frustration so disturbingly related in the interviews themselves. He warned of the "serious safety hazard to small children playing in the development" and urged BHA management to check rooftops daily, especially in buildings housing black households, "to prevent the stockpiling of beer bottles and other missiles that could be used in warfare or harassment of families." He described the lighting conditions at the project as "deplorable" and observed a "shocking" laxity about plumbing and window maintenance. Taube's account of D Street conditions, written two years later, struck a similar chord. With "no trees" and "buildings far apart," the project, he said, gave the impression that it was "merely a high extension of the sidewalk," with "grit and glass everywhere." He reported children's play areas "covered with broken glass" and observed fences with holes "gorged" through them by a car or truck. Standing in the midst of this unchecked disorder, he witnessed six BHA maintenance workers, one at work with a shovel while the others leaned on their shovels and chatted. The environmental chaos, however, appeared to him far from uniformly distributed. In fact, having toured all the twenty-five BHA family developments, Taube remarked that "in no other project" was there such an intraproject variation in cleanliness. While the B street "rear" side of the project was an "uninhabitable" mess of "broken windows, broken glass, dirt, stench, vandalism and general filth"—where even the occupied units frequently had brown paper covering the windows—the "front" sides on West Broadway and D Street appeared "relatively clean." Taube attributed the contrast to the fact that "storefronts are much better companions than empty lots and junk yards," by which he presumably meant that actively used places were far more likely to provide the informal surveillance that discourages destructive acts.[101]

Despite some better-kept areas, police records showed that D Street suffered the highest recorded incidence of vandalism of any project in Boston.[102] Beyond such formally reported destruction, the "victimization survey" of 598 D Street heads of household, conducted in 1972, revealed 376 instances of deliberate window-breaking, 172 cases of damage to walls, doors, and apartment interiors, 79 instances of arson in or directly outside apartments, and 444 incidents in which mailboxes had been broken into or set afire. In all, these 598 respondents reported 1,103 separate instances of damage and destruction to property—in addition to 112 burglaries, 204 larcenies, 151 assaults, and 31 car thefts—all *personally experienced* within the course of a *single calendar year*.[103]

In 1973, in the immediate aftermath of the Puerto Rican exodus and the Pratt killing, Boston city officials embarked on a well-publicized "turnabout campaign" at the D Street project. In July Mayor Kevin White personally launched a "D Street Days" celebration, promising that the project would once again become one of the city's best. Amid the speeches and photo opportunities, the city provided music and free food and announced summer jobs for 125 development youths, who would assist in the clean-up effort. A flurry of painting, tree-planting, and construction of a new playground soon followed. By August, however, any progress had stalled, typified by the way one union construction crew abandoned work on the tot lot before it was finished, leaving the site littered with "glass and jagged rock" instead of sand. The workers dumped the sand next to the play site, where it was left "to blow in the wind" for several months because the nonunion laborers on site were not permitted to finish the job. Press coverage of the D Street clean-up focused almost entirely on its limitations, and interviews with residents revealed a persistent skepticism. As one of the youths hired for the summer put it, "It's like everything else. They want the publicity and the votes but after they get all the good publicity, they neglect it again."

In October, one of D Street's resident priests dismissed the whole venture as a "whitewash" job, while the director of the project's Multi-Service Center failed to detect "any evidence of a sustained program" to assist the development. Others emphasized the absence of efforts to extend employment opportunities beyond the summer months and noted "no discernible improvement" in police protection, despite the findings and recommendations of the D Street "victimization study." Andrew Olins, Mayor White's chief housing adviser, refused to concede that the city had "dropped the ball." Instead, he contended, a family public housing project just cannot be judged the way one would judge a residential neighborhood: "The families in those projects have a lot of problems," he said, which do not bend to "conventional kinds of wisdom." In other words, the failure to sustain improvements ultimately lay with the tenants themselves. The physical condition of the project, Olins observed, showed the "symptoms" of both tenant problems and lack of public investment: "D Street is never going to be a garden spot."

Three months after "D Street Days," two *Boston Globe* reporters observed that once again "debris is virtually everywhere—under foot, in courtyards, in basements. No one has yet replaced the outer doors, universally bereft of either glass or wood panelling." "The development," they summed up, "looks as it did before—dingy, dirty and neglected."[104]

ASSAULTS BY THE PRESS

When reporters came to D Street to investigate the aftermath of one major altercation or another, they usually saw not the violence itself but the environment where it occurred. Like the tenement reformers of a century before, they detected close links between architecture and behavior. In so doing, however, they worried less than their predecessors had about the negative effects of the project environment on the character of its residents; instead they chronicled the evidence they saw and blamed not the environment but the tenants themselves.

For most of the late 1960s, D Street received infrequent citywide news coverage, but what little it did get was invariably negative. In May 1967 a white *Boston Globe* reporter named William Buchanan actually moved in with a black family in D Street for a week, chronicling his stay under the headline "Adults Live in Terror of Project Hoodlums."[105] He described an undisciplined world of bottle-throwing racists, parental irresponsibility, and police indifference, noting that "at times it seemed as though there are a million children" in the development. As he walked the project, Buchanan constantly discovered "some new evidence of destruction." Once outside the project, he reported, "you sensed it immediately" because "suddenly there was no broken glass under your feet . . . and no sound of smashing glass." He commented that "if Leonard Bernstein were walking with me during those days and nights he would mentally record the sounds of the D St. project . . . it would be a symphony of bottles being smashed and windows being broken."

Buchanan witnessed repeated acts of destruction, marveling that "no one walking past made a comment." When he asked adult residents to explain why no one tried to stop the kids, they told him that they feared the consequences: "Hell, if I spoke to some of these kids about not doing this or not doing that they'd break my windows or let the air out of my tires. I just hope they don't hit *my* window." Another who did complain said that, within the hour, the kids had pelted his apartment with eggs. Buchanan personally saw the racial animus behind some of these acts one night when he and his hosts were jolted by a sound he "will never forget": the "smashing of glass when a stone is hurled through the window and a voice from the semi-darkness outside, shrieks: 'Get out you niggers!'"

Although Buchanan singled out the racial attacks as the most shameful, he saw these in the broader context of rampant mayhem. He saw only one police car in the development during a week of observation and noted that the officer remained in his cruiser; "if I leave this car," the cop explained, "it may not be here when I get back." In Buchanan's depiction, D Street was caught in a cross-fire of accusations: tenants blamed the lack of police presence for the project's problems, while the police and the housing authority management quietly blamed the parenting standards of the tenants. Meanwhile, the project's "solid citizen" neighbors blamed problems on "a lot of people [who] never lived in South Boston until they moved into the project."

Buchanan recognized that this "outsider" status carried special import in other ways, too. In addition to the disdain that many South Bostonians directed at their public neighbors, the new arrivals themselves felt displaced by outside forces beyond their control. Among many residents, Buchanan concluded, "there is an attitude that the rest of the city has shipped them here to these institutionalized buildings," adding that "this does not excuse, but it might in some small way explain why [the project resident] throws rocks, marks with crayon on the walls or pokes out a window with a broomstick." In the end, Buchanan characterized the D Street project as "a great stone forest where anything goes and special rules apply" and as "a giant rug under which dirt is swept as the rest of the city goes about its business." Though he made these comments as a call for reform, his disparaging tone did not suggest much hope.

Buchanan's account of his week spent living at D Street clearly disturbed residents, who did not appreciate being compared to the "dirt" swept under the city's rug. The article prompted much reflection in the pages of the *West Broadway Bulletin,* a tenant-run newspaper founded only a month earlier. Manager Edward Meehan took it upon himself to reassure residents that the *Globe*'s journalist had missed many positive aspects of West Broadway. He enumerated several recent accomplishments, including "your wonderful monthly 'News Bulletin'; the Elderly Drop-In Center; the teenage YWCA group which numbers 100 fine young ladies who are supervised by well trained personnel; Boy Scouts; Girl Scouts; Camp Fire Girls; the fine Tenant Organizations who are working unselfishly to make this community a better place in which to live; and last, but not least, our young people who are fighting in Viet Nam." At the same time, Meehan seemed to accept much of the *Globe*'s description as distressingly accurate. "This article should now become a challenge to all of us," he argued, urging residents to show outsiders that "we do take pride in our development." He called on them to help the maintenance staff by sweeping up broken glass, and appealed to those families "who are indifferent and careless in the upkeep of even their own apartments and stair halls" to make "a more concerted effort" to supervise their children and improve their living conditions.

In the same issue of the *Bulletin,* the tenant-editor Anne Marie Neas called for a fundamental reiteration of "South Boston's Pride," ominously warning that without this the development faced an extremely dangerous future:

> In the middle of our development is a fenced [macadamized] area. It is called a ball field. Will it, this coming summer, also be called a battlefield?
>
> Adjacent to the ball field is a circular depression called a wading pool. Will it, this long hot summer, be turned into another Watts?
>
> In the center of each housing complex is an area effectively labeled drying yards. Will they, these summer evenings, be debased into drinking yards?
>
> Will the new paint on our doors and in our halls be turned into blackboards on which to display the newest forms of obscenity?
>
> Will our Senior Citizens be free to enjoy the pleasure of each other's company and their hearty round-robin discussions without the fear of attack?

> Will parents be at ease during the summer evenings knowing they can bring out their lounges and sit in comfort, enjoying the cooling breezes, expecting and receiving not only the respect of their own children but of all children?

Her eloquent editorial questions turned the manager's "you people" voice into an autochthonous outpouring of the "we," an appeal to collective morality and local tradition.

"We as South Bostonians," she continued,

> should have no use for foul play, bickering, and private grudges . . . Never let it be said that someone didn't get an even chance in South Boston!—the "little city" known for its fair play, religious endeavor, political astuteness, and the wonderful ability to "give the little guy a break." South Boston has a proud heritage, and rightly so! Let us all work together to keep it proud. Right here, in a four block area, we have exactly the ingredients that make America great. Every race, color, creed, and national origin, all working for the greater good! Americans one and all and nobody can top us! Let's talk out our differences . . . let us join in the spirit of togetherness and work to leave the name of the West Broadway Development on the pages of history as the place where there was a re-birth of the "old Southie Spirit."

Having reached her stirring rhetorical climax, Neas returned to a less certain mode in her final sentence: "Are we going to do it?"[106]

Before anyone could answer, the *Boston Globe* printed yet another disparaging assessment in early July. In the context of an investigative survey entitled "South Boston from Yachts to Rubble," D Street clearly ranked nearest the rubble. The *Globe*'s team described "the D-Street housing projects" as a "red and gray expanse" where "children play in front of open incinerators and broken glass glitters in the sun." They took note of "drunken teenagers," broken windows, and quoted the defeatist attitude of one elderly resident who described life at D Street as "worse than death."[107] This time the consoling words came not from a D Street leader but from the thoroughly bemused editor of the *Old Colony Town Crier* (another new project-based newsletter inspired by the West Broadway effort), who wrote to her friends at the *Bulletin:*

Should I offer congratulations? You made the pages of the *Boston Globe* again . . . the same old one-sided view of the picture. It's too bad they don't show the earnest effort you are making to improve conditions there. I only hope you don't get discouraged by all the adverse criticisms you've received. We at Old Colony were completely ignored by the *Boston Globe,* as they praised Old Harbor and panned "D Street." The funny part was, they described the area around us, mentioned going past Columbus Park, all the way to the Yacht Clubs, and never mentioned this development. Guess they thought we had it "too good" here, right on the ocean's edge. And we do have it "good," and we do appreciate it . . . I only wish your surroundings at West Broadway were as pleasant as ours. It would probably solve 50 percent of your problems.[108]

With "D Street Days" still few in number, however, both halves of D Street's problems continued.

As the city dailies focused on D Street's destruction, the South Boston papers treated the project's residents in more balanced ways. They saw the community not as an extension of the police blotter, but as a neighborhood that could make news for its more positive attributes. By 1969, however, even the local press coverage of D Street began to shift. Although it still made news because of its service links to the rest of the community, the development came to be identified as a source of problems, mostly internal to its own "problem families" but nonetheless threatening the broader South Boston community as well. In one column called "West Broadway Hi-Lites," The *Tribune*'s "Roving Reporter" began on a positive note, documenting the growth and importance of activities at the project's Multi-Service Center, made possible by the joint efforts of residents and neighborhood organizations—several of which provided technical assistance, staffing, and services. In the second half of the article, however, the tone changed completely, and the reporter launched a sustained attack on the inadequacy of parenting standards at the project. In contrast to the "relatively small, dedicated group of civic leaders" who worked "tirelessly and in a selfless manner to better the over-all living conditions of their community," the report stated, "many parents" had "completely abdicated" their responsibilities. Citing the widespread loss of control of teenagers in the project, the *Tribune*'s columnist summed up local opinion of publicly assisted neighbors: "One of the most frequently asked questions around D Street today is 'where are their parents?'" Although the phrase "questions asked around D Street" could easily be interpreted to refer to concerns expressed by tenants themselves about wayward fellow residents, this writer made it clear that disparaging questions came from outsiders looking in— from managers, clergy, and police. The possibility that residents themselves might actually be angered by the destructive actions of other residents seemed almost an afterthought: "Sometimes," the reporter conceded, "even the next door neighbor" might take notice.

Rather than a lament about a more general loss of parental control over teenage behavior during a turbulent period of American history, this article located the problem in one particular bounded public neighborhood. The reporter assumed that all the broken windows, and all the "frequent drinking sprees" and "constant bottle breaking," could be attributed to project teens and pre-teens. The "where are their parents?" refrain applied only to them. The questions "being asked daily" were being asked in "our" South Boston community—and not, unfortunately, in theirs. "What has happened to the 'good old days,'" the reporter wondered, "when parental responsibility was a sacred trust? When parents knew just where their children were, whom they were with and what they were doing . . . Is it too much to ask some of the local parents at D Street to inculcate in their offspring good manners, obedience and respect for law and order and the rights and property of others? Don't they care what their children are doing—what sort of lives they are living?" Although the reporter used words like "some" and "many" to describe the offending families and claimed that "this is by no means a condemnation of all the parents in West Broadway nor all of the teenagers," the column nonetheless stressed "the alarming rise in juvenile delinquency and complete disregard of parental responsibility . . . in this neighborhood." In other words, even though "all" persons were not equally at fault, it was still possible to single out this public neighborhood for special discussion. The "West Broadway Hi-Lites" were getting fewer and dimmer, and it would not be long before the community's attacks on project residents would again become racialized. For the time being, however, the condemnation remained broadly inclusive. The article concluded with a call to action: "Wake up you irresponsible parents before a tragedy happens in your very household!!"[109]

In the summer of 1973, as the first serious talk about redevelopment money for D Street got under way, a *Tribune* editorial assured its readers that "we're watching" and proclaimed that the paper had always "retained a strong interest in [the project's] well-being." Aware that some might challenge the sincerity of that statement, the editors referred readers to the paper's old files, insisting that "any program for self-help on the part of residents [of D Street] has received our support." Despite the allusions to resident initiative, the tone of the *Tribune* remained disparaging. Support for improving D Street came not out of empathy for the residents but out of collective embarrassment about the people and problems of the Lower End. The editorial concluded: "The well-being, not to say the survival of a community cannot be assured when physical and sociological conditions in a large sector of that community are less than adequate."[110] From the *Tribune*'s perspective (a view from part-way up Telegraph Hill) the problems of D Street were not just social but "sociological," a subtle distinction that reinforced the distance between a benighted public neighborhood and the rest of South Boston.

The local press picked up on prevailing neighborhood attitudes toward D Street and thereby reinforced them. As one life-long South Boston resident who lived in "The Point" put it, "We were told to stay away from the Lower End. We couldn't go past F Street. Our parents told us to stay away from the projects. They thought the people down there were different and dangerous. They wore tank tops and had no teeth. All that was just hearsay, though. I really didn't know what it was like. They were so close to where I was living but so far away. It was like two different worlds, and G Street was the line that separated them." Tellingly, even as City Point residents referred to the Lower End in its proper geographical sense, residents of other declining South Boston projects internalized the term and used it to encompass and denigrate themselves. In his trenchant memoir of growing up in Old Colony during the 1970s, Michael Patrick MacDonald described the Lower End as "the more run-down section of South Boston, with its three huge housing projects—Old Colony, D Street, and Old Harbor—and mazes of three-deckers."[111] In this way, Southie's disparately located public neighborhoods came to share a single stigmatized geography.

As conditions at D Street deteriorated, Boston's daily newspapers rejoined the fray, and they saw only the worst. In the aftermath of the Puerto Rican exodus of March 1973, the *Globe* sent its "Urban Team" to investigate attitudes and conditions at D Street. Under the front-page headline "Life on D Street—Daily Diet of Tension," the reporters detailed the depredations of "rowdy gangs" bent on revenge, harassment, and vandalism and included a separate article entitled "Puerto Ricans Are Prisoners in Apartments." The *Globe*'s reporters made clear that "the group of marauding teenagers" was "not representative" of the young people of the project, but they also cited social service agency estimates that as many as 250 D Street youths had at least fringe involvement with such activities. Despite the fact that 90 percent of the project's 2,000 residents between the ages of six to twenty did not display violent or disruptive behavior, the *Globe* had little to say about them. Instead, the reporters quoted one South Boston legal aid attorney, kept exceedingly busy defending D Street youths, as saying he'd "never seen a youth in the project carrying a book." They described the appearance of the Multi-Service Center as "reminiscent of the Charles Street jail," noted that only eighteen kids elected to join the local Boy Scout troop, and chronicled the laments of a variety of local service providers who felt unable to break through the pervasive apathy of project life. Ultimately, the bleak portrait showed only two kinds of D Street people, those who responded with violence against others and those who responded with self-directed alcohol and drug abuse. The reporters phrased their overall message in unambiguous and sweeping terms: "The kids from the lower end don't think about the future. Basically, they have no futures, and they know it."[112]

A group of D Street mothers who called themselves "The Activists Club" responded with a letter published in both the *Globe* and the *South Boston Tribune* in which they bemoaned the pattern of portrayals:

> People in D Street try to do something about the problems they live with. When they try to rise above the problems, they are more often hit with a fist than given a hand up. Negative publicity does not help. We do not get positive publicity. The good kids in D Street greatly outnumber the bad kids, but nobody wants to count them. The number of D Street kids who go to court is publicized. The number of D Street kids who go to college is overlooked. Parents in D Street have the same hopes and fears for their children as all parents everywhere . . . If society is going to put 2,000 poor kids in four square blocks and deprive them of advantages which richer kids take for granted, then those kids are going to be angry and hurt; and some of them will behave as your articles describe. Society should be grateful that all 2,000 do not turn against it.[113]

The message came through loud and clear: beware the revolt of public neighbors!

Despite such warnings, the negative portrayals remained unchanged. *Boston Globe* columnist Mike Barnicle commented that "D Street, with buildings that look like bombed out shells, could pass for Dresden or some other World War II monument," ironically using language that recalled earlier descriptions of the cleared site upon which the project had been built. As for those who could live in such a place, Barnicle observed, "It's a dull, drab, dirty section where kids learn to hate and hurt before they're ten. They learn how to steal things at the corner variety store and get away with it because the cop is too fat to chase them." Other reporters chronicled similar scenes, linking social and physical decline. Ken Hartnett, the head of the *Globe*'s Urban Team, described D Street as a "tight little universe of shattered windows and doors, garbage, dog dung, graffiti and bottomless pools of violence," calling it "clearly a place unfit for human habitation like any other project where housing officials allow too much poverty, too much ignorance, and too much failure to cluster in a dense and destructive mass." Another reporter characterized the place as "a dump, one of the roughest projects in the city, a jail." Boston's Catholic newspaper, *The Pilot*, taking note of the "commonplace . . . smashing of windows, looting and burning of apartments," wondered, "Is the Church present at D St.? Is there any Christian witness in the South Boston community?"[114]

In addition to the consistently negative portrayals in the citywide papers, D Street residents faced more parochial attacks in the *South Boston Tribune*. Worst of all, one of their own, writing anonymously in 1975, offered the *Tribune*'s readers a chance to confirm their harshest stereotypes about life in the D St. Project. The sarcastically understated article ridiculed the challenges of daily life in the project with its broken windows ("year round air-conditioning") and absence of secured entryways ("don't worry about opening the door; there is no door to open"). Its author recited the need to "check the children and see if they are sleeping with their dolls instead of rocks," and reminded residents that they had "better eat before the roaches do, or before you get hit on the head with a brick." At night, moreover, they should "be sure to wake up about 2 A.M.; there's a big fight in the hall you won't want to miss."[115]

The following week the *Tribune* printed a reply from an angry teenage "D Street Resident" who resented the implication that all such problems were the fault of tenants and wondered whether it had ever entered the writer's mind that the Boston Housing Authority could be at fault for the atrocious conditions. Moreover, the respondent charged, why didn't the writer acknowledge that most of the perpetrators of disturbances "don't even live in D Street." The author felt that the *Tribune*'s column had, in effect, referred to project residents as "animals," a galling act of disrespect to all those who have "experienced being looked upon as a 'low class punk from the D Street Project.'"[116]

By the mid-1970s, the increasingly desperate cohort of D Street residents felt under siege from all sides: from the civil rights groups' integration efforts; from Judge Garrity's forced busing plans; from the rampant devastation within the project; from the encroaching industrialization of their neighborhood around it; and from the BHA's inability to manage and maintain the project environment. To make matters worse, the residents were forced not only to contend with these problems on their own but also to face others constantly out to judge them; the disparaging accounts of the local media could disturb with their truths as well as with their fictions.

THE RESIDENTS FIGHT BACK

As problems mounted at D Street, some residents contributed to the growing climate of violence and harassment, but others found increasingly effective ways to work cooperatively. As social and physical conditions in the development worsened between the late 1960s and the late 1970s, a core group of dedicated tenants, aided by a wide variety of community-based organizations, established and sustained one of the strongest resident organizations in any Boston public housing development. In April 1967, two residents—Anne Marie Neas and Dolores Paradis—initiated the *West Broadway Bulletin,* a monthly newspaper intended "to promote a better understanding of our community and the wide scope of activities and services offered us."[117] Published "for and by the residents of the West Broadway Housing Development," the *Bulletin* had a circulation of 1,250 copies and reached beyond the households of the development itself, stressing the links between the project residents and opportunities available to them elsewhere in South Boston. Although the *Bulletin* focused on internal communication among residents, and between residents and BHA management, it provides striking evidence of the willingness of area institutions to take an active interest in the lives of D Street tenants.

The newsletter struck an intentionally cautious and diplomatic tone. Neas informed BHA Board Chairman Jacob Brier that "we will try to keep the *Bulletin* informative, rather than controversial; instructive rather than destructive; and helpful rather than critical." She asked for "any criticisms," as well as for assistance with supplies or ideas, and affirmed her lofty goal: "we will do our very best to publish the most comprehensive, informative newsletter ever in print."[118] The editors distributed copies of the *Bulletin* to every Board member and Administrator Ash, as well as to local politicians, and they received back many letters of praise.

In reprinting such letters, the *Bulletin*'s staff not only demonstrated their worth in the eyes of powerful others, but did so with an air of easy familiarity rather than cowed supplication. State Representative Flaherty described himself as "an avid reader since its first edition," and noted, "Although it is helpful to the residents of the West Broadway Development, it is doubly so, to us elected officials. It helps to keep us informed both to our constituents and their problems." "Thanks for your good words Mike" was the editor's reply. Flaherty gained more effusive editorial appreciation after he sent money to defray the cost of the October issue: "It always surprises me when someone in public office stops for a moment to lend a bit of assistance to his constituents, especially when the aid is not formally requested. Thank you Mike, and God bless you." Similarly, State Representative Bulger sent the *Bulletin* $10—an amount equal to the sum total of the nickel-and-dime contributions made by all Broadway residents during a good month of donations—and he too received a warm published reply: "It is indeed gratifying to see a public servant who is willing to support the efforts of his people in such a substantial manner. We salute you . . . Thank you Bill."[119] Even though they lived in a struggling housing project in the Lower End of South Boston, the residents of D Street could see that home-town pols like "Mike" and "Bill" still cared.

South Boston's service agencies demonstrated their concern even more directly. Making up for a frequently lamented dearth of editorial and financial support from residents, these organizations traded assistance with newsletter supplies and production costs for the opportunity to advertise their activities and the space to report forthcoming events. During the course of 1967, among many other sources, the *Bulletin* received financial or editorial contributions from the South Boston Boys' Club, South Boston Legal Aid, the South Boston Federal Credit Union, the Norcross School District, the South Boston Neighborhood Employment Center, the Laboure Center, Cardinal Cushing High School, St. Peter and Paul's Church, the Boston Public Library, Youth Forum, Headstart, the South Boston Action Council, and the D Street Residents' Committee.

The *Bulletin*'s emergence coincided not only with the acceleration of integration efforts but also with a burgeoning of project-based and neighborhood-based outposts of the "War on Poverty." Many of these organizations were concentrated just up West Broadway from the development at the South Boston Action Center, a conspicuously active affiliate of Action for Boston Community Development (ABCD). The Action Center implemented a wide range of antipoverty initiatives, including Consumer Action programs, Headstart, a summer work program, the employment center, a senior citizen program, the credit union, an egg-buying club, and Co-mart (a discount furniture-purchasing cooperative), as well as job training programs, neighborhood-improvement programs, a homemaker program, a program to promote awareness of Medicaid and Medicare, and a neighborhood orientation center.

Many other organizations operated from the housing project itself. The development's own drop-in center offered a daily program of health, education, and recreation services provided by organizations such as the South Boston APAC, the YWCA, the Urban League, the Family Service Association, the New England Medical Center, the Camp Fire Girls, and the Cub Scouts. By printing advertisements and commentary from dozens of neighborhood organizations, the *West Broadway Bulletin* helped ensure that, for the first time, project residents had ready knowledge about both new and established programs. Tenants learned that the legal aid office, conveniently located at 482 West Broadway, promised help with "housing evictions, family problems including separations, divorce, child custody, landlord-tenant disputes and welfare." They were reminded of the new Welfare office located within the development itself. They heard that fifteen day-care slots had become available at St. Peter's School, a parochial facility located next to the development's Lithuanian church. Less immediately helpful, perhaps, was the ad from the South Boston Federal Credit Union informing residents that Woodrow Wilson's portrait graced the $100,000 bill.

In all this emphasis on community outreach, however, the *Bulletin*'s central concern remained the quality of community life within the development. The bulk of each issue was dedicated to the commonplace—and the extraordinary— aspects of daily life, as expressed through a variety of letters, editorials, poems, excerpts from Cardinal Cushing's sermons on racial justice, offers of piano lessons, antidrug messages, and household hints about coping with mismatched nylons and securing shirt buttons with fishing line. Anne Marie Neas also sprinkled the *Bulletin* with pertinent quotations from such diverse sources as Shakespeare, Rostand, Emerson, Eliot, Benchley, and the Bible.

True to its stated aims as an "instructive" rather than a "controversial" publication, the *Bulletin* remained a quiet voice of reason. Manager Meehan used it to praise residents for "behaving like ladies and gentlemen" on Halloween. A new resident could write to sympathize with the "tremendous problem" and "endless job" facing housing authority management. The *Bulletin* served as a vehicle for extolling constructive behavior rather than registering complaints. When the *Bulletin* introduced a Spanish-language column (less than inventively titled "Espanol") for the development's Puerto Rican residents, it devoted its November edition entirely to discussion of how "here in the United States, we celebrate Thanksgiving Day." The paper explained how "they" mark the holiday with a turkey feast and invite the Indians, and it concluded with an assimilationist message: "So, dear friends, we are like the Pilgrims here, and we must join with them and thank God for this land which represents a new life for us." The *West Broadway Bulletin,* for all its strengths as a means of disseminating information, eschewed all forms of militancy. Its October issue concluded with a single sentence that typified its editorial stance: "All great alterations in human affairs are produced by compromise."[120]

By the end of 1967, however, the degree of outside agency support for the *Bulletin* could not overcome the paucity of residents willing to assist the weary editor. Sitting at her table at 2 A.M., working alone, Neas typed out a plea for help: "I often wonder," she wrote, "if anyone else in the development is interested in this paper besides me." As with so many other services in public housing, understaffed and intermittently funded, the *West Broadway Bulletin* soon ceased publication.

Before its demise, however, the *Bulletin* successfully promoted the "D Street Residents' Committee," the development's nascent tenant organization. By the end of 1967, at least forty different people, 90 percent of them female, had been appointed to various tenant subcommittees. Each committee, in turn, took on an outside, nonvoting volunteer advisor "to give professional guidance."[121] This structure prefigured the sort of relationship the D Street tenants would have with outside groups for decades to come. Tenants welcomed outside aid but always sought to keep it under tenant control. At times, this allowed for smooth cooperation, while often it led to bitter disagreements over authority.

The West Broadway Task Force (WBTF), as the tenant organization became known following the citywide effort to organize public housing tenants in 1968, quickly became one of the most vocal and active in the city. Though never a large group, the WBTF never seemed to be without strong leadership that could boast of good connections to local politicians and extremely deep roots in the neighborhood. Some, such as WBTF President James Orton, were even related to the veterans for whom the Ways through the development were named. Whenever something positive happened at D Street, the tenants made sure that others heard about it, even if the city dailies took no notice. In May 1968, for example, the development's Joyce-Hayes Senior Center opened with great fanfare, with Representative Bulger, three BHA Board members, Administrator Ash, and the Boston City Council president all in attendance.

A few months later, the D Street Multi-Service Center opened with a similar demonstration of political connectivity. This time Orton credited the South Boston Action Center, as well Congressman McCormack, Mayor White, and BHA Administrator Ash, for their help, but he still viewed the achievement as a demonstration of tenant initiative. It was the tenants' "dream," he claimed, and "my eight member board has shown that people in public housing can do something for themselves." The local press acknowledged the Task Force's leading role in the venture, commenting that the new center would provide "needed services to the forgotten people of the D Street Housing Project."[122] Too prideful to draw attention to their own neediness, however, the residents themselves called the new institution "the Multi" rather than "the Service Center."

In contrast to the quiescence of the 1967 *Bulletin*, the WBTF leaders adopted increasingly strident tones, willing to challenge any person or organization that diminished the quality of life in their development. They not only clamored for more financial assistance from the state and more service provision from community groups but, more fundamentally, demanded a greater decisionmaking role for public housing residents. As Orton put it when he led a delegation of twenty-five West Broadway residents to the State House to meet with several senators and representatives in April 1969, "we believe in the fundamental principle of a participatory democracy wherein residents of D Street and other housing developments have a voice in planning their future and that of their community." Testifying before the Sub-Committee on Public Housing of the legislature's Joint Committee on Urban Affairs, he decried "the atrocious state of disrepair of our apartments due to inadequate maintenance help," and he urged passage of a bill to provide substantial funds to renovate the state's public housing developments. In return, Orton promised, "we could give back to many their self-respect—let them know that living in public housing should not be a stigma nor does it automatically classify one as a second class citizen."[123] For Orton, high-quality housing marked an opportunity to demonstrate self-worth. D Street residents clearly benefited from their ample South Boston connections to all relevant legislative bodies, yet all the access in the world would have meant little without the continuous stream of strong tenant leaders ready, even demanding, to take on responsibility for themselves.

The need for such leaders grew ever more crucial as most D Street residents began losing their institutional ties to the broader community. A 1968 survey found that fewer than one-fourth of those interviewed said they belonged to any organization outside West Broadway itself. Moreover, of the three-quarters reporting limited civic connections, only 17 percent said they had any desire to join such a group. The problem operated internally as well; more than two-thirds of respondents said they had never even heard of D Street's own nascent tenant organization.[124] Despite such limited engagement on the part of residents, neighborhood organizations continued to take an interest in the welfare of D Street, and a cadre of tenant activists remained wholly engaged in the fight to improve conditions at the project.

In 1970, with "the Multi" up and running, the WBTF took up the challenge of upgrading local school facilities, located in temporary structures after a fire destroyed the Norcross School in the development's superblock. Joined in this fight by the indomitable South Boston city councilor Louise Day Hicks, who charged that "the children of this area are being treated as second class citizens," the Task Force organized meetings to promote a permanent new neighborhood school so that parents would never be faced with the need to have their children bused elsewhere. Development residents and their neighbors worked together to end this affront to South Boston. As Hicks put it, the poor conditions in the demountable buildings "would not be permitted in any other area of this city." She warned that she was "not going to tolerate it any longer."[125] When plans finally did get under way to build a new community school on the D Street edge of the development, the WBTF leaders viewed it as a new community resource. They called upon the Boston School Committee to provide facilities for the Task Force and the Multi and demanded free after-school access to school meeting rooms, ball fields, and the gymnasium.[126]

When six BHA developments received Law Enforcement Assistance funds to provide development-based security offices, the tenants at five projects readily agreed to BHA plans. At D Street, however, tenants insisted that the Authority begin by surveying resident opinions. They demanded that the BHA use some of the money to hire an outside consultant to conduct a victimization study, and they urged the Authority to listen to the tenants' own opinions about how to reduce crime and violence. The BHA director of security told the administrator that this would slow down the process, but he accepted the residents' rationale that suggestions for improving security would "stand a far better chance of tenant cooperation" if they came from the tenants themselves.[127]

In this context, it is hardly surprising that D Street residents took the lead in the early efforts to seek legal redress for the deteriorating housing conditions in their development. In 1970, five years before the decision in the landmark *Perez* case sent the BHA spiraling toward receivership, the WBTF launched its own suit, charging the BHA and the state's Department of Community Affairs with neglect that caused "irreparable harm to their health, safety, morals, welfare, and comfort." The tenant plaintiffs and their legal aid attorneys presented a great deal of evidence but failed to convince the Massachusetts courts that they had "exhausted all of their available administrative remedies." The tenants lost their last appeal on June 20, 1973, just two weeks after George Pratt's murder.[128] The courts did not yet want to accept jurisdiction for redressing the conditions of Boston public housing, but the West Broadway tenants had succeeded in raising the visibility of their plight, demonstrating their own ability to be both confrontational and constructively engaged in efforts to improve conditions.

Tenant activism now meant not just localized agitation but broad partnerships with well-connected outside service providers, as well as skillful manipulation of all possible political and legal channels. In December 1973, WBTF President Rose Hayes directly challenged politicians who failed to help D Street. She sarcastically railed against Governor Frank Sargent's veto of a mental health bill that provided matching state funds for a D Street juvenile clinic: "Your veto," she wrote, "has said to the children of D Street, Tough luck gang. The Governor of the State isn't interested in you this year. To those whose emotional problems turn them away from school and onto drugs, unwanted pregnancies, and possible prison—Hang in there baby—maybe next year." Hayes commented that "no one likes it when D Street gets into the news with our problems," but she wondered, "Who is willing to help us solve those problems?"[129] In the years that followed, Hayes also took a hard line with BHA staff, as indicated by a 1976 letter to BHA Administrator Samuel Thompson that began: "The West Broadway Task Force intends on attending the next meeting of the Boston Housing Authority Board. We want answers to the following questions: How much money has been allocated to D Street under all phases of modernization thus far? . . . Why can't we get an accurate up-date on what is going on as to why various aspects of modernization haven't been completed?"[130] The urgency of the questions, and the tone of their phrasing, gave firm notice that D Street's tenants would never be content to wait for others to act on their behalf. Torn by a decade of racial strife, decimated by unchecked vandalism and municipal neglect, and continually burned by disparaging portraits in the press, D Street had casualties too numerous to count. At the same time, however, a core group of tenants who had survived the D Street Wars stood ready to engage in a more constructive fight, and they remained well connected to the outside groups that could help them.

The Fight for Redevelopment

Even as the development descended toward its nadir during the late 1970s, D Street and its residents benefited from friends in high places. As a group, BHA tenants had won their class-action suit in the *Perez* case in 1975, but they had yet to receive assurance that any extra funds would be forthcoming. In advance of the money, however, tenants from some developments, most notably D Street, gained a great deal of attention. Robert Whittlesey, the court-appointed BHA master, lacked the staff resources to undertake a detailed study of conditions and redevelopment prospects at every BHA development. He decided to focus energy and attention on three kinds of needs: sustaining those projects that seemed to be "in stable and generally good condition," guarding those "on the verge of major change . . . with increasingly serious problems," and salvaging those already beset by "serious problems." Whittlesey's goal was to "find out the range of physical, social, security, community and other issues which must be incorporated into comprehensive plans for individual developments." He wished to develop a general approach toward development-specific planning that recognized the interconnectedness of problems, but he did so by focusing special scrutiny on two troubled developments: Commonwealth and West Broadway. The *Master's Report*, released in July 1976, explained that these projects were selected not because they were the worst off but because they epitomized project "types." Nonetheless, the very act of asserting their typicality so prominently belied any such premise.

Mastering D Street

Expectations for redevelopment inevitably arose once the master's staff descended upon the project to interview residents, service providers, and management and maintenance staff. The *Master's Report* recognized that tenants' hopes had been falsely and prematurely raised many times before, and Whittlesey's staff vowed that this would not be allowed to happen again. The *Report* called previous piecemeal modernization at D Street "a classic example of the cure being worse than the disease," and it drew attention to a Finance Committee report showing that, while the development deteriorated, the BHA had paid exorbitant materials rates for work never completed, failed to spend nearly a half million dollars of allocated funds, and "lost" the appliances for a hundred new kitchens before they could even be installed.

The *Master's Report* promised BHA reforms and sought to ensure that Boston's problems received well-publicized attention at a time when the Massachusetts legislature was considering an unprecedented expansion of modernization funding for the worst-off state-aided developments. Recognizing that the state would be wary of targeting funds to such an unreliable housing authority, the master's staff tried to identify the most promising sites for investment. In this context, the *Report*'s special focus on West Broadway and Commonwealth can be seen as part of an explicit attempt to advance the case for disproportionate state funding to realize these particular redevelopment initiatives. The *Report* urged the BHA to lobby for passage of the housing bill and to "effectively and aggressively work with [state officials] to insure that allocations are made to the BHA developments under consideration."[131]

West Broadway, selected to represent a development with "serious problems," had no trouble earning the classification. In addition to its legacy of racial strife, the development faced escalating vacancies (already 150, with a new one every three days) and no ready market to fill them. Tenants complained that the BHA sent many "problem families" to D Street "as a consequence of having no waiting list from which to select or screen." Long-time D Street Manager Joseph McNamara asserted that whenever he tried to deny the applications of undesirable tenants, central BHA staff overruled him. With everything centralized, he retained little say in matters of most concern to tenants, causing him to lose both status and effectiveness. Moreover, he added, most departing tenants left without notification (since they had paid no security deposit), allowing vacant apartments to be "vandalized overnight." McNamara explained the full dynamic of the vacancy-vandalism cycle to Whittlesey: "vacant apartments are constantly being broken into by the youths to use as a haven while consuming alcohol and smoking marijuana and, after this, the apartments are thoroughly vandalized and kitchen cabinets and fixtures stolen. All of this affects the neighboring residents who eventually move, creating another vacancy." As a member of the master's staff commented at the time, "McNamara generally feels defeated by 14 years at D Street and doesn't feel supported by downtown. He has lost his spirit and energy."[132]

The master's staff concluded that the project had "fallen apart" both physically and socially, owing to the failure of institutions "to exercise social controls over many West Broadway residents." As the *Report* put it, "Social service systems fail to reach these people, the police and courts fail to act upon their anti-social behavior, the schools and job markets do not keep them engaged in more productive activities, other families are afraid to confront them, and the BHA has no power to evict them." As long as this situation is allowed to continue, Whittlesey concluded, "the undesirable image of West Broadway will live on, 'good' tenants will move out to protect themselves, vandalism and terrorism will continue, and buildings will be destroyed."

Clearly, even the mass exodus of nonwhite families in 1973 and 1974 had not served to make D Street "safe again" in the eyes of white applicants. On the contrary, the legacy of racial problems merely added to the growing unwillingness of families of any kind to seek homes in this most stigmatized part of South Boston's Lower End. In 1976, at a time when thousands of families were on waiting lists for BHA public housing citywide, and when six thousand additional families within South Boston itself were income-eligible for public housing, only forty-six expressed an apparent willingness to live at D Street.[133] Moreover, virtually all who applied were single white individuals between the ages of eighteen and fifty-nine, most of whom had been placed on the D Street list, not because they requested it, but because as single individuals who were not elderly, disabled, or displaced they were ineligible for the federally aided housing at South Boston's other two family developments. As the exodus of existing residents continued, D Street headed from a place of last resort to a place of no resort at all.

Efforts to investigate D Street's "marketing problem" revealed several reasons potential tenants were unwilling to move to the project. According to a 1976 report, most BHA applicants who turned down a D Street apartment cited "the deplorable physical appearance of the project, and fear of what the gangs of youths would do to them or their children." They sensed that the development was uniformly dangerous, and they expressed their disapproval with "overwhelming vehemence." Many who received an offer in the mail ignored it completely but, when queried directly, provided no shortage of detailed explanations as to why they would not accept. Most were white women from South Boston who were dissuaded not by media reports but by direct observation of the project. Several expressed interest in Mary Ellen McCormack or even Old Colony but saw D Street as a place full of "roaches, rats, sewage, filthy kids, profanity, gangs, racial violence, assaults on old ladies, vandalism, alcoholism, leaky roofs, broken windows, and people who act like animals." With the prospects for reintegration judged to be "nil," Whittlesey stressed the need to rehabilitate the project in the eyes of South Bostonians.[134]

The challenge was formidable—even residents of Old Colony continued to disparage the denizens of D Street. Southie chronicler Michael MacDonald perceived all three South Boston projects as sharing the moral geography of the Lower End but remembers being warned by a fellow Old Colony kid never even to try to pass through D Street. The kids there were "white niggers" and "dirtier than Old Colony people, that's why they were called 'D Street dirtballs.'" As MacDonald notes, "It felt good to all of us not to be as bad as the hopeless people in D Street."[135] In the hierarchy of South Boston, D Street remained dead last.

Despite the understandable prevalence of hostile or defeatist attitudes, Whittlesey and his staff saw signs of hope in the quality of D Street's tenant leadership. "There are some strong individuals and families in the project who are actively engaged in an effort to make West Broadway into a more viable community," he observed in 1976. "Their efforts must be supported in every way possible, as they have a critical role to play in the rebuilding effort."[136]

The tenants did not wait for such support to arrive but forcefully sought it out. The pressure put on the Master's Office to act for D Street came chiefly from "the residents and from some of the parish people" rather than from the BHA or even from local politicians—"we were reacting," Whittlesey later recalled. The master and his staff supported redevelopment at D Street not only because "it sure needed it," but because this "big sore-point place" had "an aggressive residential bunch who were very politically connected." Here, Whittlesey thought, was a community where "you could gather enough energy to take it on."[137] Even before the state formally announced opportunities for its Pilot Modernization Program grants, the WBTF took advantage of consultants from MIT and the Boston Urban Observatory (BUO)—based at the nearby Boston campus of the University of Massachusetts—who provided *pro bono publico* assistance with preliminary grant applications. This, BHA officials later acknowledged, enabled West Broadway to prepare "a superior letter of intent" for the initial filing.[138] At the same time, D Street's leaders flexed their still-considerable political muscles. In February 1977, even before the state's Department of Community Affairs (DCA) had reviewed proposals for its Pilot program, South Boston's state representative, Michael Flaherty, made sure that the Secretary for Communities and Development himself came out to D Street to tour the facility and meet with tenant leaders. On the basis of this visit, Flaherty told the *South Boston Tribune*, funding seemed all but certain: "we can't miss."[139] Eight months later, the development indeed received initial state funding for a feasibility study and, in July 1978, was selected for a $6.5 million modernization grant, receiving fully two-thirds of the money allotted to Boston from this Pilot program.[140]

The grant money enabled the BHA and the WBTF to hire the Boston Urban Observatory in a more official capacity. Over the course of the next year, working with DCA's Pilot Program coordinator, Bernard Stewart, the tenants and their consultants put together a plan for revitalizing the development. Stewart recalls having been "initially very impressed" with the WBTF leadership, even as he endured numerous "heavy-duty raucous meetings" with them: "We came in from the State and said 'we're here to help you,' but they thought we would just continue to make promises like the BHA and nothing would happen." The groups eventually forged a more trusting partnership, with broad agreement on redevelopment goals. The Urban Observatory's Elaine Werby, who had formerly worked on social services issues for the BHA, stressed the central importance of Rose Hayes, whom Whittlesey also termed the "leading crusader." While most of the other tenants who came to meetings "were fearful of any dramatic change" and "saw security in the way things were," Hayes willingly embraced the BUO's attempt to look "beyond modernization" toward decentralization of management structures—even tenant management or contracting out to private management. The consultants talked about the intractability of the vast development and the need to "break things down" into seven smaller areas, but Hayes herself came up with the word they would later use to describe the intent: "it's like little villages." The "village" notion, so long the favored term of planners and housing reformers, thus re-entered the D Street vocabulary, not from the reports of outsiders, but from the inspiration of one of the project's own. A quarter-century later, it remains one of the most common ways for residents to identify their locations within the development.

As Werby saw it, "They labeled it and we promoted it." As is usually the case with proposals for spatial change, the idea also had a simultaneous social impetus. "[Residents] were very sensitive about living at D Street," Werby observed, "because the rest of South Boston looked down on them." The village idea "was a way to break through that and give them an identity of something else, something smaller. Psychologically it was a very helpful change and had great meaning." The BUO started with "the old organizing technique of having building captains and floor captains," intended to encourage meetings at which residents of a single building could decide things for themselves: "It was an organizing technique, but it also brought about the perception that you *could* manage something, take control and make a difference." In 1979 BUO staff took D Street residents to three housing developments in Connecticut and New Jersey "to see models where tenants were in control." As Werby recalled, "Each of the three places were minority developments, and, as frequently black tenants do, they put on this great feast, and these whites loved it. So, by the third time, as we were sitting in a basement in New Jersey having eaten this wonderful dinner, Rose Hayes says to the group— I'll never forget this—'Geez, I wish we could ask you back to come to our place, but, you know, you'd get killed if you came.' I always remember that because it was so typical of Rose and her honesty and fearlessness."[141]

Soon afterward, however, Rose Hayes got married and left Boston, leaving a temporary void in the D Street leadership. Those who remained, according to Werby, tended to be less sophisticated and less adversarial in their attitudes, although they continued to devote "an enormous amount of time" to the cause. They asked good questions but "feared the unknown," even in terms of altered apartment layouts, "and certainly they didn't go for the idea of tenant management, not at all." They thought "it was better for the Authority to do it, however badly, so you would always have somebody to blame." In these early days, Werby observed, tenants "were afraid of responsibility and power"; they were even uneasy about assuming an advisory role in interviewing potential residents. As a result, the tenant-management idea went nowhere, and a subsequent feasibility study for turning West Broadway over to private management also proved a dead end at D Street.[142]

In addition to these management initiatives, however, the BUO's *Comprehensive Plan for the Renewal of the West Broadway Development* proposed other major changes. Using the "village" concept, the team suggested reconfiguring the development into a series of courtyard-centered neighborhoods with a central "Town Hall," to be used for management and service agencies. They pointed out a variety of large and small ways to deinstitutionalize the appearance of the project, recognizing that "real community stabilization implies a significant change in the public image of the West Broadway development." Ultimately, though, the BUO team recognized that the initial $6.5 million Pilot Modernization grant would not buy very much. It could be little more than "a program for survival," a kind of "defensive strategy for protecting and extending the life of buildings and systems until more adequate resources are available."[143]

The Carrots and Sticks of Redevelopment Funding

Fortunately for the residents of D Street, Billy Bulger was elected president of the Massachusetts Senate late in 1978, a position he would hold until 1995. He did not forget his West Broadway constituents. In 1980, as the BHA went into receivership, Bulger added a $20 million set-aside for West Broadway's redevelopment into the state's housing bill, intended to ensure not only D Street's survival but its complete transformation. This infusion of dollars came none too soon.

Before signing the bill, Governor Edward King toured the development, pronouncing it "unfit for human habitation."[144] The governor's assessment of D Street merely corroborated the dispassionate gloom of Judge Paul Garrity, who visited the project just prior to ordering the BHA into receivership (Figs. 2.21–2.22). Walking through the development with tape recorder in hand, he chroni-

FIGURE 2.21 Pre-redevelopment conditions. In the 1970s, the D Street project was an asphalt landscape of litter, cars, and dying trees.

FIGURE 2.22 Dangerous passing. As the project geared up for redevelopment, even the street signs had to be amended to reflect the overall insecurity.

cled "deteriorated and vandalized" courtyards surrounded by unsecured abandoned apartments, including one that emitted steam; at other buildings he took note of interior walls that had been "literally destroyed, knocked down," basements where hot water "poured down" from leaks in the heating system, "a large number of incinerators without exterior doors," uncloseable entrance doors that had been "pretty much destroyed," all of which was surrounded by grounds that were "littered with chips of glass."

Desperate conditions prevailed in both occupied and unoccupied structures: "I am now observing 162 Orton Marotta Way," Garrity intoned. "It is a building that appears to be totally open to the elements, totally unoccupied and substantially destroyed. It has just been pointed out to me that on the second floor of 187 Orton Marotta Way several of the windows in an occupied unit are broken and it appears that the person who lives in that unit has stuffed up the windows with foam rubber. It appears to have been taken either from a mattress or a couch." Judge Garrity's conclusion about the conditions at D Street merely repeated what he had already made obvious: "There appears to be an enormous amount of vandalism that occurs at this development, and I stress the word enormous."

Interviews with three dozen long-term residents of West Broadway who lived through those days make clear that the judge's observations were an accurate representation of an environment in dangerous disarray. When residents were asked to describe conditions just before the redevelopment effort began, the litany of disasters they reported seems both never-ending and all-encompassing: "Roofs were leaking"; "Clotheslines were wrecked by kids"; "Dirty, disgusting from lack of repairing"; "Garbage everywhere"; "No locks on buildings. No security doors. Hallways weren't kept up"; "Tubs were terrible, bathroom walls were shabby, plumbing was bad"; "There were no trees. It looked like Alcatraz, like a prison. The only nice thing you could see was the church"; "It was a mess here, it was a wreck. They had boarded-up buildings, the courts were a mess, they never got cleaned"; "Never enough hot water. Paint chipping. Long wait for work orders"; "We had zero. Zilch. Roaches, lots of break-ins, no security. I lived on the first floor, so I was a prime candidate. I left things on the windowsill and they were stolen"; "There were holes in my wall. The outside looked like a jail—no trees, no nothing"; "There was garbage in the courts"; "Dumpy-looking." One 1977 arrival summed it all up: "Deplorable."[145]

Despite the horrendous conditions, BHA Receiver Harry Spence had not intended to place D Street's problems at the top of his redevelopment agenda. Spence wanted to launch the receivership by tackling troubled developments where he felt certain a turnaround could succeed, and he thought that at D Street this would be "extremely difficult." Just after he had decided that West Broadway should join the middle of the redevelopment queue, South Boston's old political clout reasserted itself. As Spence puts it, "D Street was imposed on us by the legislature, by Billy Bulger. That was not our choice." Spence immediately went directly to Bulger to discuss the matter, telling the Senate president, "You've told us we've got this money and we're to fix up D Street. Frankly, I would have done it later, it's going to be very hard to do, and I'm not sure we're organizationally ready to do that. But I understand. You are the boss, we'll do it." At the same time, however, Spence let Bulger know that he doubted that $20 million would be enough to do the whole development. In addition, the receiver made clear that redevelopment of D Street would carry two politically unpalatable consequences for South Boston. First, he warned Bulger, there would be evictions, and some people would come "screaming to elected officials." Spence's second concern was even more serious: "I told him that I was a receiver; I worked for the courts. It was an all-white development and, at some point in time—I didn't know when or how—I knew that the state could not go on investing dollars in West Broadway as a segregated development. A day would come, and it might come on my watch, when that development would have to address the racial-integration issue. I needed him to know that the inevitable consequence of investment there would be that that issue was going to get raised."[146]

THE FIGHT AGAINST FORCED HOUSING

Spence did not argue these issues with Bulger, but the racial-integration flash-point had already galvanized South Boston opinion against what now came to be called "forced housing." In early 1978, as the BHA began its planning for modest efforts to introduce selected nonwhite families back into the South Boston housing projects, someone distributed flyers throughout South Boston suggesting a forthcoming BHA plot to take over the district's public housing for minorities. In response, the BHA took the extraordinary step of distributing its own fact sheet to all residents of West Broadway, Old Colony, and Mary Ellen McCormack. The BHA claimed that it had "no plan for any kind of forced integration anywhere in the City and certainly not to move a large group of minority families into your community," assured residents that "*all* applicants, minority or *not,*" would be guaranteed "their freedom to choose where to live," and concluded that "preserving Southie as a desirable place to live is everybody's fight."[147]

Not convinced by the BHA's claim to be "a part of that fight," the South Boston Information Center stepped up its defensive posture. Promising to "keep a watchful eye on the various Housing developments," the center established a Legal Defense Fund (supported by the sale of candy and shamrocks) to assist South Boston whites arrested for "standing on their streets during legal protests," and began collecting evidence for a class-action lawsuit against the BHA, charging "discrimination against South Boston residents who wish to remain in their community." The Information Center claimed that the BHA's "Director of Equal Opportunity for Housing and Urban Development" had already issued "fighting words" on this subject. In response to a question about "what would happen if a person doesn't want to be moved to a certain Housing Project to improve integration," the housing official allegedly replied: "He has no choice. People who live in Federal Housing are wards of the State and will live where they are told." The center charged that the BHA kept delaying its planned action on integration every time local groups "got wind of it," in the hope that multiple false alarms would discredit "the groups and individuals who say it's coming"; only then would they "hit us with their disruptive plans." Meanwhile, the search was on to select a suitable South Boston flag with which to lead the charge.[148]

In April 1978, though the area was still without a proper flag, a new incident caused the center to adopt a more proactive stance. Several white South Boston families lost their homes to a fire, and allegedly the BHA refused to let them to move into vacant apartments in the South Boston projects because they were not black. "South Boston Marshalls" and Information Center volunteers responded with a "community" effort "to move our own residents into Projects in our own community regardless of what BHA policy said." The BHA ordered these "squatters" to leave and took the matter to court when they refused to do so. The Authority claimed that the apartments were "not ready" for occupancy, but the Information Center charged that the "true reason" behind this statement was that "they are being held for minorities to apply for them." With the aid of an attorney supplied by the Information Center, the white "squatters" (who were only too willing to pay for their accommodations) rapidly secured not-guilty verdicts and remained in South Boston public housing. In the months that followed, "community people moved more families in" and promised that even more would follow.

Engaging the battle on other fronts, the Information Center observed that the BHA had placed ads in a newspaper "distributed in Boston's black sections" touting the availability of South Boston public housing under "affirmative action guidelines." The center claimed that the Authority was so desperate "to get minorities to move in" that they were even "trying to get Southern blacks to come up." "They'll go to any extremes to provoke and disrupt," the center's John Ciccone insisted, "use anyone they must as pawns and guinea pigs. Then use as justification the phony reason of Civil Rights and integration." As Ciccone sardonically complained, "If Civil Rights groups filed suit against the Blizzard of '78 for dumping all white snow, it would not surprise many people."[149]

The BHA itself tried to downplay the pace and scale of its intended integration efforts and sought to interpret its tenant-assignment plan in terms least offensive to South Boston residents. Denying the statement that public housing residents were wards of the state who were given "no choice" about where to live, a BHA spokesman told *Tribune* readers that applicants could request any development they wished, but that it was the Authority's policy to offer them "a priority status at those developments where their race is in a minority." This policy, the BHA contended, actually worked to "the advantage of a community such as South Boston," since "integrated housing results in integrated schools and thereby does away with the need for busing school children."[150] In this view, forced housing was not the conspiratorial sequel to forced busing but, ultimately, could be seen as its antidote.

Even before the BHA's "secret" plans emerged, the Information Center resumed its assault on the whole idea of "pushing people of other races and cultures on one another," warning that "if trouble does come, it will be the fault of the Housing and Federal Officials who can't leave other people alone" and who "feel it's their duty to change a stable and happy community." Ciccone affirmed that his fellow South Bostonians were "determined to fight all . . . attempts to disrupt or dissolve this town as we know it." The Information Center's concern, he insisted, "isn't plain racism like the media would tell us," but instead was rooted in "a legitimate concern" about the "staggering crime rate" in "every integrated or predominantly black area in Boston." Once again, the vehemence of resistance to even token integration revealed the depth of suspicion about any public-sector activism in South Boston.

Since Southie's public neighborhoods had regained their all-white status, the Information Center staff regarded their residents as likely allies rather than as sources of community discord. Ciccone reminded *Tribune* readers that "the residents in Southie's developments play a very important role in keeping South Boston a close knit and good place to live." With tenant support, he promised, the Information Center would "use its resources and legal know-how to make sure that both the BHA and the Federal 'Big Wigs' no longer neglect South Boston's developments." By implication, Ciccone regarded integration threats as simply another form of neglect.[151]

While the controversies and rumors spread through the spring and summer of 1978, the underlying point remained moot, since the BHA could find "no minorities seeking to move into majority developments in troublesome areas." The BHA delayed its efforts in South Boston not to appease the SBIC but because it simply had no black tenants to send there.[152] That all changed in November, with the much-ballyhooed arrival of Brandeis student Faith Evans, who moved into the Mary Ellen McCormack development. Determined to implement its fair housing strategy at all costs, the BHA provided round the clock security guards, burglar alarms, police escorts to class, and "unbreakable" plexiglass window shields. These efforts nonetheless proved unable to protect either Ms. Evans or the integration policy from repeated attacks, and she moved out after only a few months. In the meantime, the Information Center complained not only about her presence but also about "how and why she was moved in" and the fact that she "received a completely renovated apartment with the best of everything, while South Boston people in this development can't even get leaky ceilings fixed."[153]

In the week following Evans's arrival, "South Boston's civic organizations" convened a community meeting of 350 residents in a packed school auditorium to protest the BHA policy. That same week, the *Tribune* used a full page to print a petition jointly sponsored by the South Boston Information Center, the South Boston Citizens Association, the South Boston Health Center Board, the South Boston Marshalls, and the South Boston Residents Group. Boldly proclaiming "We Accuse," the groups charged a variety of city, state, and federal agencies with unconstitutionally denying South Boston residents "equal access to public housing in the South Boston community." They pledged to "work towards the defeat" of all politicians who endorsed or condoned the BHA "minority preference" policy, and they promised further sustained protests and challenges to the perpetuation of such illegal "quotas."[154] A persistent fear animated their anger: "forced housing will not be restricted to the housing projects." Under the guise of civil rights, South Boston's defenders maintained, policies that began in public neighborhoods might threaten the broader community as well.

THE POLITICS OF "UNIT MIX"

Both directly and indirectly, the tense racial climate in South Boston affected the course of public housing redevelopment at West Broadway. The BHA could not disentangle decisions about physical redevelopment from a variety of social objectives and concerns. Debates phrased in terms of "unit mix"—meaning the number of apartments of different sizes and their distribution—encoded assumptions not only about the present and future pattern of demand but also about optimum juxtapositions of races, ages, and family types. Should the housing authority base its unit mix on the immediate need to rehouse existing residents? Should it be determined on the basis of the projections of the development-based waiting list, skewed toward the particular preferences of South Boston whites, 80 percent of whom requested one- or two-bedroom apartments? Or should the unit mix of the revitalized development attempt to reflect the broader pattern of Authority-wide demand? The need to work with the WBTF made close adherence to the requirements of current residents an overwhelming priority, and BHA internal memoranda show that the second priority, as of 1980, was to approximate "the demand for public housing family units *in South Boston*" [emphasis added].

BHA Design Specialist Gayle Epp acknowledged the Authority's "mandate to provide as much public housing for larger low-income families as possible or feasible." Eventually, however, the redevelopment team focused primarily on the need to reduce the density of large families within the project "to further minimize risk," and they sought to do so in a manner that was consistent with "present tenant needs." They authorized only enough large units to meet the legitimate needs of current tenants and skewed the rest of the unit mix to attract smaller families, including more elderly.[155]

At the same time, the BHA looked forward to the possibility of reintegrating the development, though its staff worried that mixing "small white families, primarily single elderly, with large minority families . . . could be problematic." Since nonwhites on the waiting list (especially Latinos) tended to require larger units than whites—and since white South Bostonians seeking small units constituted the bulk of the existing D Street demand—the redevelopment team feared that building too many large apartments would invite further tensions. If racial integration were to occur at all, their actions implied, better that it should occur among small families. As a result, only 11 percent of the proposed units contained four or more bedrooms, compared with 18 percent of those proposed for Franklin Field, where occupancy was expected to remain entirely nonwhite.

Another key decision on unit mix involved the spatial distribution of unit sizes, a matter of particular relevance for the elderly. To place all one-bedroom apartments together, for example, would segregate the elderly, but distributing them evenly could place the elderly in close proximity to large families with teenagers. The high demand for one-bedroom apartments presented an especially complex set of interrelated issues involving not just the obvious matter of family size, but also questions of race, age, disability, and neighborhood attachment. The BHA's acceptance of the need for increased numbers of small apartments reflected the desirability of housing the elderly, but it also raised the possibility that the BHA might assign some of these units to the deinstitutionalized mentally ill.[156] The BHA left the issue unresolved, at least in print, but clearly its redevelopment team wanted a unit mix that would minimize neighborhood problems at a revitalized West Broadway.

MODERNIZATION VERSUS REDEVELOPMENT

As the West Broadway redevelopment process moved into high gear, racial integration questions moved to the back burner. Few persons of any color sought entry into D Street, and, in any case, the redevelopment process would require a multiyear moratorium on admissions while construction took place. Many residents probably suspected that racial issues would eventually come to the fore once again, but their focus initially remained on improving the development's physical environment. With money suddenly available, the BHA and the WBTF needed to decide how best to use it. To assist with this decision, the BHA, acting as developer, selected two Boston firms—Lane, Frenchman, and Associates and Goody, Clancy—as architects-planners, though the tenants themselves continued to play a central role in design decisionmaking. The WBTF negotiated and signed off on all major decisions and even hired its own advisory architect, Gordon King, who had previously worked with them on the BUO plan. The WBTF also benefited enormously from the paid services of Don Gillis, who oversaw the day-to-day operations of the Multi-Service Center. Gillis, later to become one of Boston's leading economic development specialists, worked with the tenants to build on the "village" concept, hiring seven residents as village coordinators and providing them with vacant apartments for offices. At D Street, Gillis contends, in contrast to many other public housing developments, where resident involvement tended to be orchestrated by the professional organizers and social workers, "on a day-to-day basis, the process was indigenous, by and large led by the natives." The paid village coordinators essentially became advocates for their fellow tenants, helping to initiate social activities and to build trust by tracking management responsiveness to work orders or complaints.[157]

In the beginning, the residents still thought of the proposed changes in terms of a piecemeal modernization agenda, the materialization of long-sought funds needed to upgrade bathrooms and windows. This rather modest set of aspirations stood in real tension with Spence's considerable redevelopment plans, since the housing authority now resisted spending money to repair structures that might soon be torn out by more extensive subsequent reconstruction efforts. Many tenants, Gillis later recalled, simply could not understand "those people over at the Task Force talking pie in the sky." One tenant expressed the frustration of many at D Street who sought immediate repairs: "I just want to get my kitchen sink unplugged or get a lock fixed, and I can't get anything done." Slowly, however, many residents adopted the broader agenda as their own, and "talk shifted from getting bathrooms fixed to having a vision of what the community could be like." Once new bathrooms were installed, and other improvements started following, Gillis commented, "people saw that important things really can happen."

The village coordinators improved the delivery of services by prioritizing work orders and following up on them. This, in turn, encouraged more tenants to get involved. Eventually, Gillis estimates, at least a hundred people participated in some aspect of the redevelopment effort, and every meeting had at least twelve to fifteen people in regular attendance.

In addition to resident leaders, several community organizations also played significant supporting roles, especially Father Murphy of Saints Peter and Paul's Church, the South Boston Neighborhood House, and the head of the Condon Community School. The clergy from St. Peter's Lithuanian Church also showed interest, though their main objective was to push a version of redevelopment that involved greater clearance of buildings around their church, a move that served only to arouse further resentment from D Street residents.[158] Billy Bulger himself remained not far behind the scenes; he knew many of the tenants personally and continued to be a "strong advocate" for their needs, eventually securing further appropriations for additional redevelopment phases. Gillis and the tenant delegation met regularly with him at his Senate office over the next several years. "Whenever things kind of jammed up, he'd untangle them," Gillis recalled. "He was very effective at doing that, whether it meant bringing the Secretary of the Executive Office of Communities and Development to a meeting, or getting Harry Spence on the phone. He would do whatever he needed to do, whenever there was some controversy."[159]

COOPERATION OF TENANTS AND THE BHA

The perception of a good working relationship between tenants and the redevelopment team is more than a rosy recollection on the part of key participants; it is also reflected in the documents of the time. The various internal memoranda that served as negotiation vehicles demonstrate a mutual respect and a growing consensus on all major issues. At various points in the process, WBTF President Helen Young commended the architects for "following the guidance of Village Panels" and praised the "responsiveness to our concerns" of both the BHA and its redevelopment consultants. Moreover, Young made clear that residents enjoyed a broad-based consultation: "The [WBTF] Board, both personally and through our staff, have discussed the plan(s) with literally hundreds of residents."[160]

The WBTF took "serious issue" with one aspect of the redevelopment team's plan, however: they unanimously rejected the BHA's preference to stage the redevelopment beginning with the West Broadway side of the project. The WBTF stressed the need to achieve an "overall image improvement to the 'outside world'" and to put "the improvements where they are needed the most." Tenant leaders cared not only about their fellow residents but also about the opinions of outsiders. Convincing themselves that positive change had truly occurred would entail reshaping the way outsiders socially constructed their public neighborhood. Young and the other tenant leaders understood that the redevelopment effort would need to occur in phases—owing in part to the absence of full funding and in part to their own refusal to undertake off-site relocation. More important, they recognized that this phasing had both a psychology and a politics.

The tenants analyzed various staging options from the perspective of outsiders driving past their development. They wanted a plan that would convince skeptics not only that change was irreversibly under way, but also that the redevelopment deserved another round of funding. If they followed the BHA's suggestion to redevelop the West Broadway "front" of the project first, tenants feared, this would enable "West Broadway onlookers . . . to think that the entire project is finished, because they will not see the back of the site. And the Dorchester Ave. commuters and Bayview bus riders [who see only the "back"] will never know that any work has been done at all." If this were to occur, they worried, it was "foreseeable" that this "'back side' would be all but forgotten, and possibly turned into some other use . . . resulting in a totally unacceptable end product." Instead, the tenants insisted, the BHA should stage the remodeling in a way that gave passing commuters the sense that the redevelopment process was well under way but obviously not yet finished. Only this image would "provide the best possible case for D Street receiving the additional funds necessary to complete all renovation." They explicitly wished to "raise the question in an onlooker of 'well, we can't possibly leave this quarter out, if we've done all the rest.'"

The tenants also had another major reason for arguing against the BHA's plan. They all concurred that the West Broadway side of the development (especially "Village G") remained the least troubled part, and so to them it made no sense for the BHA to tackle it first. Instead, they countered, it would be much more equitable to relieve the suffering of those living under the worst conditions. On September 16, 1981, more than a hundred tenants came to a meeting with Harry Spence to advance their "rear-first" strategy. The receiver said he had come to the session "95 percent sure of starting work near West Broadway" but left it wholly uncertain. Two weeks later Spence returned to D Street (along with State Representative Flaherty and City Councilor Flynn) to join two hundred tenants at the WBTF annual meeting, at which the tenants' association voted unanimously to support the rear-first concept. Faced with such evident passion and sophisticated logic from the tenants, Spence and the BHA publicly acquiesced, a decision that not only changed the order of redevelopment but, more fundamentally, made the residents feel that their own voices carried a new order of influence.[161] Like most other key participants, Redevelopment Director Michael Jacobs later considered this BHA reversal "the most significant turning point," since it "changed the relationship dramatically between the residents and the housing authority—no longer was it a matter of just saying 'sure you can have orange tile in your bathroom'; this was a major decision about resource allocation—it changed the planning process, and issues of mistrust really disappeared."[162]

When fourteen residents who said they had played some role in the redevelopment decisionmaking were asked, a decade after the fact, to assess who had played the most important role in the redevelopment process, all gave primary credit to fellow residents: eleven highlighted the crucial role of tenant leaders, while the other three credited "all residents" for what happened. By contrast, in interviews with eighteen long-term residents who lived through the redevelopment process but said they had not taken an active role, only a minority credited tenant leaders as having played the most important role. This group gave credit to many other actors, including the Boston Housing Authority, on-site management, and architects. It is perhaps not surprising that those who saw themselves as most involved would also see their own role as central, but it is nonetheless a positive sign that the leaders—more than a decade after the redevelopment began—retained the view that their actions had mattered.[163]

The consolidation of tenant power also had its counterparts in the broader community. In the early 1980s, South Boston political clout in city and state government hit a new high. Not only had William Bulger been elected state Senate president, but Southie could also boast direct and powerful representation through U.S. Representative Joe Moakley, Massachusetts State Representative Michael Flaherty, and Boston City Councilor Jim Kelly. And in 1983, with the election of native-son Raymond Flynn as the mayor of Boston (an election in which 82 percent of D Street residents claim to have voted), the fortunes of South Boston seemed wholly auspicious.[164] Despite these connections, everyone at D Street realized that it would be difficult to obtain the funds needed to complete all phases of the redevelopment. Initially, according to Redevelopment Director Jacobs, the planners wanted to attempt to renovate the entire development using

the available money, but Harry Spence remained unconvinced of the feasibility of
that plan. Eventually, in late 1981, Spence and the Authority decided that "it made
sense to do it right," rather than simply implement "the holding action that it
would have been if we had just taken the first phase of money and distributed it
over 675 units." At that point, Jacobs recalled, "we recognized that we were just
going to have to keep going back to the legislature, but we thought that was possible, given Bulger."[165] The redevelopment team provided "convincing evidence"
to the BHA that spreading the limited construction budget "evenly across the entire site would not begin to address the numerous physical and design problems
of West Broadway," and that it was therefore "difficult to justify an investment
strategy which does not sufficiently concentrate resources to increase the potential for successful revitalization."[166]

Although the BHA–D Street–Bulger connection did eventually yield subsequent state funds to complete not only the first phase of "comprehensive redevelopment" (1982 to 1986) but also a second phase (1986 to 1989) and the first part
of a third (1989 to 1991), the pipeline to West Broadway eventually clogged.[167] It
would take another full decade of wrangling before the last quadrant (much of it
facing West Broadway) would gain redevelopment funds.

REDEVELOPMENT PRODUCTS: ARCHITECTURAL INTENTIONS

The redesign of the D Street project into the West Broadway development, as implemented by Lane, Frenchman and Goody, Clancy, seems an attempt to approximate—as closely as possible given the constraints of scale and massing—the form
of a middle-class development, while providing many of the most desired amenities of life in a single-family house. Respecting tenant preferences meant that
many of the most important improvements to the development occurred within
apartments and building interiors, though the tenant-designer team also made
many highly visible exterior changes too. Some of this reimaging aimed to alert
nonresident neighbors to the transformation, but it could also lift the self-con-
fidence of residents.

The design team thoroughly transformed the apartment units, buildings, and
site. At each of these three different scales of design, they attempted to approximate the desired spatial norms of American domestic life, despite prevailing
HUD regulations that forced them to work largely within the heavy footprints of
the existing buildings (Figs. 2.23–2.25).

At the level of the individual unit, the designers increased apartment size,
reconfiguring each unit with both vertical and horizontal breakthroughs. They

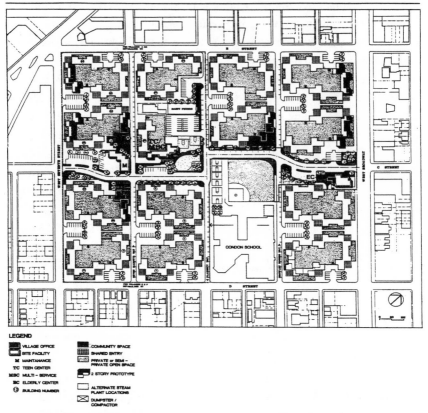

LEGEND

	VILLAGE OFFICE		COMMUNITY SPACE
	SITE FACILITY		SHARED ENTRY
M	MAINTENANCE		PRIVATE or SEMI – PRIVATE OPEN SPACE
TC	TEEN CENTER		
MSC	MULTI – SERVICE		2 STORY PROTOTYPE
EC	ELDERLY CENTER		
⑬	BUILDING NUMBER		ALTERNATE STEAM PLANT LOCATIONS
		⊠	DUMPSTER / COMPACTOR

FIGURE 2.23 Proposed site plan, after redevelopment. This plan, much of which has been implemented, reintegrated the project back into the grid of South Boston streets, relandscaped the site into a series of semi-enclosed courtyards, and introduced a set of new community buildings.

enlarged dining areas to accommodate all family members eating at once, and created a separate entrance vestibule to provide enhanced privacy for the living room. Larger apartments received second bathrooms and, at least in some phases, individual hookups for washers and dryers. More conceptually, apartments gained a clearer articulation of front and back, with living rooms facing front and more service-oriented rooms facing rear. The design provided new front stoops and backyards, semi-private areas to encourage families to regard more of their environment as being under their own control and management.

At the level of the building, the architects turned many of the multibedroom units into duplexes, permitting clearer division between sleeping and living areas.

FIGURE 2.24 Typical "open space," before redevelopment, when the area between buildings was mostly impersonal and undifferentiated asphalt.

FIGURE 2.25 New courtyard. The new landscaped courtyards, designed in collaboration with residents, featured play areas for small children.

The redesign eliminated large common stairwells, long viewed as overcrowded and unsupervisable, and prevented free access to rooftops, long the locus of illicit and dangerous behaviors. The reconfiguration added many private entrances to units and provided direct ground-floor access to the outdoors through both front and back doors for large families. More broadly, the new buildings tried to deinstitutionalize the project appearance by adding pitched roofs and other allusions to more middle-class building images.

At the site scale, the redesign dramatically reduced the density of apartments, dropping the number of units from 972 to a projected 675, through creating larger apartments and transforming some residential buildings into village centers. The new plan reintroduced much of the South Boston street grid into the superblock, another part of the effort to reintegrate this enclave into the fabric of the neighborhood. Seeking to curtail the free reign given to cars on asphalt courts, the new plan provided a more coherent way to separate cars from pedestrians. It provided parking near dwelling entrances, allowing vehicle surveillance and easy access. The designers further sought to organize the development along a new "main street," a central spine on which many community facilities could be located. Finally, in terms of landscape, the architects sought ways to encourage residents to extend their control over space outside their apartments by providing a variety of traversable, semi-traversable, and nontraversable barriers. They also worked with tenants in each village to develop play areas for different age groups, including hard and soft surfaces, with paved areas to place above-ground tenant-owned pools, wide sidewalks, and non "purpose-built" places.

The magnitude of the socioenvironmental redevelopment of project apartments into dwellings more closely resembling an American private-sector condo complex may be illustrated as follows: planners transformed a typical four-bedroom unit from a 900-square-foot flat into a 1,380-square-foot rowhouse-like duplex, providing clear separation between living and sleeping spaces, a functionally defined sense of front and rear, and semi-private outdoor space that could be treated and viewed as an extension of each family's apartment. As unacknowledged adherents to Oscar Newman's defensible-space principles, the designers of the West Broadway redevelopment sought to "assign a use and a user to every square foot." They doggedly eliminated all vestiges of the vast undifferentiated space that once characterized the project.[168] Even a public neighborhood, they affirmed, need not appear wholly available and accessible for general public use and misuse (Figs. 2.26–2.27).

FIGURES 2.26–2.27 Private entrances and private control. In many cases where families were provided with direct individual entrances to their dwellings, the residents also "privatized" nearby outdoor space. This example is shown in both its summer and its winter modes.

DESTIGMATIZING D STREET

BHA Redevelopment Director Michael Jacobs understood that public housing tenants felt "branded" by "the stigma of living in the projects." "Even though there might be an apartment building next door with as many code violations as some of our developments," he observed, "the tenants feel that the family in private housing is somehow better, even if they have exactly the same income. We saw no reason to continue stereotyping and typecasting developments as public housing. One of the goals of the design was to reintegrate D Street with the rest of South Boston. We didn't see any reason that someone should have to go by the development and say, 'That's a project.'"[169]

Stigma takes multiple forms—some physical, some social—and these forms are always closely interlinked. The cultural bias against those seen as on the government dole, and the self-perceptions of those who feel that they have been permanently relegated to life in public housing by economic necessity, will not be fully alleviated by architectural alterations. But neither are such interventions irrelevant to either internal or external perceptions of life in a public housing development.

Often with subtlety, sometimes with a heavy hand, the architects and planners of West Broadway tried to deinstitutionalize the image of the D Street project. Some residents, Don Gillis notes, even wanted to re-emphasize the official West Broadway name "because it could be the 'West Broadway Housing Development' rather than the 'D Street Project.'" "'D Street' gave it a sort of down and dirty feel," Gillis observed. Changing the name was "part of the process of changing the overall image so people would feel positively about it, to integrate it physically with the community." As one long-time tenant put it, "the Upper End always called us the D Street Dirtballs, and I think people just wanted to get out of being D Street. The only logical thing was to call us the West Broadway Development, since we are on Broadway." With a new name and a decrease of visual stigma, tenants hoped that the social stigma could be eased as well.

In pursuing destigmatization, the architects and planners considered certain aspects of the buildings' new appearance more important than did the residents themselves. While the tenants' architect Gordon King sought to find a way to make the project "look more like the rest of South Boston" and "not like the BHA,"[170] the question of pitched roofs, according to the BHA's "design specialist" Gayle Epp, seemed to arouse "no tenant feeling."[171] King added that "not much was said at the time" by tenants about "stylistic things," and architect Dennis Frenchman of Lane, Frenchman confirmed that there was little tenant concern with pitched roofs: "that's something *we* felt."[172] The designers wished to differentiate portions of the project by providing hierarchy and greater visual interest on what was otherwise twenty-seven acres of flat repetitive structures. As BHA Redevelopment Planner Pamela Goodman put it, the peaks and pitches represented "an inexpensive way to deinstitutionalize."[173]

When one actually asks a broad spectrum of tenants about the pitched roofs, however, a different answer emerges. The residents also disliked the flat roofs and urged their elimination, but they did so for different reasons. Designers and planners regarded the elimination of the flat roofs as an aesthetic and symbolic issue; for residents, the problem was security, not aesthetics. They simply wished to keep the young people in the development from using rooftops for all manner of unwanted activities. Drunken rooftop gatherings had led to numerous falls and accidents, even a death—and surely the community had not forgotten the lesson of George Pratt's murder. In any event, resident needs and designer preferences converged on a single solution.

This particular example suggests that resident design input emphasized practicality over symbolism, yet many D Street residents also cared deeply about symbolic messages. When fifty-nine adult residents were asked whether they felt that West Broadway "looks like public housing," their answers, while divergent, displayed more than a casual engagement with this question.[174]

Overall, most respondents clearly differentiated between those parts of the development that had been redesigned and those parts that remained physically unaltered. Although 40 percent said that they still believed that the whole place looked like public housing, another 47 percent thought the newly redeveloped parts no longer looked this way. An additional 7 percent said that, without qualification, West Broadway did not look like public housing, and 6 percent were unsure. Some clearly understood and appreciated the redesign techniques employed by the architects and urban designers. They spoke of specific design elements in the redeveloped part that contributed successfully to a dissociation from an earlier image of public housing, stressing the elimination of flat roofs, the addition of private entries, individual doorbells, courtyards, and gardens, and the provision of more trees and more play areas. One person even referred to the place as "like living in the country." Others spoke in more general terms about the creation of a more "modern," "homey," "organized," "cleaner," "varied," and "neater" appearance. As one respondent put it, "They fixed [the apartments] over really nice. Now they are livable and you are not ashamed to say you live here." Another said, "The outside is better looking, and the design of where you live makes others acknowledge that change came about." Someone else commented that residents were "better off" because the development was now a "place to look up to," adding that "we're people here, we're not lower than the sidewalk. The project always had a name." Another noted, "The townhouse style of apartment [presents] a better outlook to people driving by—it doesn't look like a stockade."

Many comments from residents suggest that the designers successfully effected a shift in architectural type, from housing project to "townhouses," "condos," "a nice complex," or even "individual homes." One resident of the redeveloped part proudly noted that even the phone company "has [her] unit down as one-family house not as public housing." Another pointed out that, with the new trees and greater cleanliness, "it's more like a development," and it "makes you want to take care of what you have now." Someone else added that having her own entrance made the place "look less like projects and more like private homes." Many emphasized the clear contrast between the "old" and the "new" parts of the development: "[The] new parts don't look like other projects"; "[It] looks better than public housing now—the old side looks bad—over there looks like a ghost town." For some, the contrast between old and new helped to remind them and those who visit them of the magnitude of the changes: "The old parts look like ghettos, all torn apart, a mess. The new parts don't. Relatives came to town and couldn't believe it. I think it's because of the trees and landscaping." One resident noted explicitly what seems obvious to anyone who looks at most of the private yards: "Owners are making their places look better because the development looks better." The very notion that a resident could now refer to fellow tenants as "owners" well illustrates the magnitude and power of the symbolic shift.

Still, a substantial minority of respondents were not convinced that the redevelopment had done much to change the character of the project: "It all mostly still looks like public housing"; "All parts look like public housing, because [it's] all the same buildings they were before"; "All the buildings look the same—it's all one big development." Though lacking the jargon to describe it, residents recognized the lingering presence of the superblock: "It all looks like public housing, because of they way they are set up in a large square"; "It's like a prison—building after building"; "No matter what you do it's going to look like public housing." One recent arrival to the development, a Vietnamese woman who presumably did not grow up with stigmatized images of American public housing, had to evaluate her environment through the eyes of others: "It all looks like public housing," she replied, "because friends told us it does."

Some tenants seemed to regard the transformation as a partial one, noting improvement but pointing out ways that the presence of public housing is still signaled: "[You] still can tell it's public housing"; "it's still a project"; "it all look[s] alike." Another respondent, acknowledging that the renovated sections looked "less" like public housing than they once had, noted that the revamped project "doesn't look like all plain, red blah public buildings, but people still know it's public housing. They know we're here." It is this concern for what "they" think that remains especially striking. Many respondents implied that the stigma associated with public housing inhered in the visible presence not only of its buildings but also of its residents. Even with many buildings repaired and substantially deinstitutionalized, many residents still felt part of a benighted public neighborhood. They still faced the jeers and downcast eyes of residents of "The Point" and still felt victimized by the downtown bureaucracy that controlled the selection and assignment of tenants.

Redevelopment and Reintegration

Many long-term residents, when asked about the changes that were most important to them, spoke not so much about physical design as about the construction and preservation of a viable social community. They spoke of security and privacy concerns not in terms of locks and fences and yards but in terms of the need for greater police protection. Many of their concerns centered on the racial and ethnic composition of the development, and some long-term residents recalled having cared less about what was done in the redevelopment than about *who* would be allowed in to enjoy its benefits. Many D Street tenants wanted to reserve the new West Broadway for white South Boston residents. Some became sorely disaffected when this did not happen.

As the first redeveloped apartments became ready for occupancy in 1986, discussion about admitting new tenants heated up both inside and outside West Broadway. That March, WBTF President Barbara Mellan used part of an "antiracism" grant from the Cambridge-based Lotus Development Corporation to organize a weekend retreat for twenty Task Force members, staffers, and other tenants, at which, Mellan said, "we did a lot of talking about what our feelings might be if blacks moved in." Mellan, who had resided in the development for twenty years and had once answered phones at the SBIC during the early days of the anti-busing furor, argued strongly that reintegrating D Street involved a different set of principles. With public housing, she pointed out, "nobody's being forced. When blacks reach the top of the waiting list and their names are up, they have a right to be housed. Who am I to say, 'You're black, you can't live here'? They're human beings. Besides, it's the law. When you take state and federal money, there are fair-housing codes."

Laws or no laws, Mellan's leadership soon faced the wrath of Southie's hardliners. Ciccone's April 10th column launched the counter-offensive, charging that "a tiny group of so-called South Boston people" were "holding small meetings in the projects in an attempt to prepare local people for an influx of minorities to come in the future." Two weeks later, he reported that "the Boston Housing Authority is at it again," arranging "hush-hush" meetings "with select D St. Development people to see what the feelings would be if minority tenants were moved into the Development." Their mistake, he observed, was to "continue discussing the matter in public restaurants . . . they should have remembered the old saying, 'Loose lips sink ships.'" Ciccone alleged that Mellan and other traitors were being bought off with the promise of "a job or maybe a new stove" and, employing an invidious pun, warned that "the names of those melon heads are fast getting around." He insisted that the collaborationist leadership of the project was out of touch with the majority of their fellow residents, who realized that "a policy of forced housing in South Boston will bring trouble." The following month, City Councilor Kelly rejoined the fray, cautioning that "if they're going to move in 50 or 100 or 150 minorities, that would have such an immediate change in any neighborhood, especially South Boston. There probably won't be enough police to provide security for all the people . . . I know South Boston people. There's a serious potential for violence." One of Boston's weekly papers inflamed the situation further with a page-one article entitled "Turf's Up in Southie: Preparing to Fight 'Forced Housing,'" proclaiming that "the housing battle in Southie is starkly reminiscent of the early primal fight against busing."[175]

There were certainly differences between the battles over busing and the renascent battles over housing, but many South Boston residents perceived both as the work of a distant legal system that used the excuse of public facilities to undermine the quality of neighborhood life. As Ric Kahn, the author of the "Turf's Up" piece, put it: "In Southie you don't just live in the neighborhood, you own it." The problem is, for a community composed chiefly of renters and partially of public facilities, this ownership is psychological and symbolic but not legally enforceable. Alex Rodriguez, the chairman of the Massachusetts Commission against Discrimination (MCAD) and a long-standing Jim Kelly antagonist, caustically dismissed the arguments of South Boston's more insular defenders: "Where does tenancy give you a right to the asphalt in front of your house, to the corner? Ownership gives you a right to your house. You don't own the square, you don't own the tree, you don't own the brick. That's owned by the people in common . . . Hey, it's not their Southie housing, it's my Southie housing. I own a part of it. I'm a citizen of Boston." For Rodriguez, South Bostonians wrongly defined neighborhoods in terms of nostalgia, stasis, and exclusion, and missed the extent to which all neighborhoods are characterized by change: "Forty percent of the people living in South Boston didn't live there ten years ago . . . People are born, people die, people move, people come in from out of town. People finally make it and move to the 'burbs." In resisting change through discriminatory mechanisms, Rodriguez charged, South Boston's apologists had "bastardized the concept of neighborhood" by treating it as a place "to keep people out of."[176]

As the sides hardened for renewed battle, Southie's Raymond Flynn sought ways to pursue both fair housing and neighborhood choice, but South Boston was not a place for an easy compromise. As the chairman of the City Council's Committee on Housing and Neighborhood Development in the late 1970s, Flynn had long supported the D Street rehabilitation effort, paying frequent visits to the development, and urging the city to devote at least 10 percent of its federal Community Development Block Grant (CDBG) money to the needs of public housing communities. Although he never adopted the strident line of the SBIC, he did denounce "misguided directives from social theorists which are disrupting community life while ignoring the real needs of public housing tenants." Still, to his credit, he focused attention on the dire conditions in public housing rather than on the vexed conditions under which it would be re-tenanted.[177] In 1983, when he first announced his campaign for mayor, Flynn did so at D Street, promising that "neighborhood people" would never suffer neglect in his administration. And on the day in January 1984 that he was sworn in as the first South Bostonian ever elected Boston's mayor, he again visited the rising phoenix of the D Street project. There the local-boy-made-good assured the assembled audience that he would never renounce his neighborhood roots: "The name is still Ray," he promised, "and I'm going to come to D Street to play basketball."

Many other South Boston citizens, however, viewed Flynn's public housing games as hardball rather than basketball. In late October 1987, Flynn bravely announced his intention to comply with state and federal demands to integrate South Boston public housing, including immediate, specific plans to place black families at the top of the waiting list for vacancies. Less than a week later, Bostonians overwhelmingly re-elected him as mayor, with markedly strong support from the city's black communities. Flynn won in all but two of Boston's voting districts; though he was championed throughout the city, both South Boston wards bitterly renounced their favorite son. Election day interviews conducted in South Boston confirmed that residents blamed Flynn for the housing plan. He had become yet another Boston politician intent on inflicting the will of outsiders on their neighborhood.[178]

In January 1988, just after his second inauguration, Flynn faced five hundred mostly hostile South Boston residents in the basement of a local church. He affirmed his intent to integrate the projects, but he reassured residents that this would be done without displacing current tenants, especially the elderly, even if they were currently "overhoused" in excessively large apartments. Unconvinced, representatives from the three housing projects defended their need to remain in their own neighborhood and called for the mayor to assist with housing construction in Roxbury so that more blacks could do the same. On January 24, Cardinal Bernard Law had a six-page pastoral letter read at Sunday Mass in each of South Boston's eight Catholic churches: "There is too much at stake for us to let our communities become divided by blind emotion," the Cardinal pleaded. "Every one of us should seek a reasonable, calm, open and fair resolution of the issue affecting public housing in South Boston." As time passed, many recognized the inevitability of the changes and blamed Flynn less personally. Flynn and the other Boston politicians tried to deflect the talk of integration by framing the issue in terms of fairness and freedom of choice, arguing that all citizens should be able to exercise a preference to live in any city neighborhood. This approach provided for cooler discussion, but it could hardly forestall the emotions involved once racially motivated move-ins actually began.[179]

In early 1990, with the first two phases of redevelopment complete, the BHA again accepted new residents off the waiting list into West Broadway, following a seven-year moratorium. Over the next four years, the BHA filled vacancies from a waiting list that was 86 percent minority. By 1994, nearly 40 percent of the development's population was nonwhite. This wholesale integration, accomplished on the heels of the redevelopment, became inextricably melded with it in the minds of most residents, and constitutes a major source of ongoing tension in the development. Still, despite periodic incidents, the first years of West Broadway's reintegration proceeded far less chaotically than many had feared. WBTF President Barbara Mellan anticipated "gunshots and broken windows" but was relieved to see that "all we got was fighting."[180] Compared with the sustained harassment campaigns and forced mass exoduses of the late 1960s and mid-1970s, the transformation of D Street into a multiracial and multiethnic community seems almost a model of civility. This time, backed both by the courts and by a supportive tenant organization, the BHA made the integration of West Broadway irreversible, in terms of both scale and commitment. That said, in the early years many white residents resisted integration, sometimes with silent resentment, often with outright hostility.

Given this atmosphere, many at the development credit Sister Margaret Lanen, a long-time D Street resident, with fostering a climate of greater racial and ethnic tolerance. Appointed as a paid "Integration Coordinator" in January 1990, Sister Margaret spent the next three years assisting with many aspects of the development's social transformation. She chaired an "Integration Committee" composed of fifteen to twenty residents and staff, conducted workshops, led ESL classes, hosted periodic potluck dinners, and established a mediation group in which white mothers and black mothers could meet to talk about problems with their kids. Whenever a new family arrived at the development, Sister Margaret contacted them. They received not only an eight-page booklet describing the activities of the WBTF and the "Multi," but also maps, useful phone numbers, bus schedules, gifts of candy, and guidance about local services. Most important, in the days following their arrival, she escorted the new family to meet their immediate neighbors. She chose not to bring up the long history of South Boston's racial tensions unless asked.[181]

For many long-term residents of the development, the mass influx of hundreds of nonwhites—whose otherness encompassed a broad array of races and ethnicities—proved enormously disconcerting. As one white resident put it, "It's incredible that all of a sudden I cannot talk to my neighbors. We all say 'hi, how are you,' but there's the language problem, the whole culture problem, the whole reality." During redevelopment, the tenant body (and especially its leadership) had consisted of a remarkably homogeneous group of families, dominated by female-headed Irish Catholic households who had resided at D Street for decades.

These families enjoyed a cohesiveness that made the prospect of sharing court-yard social areas with similar families quite desirable; they really did feel part of a particular "village." They refused to move off-site even during reconstruction, ne-cessitating a complex game of "musical apartments," and had sought guarantees that they would be rehoused not only in the same village but also with the same neighbors. The BHA even hired an expert from MIT to design a computer algo-rithm to maximize the ability to meet such goals.

After redevelopment, white tenants saw the desired transformations in design melded with less-desired transformations in demographics, and so for them the renewed physical environment carried unanticipated social consequences. Shared courtyards that had been planned by and for a homogeneous group of white residents were now to be shared by a multiethnic and multilingual popula-tion with different needs and practices. Fortunately, many residents pointed out, the private entrances to apartments housing large families reduced fears about en-counters with unexpected persons in hallways and stairwells. For the most part, West Broadway's old tenants accepted life with their new neighbors, but many still resisted the idea that South Boston's public neighborhoods should ever have been shared with outsiders.[182]

Serving Public Neighbors: Ours and Theirs

When fifty-nine West Broadway residents were asked about tenant selection in 1993, nearly 90 percent of white respondents called for more new tenants to come from South Boston; conversely, nearly 90 percent of black and Latino respon-dents preferred more new tenants to come from elsewhere. When asked about the fairness of BHA tenant-selection policies, white respondents almost invariably in-terpreted the question in racial terms, linking this to their desire to see South Boston's public housing reserved for South Boston residents: "It's not fair—peo-ple from South Boston don't get into their community"; "There are too many colored people coming in. We're the minority now"; "People on the list to get in are not from South Boston. All minorities are getting in and just minorities"; "The list should have been left the way it was—white people were on that list for years"; "Neighborhood people are not getting in." Black and Latino respondents, by contrast, defended the policies that allowed them to choose West Broadway.

While D Street's blacks frequently affirmed the need for further diversity to di-lute the presence of "racist" and "closed-minded" people from South Boston, white residents almost invariably defended the need to restore D Street as a South Boston resource. Although each resident was interviewed separately, white respondents seemed almost to be finishing one another's sentences: "People need public housing in South Boston so they don't have to go outside"; "They shouldn't be sent to these other places where they're getting killed"; "They should get first preference because they've lived here all their life"; "If they've lived around here, they should be able to stay where they came from"; "You shouldn't have to live where you don't want to live"; "You deserve to live in public housing when you're from the neighborhood. Why should they send you across town where you're not wanted?"; "I have a daughter that's trying to get in and they sent her to Roxbury"; "We have women without homes waiting for public housing while living with their families, and they see folks from Haiti getting the housing—it's all so crazy"; "If a person is in need of an apartment, they should have the choice to live in an area they could fit in." For D Street's whites, public housing should be a publicly subsidized extension of their current neighborhood, rather than a publicly financed pipeline for handling outside obligations.[183]

RACIAL PREFERENCES AND SPATIAL PREFERENCES

Worst of all—to many of D Street's long-term white residents—blacks and other nonwhites received not only preferential assignment to South Boston public housing but also the development's best apartments. With 80 percent of the apartments expanded, newly outfitted, and connected to a variety of carefully landscaped, semi-private courtyards and 20 percent still unredeveloped, many tenants interpreted every decision about where to place a new tenant in racial terms, even if the BHA intended no systematic bias (Figs. 2.28–2.30). When interviewed in 1993, D Street's new nonwhite neighbors voiced few complaints about their apartment assignment, whereas most white respondents reacted with anger and frustration, repeatedly insisting that the "minority" arrivals were treated "too fairly": "They" got "bigger apartments"; "the best choice"; "whatever they want"; "they automatically got brand-new apartments"; "they got everything new—from appliances to floors"; "they don't have to take an apartment they don't want"; "they take advantage of this place"; "they get treated right." Meanwhile, scores of long-term white residents had lived through the redevelopment only to find themselves still in the "old section." New arrivals, many felt, should have been made to take the old apartments, waiting their fair turn for renovated units to become available.

BHA officials pointed out that new arrivals received apartments on the basis of family size and availability, rather than on development location, but this did not

FIGURE 2.28 New streetscape, as yet incomplete. With new pitched roofs, sidewalks, streets, and trees, the development gained a new image, but the lingering quadrant of old buildings stood in stark contrast to the revamped areas.

assuage perceptions of favoritism. In fact, since the first two redeveloped sections opened for reoccupancy before reintegration began, the BHA initially repopulated them almost exclusively with whites. Moreover, reintegration commenced before the first part of Phase 3 was ready, so most nonwhite arrivals initially received apartments in the "old section," where there were many vacancies. Occupancy in some hallways there become as much as 60–70 percent minority.[184] To that point, then, new nonwhite arrivals had certainly not received preferential treatment. A much better case could be made to suggest just the opposite.

More plausible charges of minority favoritism surfaced only in 1991, following completion of fifty-five new apartments in Phase 3a. For the first time, BHA officials had to decide how to allocate the new housing between new nonwhite arrivals and D Street's long-term white residents who still remained in the old part. The BHA and its planners remained committed to a policy of integrating all parts of the development as equally as possible, but they soon faced an unanticipated roadblock.

Many new arrivals had young children, and BHA officials determined that

FIGURES 2.29–2.30 A tale of two pools. For those living in the new landscaped courts, playtime could be pleasant and supervised. For those in or adjacent to the old parts of the development, there were fewer options. Eventually, the BHA boarded-up all the non-redeveloped buildings, to await funding for the last phase of construction.

apartments in the old section presented a potential lead paint hazard; under the strict Massachusetts laws of the time, the housing authority could not use these buildings for families with children under age seven. As a result, the BHA sent many young, nonwhite families to the new parts. Correspondingly, this tended to consolidate families with teenagers in the older parts, sometimes uneasily mixed in with the many elderly still living in nonrenovated "Village G." In this way, the lead paint externality rapidly unraveled almost a decade of careful planning about "unit mix."

With redevelopment incomplete, every tenant assignment forced an acknowledgment and a revisitation of the gnawing inequity. As long-term white residents still living in the old sections of the development stood by while nonwhite newcomers received apartments in the redeveloped sections, frustrations mounted. One woman who had previously been supportive of the integration effort described her reaction to observing young black families walk from the old section to their renovated apartments in the new parts: "These people had been homeless—I'm not condemning them—but there they were moving furniture I would *love* to have. And the truth of the matter was that they were all minority, and I sat there and I cried because, God, I was so angry. I called Sister Margaret the next day and said, 'Sorry but I'm off the Integration Committee.' It doesn't mean I hate these people, but I resent the way it was done." Left back in the old part, she felt doubly scorned: "When they bring the minorities here to show them my apartment, they don't want it—they don't want to live in that hall where dummies have lived for seventeen years. It was all very unfair." Another, older white tenant added that the black families were "delighted" by the lead paint problem, charging that "one couple moved in to the old section and got pregnant very quickly and . . . zooooom—off to the new section . . . so long!" As the racial conflicts took on spatial manifestations, West Broadway Manager Sally McAward felt completely caught in the middle. "There was a lot of racial tension," she recalled, "and no matter what you did each group thought you were biased against them." Even though many old-timers who had worked so long for redevelopment understood "that if there was lead paint, there was danger," this intellectual understanding could not stop "a different emotional gut reaction."[185]

RACE, CRIME, AND PUBLIC NEIGHBORHOODS

In the early 1990s, Jim Kelly (by then the president of the Boston City Council) and other South Boston community leaders repeatedly insisted that their neighborhood's problems had grown in tandem with the arrival of minorities in the housing projects. In the fall of 1994, hundreds of residents joined in a "flag-waving protest march" and assembled for a raucous meeting where they blamed "outsiders" for making their streets more dangerous. Always skeptical of South Boston's hard-liners, the *Boston Globe* launched its own, more systematic investigation of the matter, assigning a team to examine the previous six years of police records and to review a thousand criminal case files at the South Boston District Court for three-month periods in 1989 and 1994. After a month-long investigation, the paper reported that "despite a belief of many white South Boston residents that minorities have brought more crime into the neighborhood, blacks there are arrested no more frequently" for violent or drug-related crimes than their white neighbors. Overall serious crime had dropped by 18 percent in South Boston during the first six years of public housing reintegration, and, the *Globe* noted, court records showed that South Boston's whites were "eight times more likely to be victimized by another white than by a black or Hispanic." South Boston whites continued to complain about black-on-white crime, but figures supplied by the Boston Police Department's Community Disorders Unit showed that, for the first ten months of 1994, two-thirds of the district's eighty-six perpetrators were white and two-thirds of the eighty-five victims were nonwhite. Kelly called such findings "totally irrelevant"—they only showed that "obviously a lot of perpetrators who are black were not arrested."[186]

Whatever the district-wide statistics showed, they clearly missed the underlying dynamic of fear and hostile rhetoric that continued to swirl around the housing projects. The *Globe* fully acknowledged the growing incidence of South Boston "hate crimes" during the early 1990s—a plateau rising seven times higher than the preintegration level—and also pointed to a substantial increase in arrests at the housing developments themselves. At a time when overall crime in South Boston declined, arrests in its housing developments doubled between 1989 and 1994. A BHA spokesman explained this as an outcome of more aggressive police work rather than more crime, but many project residents and neighbors remained convinced that the new neighbors had brought trouble, owing in part to lax screening by the BHA.

In the first three years of the public housing reintegration push, South Boston accounted for between 26 and 31 percent of all bias crimes reported citywide. And in 1992, two-thirds of South Boston's sixty-six reported racial crimes occurred in the housing projects. Thirty-three of them—fully half of the entire district's total—occurred at West Broadway itself. Despite police efforts to try to sort out racially motivated crimes from other incidents, many of those interviewed at the development during the early 1990s stressed that much of what got interpreted as a racial matter actually had nonracial roots. A South Boston detective concurred: "Sometimes you've got to tell people that, when they get robbed, the only color involved is green. They want the money. And sometimes people have fights, not because they don't like the color of the other guy, but because they just don't like the other guy."[187] Police investigated West Broadway's largest post-redevelopment disturbance—a melee involving up to 150 whites and blacks during a Monday afternoon in June 1993—as a racial issue, but many at the time claimed that it was touched off by other factors. As one witness explained, "It was just a normal fight, wasn't nothing racial at first. But when people went outside and saw a white guy and a black guy getting into it, everyone started to say stuff, and started jumping in."[188]

SUCCESS AND DISTRESS

Despite clear evidence of success in many aspects of the West Broadway redevelopment, significant problems remain. Residents complain especially about the looming presence of racism and drugs. These problems, while certainly endemic to the larger society, are not without special connection to the processes and products of public housing redevelopment. In most interviews with West Broadway residents, despair about drugs ranked even higher than concern over race relations.

In trying to assess the success of the West Broadway redevelopment, one is left with a puzzle: residents spoke warmly about design accomplishments but still faced extreme socioeconomic disarray. More than 80 percent of respondents said they were "somewhat" or "very" satisfied with living at West Broadway, and fully 40 percent of those from the redeveloped part liked their apartments so well that they could think of nothing that they "liked least." Yet residents also acknowledged rampant drug use and drug-related violence in and around the development, and BHA statistics from the early 1990s showed that only about a quarter of households in the development reported employment as their major source of income. Through the 1990s, the development lacked organized job training, adult education programs, or day care. In some years, the Task Force submitted seventy to eighty grant applications and received funding from dozens of government agencies and private foundations, but the WBTF still could not provide the comprehensive service program that residents needed.

Whatever the improved appearance of their homes, the consolidated and accumulated socioeconomic desperation of West Broadway's residents left them outside the American mainstream. As Sister Louise Kearns, a D Street resident who has spent two decades providing "family learning" services to South Boston's female public housing tenants, put it, "South Boston is an open-air clinic." The problems of its residents fester "not because of busing and not because of racism, but because of self-esteem." Sister Louise found deeply rooted problems in the women she attempted to assist: "If you come from layers and layers and generations of poor self-esteem, you sense that there's too much going on in life and you're a victim." This enables people to perpetuate violence and distrust: "You end up turning your anger on the next group, whomever it happens to be."[189] White and nonwhite, the denizens of South Boston's Lower End felt victimized from all sides: by The Point's ongoing disdain for "D Street Dirtballs," by the media's insistence on "stirring trouble" rather than reporting progress, and by the Boston Housing Authority's legal obligations to bring in alien (and equally impoverished) new neighbors. As Lieutenant William Johnson, the commander of the Community Disorders Unit, put it in 1993, "There was a time in South Boston when they blamed people in the projects for everything. Now they blame the black people in the projects. And before they blamed the projects, they blamed the Lower End. People are frustrated, in some cases justifiably, but blaming whole groups of people, instead of individuals, is dangerous."[190]

Over time, however, the dangers and the tensions of West Broadway's dramatic integration effort have dissipated markedly. While South Boston's other two developments, Old Colony and Mary Ellen McCormack—as well as the Bunker Hill development in Charlestown—faced serious incidents and ongoing civil rights violations through the 1990s, West Broadway remained largely peaceful. Between 1995 and 1997, the BHA did evict a dozen families (seven white, three black, and two Latino) from the development for civil rights offenses, drug dealing, or assault—but this was less than half the number forced out at the more racially troubled developments. By 2000, little more than a decade since the project was all-white, West Broadway's tenants were as diverse as any community in the city: still 40 percent white, but also 29 percent Latino, 17 percent black, 12 percent Asian, and 1 percent American Indian.[191]

Although South Boston's public housing led the way toward a more ethnically and racially varied neighborhood, the three projects remained centers of stultifying poverty. In 2000, only 29 percent of adults aged eighteen to sixty-one at West

Broadway reported full-time employment, and an equal percentage listed themselves as disabled. Moreover, South Boston's housing projects, whatever their numerous strengths, continued to harbor many highly depressed individuals, especially youth. In 1997 the *Globe* editorialized about the need for "suicide prevention in Southie," calling attention to "an air of fatality" that also contributed to widespread drug addiction and overdoses. *Globe* columnist Barnicle warned that "heroin menaces South Boston" and concluded that "South Boston has been staggered by suicide and drugs." He quoted one local police officer: "It's a bizarre form of equality. Many of the white kids in D Street or Old Colony are in the same position as a lot of black kids in Roxbury and Dorchester. They have no shot and they know it by the time they're 15." One such white fifteen-year-old, West Broadway's Tommy Mullin, hung himself in a project stairwell, while facing investigation for alleged involvement in a case of racial harassment. The tabloid *Boston Herald* headlined its account of the suicide "Down and Out on D Street," thereby implicating the entire development in this tragedy (Fig. 2.31). Many young South Boston males felt better understood by their multilayered portrayal in the 1997 film *Good Will Hunting*—which showcased fierce loyalty and quick wits as well as cocky and profane aggression—than they did by the local media. Michael MacDonald's gripping *All Souls,* published to intense local interest in 1999, chronicled the travails and coping mechanisms of "the hidden Southie." Near the end of his account, MacDonald describes a vigil to remember 250 neighborhood residents who had all died young, "most of them victims of the drug trade, crime, or suicide." MacDonald intended this as an important counterpoint to "the usual articles by the South Boston Information Center, about how our biggest problem was black people bringing drugs into the neighborhood."[192]

As the twenty-first century begins at West Broadway, the community remains troubled but far more tolerant and welcoming of diversity than many would have expected, given the horrific excesses of the 1970s. As one man who works across the street from the development at the Teamster's union office puts it, "There used to be controversy about black families moving in, but it's not like that anymore." The proprietor of a variety store adjacent to the development, who has lived in Southie for sixty years, observes that "this used to be a tougher neighborhood. You would see people stealing stuff off the back of trucks as they came down the street. There used to be gangs around here, but there are no more gangs. The problem now is drugs everywhere." He dismissed the issue of integration: "There were no problems when the minorities moved in. It was nothing like

FIGURE 2.31 Down and out on D Street. Following a suicide at the development in 1997, the Boston press once again investigated conditions at the project.

busing, yeah believe me, nothing like busing. Don't get me wrong; there were fights, but it went both ways, you know. Whites beat up blacks, but blacks were beating up whites, too." A local police officer concurred that most initial anxieties have waned: "The development is quiet, though that wasn't the case a few years ago." As the 1990s ended, HUD issued a report praising the turnaround in civil rights enforcement by the BHA. Since 1996, under the leadership of Administrator Sandra Henriquez, the Authority has changed its response to bias complaints and drastically reduced harassment and discrimination. HUD described the transformation as "a national model to be replicated by other housing authorities." South Boston clearly gained from the reduced tensions. By 2000, as one marker of just how far the neighborhood had come, it was quite possible—without the least incident—to repeatedly send a black research assistant into the neighborhood to interview Southie whites. Clearly, this was a new South Boston.[193]

GENTRIFYING SOUTHIE: FROM LOWER END TO WEST SIDE

By the mid-1990s, the real estate section of the *Boston Sunday Globe* could tout South Boston as "one of Boston's hottest neighborhoods." Between 1992 and 1996, median home sale prices rose more than 30 percent, outpacing all but one other neighborhood in the city. A few years earlier, Southie-based realtors did not even choose to advertise beyond the *South Boston Tribune.* Now, however, they touted South Boston as a citywide resource for housing bargains, even as those bargains rapidly disappeared. After 1996, as in many other Boston neighborhoods, home prices in Southie continued to rise dramatically. Between 1996 and 1999, the median sale price of a condominium increased by 41 percent—and that of a three-family dwelling by 61 percent—outpacing citywide averages. Similarly, during the same period, median rents for a two-bedroom apartment soared by 58 percent.[194]

Some of this increase was due to the booming local economy and to the end of rent control citywide, but the looming prospect of nearby development projects also played a significant role. After many false starts, large-scale redevelopment of Boston's seaport district began in earnest during the late 1990s. Located on harborfront landfill adjacent to the residential areas of the Lower End, this area offered an unequaled opportunity to expand Boston's downtown, bringing it across the Fort Point Channel. City officials championed the replacement of the piers and waterfront industries with a mixed-use district composed of office buildings, apartments, hotels, and the massive Massachusetts Convention Center, located just a few blocks down D Street from the West Broadway development (Fig. 2.32).

Southie's Jimmy Kelly, the City Council president, refused to view the new neighborhood as some generic Boston Seaport District; he saw it as an intrinsic part of the South Boston Waterfront. Critics pointed out that the Fan Pier (site of the first major building, a federal courthouse) was located no closer to the heart of City Point than it was to the South End, Charlestown, East Boston, Beacon Hill, or the Back Bay (and much nearer to Chinatown), but Kelly successfully lobbied to make "South Boston Waterfront" the official name of the district. Reflecting this bias, in 1998 he quietly negotiated a "memorandum of understanding" with Mayor Thomas Menino to give Southie the lion's share of linkage fees and community benefits being charged to developers to compensate impacted neighborhoods for the strains such massive redevelopment could bring. Having extracted

FIGURE 2.32 West Broadway development and the South Boston Waterfront. By the end of the 1990s, Southie braced for gentrification. This aerial photo, showing the area between B Street and C Street, reveals the close relationship between the development and the site cleared for the Boston Convention Center.

all he could from the mayor, Kelly voted to support city funding for the convention center.[195]

In May 2000, just as work on the convention center broke ground, the *Boston Globe* precipitated a major public outcry when it revealed that Kelly's "backroom deal" could yield at least $65 million in benefits for South Boston. The funds were to be "funneled through an obscure organization" called the South Boston Betterment Trust, a group tapped by Kelly and South Boston's two other principal political figures, State Senator Stephen F. Lynch and Representative John A. Hart, Jr., to build housing with seaport-development proceeds. Bringing Southie's neighborhood politics full circle, Kelly nominated John Ciccone—of South Boston Information Center fame—as one member of the Trust, positioning him as a "first stop for developers who are negotiating community benefits." Black leaders and affordable housing advocates pounced on the arrangement, charging that the Trust could allow community benefits to circumvent fair housing laws in the effort to serve only those Kelly termed "our people." Others chided the Trust's "heavy-handed tactics" and "potential conflicts of interest." Almost immediately, Kelly and the others faced intense pressures to reopen consideration of the deal, eventually contributing to Kelly's downfall as City Council president. In South Boston, however, residents were outraged by the demise of the deal; civic groups (including the Lower End Political Action Committee) ran full-page ads in the *South Boston Tribune* claiming that Mayor Menino "will destroy this neighborhood if we don't stop him." In an impassioned speech to the City Council, Kelly charged that tens of millions of dollars in HUD and community development funds regularly went to "certain neighborhoods" (meaning those dominated by minorities), and rhetorically asked why all talk of "justice and equality for everyone" evaporated once South Boston was seen to be "getting benefits." Acknowledging that rents were rising everywhere, he nonetheless blamed the decision to site the convention center in South Boston for sending "rents through the roof" in that area. "The neighborhood of South Boston is going to suffer, and suffer big-time. Our neighborhood's been turned on its head."[196]

Much of this head-turning was well under way before the convention center, however. As perhaps the most telling portent of change, realtors primed the Lower End for gentrification by redubbing it South Boston's "West Side." Although City Point still boasted the highest rents and priciest condos, by 1997 real estate brokers regarded property on the West Side as the "best investment in Southie." As one broker told the *Globe,* "Historically, it's been the less-desirable end of town" and "that's still reflected in the prices," but "it's the area that will realize the most appreciation as the waterfront developments come on line." With every passing year, new households discovered the convenience of South Boston, and the district began to "lose the psychological isolation provided by the belt of underused land separating it from downtown." At the end of the 1990s, fully 37 percent of Southie's residents consisted of those who had not lived in Boston (let alone *South* Boston) when the decade began. Nearly three-quarters of these newcomers held at least a bachelor's degree, compared with barely one-third of adults in more-established Southie households. As the *Globe* put it in June 2000, "Old and new Boston are colliding in this neighborhood as nowhere else in the city."[197]

Interviews conducted with a variety of neighborhood residents during the summer of 2000 confirm a widespread belief that the coming of the convention center is symptomatic of a broader gentrification of the area. For long-term business owners, the apparent economic upturn holds great promise, yet it portends great change to the old neighborhood (see Fig. 2.33). An owner of the family-run Broadway Lock Company, located a block up West Broadway from the development, welcomes "the yuppies" who are bringing "a lot of new shops around here

FIGURE 2.33 West Broadway streetscape, 1990s. As the twentieth century closed, the strip of West Broadway across from the development awaited a new round of retail opportunities.

with different foods," but is bemused by their behavior. "They come in here to cut keys for their Saabs and can't believe it only costs two dollars. People don't know the good ol' Southie is gone. Pretty soon you're gonna get people coming over here from the convention center to park because it's cheap, and they don't wanna pay fifteen, twenty dollars." Already, she observed, the increased number of condo conversions had brought more people with cars, without any increase in parking. She feared for the future of any small business that had to rent its space: "I am OK because my family owns this building, but what will everyone else do?" Another local businessman added, "The convention center is gonna be good, but it will mean property values going up. Then you will have taxes going up, which will mean higher rents. It's a Catch-22. You like the convention center because it may bring some jobs and help the neighborhood get more attention, but then you will have higher rents in the long run." Near the close of his memoir, Michael MacDonald describes his reluctant visit to one of "the new espresso shops that had opened for the yuppies": "I waited in line with the 'outsiders,' resentful of their proud talk about 'bringing the neighborhood up.' I cringed as they all pronounced the 'r' in the sugar that went into their grande-double-shot-skinny-mochaccinos."[198]

To some local proprietors, the arrival of more upscale outsiders during the 1990s caused the neighborhood to be both better patrolled and safer. A worker at Ross Discount Auto Parts on West Broadway, which used to have break-ins "once a week," observed that "nicer people are moving into the neighborhood and crime is down." A few doors away at Al's Bottled Liquors, the managers concurred that the neighborhood had changed a lot since the days when they were forced "to sleep here at the store" to defend its merchandise. "Crime has gone way down," one added, because "they started evicting low-life scum."[199]

COMPLETING THE REDEVELOPMENT

Old and new Boston collided most dramatically at the corner of West Broadway and D Street, where, after a decade of stalemate, plans moved forward to renovate the last quadrant of the West Broadway development. Seeking to convince the state government to invest further money in the unfinished redevelopment, the BHA commissioned a market analysis. The Authority asked consultants to consider two basic options: market-based commercial and residential development or mixed-use development with mixed-income housing (either financially self-sustaining or requiring a limited infusion of capital grant funds). The study, issued in February 1998, clearly recognized the ongoing gentrification of the "West Side" and concluded that the site could support market-rate housing. To the astonishment of BHA officials, the consultants concluded that a three-bedroom apartment could rent for $1,760 a month. Such apartments, local realtors confirmed, would most likely be occupied by newly formed households composed of unrelated roommates pooling their individual incomes. Given this infusion of young professionals to the area, the remainder of the West Broadway site could be developed entirely for market-rate housing and retail. The consultants viewed the existing public housing as a kind of tolerable liability, since it "should not unduly impact the ability of the site to command the rent levels seen at the comparables." The state pressed BHA officials to redevelop the site for its "highest best use"— either market-rate apartments or commercial retail that would spin off enough cash to help subsidize the remaining housing.[200] Meanwhile, rumors about the future of the site swirled about the neighborhood. Some nearby merchants said they expected condominiums; others guessed a strip mall, a department store, a market, a cinema, or townhouses. Another hoped for a parking lot or elderly housing. The proprietor of Al's Discount Liquors correctly surmised that the BHA planned to build more family housing, and wryly commented, "I sure hope they will be heavy drinkers!"[201]

In March 2000, the BHA announced plans to raze the remaining seven boarded-up reminders of the old D Street project, replacing 244 dilapidated units with new buildings. The new housing plan, prepared by the successor firm to Lane, Frenchman, envisioned brickfronted buildings along West Broadway and less expensive clapboarded structures elsewhere. It provided for 133 apartments, all of which could be marketed to those earning less than 60 percent of the area median income (using Low Income Housing Tax Credits), with about one-fifth of the units targeted to those with very low incomes (Fig. 2.34). The state's Department of Housing and Community Development (DHCD), stung by a cost estimate of $28 million, insisted that designers avoid any sense of over-embellishment, fearing repercussions from those in the previously redeveloped sections of West Broadway, or in other state-aided developments that had not received comparable investment. Instead of a commercial component, the BHA and DHCD decided to anchor the corner of West Broadway and D Street with a headquarters facility for the Laboure Center, a Catholic social services agency that could serve the broader neighborhood as well as those in the development (Fig. 2.35). The Laboure facility, welcomed by the tenants, offered the prospect of day care, after-

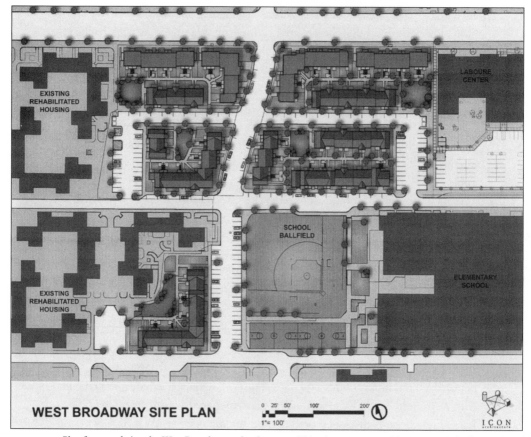

FIGURE 2.34 Plan for completing the West Broadway redevelopment. This plan, as proposed in 2002, promised 133 units of new public housing for the development's last remaining quadrant (partly shown in Figure 2.32). It also provided for greater connectivity with surrounding streets.

school tutoring, and programs for seniors that went well beyond anything the West Broadway Task Force could provide.[202]

To BHA Administrator Henriquez, the changes in South Boston meant "high marketability" for West Broadway: "We'd better hurry up and get it done," she commented in early 2000, "because it feels like W. Broadway will be a major gateway into Southie and into the convention center. You can come right to the corner and hang the left and go down D Street to get to the site." The skyrocketing rents and nascent cachet of Southie offered the BHA a rare opportunity to reach beyond its usual applicant pool to target some of the new apartments to those with

PROPOSED
COMMUNITY SERVICES CENTER
LABOURE CENTER

THE R.F. WALSH COMPANY, INC.
DEVELOPMENT AND CONSTRUCTION MANAGEMENT

HOLMES & EDWARDS, INC. ARCHITECTS
APRIL 26, 2000

FIGURE 2.35 Cornering the market on services. At the corner of West Broadway and D Street, the BHA proposed construction of a large community services center. In its form and massing, the new construction recalls the streetscape demolished to make way for the housing project shown in Figure 2.10.

incomes closer to the legal ceiling for public housing—which in Boston was about $55,000 for a family of four. At the same time, however, the BHA resisted the temptation to shift some of its housing to market-rate apartments.[203]

Even as the BHA prepared its plan to attract a range of incomes to the last quadrant of the former D Street project, the old public neighborhood retained some of its isolation. As one store proprietor who works less than a block away commented, "I don't know many people down there." Another local merchant noted that his contact with project residents mostly involved dealing with their frequent pleas for free cigarettes. The proprietor of the Broadway Laundry Wash & Fold on the corner of West Broadway and B Street observed that since the housing development had added its own washing machines fewer project residents came by to make trouble, bang on machines, and scare her. Another local merchant opined, "I know there is a big heroin problem and a lot of teen pregnancy," adding resentfully that "there are a lot of people living there that probably make more than I do, but they get special preferences. I don't think it's right. I was raised to work hard and earn what you get and not to take handouts." A few doors down, an elderly white man who has run Strand's Barber Shop since the

1930s leaned over and said with a smirk, eyebrows raised: "It is all integrated now with those people. Mixed people coming in with drugs and poor families. I don't go over there or have any contact with them. It's all depressed over there with crime, drugs, and poor people."[204] Clearly, at least in some minds, all the hype about South Boston's West Side had done little to challenge the stigma of the Lower End.

Listening to the voices of his changing neighborhood at the end of the 1990s, Michael MacDonald acutely sensed the stinging contradiction between gentrification and despair: "Gentrification had added to my neighbors' sense that they were walking on a sinking landfill. Maybe that's why I heard more honest stories of poverty and lack of opportunities for young people, even as one of the biggest development projects in the country was visible from the rooftops of the D Street Housing Project, where black and white teens were still distracted by race, still standing their ground, and still going nowhere. Southie's waterfront, former home to manufacturing and shipping jobs, was set to become 'the Seaport District,' with plans underway for billions of dollars in development, luxury condos, and jobs that these Boston Public School kids—graduates and dropouts alike— would not be educated for."[205] In this way, the success of redevelopment at this sprawling public neighborhood, however substantial, remained incomplete.

Despite its mixed messages (or, perhaps, *because* of them) the long saga of West Broadway carries many lessons. Looking back across two hundred years of development history, the tale of D Street and South Boston's Lower End is an intense demonstration of the many ways that stigma can be constructed in an American urban neighborhood, even one predominantly inhabited by whites. Repeated denunciations in the press, dismissive assessments by neighbors, and sustained assaults on the physical fabric of the place—set against the backdrop of widespread industrial restructuring and the managerial collapse of the local housing authority—all contributed to festering self-doubts, anger, and depression among residents. At the same time, West Broadway is a story of dramatic tenant-led struggles to destigmatize an environment and rebuild a community. D Street's tenants were the first to sue the housing authority. They did not simply complain; they demanded restitution, formed one of the city's most active tenant organizations, produced and distributed their own community newspaper, rallied at the State House, threatened to arrive en masse at BHA Board meetings, and repeatedly exploited their long-nurtured connections to South Boston's wide array of Irish Catholic elected officials. Through engaging in a protracted but politically savvy redevelopment process, tenants worked constructively with the housing authority, planners, designers, and service providers, while retaining psychological ownership over the results. By subdividing a vast public neighborhood into a more manageable and imageable set of smaller "villages," tenants regained control over public spaces and enhanced their own privacy and security. Clearly, even the most victimized public housing residents do not always act like victims.

West Broadway's history is a chronicle of virulent racism fanned by public policies that placed integration of schools and housing projects ahead of neighborhood cohesion, yet it is also an account of the more recent ability of a community to accept broadly rooted racial and ethnic diversity with little semblance of the previous violence. This long struggle shows that racial and ethnic integration—when attempted at more than token levels and when backed with support mechanisms and firm civil rights enforcement—can occur successfully even in a place like South Boston.

Despite these notable successes, however, the fifty-year trajectory of the project is still one of economic decline or stagnation. The story of West Broadway can serve as an example of how public housing can be reclaimed as a resource for low-income people, but without contributing much to the incipient economic dynamism of the surrounding neighborhood. Still, at a time when many want to see public housing redevelopment as another path to gentrification, the story of West Broadway's transformation serves as a significant counterweight.

THREE

Franklin Field: Public Housing, Neighborhood
Abandonment, and Racial Transition

BOSTON'S FRANKLIN FIELD public housing project, built
under the terms of the same legislation that sponsored West Broadway, could
hardly be more different from its South Boston counterpart. West Broadway was
an integral part of the Southie streetscape, a four-thousand-member community
that retained central political importance, even once it became widely viewed as a
community liability. The massive square project constituted its own census tract,
located just beyond the shadows of the downtown financial district. Its long public front on West Broadway formed a perpetually visible presence on South
Boston's main commuter artery and parade route. West Broadway's tenants were,
for several decades, principally composed of white Irish Catholics, the same influential constituency that staffed the city's public housing bureaucracy and dominated the rest of local government. By contrast, Franklin Field was marginal in
every way.

As with almost all of Boston's other postwar projects, Franklin Field was built
using peripheral city-owned vacant land rather than a slum-clearance site closer
to downtown. Instead of a piece of hotly contested territory in the heart of a bus-
tling urban neighborhood, Franklin Field began life as a quiet backwater in an
area originally built as a streetcar suburb (Fig 3.1). Unlike West Broadway with its
neighborhood of dense tenements and industrial enterprises, Franklin Field was

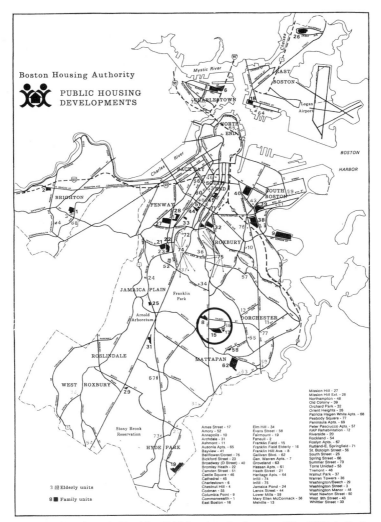

FIGURE 3.1 Dorchester's Franklin Field housing development. The BHA built the Franklin Field development on a portion of its namesake field, adjacent to the vibrant commercial strip of Blue Hill Avenue.

constructed on its namesake parkland, and it abutted a cemetery. Its neighboring residences were twentieth-century houses rather than nineteenth-century cold-water flats. In an area rapidly colonized by successful speculative construction, vacant lots were virtually unknown.

Socially, Franklin Field differed from most public housing in Boston in that it was built primarily to serve Jewish war veterans and their families, rather than to help the usual coterie of Irish or Italian Catholics or to make sure that black families could remain in a discrete area. Although Franklin Field, like West Broadway, began life as a public housing project for whites, its eventual integration bore no resemblance to the painful introduction of "pioneer" families at D Street. In contrast to South Boston, where the BHA asked public housing to lead the way in racial integration—making the public neighborhood the experiment station for the surrounding area—at Franklin Field, the wider neighborhood rapidly changed from white to black, and the project "tipped" as well, decisively and irreversibly. In these ways, socially as well as spatially, Franklin Field was repeatedly marginalized.

In more subtle ways, too, this particular project stood apart from its neighborhood in ways that would have been inconceivable in South Boston. In stark contrast to the high public visibility of West Broadway, Franklin Field lacked a commercial face. Although built adjacent to one of the city's most vibrant retail strips, Blue Hill Avenue, the project reached out to the thoroughfare only with its westernmost point. The rest was tucked well away from heavily trafficked areas. This could have been a distinct advantage for those seeking a quieter style of life, yet it was undercut by the fact that Franklin Field seemed to belong to no particular neighborhood. When most shop owners abandoned the neighborhood during the time of racial transition, the area's lack of clear neighborhood affiliation hampered reinvestment efforts. To this day, there is no consistency in the neighborhood identification of Franklin Field, either by "official" city documents or by more informal sources. Most often it is recognized as part of North Dorchester, but the area is also sometimes listed as part of South Dorchester or Mattapan. Others continue to identify it with Roxbury, confusing Franklin Field with Roxbury's nearby Franklin Park. Sometimes, acknowledging the primacy of the Field itself, people will refer to the neighborhood as "Franklin Field," a designation that does little more than beg the question.

At mid-century, when the Blue Hill Avenue corridor passing from Roxbury to Dorchester to Mattapan was still heavily—almost uniformly—Jewish, the particular name of the neighborhood mattered little. Franklin Field stood at the heart of a cultural conurbation. "Ward 14" or "Blue Hill Avenue" could serve as widely understood metonyms that immediately conjured images of "Jewish Boston." By 1970, however, with the Jews mostly dispersed into suburbia and ward-based City Council representation minimized, Franklin Field marked little more than an empty center, housing residents with little attachment to any one particular neighborhood. And, of equal import, no one particular neighborhood exhibited any special attachment to these public housing residents.

In practical terms, the neighborhood and the project within it lacked an easily identifiable geopolitical status. Unlike the Lower End of South Boston, no larger entity ever considered Franklin Field its responsibility. When built, the project never served as much of an amenity for Dorchester; when it declined, no one thought to treat its horrific conditions as an affront to the dignity of the larger district, as was so clearly the case in South Boston. Instead, Bostonians left the Franklin Field project to sink or swim on its own as a public neighborhood, with the flagging BHA as its increasingly unreliable lifeguard.

Franklin Field's ambiguous neighborhood status also let it slip between the nets of Boston's neighborhood newspapers. In part because it was only half the size of West Broadway, but more important because it had far less than half its clout, Franklin Field rated nary a mention in the various local papers that could have chosen to embrace or condemn it. Whereas the *South Boston Tribune* and the *South Boston Gazette* paid frequent—if often disparaging—attention to life at D Street, local newspapers essentially ignored Franklin Field. Neither Dorchester-specific papers nor ethnically specific citywide papers such as the *Jewish Advocate* (or, later, the black-oriented *Bay State Banner*) bothered to take special note of events at Franklin Field, whether these were positive community-oriented activities or violent incidents of community unrest.

By the late-1960s and early-1970s, the residents of Franklin Field public housing were markedly worse off economically than their privately housed neighbors, but conditions in the broader neighborhood also reached such depths of turmoil that the distinction could easily be lost. The Franklin Field project lacked the newsworthy horror of racially motivated killings like that of George Pratt, and it was not a hotbed of public policy experiments gone awry. Instead, it was one outpost of disorder in a broad swath of neighborhoods undergoing a protracted period of racial transition, violent crime, disinvestment, and abandonment. Franklin Field's decline simply did not stand out in the same bold relief that prevailed in Irish South Boston. The comparative lack of attention to Franklin Field typified the treatment accorded to housing conditions affecting Boston's minority population. Most Bostonians found West Broadway intrinsically more newsworthy because its atrocious conditions affected chiefly poor whites.

Along Blue Hill Avenue, public housing's problems paled before the even greater problems that public policy decisions had foisted on the area's private housing. As the city's growing black population expanded southward into Dorchester and Mattapan, a consortium of the city's banks known as the Boston Banks Urban Renewal Group (BBURG) sought to encourage higher levels of black homeownership in these areas. In providing two thousand mortgages with minimal down payments, however, they inadvertently destabilized these neighborhoods by introducing more than a thousand new homeowners who were financially unprepared to maintain their properties. The new black buyers frequently paid too much for houses that were in ill-repair, and they soon faced foreclosure or chose to abandon their investment completely. The entire BBURG venture, coming in the wake of a long Jewish exodus, took place in a fearful climate of racially motivated blockbusting engineered by unscrupulous realtors, and contributed to a vacant and vandalized neighborhood landscape that mirrored the decline in the Franklin Field project itself.

As Franklin Field's conditions worsened during the late 1960s and throughout the 1970s, tenants certainly complained, but their protests never approached either the organization or the vehemence of their counterparts at West Broadway. Franklin Field's tenants lacked either the means or the spirit to make bold claims upon those in positions of power. Despite some strong and committed individuals, Franklin Field's nonwhite leadership had far greater reason than D Street's tenants to distrust all those who potentially were in a position to help them. The double weight of race and class bias, pressing down on a neighborhood already riven by such tensions, made any effort at public housing redevelopment a particularly daunting proposition.

When substantial redevelopment funds did finally come to benighted Franklin Field in the early 1980s, the millions came mostly out of a sense of governmental obligation to throw some money at a distressed black project, a politic way to balance the effort made at West Broadway to help whites. Franklin Field tenants welcomed the funding but never fully invested themselves in a process that always seemed to be something done *to* them, or perhaps *for* them—never something that was done *with* them or *by* them. Not surprisingly, the results of the Franklin Field redevelopment effort proved disappointing to all concerned. Even worse, in the 1990s, several Franklin Field residents were brutally murdered, triggering a barrage of negative generalities in the media about people in the development. The saga of Franklin Field, then, is a tale of repeated institutional failure, set against a backdrop of escalating neighborhood violence that outlasted twenty-five years of efforts to restore peace to the project.

FRANKLIN FIELD'S ORIGINS: THE GEOGRAPHY OF MARGINALITY

Franklin Field's uncertain neighborhood nomenclature is a direct legacy of the area's nineteenth-century development history. Because it was distant from any true center, its identity depended chiefly on its relationship to the Field and to the commercial strip of Blue Hill Avenue. As Sam Bass Warner, Jr., puts it in *Streetcar Suburbs,* "there was nothing in the process of late nineteenth century suburban construction that built communities or neighborhoods; it built streets." Between 1870—when Boston annexed Dorchester—and 1900, Dorchester's population increased from 12,000 to 80,000, spurred by the electrification and extension of streetcar routes.

Boston's Park Department proposed the site of Franklin Field as an open space in 1891, at the suggestion of Frederick Law Olmsted. Olmsted viewed this place as necessary for "diverting undesirable uses" from nearby Franklin Park, the crown jewel in his "emerald necklace" of Boston parks. Franklin Park, Olmsted observed, had become "a battleground for competing interests," and its commissioners felt constant pressure to allow it to become overrun by mass gatherings (including labor rallies and prayer meetings) and active sports activities, for which its mostly hilly terrain was felt to be unsuited. As Geoffrey Blodgett observes, "Olmsted wanted no men's athletic teams playing there; he wanted labor agitators and other speechmakers barred from its grounds; he wanted schoolchildren trained in dutiful respect to its peaceful influences." The matter came to a head on September 18, 1891, when the 9th Infantry submitted a request to hold its annual drill in Franklin Park. Concurring with Olmsted, the Boston Park Commission denied the petition, viewing "the fighting of a sham battle or military maneuvers and exercises of this character" as "incompatible with the proper purposes of Franklin Park" and "inconsistent with public interests." Olmsted viewed his parks as tranquil oases—counterpoints to the "excessive nervous tension, over-anxiety, hasteful disposition, impatience, [and] irritability" of urban life—and he worried about the growing public predilection for more active forms of recreation. Franklin Field would provide the necessary outlet for such urges, shifting them to a less-developed jurisdiction.

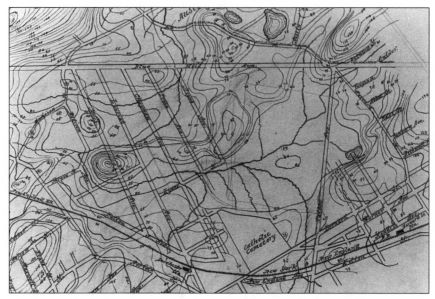

FIGURE 3.2 The lowland site of Franklin Field. Frederick Law Olmsted designed Franklin Field to divert unwanted activities from nearby Franklin Park. He located the site on a floodplain criss-crossed by streams and bordered by Blue Hill Avenue, Talbot Avenue, and a Catholic cemetery. He considered most of the land undevelopable, yet one day part of it became home to the Franklin Field housing development.

The delayed development of this particular site was no mere coincidence. Olmsted considered at least two-thirds of the land unbuildable, and it marked the last empty zone in an area criss-crossed by proposed streets awaiting new public transportation and new houses (Fig. 3.2). Framed by a Catholic cemetery and by two major roadways (Blue Hill Avenue and Talbot Avenue), the land was mostly peat meadow, crossed by streams feeding the nearby Neponset River watershed. To a committee of the Harvard Improvement Association of Dorchester, this "tract of low land" would remain "a source of danger in a sanitary way unless taken by the City for improvement." Dissuaded by engineers from turning it into a lake, Olmsted nonetheless observed that fully 80 percent of the site could be flooded in winter for ice skating. In summer, it could serve as "a large public ground for mass meetings, parades, sports and like uses," or even a place "for the display of fireworks and balloon ascensions." The firm initially referred to the Peat Meadow as a future Muster Ground, then termed it a Parade Ground, but consistently regarded it as a drained and flattened area for athletic competition

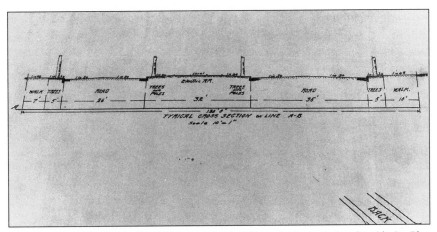

FIGURE 3.3 Olmsted's plan for Blue Hill Avenue. In 1895 Olmsted submitted plans for widening Blue Hill Avenue as it passed Franklin Field, anticipating the arrival of the electric streetcars that would shortly jump-start the development of this area.

and public grandstands, fringed by carriageways. The curved southern edge of the resultant Franklin Field is a vestigial reminder of the firm's desire for a boulevard linking Franklin Park past the Field and around the cemetery, all the way to the Dorchester Station of the New York and New England Railroad.[1] More than a half-century later this same curve would form the southern edge of the Franklin Field public housing project. More ominously, the legacy of the peat meadow and the buried waterways would also undermine the quality of life in that project, as well as in its surrounding neighborhood.

Franklin Field predated the residential areas that soon grew up around it. In 1895 Olmsted laid out a 120-foot right-of-way for Blue Hill Avenue, doubling its width in preparation for the arrival of electrified streetcar service. He envisioned a dramatic boulevard, with four rows of trees alternating between dual carriageways and pedestrian paths, and the streetcar line running down the center (Fig. 3.3). In 1899, a year after the electrified streetcar system had been extended along Blue Hill Avenue to the Field, only a clubhouse marked the area. Within a few years, though, developers began to construct houses—most for single families, some divided into three flats. In 1906, the Blue Hill Avenue streetcar line was extended further south, meeting up with an older area of settlement in Mattapan Square. The streetcar line spurred the rapid layout of further side streets and small lots, ready to receive waves of speculative builders. By the 1920s, developers had almost wholly outfitted the neighborhood with modest wooden houses, and Blue Hill Avenue itself housed a variety of shops to serve these local residents.[2] As Warner puts it, Blue Hill Avenue was typical of the new suburban order—"a commercial strip which followed the main transportation lines and had no center at all."[3] Dorchester did have its historic village clusters and other squares and "corners" that emerged as a result of the streetcar network, but the pattern of development near Franklin Field bore little relation to any such node.

For much of the first half of the twentieth century, however, this strip of Blue Hill Avenue became a kind of linear center, home not only to a myriad of small shops but also to many of the religious and cultural institutions that served Boston's Jewish community. By 1920, in addition to the large Jewish presence along the more northerly parts of Blue Hill Avenue where Dorchester intersected with upper Roxbury, about 10,000 Jews had settled in homes on either side of Blue Hill Avenue further south, between Franklin Field and Mattapan Square (Fig. 3.4). The old New York and New England railway line formed a prominent boundary that separated the Jewish district from areas to the east and south that remained overwhelmingly Catholic.[4]

In the early 1930s, half the Jewish population of the entire Boston metropolitan area lived along the Blue Hill Avenue corridor in upper Roxbury and Dorchester, forming a narrow strip of neighborhoods with Franklin Field at its geographical center. Writing in 1944, Wallace Stegner described the area as "perhaps the most solidly Jewish neighborhood in the United States." The Jewish population of the district peaked at about 77,000 in 1930 and remained relatively stable until the early 1950s.[5]

Hidden in the relative consistency of numbers through the early 1950s, however, are powerful changes in neighborhood composition that had been well under way since the 1920s. Even though the Blue Hill Avenue corridor remained predominantly Jewish, it suffered mightily from the gradual exodus of its more affluent members. With the departure of the Jewish middle and upper-middle class to burgeoning Jewish suburban areas such as Brookline and Newton, many of the institutions that depended on the patronage and financial contribution of wealthier Jews either followed their patrons to the suburbs or were forced to shut down.[6] Beginning in the 1920s, Gerald Gamm argues in *Urban Exodus: Why the Jews Left Boston and the Catholics Stayed*, "the number of middle-class Jews supporting the area's institutions diminished year by year. From the middle 1920s onward, these institutions reckoned with financial crisis." This situation was exacerbated by the Depression, and many congregations could not afford to hire a

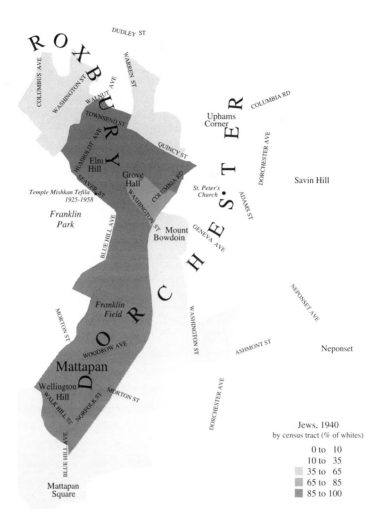

FIGURE 3.4 Blue Hill Avenue Jews, 1940. In 1940 Boston's Jewish population was clustered in a long strip paralleling Blue Hill Avenue in Roxbury, Dorchester, and Mattapan. The future site of the Franklin Field development was in the heart of this zone.

permanent rabbi. By the late 1940s, the four major Hebrew schools in Dorchester and Roxbury were insolvent, requiring annual subsidies to stay open. Because Jewish institutional life had encouraged a profusion of competing synagogues and schools (as opposed to the single territorially based institutional monopolies employed by Catholic parishes), the neighborhoods had been especially dependent on "the overstretched resources" of the rapidly vanishing middle class. Without them, the synagogues that struggled to stay put in Roxbury and Dorchester were forced to deplete their cemetery funds to maintain operations. By the mid-1950s, major schools and temples began to "cast their lots with the suburbs," recognizing that relocation was the only way to survive. The Jewish institutions located south of Franklin Field lasted longer, but the exodus continued to gain force: "First in Roxbury, then neighborhood by neighborhood in Dorchester, the evisceration of institutional life proceeded more suddenly and more decisively than contemporary population movements."[7] By the 1950s, Hillel Levine and Lawrence Harmon concur in *The Death of an American Jewish Community,* "the Jewish lower middle class was being abandoned." In Boston—as in the rest of America—low interest rates and postwar housing finance programs fueled a boom in suburban mass-produced housing, placing the American Dream of the single-family house and yard within the economic reach of most of Dorchester's Jews.[8]

The old streetcar district they left behind became transformed into a working-class ethnic neighborhood, temporarily still vibrant, but profoundly weakened by a loss of social and financial leadership. In Gamm's succinct terms, "The ascendancy of the ethnic neighborhood was brief. The ethnic era was bracketed on one side by socioeconomic succession, on the other by racial succession." Gamm's perceptive analysis of neighborhood transformation provides a convincing account of the history and sociology of this sea-change of population along Blue Hill Avenue. His account is not a story of white flight from racially changing urban neighborhoods. Rather, it is centered in a longer and earlier saga of white exodus from neighborhoods when they were still white.[9]

For Gamm, the fundamental reason the Roxbury-Dorchester Jewish community declined is that its institutions were autonomous and mobile, thereby markedly reducing the social costs otherwise associated with upward economic advancement and neighborhood abandonment. In sharp contrast to Boston's Catholics, who were rooted to one particular parish by rules that tied church membership to parish residency, the institutional structure of Boston's Jewish community provided no comparable incentives to remain tied to a particular location. Unlike parish churches, Jewish temples could relocate. Similarly, in contrast to Catholic schools and parish churches that received financial support from the central archdiocese if their continuing function should be threatened, the comparable Jewish institutions rose or fell largely according to the will of their own congregations. As Gamm puts it, "The relative strength and stability of neighborhoods is determined not by external pressures but by each neighborhood's internal structure. Institutions play a profound and independent role in the capacity of a neighborhood to resist change and, when change comes, to deal with it in orderly fashion."[10] Many of the upwardly mobile Jews who left Blue Hill Avenue kept up their ties to the old neighborhood for a few years, but soon consolidated their new personal and institutional connections in the suburbs. By the early 1970s, every one of the more than fifty Jewish community centers, Hebrew schools, and synagogues that had once permeated this part of Roxbury and Dorchester had dissolved or relocated.[11] Public housing came to Franklin Field in the middle of this profound social transition.

HOUSING VETERANS ON FRANKLIN FIELD

With the advent of United States involvement in World War II, federal, state, and city agencies sought ways to develop housing to assist the war effort; once the war was over, local Boston officials faced a different sort of housing problem: the return of veterans to a city that lacked adequate facilities to house them. City-owned open land near transportation lines provided a tempting target for development, and Franklin Field fit the bill perfectly. In 1946, using a combination of city and state funding (authorized by Chapter 372 of the Acts of 1946) with supplemental aid from Title V of the federal Lanham Act, the BHA gained the authority and the funding to build a temporary housing project for veterans on Boston Parks Department land. The *Dorchester Beacon* applauded the action, commenting that "this will absorb in part the G.I. housing problem for that part of Roxbury and Dorchester."[12] Given the desperate need and patriotic cause, no one seems to have questioned the incursion of public housing into valued parkland. Soon afterward, contractors transformed the southern portion of Franklin Field, which abutted a residential neighborhood, into eighty-one four-unit, single-story wood-frame rowhouses, each containing paired semi-private entrances with awning-covered stoops and a pitched roof (Fig. 3.5). The temporary housing rented for an average of twenty-seven dollars a month, a great bargain, and approximately half the rent prevailing in the triple-deckers just across the street. No longer a Muster Ground, Franklin Field had gained a new peacetime military use.[13]

With the advent of the state's Chapter 200 Veterans Housing legislation in 1948 and passage of the federal Housing Act of 1949, many parts of Boston clam-

FIGURE 3.5 Temporary housing for veterans on Franklin Field. Shortly after the end of World War II, the BHA built 324 units of temporary housing for veterans on the southern side of Franklin Field.

ored to get housing projects located nearby. Franklin Field, as the site of Boston's largest temporary housing facility, seemed a logical choice for further consideration. Geographic distribution played some role, but political influence was even more important. Fortunately for Dorchester's veterans (especially its Jewish ones), the district had Julius Ansel, Boston's only Jewish city councilor. Ansel, whose campaign slogan was "My heart belongs to Ward 14," helped his constituents gain accessible public housing in a dual capacity, first as a member of the Boston City Council and subsequently as a state legislator.[14] In the burst of public housing activity in Boston in the early 1950s, this small section of Blue Hill Avenue gained two projects: 375 units at Franklin Hill Avenue, a federal project that opened in 1951, and a larger, state-funded development sited on Franklin Field.

As the deadline for disposition of the temporary veterans housing approached, Councilor Ansel (widely referred to as "The Lion of Dorchester") forcefully urged demolition and new construction of permanent public housing on the Franklin Field site. The BHA also regarded Franklin Field as an ideal location, since it abutted "a stable middle-income neighborhood" with "no adverse influences" present. In financial documents assembled to convince the State Housing Board to fund the project, the Authority praised the location for its accessibility

FIGURE 3.6 Blue Hill Avenue in 1951. In 1951 the thoroughfare still had its old streetcars, its new buses, and its legendary bustle. This view is from Morton Street, just south of the Franklin Field development.

to public transportation, noting that the Mattapan-Egleston Station carline of the Massachusetts Transit Authority (MTA) passed the development along Blue Hill Avenue, making the "large shopping district" of Mattapan Square just a five-minute ride to the south (Fig. 3.6). In an east-west direction, the Ashmont-Dudley Station bus line traversed Talbot Avenue, just 200 yards north of the development, providing similarly easy access to Codman Square.[15] With the remaining acreage of Franklin Field serving as an unparalleled recreation resource, this spot seemed nothing short of ideal.

For well over a year in 1950 and 1951, the Boston Housing Authority and State Housing Board squabbled over the size and form of the prospective project, although there seemed no doubt that one would be built on this site. Still, one potentially serious hitch arose: the U.S. Army proposed using Franklin Field for stationing armed personnel and developing a base for radar activities. Undaunted, Ansel got his City Council colleagues to pass an order requesting the Army to find another site; slowly but surely, the remaining barriers to construction fell away.[16] Even Boston's Board of Park Commissioners unanimously agreed that this site was "no longer required for park purposes" and committed to selling it at the bargain rate of thirteen cents per square foot.[17]

Once the land was out of Park Department hands, attention to its natural assets quickly succumbed to the exigencies of site preparation and grading. Even in cases where the BHA's architects proposed retaining mature trees, the State Housing Board—which held the purse strings—raised objections. The Board proposed removing four imposing elms along Stratton Street, for instance, because "most" were to be within twenty feet of a building: "Cost of removal later and mangling of trees during the construction period offset the possible beauty of the trees," the State Board opined. As further incentive to take a preemptive axe to such arboreal budget-busters, the State Board proposed a penalty clause for contractors who subsequently damaged any tree that had been designated for preservation. Clearly, the State Board believed, it was simply more cost effective just to plant new small trees.

The BHA originally planned Franklin Field as 840 units in three-story walk-up apartments, but the State Board preferred a smaller development of no more than 364 units, arranged in two-story rowhouses. Eventually, after a series of counter-proposals, a compromise prevailed. Planners decided to reserve the eastern portion of the site, abutting the Catholic cemetery, for future development, and build Franklin Field as a complex of 504 apartments arranged into 19 three-story, walk-up brick-faced buildings. The BHA dedicated the complex on June 18, 1954 (Figs. 3.7–3.8). Following a rendition of the National Anthem played by the Boston Firemen's Band and a flag-raising ceremony, Rabbi Samuel Korff, the spiritual head of the district's most influential synagogue, delivered the invocation before a wide array of state and local politicians and assembled guests. Speakers included both Mayor John B. Hynes and Lieutenant Governor Sumner Whittier, and the dedication exercises concluded after a group of grateful community citizens presented a citation to members of the Boston Housing Authority.[18]

At a time when most Boston public housing was built in Irish Catholic neighborhoods to serve predominantly Irish Catholics, Franklin Field marked an exception. As at the nearby Franklin Hill project, an ethnically diverse population initially tenanted Franklin Field, but Jews formed a clear majority. Oddly enough for a project that was clearly championed by Julius Ansel, only 42 percent of the original tenants came from either Ward 14 or its Dorchester neighbor, Ward 17. Since the five BHA Board members retained the largest control over the patron-

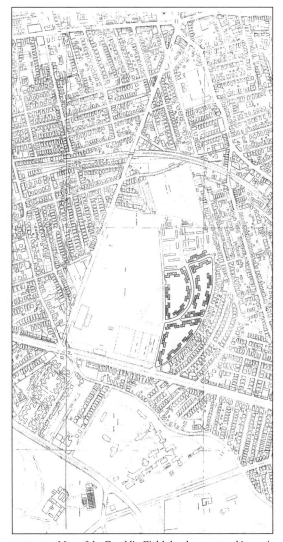

FIGURE 3.7 Map of the Franklin Field development and its environs. The BHA obtained the southern section of Franklin Field from the Boston Parks Department to build its housing development, which took the form of three large superblocks completed in 1954. The Authority reserved the eastern portion of the site, closest to the cemetery, for future construction. Between 1962 and 1964, the BHA used this land to build housing for the elderly, in a series of bar-shaped low-rise buildings.

FIGURE 3.8 Dedication of Franklin Field development, 1954. The BHA dedicated Franklin Field on June 18, 1954, with the usual coterie of state and local officials sharing the podium.

age associated with tenant assignments, the pull of one local councilor had its limits. Still, 42 percent was more than twice the rate of neighborhood draw enjoyed by South Boston's West Broadway project, and the figure attests to the extent to which Boston's lower-income Jews—for whom Franklin Field and Franklin Hill would have been the projects of choice—were concentrated in areas along Blue Hill Avenue. That said, Franklin Field—like the other new veterans' projects—was a citywide attraction. While some, like Saul and Shirley Levine, simply moved across Stratton Street when the project opened, others came from all over Boston. Ten families, in fact, relocated to Franklin Field from West Broadway.[19] Few if any relocated to Franklin Field from an area of concentrated poverty. Most of those who came from outside Dorchester-Mattapan seem not to have been Jewish (if surnames are to be trusted as a guide to such matters), but the project nonetheless served as a magnet for marginally poor Jewish veterans. The key to admission for such Jews, it seems, was the ward heeler Sam Levine, a local funeral home operator known to all as "the Chief." As one long-time BHA employee who spent his youth campaigning in the Franklin Field area recalls: "if you wanted to live in either Franklin Hill or Franklin Field, you had to know Chief Levine. That's how you got into one of those developments. He knew one of the Commissioners."[20]

Given the economic stability of the intended applicant pool, it did not seem to matter that the BHA initially set its "minimum average monthly rent" for Franklin Field apartments at $49.62, more than 25 percent higher than the average rents prevailing in the district as a whole in 1950, and nearly double what had been charged for the temporary housing. The BHA welcomed tenants with incomes up to $4,300 for a family of four, a figure that was 44 percent higher than the median income of those living in the neighborhood.[21] As before, the new public neighborhoods of the early 1950s sought out barely poor exemplary families, nearly all with two spouses, at least one of whom held a steady job. Perhaps 90 percent of the adult women in the project considered themselves "housewives," whereas the men reported more than a hundred different occupations. Sixty-one of them described themselves as clerks or salesmen, but there were also numerous taxi drivers, mechanics, machinists, electricians, foremen, butchers, managers, and accountants, as well as the occasional pharmacist, optometrist, and attorney. Fewer than a dozen of these veterans reported ongoing occupation with any branch of the U.S. military, but the project did house no fewer than ten Boston police officers and six firemen. It also accommodated twenty-six chauffeurs—one can only speculate about the political pull of their passengers. Most families consisted of a young couple (average age thirty-three) and a pair of children. As at West Broadway, though, the initial tenant cohort of the project was economically better off than those in the neighborhood, a neighborhood that—as has already been mentioned—was rapidly losing its middle-class residents to suburbia.[22]

Tenants living at Franklin Field had, within a short walk, three movie theaters, two bowling alleys, a roller-skating rink, and a variety of other child-friendly establishments. On the Field itself, the male youths of the development had access to both Little League baseball and Pop Warner football. One former tenant, Tony Fonseca—who grew up at Franklin Field during the 1950s and 1960s—recalls that "the entire neighborhood was child-oriented; you felt good about being a kid." Moreover, every place "had an adult that was central to that activity, who told you

what was right, what was wrong; if you wanted to partake, you had to behave."
He particularly appreciated the proprietor of Harry's Variety Store, who let
kids "charge" their penny candy, recording the transaction on a little notepad.
Through the 1950s, Fonseca remembers, "every single store on Blue Hill Ave.
was vibrant; you didn't have to leave this Ave. to get anything you wanted, from
fresh produce and meat and fish, to clothing, bicycle parts, furniture, and cars.
Many people didn't own cars, but it didn't matter because everything was there."
As Fonseca remembers it, "99.9 percent" of these neighborhood establishments
were owned by Jews. Even within the span of Fonseca's own childhood, however,
these neighborhood amenities slowly but surely began to disappear.[23]

Tellingly, the *Jewish Advocate*—the principal journalistic arm of Boston's Jewish community—did not even bother to cover Franklin Field's dedication, despite
the presence of Rabbi Korff and the various distinguished politicians who had assembled for the occasion. By 1954, the *Jewish Advocate* was far more likely to take
note of new plans for suburban synagogues, or Jewish-related activities at area
universities, or new ranch house subdivisions; it did little to advocate the needs of
Jews who remained in central Boston.

THE LONG DECLINE

FRANKLIN FIELD'S PROBLEMS BEGIN

Despite their relatively stable employment status, both the Jews and the non-Jews
who constituted Franklin Field's initial tenants faced some urgent needs. In contrast to other Boston public housing projects, where the early years of occupancy
seem to have been relatively problem-free, Franklin Field seemed somehow
cursed right from the start. The BHA's project file for this place is an unusually
thick one, due not only to the multiyear delay in deciding how large a project to
build (which initiated tensions between the BHA and the State Housing Board),
but also to the consistent problems that befell the project and its occupants almost immediately following first occupancy. Beginning in 1955 and continuing almost annually thereafter, the BHA conducted studies and budgeted funds to try
to discover why this project faced persistent leaks in its walls and roofs and suffered from flooded basements. Internal memoranda argued about "the difficulties
involved in making the buildings weather-tight and water-proof" and complained
that repairs should not be "entrusted to any fly-by-night concern." Meanwhile,

various consultants and bidders gave wildly different accounts of what was needed to correct the problems; state housing officials rejected ambitious proposals as too costly, arguing in 1959 that "there is absolutely no need to waterproof this entire project." Even as the local press gave thorough coverage to the leaks and seepages, no one seemed to remember that the entire project had been built on a buried floodplain.[24]

By 1960, however, BHA officials acknowledged that "conditions, uncorrected as they are, have worsened to the extent that bricks are crumbling at several outside corners and fragments are falling from the parapet." "Serious injury to the passer-by," Board members worried, "could, and may, result from this condition." As the problems persisted, they feared the legal consequences of continued inaction. By late 1960, the district's state representative also fielded tenant complaints about rats in the development, despite three visits by exterminators. Newly appointed BHA Board Chairman Edward Hassan defensively insisted that "the rats do not originate in this development," blaming their presence on the adjacent graveyard and on the Supreme Market (located all the way on the other side of Franklin Field, on Talbot Avenue). Intent on defending the integrity of his public neighborhood, he called on the Health Department to investigate the development's private neighbors, noting, "It will not do any good if we alone employ an exterminator."[25]

Meanwhile, as rats prowled, Franklin Field residents reiterated older concerns. One report from 1961 summed it all up: "Tenants started registering complaints about leaky walls shortly after they moved in and the complaints have continued to the present day." Chairman Hassan visited the development in March of that year during a heavy rainfall and, after a six-month delay, conveyed his frustrations in a letter to Leo Benoit, the chairman of the State Housing Board. Franklin Field's dire conditions, he commented, were "realistically brought to my attention" when he encountered water "dripping steadily in several rooms of each apartment," and tenants declared this was a "regular occurrence." "I have been informed, reliably," Hassan told state authorities, "that these conditions have existed since shortly after the first occupancies, and, that the complaint is general throughout the Development." With no permanent solution in sight, Franklin Field tenants continued to complain. BHA Director of Management Albert Palmer unconvincingly assured one such resident that "in some areas of the development corrective measures have been taken to some degree of success," and suggested that, given "the advance knowledge of storms," the tenant "take the

necessary precaution to protect personal property." Six years later, after continued unsuccessful attempts to stop leaking walls, residents were still complaining.
Palmer told one fair housing advocate that the Authority was "thoroughly familiar" with the damage caused by one particular heavy rain, but he reassured her
that the storm "also affected many private well-built homes."[26]

Many of these water-related problems surely had more to do with faulty construction than with underlying hydrology, but the lowland character of the site
continued to plague the area. In the place Olmsted once proposed for a skating
rink, heavy rains not only caused problems for the development but inundated
parts of the adjacent Field. As Tony Fonseca recalls, "To an adult it might have
been a problem, but to us kids it was a thrill. Depending on your height, the water
would be up to your knees or your hips, and you could go and splash around."[27]
To children, the Franklin Field area offered multiple opportunities for adventur-
ous play; for their parents, the place represented more of a waystation.

In the development's early years, those tenants who could afford to rent or buy
private homes of their own moved on quickly. Of the initial tenant cohort, one-
third stayed no more than two years, and each year in the late-1950s approximately 6–8 percent of the households earned too much income to be eligible to
remain. By 1961, more than three-quarters of the original tenants had left Franklin
Field's rats and leaks behind. City directory records suggest that as many as half
of these first tenants moved directly to the Boston suburbs or left the area completely. Most of those who left Franklin Field but remained in the city moved to
neighborhoods with similar working-class incomes, close to the Boston median.[28]
Armed with a wide array of government programs to assist veterans with housing,
and spared the racial discrimination that constrained the housing choices of nonwhite Americans, most of those who wished to leave Franklin Field could afford
to do so.

Those who remained not only faced the unwelcome intrusion of water into
their walls and basements but also coped with the lingering paternalism of the
BHA. In April 1958, the chairman of the State Housing Board asked the BHA to
distribute a "friendly reminder" about the advantages to and procedures for
"Spring Cleaning," and the Authority dutifully circulated the State Board's flyer.
The flyer described cleaning as "one of Spring's most rewarding customs," noting that "if each of us puts our best effort into making sure the inside and outside
of our homes are in order, we can all share the benefits of an attractive and pleasant development." Rather than assume that tenants already ascribed to adequate

standards of cleanliness and were capable of caring for their apartments on a year-round basis, the State Housing Board defined "Spring Cleaning" to include not just those tasks commonly left by most families to annual consideration, but also more frequently pressing matters such as washing kitchen floors and cleaning the refrigerator. Moreover, these public neighbors were asked to undertake such efforts during a specific week in May, since "Officials of the State Housing Board" would "soon be making their annual inspection of the premises."

With such an inspection in the offing, the Board also asked tenants to assist with "outside cleaning." The flyer urged them to "spruce up the yard and lawn areas" by raking up and disposing of the "accumulated debris," and promised to supply grass seed and fertilizer. Closer to their dwellings, residents were asked to "remove all crayon, chalk and other marks off the buildings and walls" and, using anglicized spelling, the Board could not resist scolding the tenants for having previously countenanced "this type of behaviour." Adopting an ambiguously inclusive paternalist voice, the Board commented: "we should see that our children do not repeat such activity." In the end, the flyer appealed to collective neighborhood pride and to partnership between tenants and management. The flyers were designed to be distributed at every state-subsidized development, but the Board deceptively individualized the wording, pointing out that "if the whole family pitches in and takes sufficient pride in the job to be done, we'll have the finest project in the state." Then, shifting pronouns, the State Housing Board referred to its own visiting inspectors in the third person, charging residents to "show them . . . that they can be proud of our project." The document concluded with a final exhortation: "ALL RIGHT FOLKS—*LET'S KEEP IT CLEAN!*"[29]

In the late 1950s Franklin Field's chief problems remained architectural, not social. Still, the BHA clearly recognized ways that tenant behavior could have negative impacts on project conditions. In keeping with the spirit of the Spring Cleaning program, the Authority desperately sought to keep up the external appearance of its developments, even as it proved increasingly incapable of maintaining the buildings. At Franklin Field, after only four years of occupancy, many of the new trees that had survived the construction now suffered from the play habits of two thousand new residents. In 1958, the BHA requested $22,000 to install one mile's worth of four-foot chainlink fences around lawn and tree areas to "stop the future loss of landscaped areas."[30] The Authority found it easiest to fence in or pave over what it could not maintain. Frederick Law Olmsted would not have approved.

HOUSING ELDERLY JEWS

None of these problems dissuaded the BHA from pressing for additional housing on the remainder of the Franklin Field site, east of the existing development. Prodded by Julius Ansel and other Dorchester-based politicians, the state government funded Boston's first public housing project for the elderly on this spot—eighty two-story apartments that opened in April 1962. John Murphy, who later became the BHA's director of tenant selection for more than a quarter century, recalls that "the elderly developments were added . . . to accommodate the elderly people that had already lived in the family development and wanted to be separated to some extent but still wanted to be in that neighborhood, in that area, so they could go to the synagogue. That's why they built it where they did." Although BHA rules initially prohibited this kind of internal transfer, the Authority soon dropped the restriction. Meanwhile, Chief Levine had little trouble finding new elderly Jewish tenants. In August 1962 State Senator Samuel Harmon told *The Jewish Advocate* that "in Ward 14 alone, we still have over 2000 senior citizens who need and want this type of housing," adding that the first eighty units housed "a very happy group" who benefited from Boston YMHA–Hecht House programs. The NAACP's Melnea Cass saw distinct signs of bias and complained directly to Boston Mayor John F. Collins: "There are lots of rumors about the Franklin Field *Elderly* Project. I called about it sometime ago to let you know. It is to be for Jews *only*—no Negroes. This sounds bad. I hope it will be well integrated. I am sure it will be if you know about it in time."

Cass's plea had little effect. For at least a little while longer, the BHA preferred to regard Franklin Field as one of its "better projects." The Authority cultivated an overwhelmingly white occupancy and aggressively resisted housing low-income, welfare-dependent applicants of any race. As the tenant-selection chief James Crowley put it to one woman applicant in 1964: "In the interest of solvency the Authority is not accepting as applicants, for the Franklin Field development, those whose incomes, such as yours, call for the minimum rental." BHA Administrator Ellis Ash, who took office in 1963 committed to reform and desegregation, ruefully acknowledged later that the BHA built the Franklin Field elderly annex to "accommodate special interests of groups and persons known to members of the Housing Authority Board." In 1964 eighty additional units opened immediately adjacent to the first group to instant popularity; half the one thousand elderly households that applied for BHA apartments citywide specifically requested placement in the new Franklin Field housing. That year, only sixteen nonwhite households resided in all of the Franklin Field development.[31]

TWILIGHT OF THE BLUE HILL AVENUE JEWS

Public housing came to Franklin Field just as the neighborhood entered the throes of ethnic and racial change. The new housing became both a mirror and a participating force in the transformation. Franklin Field could still be considered a "Jewish project" when it opened and when elderly housing annexes were added, but it fronted on a Jewish community very different from that of a generation earlier. Although 47,000 Jews remained in the area as late as 1960, they no longer constituted the "emerging middle class" of earlier decades. As Gamm puts it, "Dorchester and Roxbury had become a distinctively working-class enclave." The Jews who remained were increasingly blue-collar workers with low incomes and little education.

Blue Hill Avenue in the 1950s was three miles of bakeries, grocery stores, and fruit shops, interspersed with more than sixty kosher butchers and a variety of delicatessens. As one former denizen described it, the avenue was "the central fact of Ward 14, of the Jewish district . . . a mighty river of traffic, a double helix of asphalt around which the tributaries, the life of the Jews in Boston, spun, cohered, developed."[32] At the place where Franklin Field touched the east side of Blue Hill Avenue a 1,200-foot-long low stone wall provided an unparalleled source of seating to survey the scene. As Hillel Levine and Lawrence Harmon describe it, this was especially true during the High Holy Days:

> At the end of services synagogue goers would descend on the wall from all directions, some muttering that the apostates who avoided synagogue had already secured the best spots. The wall at Franklin Field was the one opportunity for all of the disparate neighborhood characters to connect. The members of the socialist Workmen's Circle, which ran a popular Kinder Ring summer camp for neighborhood youth, would share wall space with followers of the Hassidic Bostoner Rebbe, Levi Horowitz. Even the modest rebbetzins (rabbis' wives) would nod to the prostitutes who made their living in the back room of a barber shop on Erie Street. By early afternoon, the field would be filled with Jews.[33]

Hecht House, which relocated to the Franklin Field neighborhood from the West End in 1936, constituted the area's major Jewish community center. This center became a prime viewing spot to watch the decentering of the community. By 1960, when the staff at Hecht House met to discuss why "Jewish people no longer aspire to live" in the Blue Hill Avenue corridor, the answer was clear: "fine institutions (educational and religious) have moved to the suburbs."[34] Other institutions remained, but they changed their role in the community.

For decades, the most famous destination in the area had been the storied G & G delicatessen at 1106 Blue Hill Avenue. Julius Ansel, as Dorchester's most influential politician, used a corner table at the G & G as his "main office," and through the 1950s the deli "stood at the epicenter of Ward 14's political life." Levine and Harmon summon up the ambiance of the G & G at its peak: "Jewish leaders and lobbyists did not need to advance their causes by having breakfast with their senator in the Senate Dining Room. The national leaders, instead, came to the G & G. . . . The restaurant was positively electric on the eve of local and national elections. An enormous wooden bandstand was erected outside the delicatessen, where recorded jingles and live political pitches from scores of soundtrucks competed at a deafening volume for the precious votes of tailors, mechanics, rabbis, pharmacists, and bookies."[35] Outside of election times, the G & G was central in other ways. As Mark Mirsky, the son of another prominent Dorchester Jewish politician, recalls it, "On the tables of the cafeteria talmudic jurisprudence sorted out racing results, the stock market, and the student could look up from his 'desk' to leer at the young girls sipping cream sodas under the immense wings of their mothers; watch the whole world of Blue Hill avenue revolve through the G & G's glass gate." Yet even in the 1950s, Mirsky acknowledges, the center of Jewish life was shifting to Brookline, to Coolidge Corner sandwich shops like Jack and Marion's: "The ranks of the G & G were not yet thinned noticeably but the seed crop was gone. The loins of Israel sat in Jack & Marion's."[36]

What remained in Dorchester were the seeds of conflict, slowly becoming racialized, yet still dominated by ongoing tension between Jews and Catholics. Writing in the mid-1940s, Wallace Stegner described Catholic gangs roaming Franklin Field "in search of cross-lot walkers" and lying in wait for Jewish boys coming out of nearby Hecht House; "Sometimes they appeared in cars, which pulled up beside Jewish youths to disgorge half a dozen attackers."[37] Having consulted the records of the Jewish Community Center and other sources, Gamm concluded that this kind of violence remained a "major concern" of the Jewish community into the 1950s.

The departure of Jews dramatically affected the composition of the local public schools, a reconfiguring that was exacerbated by Boston's Racial Imbalance Act of 1965 whose "open enrollment" policy allowed students to attend schools outside their home district. The Solomon Lewenberg Junior High School, located just south of Morton Street, had an enrollment that was 80 percent Jewish in 1963; six years later its students were 90 percent black.[38]

The Jewish population of the Blue Hill Avenue corridor dropped from 70,000 in 1950 to 47,000 in 1960; thereafter, the decline accelerated. By 1967, only 25,000 Jews remained. In 1960, the neighborhood between Franklin Field and Morton Street had housed 13,400 Jews and was 99 percent white; seven years later, only 6,500 Jews remained, and the population of the area was nearly half black. Three years after that, in 1970, black occupancy stood at 73 percent. As the Jewish exodus to the suburbs accelerated in the 1960s, Blue Hill Avenue became "the principal route for the expansion of black settlement into Dorchester." As Gamm puts it, it was not that Jews fled because they feared black neighborhood succession; more fundamentally, the process worked the other way around: the "Jewish exodus itself" made room for blacks to move into formerly Jewish neighborhoods. Whatever the true dynamic, it seems clear that the residential movement of each group impacted the other.[39]

Some synagogues remained in this area, but they became increasingly cut off from the last concentrated zones of Jewish settlement, located further to the south.[40] A Jewish observer in 1967 described the area adjacent to the Franklin Field development as "a neighborhood already beset with deterioration, blight, crime, and general slum conditions," adding that "most of the Jews who could have already moved out of this section."[41] Eventually, as Gamm puts it, what had begun in the 1950s as "a simple matter of upward economic mobility began to be driven also by panic selling, blockbusting, crime, and racial fears." Ruth Botts, a black woman who moved with her parents in 1965 to Floyd Street, a block south of the development, recalls being relatively well received by white children. Soon afterward, though, "the realtors came through scaring everyone." The assassination of Martin Luther King, Jr., made matters much worse by precipitating riots along Blue Hill Avenue. Although most violence occurred in Grove Hall, well to the north of Franklin Field, angry blacks nonetheless were involved in substantial looting at least as far south as Morton Street. After that, Botts recalls, the Jews "just fled." If they had stayed "the stores just wouldn't have disappeared overnight," and the neighborhood would still have had the Jews' "resources for political power." Wilhelmina Hardy, another black woman who once lived in the area, concurs: "I think the Jews would still be there now, if [the blacks] didn't burn and burglarize their stores. It happened so fast, you could bat your eyes; one minute you'd see all the whites, and the next minute you'd see all the blacks moving in."[42]

BBURG: Banking on Racial Change

For more than thirty years, much debate about the fate of the Blue Hill Avenue corridor has centered on the nefarious activities of one long-defunct organization, the Boston Banks Urban Renewal Group (BBURG). This group, a consortium of local thrifts, had been established in 1962 during the Collins administration to commit funds for rehabilitation and homeownership loans in Roxbury's Washington Park Urban Renewal area. In 1968, in the wake of racial tensions following King's assassination, Mayor Kevin White revived and expanded the program, viewing it as a way to "accelerate housing rehabilitation and new construction for low income families" and as a means to increase the availability of mortgage funds for "greatly expanded home ownership in the inner city."[43] Over the next three years, twenty-two Boston banks processed $29 million in loans, enabling more than two thousand families—most of them black—to become homeowners. Offering the same advantageous FHA (Federal Housing Administration) loan guarantees to blacks that had long been guaranteed to whites, BBURG's bankers facilitated mortgages with down payments of as little as 3 percent. With the federal government assuming the risk of the loans, the banks set up an office in Roxbury to find their new market among Boston's blacks. As a fair housing advocate put it, BBURG served "very small numbers" of Boston's low-income whites "because the office was located in the black community and it was obviously designed for the black community."[44] In 1968, BBURG leaders noted with satisfaction that "the new office in Roxbury seems to have been declared off-limits by the radical element," leaving this outpost of social progress "unscathed, although there has been unrest and damage all around us, even as close as next door."[45] The BBURG pamphlets made no explicit mention of race, but proponents illustrated them exclusively with photos of a potential black buyer and the helpful black BBURG official who would presumably be there to assist him (Figs. 3.9–3.10).[46]

What on the surface could seem to be a commendable initiative to extend homeownership opportunities to nonwhites soon drew much criticism, culminat-

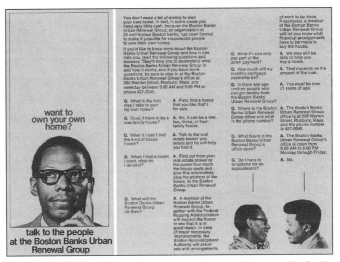

FIGURE 3.9 BBURG: Soliciting black homeownership. The Boston Banks Urban Renewal Group (BBURG) actively recruited potential black homebuyers.

ing in three days of antitrust hearings conducted by a U.S. Senate subcommittee in 1971. At base, the BBURG program—in its design and in its implementation—fell victim to the pervasiveness of racial discrimination in American housing markets. Providing advantageous loan terms to blacks did not protect them from unscrupulous FHA appraisers, greedy speculators, and corrupt realtors, all of whom preyed on the worst fears of white homeowners. As one analyst found, "Even though the suggested real estate commission on residential sales during the BBURG program was 6 percent, brokers were selling houses with commissions at 10, 15, 20 and 25 percent. Speculators bought homes at low prices as a result of white fears and then resold them with minimal repairs and with often more than 100 percent price increases to BBURG purchasers."[47] Caught up in a broader climate of blockbusting, many white homeowners sold out at fire-sale prices to such middlemen, who then resold the homes for inflated amounts to blacks, pocketing the profits. At the same time, the cursory inspections associated with the appraisals failed to disclose that most of these homes needed major repairs. New black homeowners, having been given inadequate counseling before their purchase, thus faced unanticipated expenses. Because funds for rehabilitation had not been included as part of their loan, BBURG ultimately led to widespread foreclosure and housing abandonment in the very neighborhoods it was designed to assist.[48] Whites received too little for their houses; blacks paid too

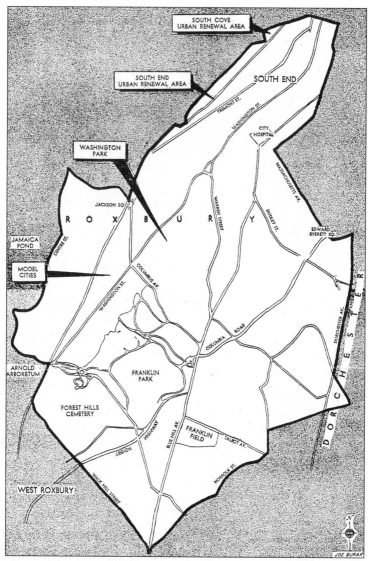

FIGURE 3.10 The BBURG line. BBURG expected to make its housing loans entirely within one section of the city, encompassing the neighborhoods of highest black occupancy and preferred black expansion. Its supporters drew a blue line to delineate several of the major urban-renewal areas as well as a section of Dorchester and Mattapan. Franklin Field was near the southern end of this zone. The *Boston Globe* published this version of the BBURG map on June 3, 1971.

much; property conditions declined, and neighborhood racial and ethnic tensions continued to mount.

Many blacks wished to use their newfound homeownership resource as an opportunity to escape the ghetto, so the avowed purpose of inducing investment in the federally subsidized Model Cities and urban-renewal areas frequently backfired. In many instances, the most upwardly mobile individuals used the loans to leave, depriving the community of actual and potential leaders; in any case, homeownership could do little to stabilize any neighborhood if the loan terms did not take account of the costly major repairs that many of these homes so sorely required.[49] Although intended to stabilize Roxbury and Dorchester, BBURG did little to finance reinvestment in these areas, and instead facilitated the departure of many upwardly mobile blacks to adjacent areas, into which they unwittingly imported the new financial distress foisted on them by the terms of their loans and the conditions of their new homes. Most ominously, because BBURG limited its loan activity to a prescribed area within Boston—an area circled with a blue line—the program allowed the banks to dictate the neighborhoods in which most Boston blacks could buy homes. As one community organization put it at the time, "The 'red line,' cutting off the ghetto from loans and insurance, became the 'blue line,' guaranteeing loans within these communities—but the net result was still to combine black families." The fair housing advocate Sadelle Sacks put it even more pointedly: "The BBURG coalition had decided where the black communities could live."[50]

Defending the program before the Senate investigators in 1971, the former BBURG chairman Joseph Bacheller argued that the BBURG line—formalized on well-publicized maps in January 1971—was intended to disassociate BBURG from the blockbusting that was rampant just south of its boundaries.[51] Ignoring the evidence that suggested most loans were made outside the urban-renewal/Model Cities area targeted for rehabilitation, he insisted that BBURG was intended to "help rebuild an area of the city that was festering with decay," and that the program marked "a public-spirited commitment to halt this decadence and assist the disadvantaged." "We were asked," he pointed out, "to make these loans in those areas because otherwise these poor people could not get any loans at all."[52] To Bacheller and the other bankers, BBURG, whatever its flaws, represented progress.

Yet the bankers acted from a tangle of mixed motives. Forged in the simmering heat of urban unrest, BBURG was seen by many as an insurance plan. "Our primary objective," George H. Robinson, the vice president of the Boston Five Cents Savings Bank and the director of BBURG's Roxbury office, declared, "is to provide homes for the rootless in the ghetto area and thus help avert or minimize disorders."[53] Seeking to inject the stability of middle-class black homeownership into troubled black neighborhoods, the bankers also sought to sustain the stability of Boston's many all-white communities. The BBURG banks were heavily invested with mortgages and construction loans in these other neighborhoods, and they certainly did not wish to see their investments jeopardized by racial unrest that could reduce appraisal values.[54] The BBURG bankers saw themselves as social progressives—offering homeownership chances to lower-income blacks who had been denied such affordable opportunities previously. Yet, with incomes that were well above the median income citywide, many of these black families could have afforded homes in other areas. By consolidating the supply geographically and containing the demand for black-owned homes financially (by limiting the number of loans), the bankers kept BBURG's blacks far from racial hotbeds like South Boston, Charlestown, and East Boston—not to mention suburbia.

Instead, as Levine and Harmon stress in their book, the BBURG line, while explicitly avoiding the city's Irish Catholic strongholds, deliberately encompassed a substantial piece of Boston's remaining Jewish enclave. This inclusion, they observe, made financial sense because these neighborhoods had become economically "dead areas" for the banks: "elderly Jewish homeowners had paid off their mortgages years before or had 4 1/2 percent loans, available during the 1940s and 1950s."[55] In 1970, with markedly higher interest rates in place, encouraging new homeownership in this area increased the value of the area to BBURG banks, even as new black homeowners paid inflated prices for homes in which they held little equity, and which many could not afford to maintain.[56] Among other things, then, the location of the southern portion of the BBURG blue line meant that the program considerably impacted the neighborhoods on all sides of the Franklin Field public housing project.

BBURG's backers drew lines to encompass the existing black communities in the Model Cities and urban-renewal areas, as well as to allow room for black expansion. As BBURG Steering Committee Vice Chairman Carl Erickson put it, the black community was "starting to expand into the expanded line we created," a growth that was mostly to the south and west, paralleling Blue Hill Avenue. The bankers wished to infuse the black ghetto with the presumed stability of homeownership, but they did not wish to provide loans *only* in this area because such a move could imply "discrimination against whites."[57]

The city's growing black population—squeezed out of affordable housing by urban renewal—moved outward from Roxbury into expanded portions of Dorchester, where families faced uncertain welcome. As Levine and Harmon put it, "the residents of largely Irish neighborhoods of Dorchester had not exactly put out the red carpet for black house seekers."[58] The situation may not have matched the harrowing experience of black "pioneer" families moving into BHA properties in Irish South Boston during this same period, but the power of racial antipathy remained immense. In this context, the southward swath of homes made available by departing Jews seemed much less dangerous turf than Southie for incoming blacks. As Levine and Harmon put it, "Black parents in Roxbury knew their children might be greeted with taunts, fists, or worse in schools in South Boston, East Boston, and Charlestown, but in Mattapan they would be free to learn. Jews would not throw rocks at their children."[59]

No one disagrees about the extent to which the formerly Jewish corridor of settlement north and south of Franklin Field became transformed into predominantly black neighborhoods. At issue are questions of pace and causality. Hillel Levine and Lawrence Harmon charge that "2,500 low-income black families were . . . funneled into a small, cohesive Jewish neighborhood by the chairmen of twenty-two Boston savings banks," an act that "essentially walled off the city's Jewish community."[60] Gerald Gamm, however, counters this argument at every turn. He demonstrates that the stability of the Mattapan Jewish community had begun to erode well before BBURG, with panic selling already occurring in the winter of 1966–67. Moreover, he points out that the BBURG line encompassed one-third of the entire city of Boston, a vast zone that was less than 8 percent Jewish. In fact, Gamm calculated, most residents within the BBURG line were not even black; the zone actually housed a majority of white non-Jews. Further, he shows that Jewish areas outside the BBURG line also experienced widespread panic and flight. As Gamm puts it, "The Jewish exodus had entered its final stages before the line was drawn."[61]

At the heart of the dispute between Gamm and Levine-Harmon is the question of whether the BBURG boundary line was drawn to target Jewish neighborhoods for future black occupancy. Gamm correctly notes that the overall BBURG area encompassed large sections of predominantly Catholic white neighborhoods and actually *excluded* key areas where heavy Jewish concentration still existed, in particular, those areas located to its south around Mattapan Square (Fig. 3.11). Levine and Harmon do not contest the fact that the BBURG bankers nominally drew the line to encompass many non-Jewish areas; their argument is that—

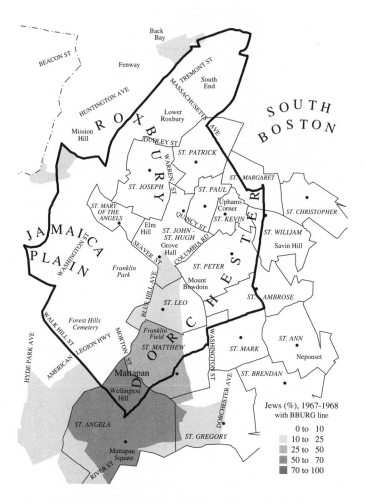

FIGURE 3.11 BBURG and the Blue Hill Avenue Jews. Gerald Gamm argues that most of the BBURG territory encompassed predominantly white Catholic neighborhoods, whereas some of the heaviest areas of Jewish occupancy remained outside the line to the south.

within this broad zone—they disproportionately and discriminatorily concentrated the "vast majority" of properties actually sold to blacks under the subsidized mortgage plan in the small part of the BBURG territory that was struggling to remain predominantly Jewish.

Curiously, neither of these books about the neighborhood actually attempted

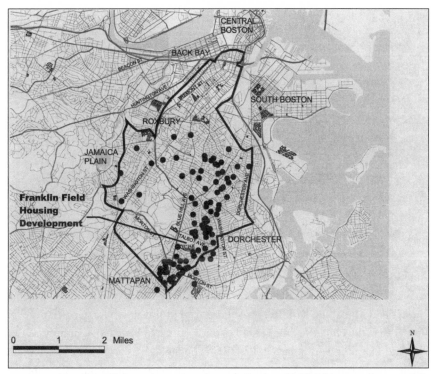

FIGURE 3.12 Map of BBURG purchases. A random sample of 100 BBURG home purchases made in 1968–1969 shows that most occurred just east of Blue Hill Avenue. The Franklin Field housing development was near the epicenter of this activity, so its residents shared in the consequences.

to map the pattern of BBURG loan activity. When one does so (Fig. 3.12), the results provide less than ringing support for Levine and Harmon's more conspiratorial interpretations. Yes, the locational distribution of BBURG purchases closely mirrored the distribution of majority-Jewish neighborhoods, but the match was with the Jewish neighborhoods of 1940, not 1968. An analysis of a random sample of one hundred BBURG-assisted purchases made in 1968 and 1969 (approximately one-fourth of the loans processed to that point) shows clearly that they overwhelmingly fall in a one-by-three-mile rectangle paralleling Blue Hill Avenue, an area within the BBURG boundary that includes parts of the Model City area in the north and extends south to reach the northern limits of the remaining area of concentrated Jewish settlement.[62] Only 20 percent of the homes are in this heavily Jewish zone—Mattapan below Morton Street—the area that Levine and Harmon single out as the "area of greatest loan activity."[63] This may well have been the area of greatest activity *within the Mattapan portion* of the BBURG territory, but it hardly seems to have been the concerted focus of the "vast majority" of home purchases overall. In viewing the whole BBURG fiasco through the lens of the "death" of the Jewish community, Levine and Harmon let one aspect of the story appear central. If there was discriminatory targeting of the Jewish community as one reserve area for ghetto expansion, this pales before the discriminatory assumption of the program as a whole, sorely constrained by insistent patterns of racially segregated housing. Seen another way, BBURG marks a late chapter in the decades-long transformation of a predominantly Jewish corridor of settlement into a predominantly African-American one. If BBURG can be said to have had a spatial focus, it was not on Mattapan; rather, as Figure 3.12 suggests, the centroid of greatest loan activity occurred on the streets above and below Franklin Field.

It is debatable how significantly BBURG contributed to "the death of an American Jewish community," but it undeniably reinforced boundaries for lower-income black residential expansion and contributed to growing unrest in Dorchester and Mattapan. BBURG must be placed in this much longer perspective. Rather than the chief executioner of Boston's principal Jewish community, as Levine and Harmon would have it, BBURG is better seen as a prominent nail in its coffin. More a symptom of change than a cause, it became the principal symbol of the neighborhood's protracted social tension. Touted as a means to promote investment and homeownership in troubled communities, it ultimately catalyzed further trouble elsewhere. Even if BBURG were not the proximate cause, it contributed to the climate of uncertainty facing Blue Hill Avenue's remaining Jews, many of whom still clung to public housing apartments at Franklin Field and its elderly housing annex.

BBURG, by definition, was a program targeted to (or at) homeowners, yet more than two-thirds of the Jews who lived in the most heavily affected part of Mattapan were renters rather than owners. This, Gamm argues, is because most of the homeowning Jews had already left: "Over two decades of racial change and in virtually every Jewish neighborhood, the Jewish exodus was led by homeowners."[64] Those renting in the Franklin Field public housing project belatedly joined in the flight.

Franklin Field, 1970: Entry and Exodus

In 1970 alone, nearly 25 percent of the families living in Franklin Field left the project. The 124 new households that arrived to replace them were a far cry from the original tenant cohort of fifteen years before, epitomizing the desperate economic straits of those seeking public housing. In contrast to the two-parent, reliably employed families of the 1950s, three-quarters of the new families were headed by a single parent, and most were dependent on public assistance. Fifty-six percent came to Franklin Field from outside the immediate neighborhood, but nearly all came from the city's black districts. In most Boston neighborhoods, the BHA struggled to find black families willing to move into white-dominated projects; at Franklin Field, however, the BHA's Advisory Committee on Minority Housing found that nonwhites "were accepting assignments, as this neighborhood is a changing one." In 1969, the project was still two-thirds white; three years later, it was 90 percent black.[65] In short, the movement into Franklin Field was a microcosm of the broad black migration southward within the bounds of the BBURG territory. Whereas BBURG brought black homeowners (who then imported less affluent black tenants), Franklin Field attracted the least advantaged blacks of all.

Researcher Gerald Taube surveyed tenants in the Franklin Field project in 1969, just as the development was beginning its racial "tip." He found a place that was rapidly turning inward; although tenants kept "tightly-drawn shades," 88 percent still claimed to feel "safe." Socially, however, they reported having few friends either inside or outside the development and demonstrated little interest in becoming involved in neighborhood organizations. Within the development, residents had not bothered to form a tenants organization, and 80 percent indicated there was nothing they wanted a tenants' council to do. To the extent that they perceived "trouble" in the project, they attributed it to other tenants. They wished for improved laundry facilities and recreation areas, but they expressed few complaints about BHA maintenance and did not report problems with noise or cleanliness of the hallways or grounds. Two-thirds doubted whether managerial responsiveness would be any better if they lived in private housing.[66]

Taube himself found more to disparage. From the outside, the buildings appeared "defaced" and "marred by litter," with parking areas "filled with glass":

> A few trees and saplings, protected by chain link cages around their trunks, are not sufficient to alleviate the barrenness that the absence of grass permits. Small patches of grass, protected by low green bar fences, do appear in front of each building. The rest is asphalt . . . Despite its size, the project manifests very few signs of life . . . As a

result, even the absence of litter on the walks leads one to conclude that there is not enough life to generate it.

Inside, however, Taube found the buildings to be free of litter and without "foul aromas." Exterior doors remained in good repair, and he concluded that, overall, the project was "reasonably well maintained."[67]

For the elderly at Franklin Field (whether living in the "family" development or in the newer, elderly-oriented additions), living conditions continued to deteriorate. As early as 1966, forty residents sent a petition to Mayor Collins, complaining about "the abuse of the Hoodlums who infest our section, 20 or 30 at a time":

> There are three groups who come down from the *Big Project* after school and on Sat., Sun. and Holidays with guns and scream and shout and give all kinds of abuse. They come in the front and back halls and use it for a toilet and on several occasions have lighted matches and thrown [them] in the doorways—also setting fire to the grass.
>
> The girls and boys on bicycles are on all our walks and tell us to get the Hell off the walk or they will run us down.
>
> There is Franklin Field, plus other Playground sections, a skating rink, and a swimming pool for them to use.
>
> Many of our residents are ill and cannot take the abuse.
>
> Surely it is not asking too much to have protection from these hoodlums? All we ask is to live out our lives in *peace* and *quiet*.

The police agreed to help patrol the area, but problems mounted. In late 1969, 120 residents attended a public meeting of the Boston City Council's Committee on Public Housing, held at Franklin Field. One after another, 21 tenants described stories of muggings and other lawlessness and pleaded for a greater police presence. Sergeant Lawrence McCarthy of the local station told them that a patrolman was present, but that residents needed to work with him more closely: "When you see an officer, talk to him. Explain which are the bad hallways. Tell him which groups should be moving. That's what people used to do." The *Boston Globe* sent a reporter to investigate conditions at the development. His report, entitled "They Live in Fear at Franklin Field," contained a litany of horror stories: a woman whose blind husband was beaten several different times and pulled down a flight of stairs; a man whose car had been stolen twice within a month; a BHA social worker for the area who said she was "constantly trying to appease people who are petrified by the many muggings, bag-snatchings, and housebreaks in this project."[68]

A year later, in December 1970, a reporter for the *Boston Herald Traveler* singled out Franklin Field in a page-one exposé provocatively headlined "City Housing Project Crime Soars: Tenants Live in Terror." Long-time BHA management supervisor Kenneth Gralton observed that Franklin Field had gone from one of the city's most desirable projects to one of its most troubled in a matter of only five years. Tenants recalled a neighborhood that had been a "garden spot" as recently as the mid-1960s, "the kind of place where you brought people to show them how good public housing could be." Now, residents regularly paid to have third locks added to their doors but still faced break-ins through their windows, often while they were present. The BHA eventually installed "security screens" in all apartments, but tenants observed that these could be "entered at will with the use of a pair of scissors." Elderly residents consistently reported experiences with assault, robbery, and burglary and—almost uniformly—kept dogs in their apartments for added protection, even though this violated the no-pets clause of their lease. A black woman feared for her life after having BB pellets shot into her third-floor apartment, and white tenants reported muggings inside their hallways, as well as throughout their neighborhood. Predators looking to steal welfare and social security checks destroyed most of the project's mailboxes, so that the mailman stopped delivering the checks unless their intended recipients were home to receive them in person. Assistant Manager Edward Ryan's desk was piled with tenant applications to transfer out of Franklin Field, each with the same reason: "Afraid of area—doctor's letter attached."[69]

By late 1970, the BHA began to acknowledge the seriousness of the security problems at Franklin Field. Director of Management Leo Donovan placed an "emergency requisition" for dead-bolt locks at the project, and the Authority hired a private security firm to patrol the development from 10 A.M. to 10 P.M., supplementing the patrols of Boston police officers assigned to pass through from 8:30 A.M. to 2:30 A.M. The private firm, SLED Protective, described its challenges as preventing vandalism while protecting residents from "undesirables who live in the surrounding area; teenagers who have been known to snatch purses from the elderly; and children, on bicycles, who knock over the elderly."[70]

For older residents of Franklin Field, the options were few. Some complained that even the police had started telling them to "get out of here, not to live here."

"They're not being sarcastic," one elderly man said, "they are trying to tell us to leave here because we're old and helpless. But where can we go?" Another commented: "We shouldn't have to go anywhere. We are American citizens and this is public housing, isn't it? Why should we have to leave? Everybody talks about freedom, but some people can't digest the freedom they have and so they beat us and rob us because we're too old to stop them and we can't go anywhere else."[71]

Because it was tucked in between a field and a cemetery, the Franklin Field project had always been rather isolated from services. As long as the neighborhood was safe and as long as most of the residents were relatively young and mobile, tenants found the long walk to shopping merely a minor inconvenience. Once the BHA located the Franklin Field housing for the elderly at the point furthest from Blue Hill Avenue and public transit, however, the situation grew more serious. Within a few years after these annexes had been built, the BHA struggled to find anyone who wanted to live there. As BHA tenant-selection chief Murphy observed, during the course of his long career the "Franklin Field elderly developments were the only ones that never had any demand." Once the original elderly tenants "either died or left," Murphy explains, "others weren't interested in having to go all through a family development to get home. The transportation was very poor and they had to deal with the kids in the family development, and the kids in the Field. And, living next to the cemetery, they could look out and see where they were going to end up, a reminder every day."[72]

As early as 1965, elderly Franklin Field residents urged State Senator Samuel Harmon to convince the Massachusetts Bay Transportation Authority (MBTA) to route scheduled buses through the development, to take them to Blue Hill Avenue for shopping and enable them to "carry back their heavy packages." As Harmon put it to an MBTA official, "the entire Golden Age group in the Franklin Field project is on my back for this service, especially in view of the fact that they are willing to pay the dime carfare." The MBTA denied the request and continued to resist adding bus service for six more years.

Sometimes MBTA officials told residents and BHA officials that adding the desired bus route would set a bad precedent ("a concession here might result in future demands in other project areas for similar service"); at other times, they deflected the matter for reasons of costs and logistics. In the meantime, the stakes for Franklin Field residents had risen dramatically. No longer was bus service simply a convenience for an aging population largely without access to automobiles; it had become, by 1969, an urgent matter of personal safety. In November

1970, BHA Administrator Daniel Finn pleaded with the MBTA again, citing a "continuing series of serious crimes," and noting "numerous and unceasing requests on behalf of the tenants organization, the elderly, the social service agencies and our own security office." MBTA General Manager Joseph Kelly again refused to help: "This Authority is sympathetic to the problems of the elderly in the Housing Project," Kelly wrote. "However, this particular problem is not a transportation matter, but a problem of protection by law enforcement authorities."

Undaunted, the tenants took their complaints through a case worker to Julius Bernstein, the new BHA Board chairman who was both a champion of tenants' interests and a Jew. The tenants documented a daily increase in criminal attacks, including an assault on Esther Schneider, the president of their tenants group, who was forced into a nursing home because of a particularly brutal mugging. Still, in late December, Kelly once again informed the BHA that the MBTA could be of no assistance: they did not wish to disrupt the existing "continuity of service," eliminate other popular stops, or face added expenses. Moreover, using language that furthered the dismissive tone of his response, Kelly added, "There is no question that it is a minority group issue."

In February 1971, Franklin Field tenants met directly with BHA Chairman Bernstein and two representatives of the Jewish Community Council of Metropolitan Boston (JCC). Two weeks later, a JCC leader interceded with the Massachusetts governor's office and, in March, the Franklin Field tenants finally got their bus service.[73] By this time, however, all these buses could do was to take residents to other parts of a neighborhood in turmoil.

Abandoning Blue Hill Avenue

In 1969 Ward 14's representative, Edward Serlin, grimly told the *Boston Globe* that "there's no future for the Jewish people in the Ward 14 area anymore. Only the poor, the sick and the elderly are here and in five years they will all be dead." Writing in the *Jewish Advocate,* Serlin compared the area's remaining Jews to those living in "Germany in 1939": "Numerous times every week my wife and I receive telephone calls from these poor people to bring them milk and bread, as they are fearful of venturing out to buy necessities of life. Even if they would go out, almost every business on Blue Hill Avenue has had its Crystal Night, and still the so-called Jewish leaders look the other way. It is actually safer on the border between Israel and Jordan than walking on Blue Hill Avenue in the day time, let alone at night."[74] Arsonists destroyed the last drug store in the Franklin Field neighborhood in 1970, two years after its owner had been robbed of $1,000.[75] Jewish cultural life departed along with the businesses. Hecht House (which had merged with the Young Mens Hebrew Association [YMHA] a decade earlier) itself was sold in 1970, and Dorchester's remaining synagogues all closed by the early 1970s.[76]

Levine and Harmon's informants relay accounts of massive unrest caused by blacks in and around the local public schools: "At the end of the school day, the Lewenberg open-enrollment students burst down Wellington Hill toward Blue Hill Avenue. Nothing, it seemed, was safe along their path—tricycles were smashed and carefully planted rows of flowers were tramped upon; those unlucky enough to get caught in their path were fortunate to escape with just a shower of verbal abuse. Along the Avenue, vendors scurried to remove their goods from sidewalk stalls and dropped their iron grates before the Lewenberg wave broke over them. Those who moved too slow could expect to spend the next few hours salvaging fruit from overturned carts or trying to match left shoes with right." For Levine and Harmon, the black-Jewish tensions at the Lewenberg Junior High School were "a dress rehearsal for the desegregation crisis that would rock Boston in the middle 1970s."[77]

Even before the mid-1970s, however, Franklin Field residents became caught up in the new round of racial violence that engulfed Boston over questions of school desegregation. In 1971, the State Board of Education voted to withhold state aid from Boston because the Boston School Committee refused to cooperate on the matter of open enrollment. The State Board wanted Boston to limit open-enrollment transfers to cases where the move would relieve racial imbalance, whereas the Boston School Committee wished to continue its usual practice of granting routine transfers to white students whose parents "knew the system," while making it difficult for black students to have comparable choices. The issue came to a head over the brand-new Joseph Lee Elementary School, located on Talbot Avenue just adjacent to Franklin Field. The school had been built using state funds with the stipulation that it would open with a racial balance (a slight white majority); while it was under construction, however, the neighborhood shifted to nearly all-black occupancy, and the State Board agreed to release Boston's share of the state education funding only when the School Committee reassigned hundreds of white students to this new school. Many white parents, fearing for their children's safety, saw the Lee School as a serious liability; residents of Franklin Field, by contrast, regarded the Lee as a great new resource that too few of their children would get to use. Instead of attending this nearby school (so close by that "your mouth waters when you look at it," as one black mother put it) with a modern gym, a pool, a theater, carpeted classrooms, and a curriculum described as "one of the finest in any elementary school," their kids were to be bused to older schools in white neighborhoods. When school opened in September, 250 white children refused assignment to the Lee School, while many black parents gave false addresses in the attempt to gain eligibility. Soon afterward, the School Committee bowed to community protests and agreed to prevent forced transfers of white children to the Lee; the State Board responded by withholding $14 million from Boston and suspending approval of all new school construction in the city.[78]

The politics of the Lee School continued to simmer for several years, as court-ordered busing tore the city apart. Still, busing did little to add to the ample violence that already plagued this particular neighborhood. In sharp contrast to the altercations that marked the advent of busing in white strongholds such as South Boston when blacks were bused in, there were no comparable attacks on whites bused to Roxbury and Dorchester. Throughout the mid-1970s, the black-oriented *Bay State Banner* continued to praise the city's black community for its "extraordinary reserve and compassion . . . in the face of extreme provocation," and asserted that "busing is working and will continue to work."[79] Whatever its promise, the arrival of busing forced some Franklin Field children to split their daily lives between a home neighborhood where they were not safe and a school neighborhood where they were not welcome.

The neighborhood flux that engulfed Franklin Field had additional consequences. Many area residents noted a distinct decline in city services (such as snow removal and trash pick-ups) and a decreased ability to obtain low-interest home-improvement loans once their neighborhood became predominantly black.[80] The changes operated in more subtle ways, as well. When the neighborhood was still Jewish, many residents relied on the services of eighty small credit unions, legal or otherwise, that had operated throughout Jewish Dorchester and Mattapan and were used to finance everything from college tuition to car purchases to vacations. Many of these credit unions did not even require two additional cosigners for their loans, since "the collateral in the Jewish financial district was one's good name."[81] With the departure of these institutions and the tight community that supported them, the area lost another key layer of its social infrastructure.

If Franklin Field's new black majority felt unwelcome, unsafe, and under-served, so too did the area's remaining Jews. The attacks on Franklin Field's elderly were part of a broader pattern of violence. Beginning in the late 1960s and culminating in 1970, several attacks on Jewish persons and property gained widespread publicity and fueled further fears. In 1969, two black men allegedly threw acid in the face of a Dorchester rabbi, and in May 1970 arsonists attacked two Mattapan synagogues.[82] As the *Boston Globe* put it, "The Jewish community viewed the attacks upon their temples as 'part of a pattern' and a continuation of a campaign to scare the Jewish residents out of the area.'"[83] Zezette Larsen, a Holocaust survivor who staffed the elderly services component of the Combined Jewish Philanthropies' multiservice center in Mattapan (belatedly opened in 1970), worried particularly about the remaining Jewish elderly residents in the Franklin Field project, spending much of her time helping some of them relocate to Brighton. "The elderly residents who were transported to the center for a kosher lunch program told horror stories of being assaulted and humiliated by young, rootless teens," she recounted.[84]

In late 1969, the *Bay State Banner* tried to come to terms with the spate of attacks along this part of Blue Hill Avenue, acknowledging that "many of the victims are white," but editorializing that it was an "illusion" to think that the attacks had racial overtones; the elderly were being attacked "because they are old not because they are white." The *Banner* sought to shift discussion to broader questions of "urban poverty" and called for all ethnic groups to mobilize to "stop the terror." With the arrival of armed patrols organized by the Boston branch of Meir Kahane's Jewish Defense League, however, the tensions could not be so easily disentangled from the open hostility of ethnic turf battles.[85]

In 1972 a report summarizing interviews conducted with Jews in Mattapan concluded that "they are basically frightened by what has happened in the neighborhoods immediately north of theirs and they see the beginnings of similar disruptions in their own neighborhoods." Specifically, "there is a deep sense of abandonment by the institutions that support community life, i.e. synagogues, professionals, stores, etc. They now feel trapped even though a significant percentage live on good streets, relatively safe in comfortable, modest single-family homes, etc. They talk about wanting to leave." Many business owners along Blue Hill Avenue moved their families away but retained their businesses as long as they remained profitable.[86] In 1973 the *Bay State Banner* editorialized about "madness in Mattapan," concluding that "only the most hardy continue to operate their stores along Blue Hill Avenue in the Morton Street section. What was once a thriving commercial section is fast grinding to a halt." That July, one such merchant was gunned down while trying to prevent the latest in a series of robberies at his fish and chips restaurant; later the same month, his widow was robbed again at gunpoint. The central problem, according to the *Banner*, was not just that older Jewish businesses had left once their customers had departed; it was that the businesses that did exist were too crime-ridden to support the many area residents eager to patronize them: "The few who remain find it difficult to do business in an area where potential customers stay away because of the fear of purse snatchers and other street crime. Now the streets are empty when they should be filled with shoppers." The Franklin Field Lumber Company, located on Talbot Avenue near Blue Hill Avenue, survived because it served a real neighborhood need. As the owner, Mort Kane, comments, "We were doing a decent business because of where we were—It's kind of a shame to make a profit off of the crime and vandalism in the neighborhood but—because of break-ins—people were constantly replacing their doors, and buying locks and security devices. We had a great market for some of that stuff."[87]

Not long afterward, the Boston Redevelopment Authority referred to Blue Hill Avenue as "the most striking physical personification of the many ills besetting Boston's low to moderate-income population; it is a four-mile stretch of roadway characterized by boarded storefronts, abandoned multi-family housing, and all-too-visible expanses of vacant land."[88] As area resident Janice Bernstein put it, "All your local stores leave you. The school is in complete chaos. There is no safety at all. What is there to stay for when you have that?[89] Kevin White, Boston's mayor since 1968, later reflected that he was surprised not to get more complaints from the city's Jews: "The Jewish community was not making any noise. Swift change and they were not making noise."[90]

Various groups belatedly arose to try to combat Blue Hill Avenue's decline, but the forces arrayed against them were large and diverse. It was not just that the area was in the throes of violent change; it was also that the very nature of this type of retail strip was under harsh challenge from automobile-centered shopping centers elsewhere. Blue Hill Avenue's neighborhood-oriented variety and food stores first lost their trolley line in the 1950s, then lost both the intimate social and cultural connection with their customer-neighbors as well as the economic ability to compete with chain supermarkets and new malls located along the American Legion Highway and elsewhere. Instead of the fine-grained pattern of local shops, Blue Hill Avenue gained "too many gas stations, car washes, fast food joints, clubs and restaurants, real estate offices, and just plain abandoned buildings."[91] When surveyed in 1976, residents said they wished that Blue Hill Avenue could be "restored" to a node of drug stores, shoe stores, and other conveniences, but the BRA concluded that the old commercial strip was "history," pointing out that "to restore Blue Hill Avenue to its original character would not be in tune with the present time."[92] The once vibrant streetcar suburb was no longer vibrant, suburban, or even served by streetcars.

Blue Hill Avenue's collapse as a retail strip was the most visible neighborhood scar, but it was inseparable from the damage that had been done along the residential sidestreets. Much of the growing residential abandonment in the area could be traced, directly or indirectly, to the ill-fated homeownership experiment of BBURG. Amid racial change and rampant disinvestment, many of the new homeowners had trouble attracting good tenants to their rental apartments, and without good tenants they faced increased difficulty in meeting mortgage payments. "In the early 1970s," Levine and Harmon report, "more than 70 percent of B-BURG-assisted homeowners were unable to keep up their mortgage payments, because those payments far exceeded their earning power or because they were faced with repair costs about which the FHA appraisers and loan officers had failed to warn them. The banks foreclosed on more than a thousand single-family homes and multiunit dwellings in the area" (Fig. 3.13). In 1974 the *Boston Globe* described a rising surge of foreclosures in the Franklin Field neighborhood: "Tripledecker homes . . . are being cashed in by Boston banks like poker chips in a card game." HUD, which took title to the homes under the terms of the federal mortgage insurance program, quickly became "one of the city's largest property owners," acquiring a new house at a rate of almost one every other day.[93] As Levine and Harmon concluded,

> B-BURG buyers were far more likely to lose their homes through foreclosure and abandonment than to realize capital gains on their purchases. With little or no down payment, the new buyers enjoyed no equity. For those who had difficulty meeting mortgage and up-keep costs and who had no reserves to cover the needed repairs that inefficient or corrupt FHA appraisers had failed to report, it was often more prudent to walk away than to persevere. . . . More than one-half of all B-BURG purchasers would lose their homes

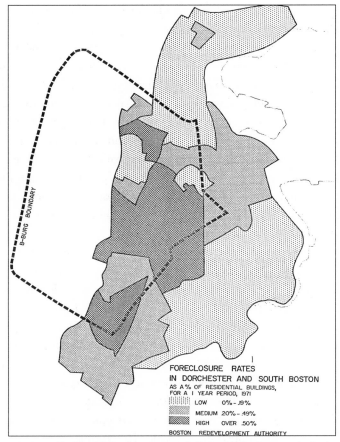

FIGURE 3.13 Residential foreclosures, 1971. A Boston Redevelopment Authority study found very high rates of residential mortgage foreclosure along the Blue Hill Avenue corridor within the BBURG boundary, with the highest concentrations located just north and south of Franklin Field.

by 1974. The effect on the city's black community would be devastating.[94]

By the middle and late 1970s, the neighborhood located just south of Franklin Field experienced what the BRA termed "highly concentrated abandonment." In one small area centered on Lucerne and Arbutus streets, residents abandoned 110 buildings, "indicating the concentration of blockbusting during the BBURG program years."[95] In this area, which extended three blocks south from the Franklin

Field project, vacant lots and abandoned buildings actually outnumbered occupied structures, becoming common sites for illegal dumping. In other parts of the neighborhood, those residual white homeowners who could not find buyers moved to the suburbs and continued to operate their old homes as absentee landlords; others sold their homes to real estate investors who "milked" them for maximum rent while providing virtually no maintenance. During the 1970s, the district as a whole lost more than 17 percent of its housing stock, as deferred maintenance, absentee ownership, foreclosures, abandonment, and city-sponsored demolition combined to transform the landscape.[96] Beyond these socioeconomic causes, the same hydrological problems that plagued Franklin Field may also have, quite literally, undermined some of the houses built upon the buried streambeds that once traversed the neighborhood. The full ecopolitics of housing abandonment surely warrants further exploration.[97]

Whatever the nature of contending forces, beginning in the late 1960s and continuing to the present day, all manner of neighborhood and city groups have sought ways to revitalize this part of Blue Hill Avenue, all with limited success. In 1960 commercial and residential real estate along Blue Hill Avenue between Talbot Avenue and Morton Street experienced only a 7 percent vacancy rate; by 1968, this had jumped to 19 percent, and by 1974, fully half of the businesses and apartments stood empty. The Mattapan Organization, formed in 1967, tried valiantly to curtail panic selling just south of this area, but the group was dissolved in 1969. The city of Boston also tried to help, awarding the "Franklin Field Neighborhood Business District" $45,000 in demolition grants to try to eliminate the eyesore of "selected abandoned stores on Blue Hill Avenue." Boston's Neighborhood Housing Improvement Program dispensed 20–40 percent rebates to residents for housing rehabilitation investments in an attempt to "help boost lagging neighborhood confidence," while the Lena Park Community Development group belatedly received funds to provide housing counseling to area families facing potential mortgage default. The city sought federal Community Development Block Grant funds for improvements to Blue Hill Avenue sidewalks and low-interest commercial development loans, plus funds to support housing rehabilitation and energy conservation. Beyond such efforts, the BRA proposed "a major public relations effort to promote confidence on the part of current residents, and also to encourage replacement buyers to seek housing in Dorchester, Franklin Field, and Mattapan." It called upon the city to publish "promotional brochures" to highlight "the general quality of life available in this area of Boston." At the same time, the BRA fully recognized that the neighborhood's decline had already taken a dreadful toll:

> The condition of the housing stock and commercial area has caused a situation where individuals have become so depressed that neighborhood pride, individual confidence, neighborhood unity, individual goal vocation, health and welfare services have affected the mental attitudes of residents of this area. This mental depression is so obvious and so deep that the need for social service has become extremely demanding. This depressed state for individuals also affects their attitudes towards home ownership, renting, neighborhood interaction, credit and the capitalistic system of government and ultimately the family.[98]

Located at the center of such sweeping social, economic, physical, and psychic devastation, the BHA's ill-fated Franklin Field public housing project continued its own downward spiral.

THE COLLAPSE OF FRANKLIN FIELD

By the mid-1970s, Franklin Field's residents as a group were the most economically desperate in the entire BHA system. An "alarmingly high" 95 percent of households lacked a wage-earner (a number higher than in any other Boston project), and 85 percent were headed by a single parent. For every adult male legally residing in the development, there were eleven children present. Nearly half of the households in the development were headed by persons under the age of thirty—a figure more than twice the Authority-wide average. Conversely, another one-third of household heads were over the age of sixty, also above the BHA average. Both segments of this bifurcated population faced distinct vulnerabilities. The incomes of residents of Franklin Field were among the lowest at any BHA property. Nearly two-thirds of households depended on AFDC payments—twice the BHA average—and the number of such households had grown by 92 percent since 1969. By 1975 more than half of all Franklin Field households had fallen more than a month behind in their rent. This uncommonly needy population nonetheless received "extremely limited" direct community services; even the project's day-care center—located in a basement—had to be shut down following repeated break-ins. More generally, as one report put it, "those services that are provided as part of the larger service delivery system are often inadequate, ill-designed, overlapping and uncoordinated." To the BHA, all this resulted in a thoroughly destructive living environment characterized by "tenant apathy, hopelessness, and helplessness."[99]

Tenants—98 percent of whom were nonwhite by 1975—continued to complain to the BHA and to the local police throughout the 1970s, with little relief. At one community meeting with BHA representatives in December 1974, Franklin Field resident Essie Johnson described repeated break-ins, reporting that many tenants had resorted to hiring house-sitters to guard their apartments whenever they ventured out to shop or take children to day care. A nascent Tenant Task Force with three voting members organized a system of building captains to help with cleaning, painting, and fixing lights in common areas but managed to staff fewer than half of the project's entryways. Most tenants were either too traumatized or too hopeless to even attend community meetings. Many such tenants relied on Marilyn Rollins to serve as their spokesperson. Rollins, a nurse from nearby Boston State Hospital who visited the project to provide assistance and counseling to parents and children, told BHA officials that conditions at Franklin Field had become "deplorable"; tenants suffered from unlit corridors and undrained sewage; large rats roamed the buildings; and a number of children had needed to have large roaches removed from their ears. The place, she concluded, had become "an absolute jungle." In response, BHA officials blamed both their own staff and the tenants. "We don't have any money to assist the projects," one BHA representative stated. "Maintenance staff doesn't care. They are only interested in collecting a pay check. Lights have been on order for three years. They have just started putting them up but we wouldn't venture to say when they might complete the job." The BHA official also struck out at residents, claiming that more than a hundred had refused to let exterminators into their apartments to do their job: "We don't know what's wrong with those people. They seem to be afraid to open their doors for their own good."[100] The BHA administrator's own interpretation of the security situation was less than wholly reassuring: "Our honest assessment of the Franklin Field area is that we meet our security standards at times."[101]

In 1975 a BRA report blamed Franklin Field's decline on a "lack of maintenance and modernization" and noted that increasing vacancies also detracted from the project's "image and security." "If these trends continue," the city's planning and development agency commented, "fewer and fewer people will be willing to live there if any other choices exist"; as a result, Franklin Field could become a "center of deterioration and crime."[102] The BHA's own State of the

Development Report for 1975 ranked Franklin Field's "problem score" nineteenth out of the twenty-three developments it evaluated, calling attention to the project's deferred maintenance and high levels of crime and fear. In 1975, apartments turned over at an annual rate of 22 percent, but the housing authority proved incapable of re-renting many vacated units. A major effort to reduce vacancies that year briefly managed to cut the vacancy rate to 1 percent, but it soon ballooned to 20 percent by 1978, and 32 percent in 1979, finally peaking at 40 percent in 1982. When a team from the BHA master's office paid a site visit to Franklin Field in June 1977, they found a "number of open vacant units with no windows" and heard a litany of complaints from the site manager, Rupert Garvin. Garvin said he could get an electrician once a week, but that the fellow rarely had the necessary parts, served too many projects, and "has no loyalty to or understanding of any one of them." Other work orders were phrased so generally (for example, "repair plumbing") that they yielded many wasted calls; often, a tenant was not home to let the workmen in when they came because the tenant had never been notified. Garvin added that most maintenance supervisors were unqualified, used the very cheapest materials, and gave their increasingly resentful craftspeople no useful input. Even worse, Garvin claimed he could get a plasterer "maybe once in 6 months" ("it's like going to heaven"), and that he would only come for court-ordered work. "Tenants are realizing that they will get certain repairs only if they go to court," Garvin noted, "and are doing that increasingly." Although he understood why they did so, he was offended that "squeaky wheels get the grease." He told the master that he could fill forty of Franklin Field's vacancies if only he had refrigerators to put in the apartments.[103]

Tenants who met with the master blamed vandalism on other tenants, but they pointed the finger at BHA employees for stealing appliances. They complained that "maintenance staff spend more time resting than working," and that Garvin "doesn't walk the project enough." The tenants also expressed the view that the manager doled out maintenance attention inequitably, with the Tenant Task Force members receiving special consideration. A later study of BHA maintenance practices concluded that such intraproject inequities paled before the larger pattern of racial discrimination in the assignment of maintenance resources to particular projects. The study, conducted for the BHA's civil rights division, confirmed widespread "allegations that predominantly white developments and/ or districts receive a larger share of maintenance resources than non-white districts and developments." Wilbur Best, the director of the management zone that included Franklin Field, also concluded that "non-white developments and districts do not get the resources white ones get."[104] With favoritism and racism working in unplanned concert, Franklin Field faced a climate of widespread mutual distrust and growing destruction. More than three hundred families—all of them black or Latino—remained on the waiting list for apartments at the development, yet, increasingly, prospective tenants simply refused assignment to the devastated project if offered a vacant unit, while other tenants continued to move out without even notifying the manager.[105]

At base, according to Manager Garvin, the vacancy rate escalated because—as at West Broadway and elsewhere—the Authority could not manage to re-rent apartments before they were vandalized: "90 percent" of the time, Garvin charged, "the applicants are either not located, don't respond, or are no longer interested. During this period of waiting for this non-response and sending for another case, the apartment which was repaired is either seriously vandalized or demolished." "During this same period of destruction," he observed, "several persons are turning up at this office inquiring for housing, they are all turned away and referred to the Tenant Selection in the Central Office." Clearly Garvin wanted the BHA to give the local site manager complete control over filling vacancies.[106] This did not happen, however, and by 1982, when redevelopment finally became a reality, 40 percent of Franklin Field's apartments stood empty.

As neighborhood conditions worsened and BHA maintenance efforts collapsed, the physical fabric of the Franklin Field project declined ever more rapidly. At a place where faulty construction had caused building systems to deteriorate as early as the 1950s, the added pressures of aging structures, inadequate funding, and incompetent maintenance staffs made matters worse with every passing year. Even when the BHA received and allocated modernization funds, nothing guaranteed that these monies would be appropriately spent. In 1975 a Finance Committee report found that Franklin Field had been allocated $710,709 in modernization funds, but that almost half that amount had remained unexpended; moreover, the BHA often billed the same labor costs twice or paid for work that was not completed. In many cases, buildings lacked not only long-promised security doors but any exterior doors at all. In 1978, the BHA acknowledged that "in many instances facilities are not fit for human use or habitation," owing to vandalism and lack of maintenance: "Specifically, the buildings are not weather tight, requiring major repairs to roofs, parapet doors, entrance doors and windows. In many occupied dwelling units, walls and ceilings are severely cracked with much falling plaster, and bathroom and kitchen areas are inadequately ventilated."[107] From 1975 to 1978, tenants reported 42 different roof leaks, most of which the BHA seemed unable to repair. By 1979, when the housing authority inspected buildings in response to another round of roof leaks, they found roofs "loaded with debris"—not only things like broken glass, bottles, cans, and rags, but such detritus as wagon wheels, tree stumps, doors, table tops, and a TV antenna embedded into the roof surface.[108] In September 1979 alone, the BHA faced 691 separate active work orders at the development. Tenants blamed the BHA for poor maintenance, while the BHA blamed maintenance problems on poor tenants.

In some cases, the tenants themselves took the lead in criticizing other tenants. Tenant Task Force Chairperson Gladys Sanders complained to the BHA tenant-selection chief, John Murphy, about the inadequacies of tenants transferred to Franklin Field from other developments, especially those assigned to vacant one-bedroom units. She called for the BHA to "rent those apartments to single persons such as student nurses and college students rather than to persons on General Relief and SSI because in the past we have only gotten alcoholics or worst— Drug Addicts." "The Task Force goal," she continued, "is to upgrade the class of people moving into public housing, rather than excepting [sic] what no one else wants."[109] To Sanders, Franklin Field faced a severe public-neighbor problem. Desperate to fill vacancies, the BHA tenanted empty apartments with persons judged to be further destabilizing the project.

Interviews conducted with long-time Franklin Field residents suggest that the project's steepest decline began only after 1970. Among two dozen black interviewees who moved in between 1962 and 1979, those who arrived before 1970 uniformly recall viewing their new home very positively; those who arrived thereafter carry much darker memories. To those who arrived in the 1960s, Franklin Field was "clean and peaceful, a beautiful place where most of the neighbors watch out for you"; it was a place "where everybody used to stick together, without as much violence"; it had "real neighbors, and we could mix with white people"; it was "friendly, much quieter, and children could play basketball outside, even after dark." Through the mid-1960s, Ruth Botts, a neighbor of Franklin Field, recalls, "I remember that African American families could still come in with pride. I don't think we even called them 'projects'; we just thought they lived in brick houses. There was no fear about walking through there to get to the Field." Janie Gibbs, who arrived at the development in 1971 and would later become one of Franklin Field's principal tenant leaders, initially viewed the development as a place where management was "handled with firmness and respect." "As the years passed and as the development became predominantly African American," however, Gibbs saw "numerous changes"—"management of the development fell way below any decent standard. Tenants had to suffer unbelievable conditions: broken windows, no hot water, no heat when it was needed, no response to emergencies."[110]

Those who arrived after Gibbs noticed the negative changes right from the start. One who came in 1972 as a twelve-year-old chiefly remembers a sense of profound disorientation: "My first impression was that the buildings looked alike—I got lost when coming home from school. The only way I could find my building was words written on the back door." Another 1972 arrival recalled that her car was stolen by kids from the project; a third comments that "the whites moved out and services got worse"; a fourth remembers a "rough, depressed area, lots of crime, lots of drugs, a scary place." After 1975 the reports grew even more grim. One resident who came to Franklin Field in 1976 remembers thinking the decision was a big mistake: "I wished I had never accepted it. I hated this place. The apartment was painted an ugly gray color, and I spent a lot of money staying away." A ten-year-old newcomer in 1978 remembers "hunting down big rats, [living with] some disrespectful kids, and some people who needed help mentally."[111] As always, tenants struggled to separate the physical conditions of the project from the social conditions of those who lived there or paid unwelcome visits.

Planning and design consultants who were asked to assess the development concluded that the buildings and the site were "largely worn out" and had become "seriously inadequate for the needs of the families now living there." The common stairwells that served twelve apartments were "unworkable for families with many children." With small apartments and no on-site recreation facilities, the hallways inevitably had become indoor play areas, leading to lapses of security and maintenance problems. The brick facing of the buildings continued to spall away in many places, while basements had become "useless trash collectors with no security."

Inside the apartments, tenants struggled with small kitchens and with bedrooms that could not fit two twin beds, dressers, and desks. The units had no dining rooms and the living rooms were laid out to function as hallways. Even the largest apartments had only a single bathroom, and they lacked hookups for washers or dryers. More conceptually, the apartments had "no useful relationship between inside and outside" and "no outdoor private space for small children's play or other family use." With so little definition of territory and so little attention given to maintenance, the site conditions had continued to degrade. By the late 1970s, the only "landscape" that remained around the buildings consisted of concrete walks, abandoned drying yards, expanses of dirt, and broken asphalt parking lots—occupied by derelict or temporarily out-of-service cars or, in some cases, used by car thieves for hiding stolen vehicles. Unlit and so dangerous that women walking alone avoided them even during the day, these parking areas could not even accommodate children at play.[112]

By the end of the 1970s, two dozen residents who were interviewed years later all agreed that conditions at Franklin Field had reached their lowest point. Their memories echo the comments made at public meetings at the time. Everyone suffered from issues of building maintenance—leaks, dirt, odors, broken or insecure windows and doors, problems with rats and "thousands of roaches," the absence of mailboxes, and apartment vacancies. Despite such conditions, several residents took pains to point out that the interiors of their apartments, against all odds, were still "all right." In particular, they praised the solidity of the walls ("more theft proof," "heavy duty," "the real McCoy"), and the quality of the heating.

Unfortunately, things continued to heat up beyond the walls of the project, as the neighborhood continued to decline in use-value to Franklin Field residents. In Franklin Field and its neighborhood, ongoing residential disinvestment carried consequences for the broader commercial viability of the area. Although Franklin Field residents could, in theory, walk to a small laundromat, a storefront variety store, and some sandwich shops, to reach any large commercial area required a round-trip bus ride of about an hour, not counting time spent shopping. The MBTA made matters worse in December 1978 when, without notifying local residents of its plans, it discontinued the Franklin Field bus service that had provided elderly residents with a lifeline to services for more than seven years. The curtailment, ostensibly due to low ridership, left many residents a long distance from the nearest bus line; some claimed that "the cancellation made it virtually impossible for them to go shopping or keep medical appointments." Two months later, following protests by a Mattapan state senator, the service was resumed.[113] Once again, the residents of Franklin Field had to fight more than their share of battles, and often had to fight the same ones repeatedly.

Meanwhile, even with bus service, the nearest supermarket was very remote, so residents instead reluctantly supported two on-site "stores"—one in a truck near the elderly complex, and one operating out of an apartment. As one consultant observed, "These stores charge outrageous prices, the advantages of proximity being great." The Blue Hill Avenue situation continued to deteriorate—with commercial vacancy reaching more than 50 percent—and contributed increasingly little to the needs of Franklin Field residents.[114]

Franklin Field Park, seemingly the development's most benign neighbor, also remained a liability. A BRA report found that parts of the park were "nothing more than weeds," calling it a blight that "lowers both the quality of the area and the amount of active space."[115] Franklin Field residents resisted using the park because of poor conditions and because there was no one at the development to organize recreational activities. Parents reported that their children were often harassed or physically abused on the other side of the park because of territorial claims established by neighborhood youths, often those who lived at Franklin Hill and viewed the field as a boundary line. In addition to concerns about "turf," residents cited other kinds of physical dangers in crossing the park: automobiles and pedestrians shared the same narrow unlit path, one that the city did not even bother to plow after snowstorms. On weekdays during the warmer months, residents reported, "young men not from the development hang out in the vicinity of the basketball court and edge of the field, drinking, smoking and making life difficult for the residents of Westview and Stratton Streets." On the weekends, the influx of park visitors deprived residents of parking places and caused them to fear that their cars would be vandalized if they parked on Westview Street, facing the field. Even as Franklin Field residents themselves felt excluded from the park, continued heavy weekend use by the general public frequently spilled over into the development, as unthinking visitors used the project for waste disposal and for relieving themselves. One former Franklin Field manager recalled the "awful way that the community treated the public housing development." Those who played soccer or cricket in the park on Sundays would "run across the street and urinate in the hallways or in bushes." Meanwhile, she noted, neighboring homeowners "would throw their trash in the dumpster and then call me to complain about overflowing dumpsters. I finally said to the [maintenance] guys, 'let's go look through the trash.' I made them put the gloves on and then I could knock on [the complainer's] door and say, 'Well, John Q. Homeowner, you called me last week, and I have a bag of your trash in my dumpster.'" In increasing ways, the relations between the public neighborhood and its surroundings continued to slide.[116]

Bounded by a neighborhood that seemed to have lost all its once plentiful amenities, Franklin Field's economically strapped residents lacked the social service
connections that might have helped them cope. No programs operated on-site,
and those in the surrounding area were few, underfunded, and had long waiting
lists. In terms of day care, adult education, job placement, and training referral,
the needs of Franklin Field's tenants remained entirely unmet.

The vast majority of BHA family projects faced comparable social, economic,
and physical conditions in the late 1970s. With the Authority headed toward receivership, the BHA itself judged that only two of its twenty-five family developments were still "sound." Six others were "slipping," four more were "in danger,"
and all the rest—including West Broadway, Commonwealth, and Franklin Field—
were already judged "seriously distressed." The BHA viewed its developments
for the elderly more optimistically, finding that 1,950 units in sixteen developments were "sound," 855 units in nine developments were "slipping," 531 units in
seven developments were "in danger," and only 447 units in four developments
were "seriously distressed." Not surprisingly, the elderly housing projects at
Franklin Field fell into the last category.[117] Slowly and fitfully, the time for action
drew near.

Lurching toward Redevelopment

The Racial Politics of Redevelopment Funding

In 1978 the Massachusetts Department of Community Affairs (DCA) considered
which few developments would receive state modernization funds under a new
pilot program. Greater Boston Legal Services attorneys appealed directly to Governor Michael Dukakis to include funding for Franklin Field, while also calling
for West Broadway to be funded at a level adequate to meet its needs. In essence,
the attorneys simply staked out Boston's claim upon statewide public housing
funds by emphasizing the high political costs for the city if the state failed to act
equitably. They recognized that Senate President Bulger's wishes made funding
for D Street already a done deal, but they foresaw dire consequences if the state
funded *only* the South Boston project: "It cannot be forgotten that the tenants at
D. St. are predominantly white and the tenants at Franklin Field are predominantly black. Any decision by DCA that would provide 'pilot' funding to one of
these projects while denying it to the other, would seriously aggravate racial tensions in public housing in Boston." Soon thereafter, the state chose to contribute

major funds to both West Broadway and Franklin Field. As Harry Spence, who took over the BHA as receiver-administrator in 1980, later put it, at a time when racial tensions were still high over busing, "it would have been simply too crude and too evidently racist to give a big chunk of money to a South Boston development and not do something for a black development." Bernie Stewart, who served as the state's coordinator of the pilot program, saw it much the same way: "We were not far removed from court-ordered desegregation" and needed "some balance in terms of minority and 'majority' communities." DCA was staffed by "'60s liberals," Stewart commented, and "didn't need to be told this by the legislature."[118]

As a result, Franklin Field received its funding not because the BHA could make a convincing case that a redevelopment investment would most likely succeed, but because the state's South Boston delegation needed to cover itself politically. The matter came to an even bigger head in 1980 once Senate President Bulger inserted a $20 million set-aside into the state's housing bill to fund the first phase of the West Broadway redevelopment; the BHA saw an opportunity to play Boston's racial politics for its own gain. Spence sent his deputy John Washek to ask State Legislator Doris Bunte to help get Franklin Field included in the pending legislation. Bunte, a black former BHA tenant who had previously served as a member of the BHA Board during its brief interlude of tenant-oriented progressivism in the early 1970s, viewed herself as a champion of public housing. She "never went for just South Boston, obviously," and jumped at the chance to include Franklin Field, even though it was not expressly located in her district. "I don't think anybody intended there to be a second [Boston] development," Bunte comments, "but I presented myself as the public housing person, and there was going to be a second development because we amended it on there." Even though she "didn't have the clout of the people who had gotten the promises of funding for D Street, the pressure came from me because I was the public housing person."[119]

Harry Spence downplays his own involvement in the funding effort, since the financial linkage had originated in pilot program politics prior to the receivership. "When D St. was identified as the one they were going to put money into, Franklin Field went along with the package. We had nothing to do with that choice," he says. Once the odd coupling of West Broadway and Franklin Field had been established, however, Spence observed, "Franklin Field always got kind of a free ride on whatever D Street got. If you give money to D Street, you had to give money to Franklin Field."[120]

Soon afterward, the BHA's own sophisticated study entitled "Site Selection Criteria for Substantial Rehabilitation"—intended to identify the developments where investment could have "the greatest impact as well as the greatest likelihood of success"—revealed the immensity of the challenge that this largely unsolicited statehouse "gift" had presented to the Authority. On the basis of a study of the BHA's ten most troubled developments (a group that also included both West Broadway and Commonwealth), the BHA's own planning department ranked Franklin Field as the one place where redevelopment would be *least* likely to succeed. In many categories of analysis, it ranked at or near the bottom. In terms of "site accessibility," for instance, Franklin Field suffered from its distance to any subway line or nearby shopping. Its surrounding neighborhood ranked very low in terms of public and private investment in housing improvement and dead last in terms of high unemployment (21.6 percent). Ironically, given the deteriorated condition of housing and the histrionics of the BBURG experience, the project gained points for being located in a neighborhood with an unusually high percentage of owner-occupied buildings.

Most of all, though, Franklin Field's rating suffered from the way the BHA assessed the characteristics of its tenants, who were seen as contributing heavily to its problems of management and maintenance. By this point, fully 92 percent of households were female-headed, and 74 percent of all residents were children—by far the highest child-adult ratio of any development. Only 3 percent of Franklin Field's adults reported working, a markedly smaller percentage than at any other BHA development (all of which had at least 10–15 percent of tenants reporting employment). None of this ratings exercise really mattered, however, since Franklin Field had already been preselected by the state for redevelopment.

Even though tenants had helped to prepare the pilot program application, achieving a successful "turnaround" appeared extremely difficult. As Spence comments, "Franklin Field was much the hardest, above all, because it had no meaningful tenant organization whatsoever." DCA's pilot program coordinator, when asked twenty years after the fact about the choice of Franklin Field, merely shrugs, speculating that the DCA may have been given encouragement by the "umpteenth plan for the rehab of Blue Hill Avenue" but conceding, "Maybe we were naive."[121]

FROM PILOT PROGRAM TO REDEVELOPMENT

In 1980 the BHA appointed Basil Tommy, a black South African, as project manager for the Franklin Field redevelopment. To Tommy, the Franklin Field community he met seemed "a non-community." This was more than a matter of "apathy," he recalls; the residents also exhibited "a lot of antagonism and antipathy . . . toward each other and certainly a great deal of hostility toward the Authority." The tenants had endured well over a decade of neglect of development maintenance, and they continued to blame the BHA for inadequate security. Even when selecting a consultant to help them prepare the pilot program application, the tenants felt frustrated; the DCA disqualified their top two choices (out of ten bids) because other housing authorities in Worcester and Springfield already had them under contract. Whereas the West Broadway redevelopment got off to a highly productive start through its relationship with the Boston Urban Observatory, at Franklin Field the tenants struggled to find supportive partners and viewed both the city and the state housing bureaucracies as serious impediments.[122]

As Harry Spence sees it, the BHA had to take the lead because Franklin Field "had no tenant organization, and we were having to try and build one from scratch." He was constantly struck by the contrast with West Broadway. "D St., in spite of high levels of violence, had always been able to turn out 200–300 people for a public meeting. You could go to meetings at Franklin Field and three people would come if you were lucky." Pilot Program Coordinator Stewart found much the same thing: "You'd have a meeting where you got ten to fifteen to twenty people, but at the next meeting there'd be six, and four of them would be faces you never saw before." He recalled multiple discussions "where the theme was 'weakness of the tenant organization'"; even Gladys Sanders lamented that it was "very difficult to get people involved." Spence viewed the lack of resident involvement as a symptom of "a very deeply discouraged community" that remained "geographically isolated, on that bombed-out stretch of Blue Hill Avenue." To Bernie Stewart, residents seemed to have "given up"; "there was a sense of resignation around the meetings," despite the availability of money and organizing efforts. Even though "there was some genuine spirit on the part of some people to want to stick in there and make sure things got better, you just never get the sense that you did in the other developments that the residents had taken part ownership of what was going on. No matter how many meetings or discussions, community organizers or not, they never truly bought in to the 'ownership' piece, which is so fundamental to the turnaround of a development like that."[123] Spence, who "spent loads of time at Franklin Field trying to get the tenant organization off the ground," felt that the community had internalized all the worst things being said about its members. At early meetings, he recalls, people were saying, "Why are you doing this? We're just going to destroy it again."[124] As one tenant leader, Janie Gibbs, put it: "People don't think very much of themselves now because they're living in such bad conditions."[125] Despite the lack of tenant response, Stewart insists that the state and the city always afforded Franklin Field an "equal commitment."

Leslie Newman, who served as the tenant plaintiffs' lead attorney throughout the receivership, spent an "enormous amount of time at Franklin Field," beginning in late 1980. She did so not because the litigation demanded it but because she saw the need for a community effort at this particular place. Newman traveled to the development by herself, sometimes as often as three or four nights a week, to seek out tenants. She helped spread leaflets around the project, urgently searching to identify the issues that would get people to attend meetings and allow Franklin Field to replicate the kind of strong tenant organizations found at D Street and elsewhere. She talked with residents about the nature of the tenant-landlord relationship, and explained that if the landlord failed to deliver, tenants didn't have to pay all the rent that the Authority said they owed. Newman found one "extremely powerful" tenant leader in Peggy Santos, who was quite active in the citywide Tenants Policy Council. Unfortunately, Santos was not representative of most Franklin Field tenants. Meeting places shifted because the micropolitics of the development determined where they could be held; some tenants would boycott a meeting just because of its location. Sometimes meetings had to be held in Peggy Santos's apartment, and there had to be "premeetings" beforehand to try to minimize the likelihood of further setbacks. Lacking any breadth or depth of tenant involvement, Newman later observed, Franklin Field was "not poised for redevelopment" but remained "entrenched in its debilitated state."[126]

As the pilot program got under way, the BHA struggled to manage the site. In the first six months of 1980 alone, the Authority assigned Franklin Field three different managers, and the development went through three different pilot program coordinators. Despite the leadership flux, plans proceeded for rehabilitation of scattered vacant units, electrical upgrades, consolidation of vacancies, and substantial renovation of the first eighty-four units. Meanwhile, the state legislature established a separate bonding instrument that enabled Massachusetts to use federal Section 8 subsidies, in addition to state modernization funds, for public housing redevelopment. Beyond the initial pilot program grant, the BHA and the state now marshaled more than $20 million in additional funds, judged to be sufficient to rehabilitate the entire project.[127] Although full financing of redevelopment appeared to be in place in 1980, the entire package would not be clarified and secured until 1983. In the meantime, the BHA lacked a secure and well-managed environment in which to carry out redevelopment.

Sandra Henriquez—a young black woman who had worked for BHA Master Bob Whittlesey since 1977 and had joined the BHA itself after the receivership began, became the manager of Franklin Field in June 1980, just as full-scale redevelopment plans were being clarified. Her first day on the job was anything but auspicious. She arrived early, wearing a "nice black suit with a little bow tie and my patent leather heels," and wandered into the unlocked, wide open stairwell of a building; once inside she immediately slipped in dog excrement. By the time she met with maintenance staff later in the day, she felt quite familiar with the project—its unlocked doors, its dark and dirty hallways, and its "chest-high" weeds. The maintenance personnel she met exuded a "warm camaraderie." They were "not malicious"; they just had markedly low expectations about their jobs. Their guiding notion was "If we just do the minimum, it's OK because these are poor people." Henriquez found it a major challenge "just trying to get control of the property, and get people responsive on a timely basis." Frustrated residents barraged her with "abusive phone calls," and she discovered that the few who were active in the tenant organization were also paid employees of the BHA. Henriquez found this relationship "difficult" because they were "both my employees and also my constituents," so "taking any action with them as employees" was especially problematic. To her relief, the BHA promoted her to area management director a few months later.[128]

As management problems continued, tenant concerns about personal security remained acute. The residents made at least three proposals for new security initiatives, including a pilot program for building captains and uniformed tenants, all of which were rejected for funding reasons. Residents told consultants hired by the BHA to assess "security in public housing" that crime was their biggest problem, blaming both residents and nonresidents of all ages for assaults, burglary, auto theft, and vandalism. Management staff blamed nonresident juveniles for most problems, although the elderly often complained about kids from the family part of the development. The worst problems, according to Franklin Field management, were burglary, alcoholism, tenant fights, and "purse snaps." All this led to an environment of "high crime" and "high fear," the consultants concluded.[129]

In 1980, twenty-six-year-old Tony Fonseca—who had grown up in the development between 1954 and 1968—returned to his old neighborhood in a new role: team police officer assigned to the Franklin Field and Franklin Hill developments. He used stories of his own upbringing at the development to make a connection with current teens, yet he also had to tell them just how much had changed. As Fonseca recalls, "Living here then and living here now are two different things altogether. At the age of thirteen, I did not have to worry about losing my life, or worry about making my way past drug dealers in the hallway, or worry about getting beat up if I didn't belong to a gang, or consider 'should I carry a gun, or should I not?'" Thirteen-year-old kids at Franklin Field during the early 1980s "had to seriously contemplate those things."[130]

Basil Tommy insisted that any redevelopment team hired to transform the project would need to be very experienced in community participation, so that the redevelopment would not only change the buildings but also "develop the community." He wanted the residents to feel that "the end product was going to be theirs" and that they had been empowered to make "many of the decisions that led to that product." Tommy and the tenants' representative Peggy Santos agreed that the team of Carr, Lynch Associates (CLA) and Wallace, Floyd, Ellenzweig, Moore (WFEM) seemed the best choice, and they helped convince others at the BHA of their view.

Steve Carr and David Wallace submitted their proposal in December 1980, calling the Franklin Field redevelopment project "a realistic opportunity to demonstrate that public housing does not have to be a dehumanizing environment." Their team included not only the principals from two distinguished firms (a group that included the world famous urbanist Kevin Lynch), but also the well-respected landscape architect Michael van Valkenburgh and the environmental psychologist Florence Ladd, famous for her studies of minority teenagers. Wallace, Floyd headed up the building design, while Carr, Lynch took charge of the site design and community-participation issues. The CLA-WFEM team rejected the claims of "housing experts" who insisted that "a development such as Franklin Field which concentrates large, very low income, single parent families in a project big enough to be a small neighborhood but lacking in social and commercial services, set in a larger deteriorating area which also lacks commercial services as well as employment opportunities, cannot be viable." This conventional view, they opined, would lead only to "defeatist attitudes." They suspiciously viewed "the recent excitement about ideas for making such environments 'defensible' instead of 'pleasant' or even 'livable'" as "an extension of this attitude." "It seems to be forgotten," Carr and Wallace wrote, "that those residing in public housing developments seek an environment which provides many of the same values and opportunities which are enjoyed by wealthier members of the society." Their proposal not only spoke about design issues but actively raised the "related institutional issues which must also be addressed in the planning process." They wished to take on the full range of tenant needs, seeking ways to reduce crime and drug and alcohol abuse; to meet needs for social services, including job referral and training, child care, education, and health services; and to develop an effective structure for ongoing management and maintenance. "Physical and institutional decisions," they averred, "must be joined in a single strategy." With those words, they sought and won the daunting assignment to redevelop Franklin Field.[131]

Not everyone at the BHA agreed with the choice of CLA-WFEM. In selecting them, Tommy and Spence had to override the strong objections of the BHA's deputy administrator for construction, who preferred a different team, one more limited to a bricks-and-mortar approach. The disagreement, Tommy observes, "started the project off badly" because "the branch that saw to the implementation of the design felt slighted that my word rather than theirs was taken." In a bureaucracy trying to regain credibility, pettiness carried a price: "In a sense, they wanted the project to fail, so they could tell Harry, 'see, we told you so.'" BHA Design Consultant Gayle Epp, who watched the "in-house fighting" develop over the selection of the architect, worried right from the start that the Franklin Field process lacked the "necessary consensus building with all the partners." Despite all the efforts to develop a participatory process, "there was not a great deal of trust developed between the housing authority and the residents."[132]

In June 1981, after several months of internal meetings between BHA staff and CLA-WFEM that did not appear to include residents, the design consultants resolutely sought to bring the tenants on board. By this time, to a large extent, they used meetings with tenant representatives to "explain/clarify" the major design and programming decisions that had already been made.[133] Although their planning process made a real push to involve tenants, it did so belatedly, at a time when budget constraints had become increasingly evident. Carr, Lynch's community planner, Imani Kazana, circulated a letter (in English) to all Franklin Field households, informing them about the upcoming redevelopment and affirming that CLA and WFEM wanted "to include as much participation by the residents as possible." The letter included a "Resident Fact Sheet" with questions about age and employment status for each household to fill out if members were interested in participating. CLA-WFEM wished to "select a representative group of about 50 residents (ages 15 and above) to work with our team in about six meetings during June and July." The planners told tenants to expect a voice on such "broad issues as placement of recreation space and fine details such as the colors of paint for the interiors."[134] This strategy seems to have yielded sufficient tenant participation to proceed, but it fell short of BHA hopes.

To improve tenant participation, the BHA proposed a "community capacity building program" and used $50,000 of the pilot program money to hire a community organizer and two assistants. The Authority asked the community organizer to develop a program of tenant responsibility for maintenance and security of common areas, produce a community newsletter, increase the presence of local social service providers, work with youths in the development, strengthen the Task Force "and assist it to develop a cooperative relationship with management," and solicit additional grants from private sources.[135] From Tommy's perspective, the first tenant organizer, Phil Horne, was "a disaster." He saw himself as "only being effective if he badmouthed the Authority. He'd make excessive demands that the BHA could never meet and that he knew they could never meet." His approach was to get tenants excited about things they could never have and then assert that the BHA was "willful in denying them these sorts of things."[136]

Carr, Lynch and the BHA also actively tried to engage the surrounding Dorchester community in discussions about how to redevelop the project. When community representatives came to meetings, however, their chief goal was to shift all access to the development to the Field-facing side of the project, thereby minimizing any potential neighborhood contact with Franklin Field residents. The designers, however—like their counterparts working at West Broadway—assiduously argued for ways to integrate the development into its neighborhood, hoping to make the Stratton Street edge seem more like the private housing across the street. The viewpoints were fundamentally irreconcilable; Franklin Field's neighbors—despite their own problems—still wished to remain at least as separate from the project as they had been prior to redevelopment. Tommy found their viewpoint to be "psychologically understandable": "People who live in the housing development are the failures in the society. They end up there because they don't have the wherewithal or the ability to do anything better. And so, even though you're just one step removed economically and otherwise, it's important for your psyche to keep that distance." Once again, the stigma of the public neighbor reemerged.[137]

The longest policy discussions centered on questions of "unit mix"; namely, what proportion of various sized apartments to build and how best to arrange them. Not simply an architectural issue, questions of unit mix always carried social and policy overtones. To accept the high demand for large four- or five-bedroom apartments would, in practice, be to increase "the probability of anti-social behavior and overcrowding (and their associated strain on management resources)." Yet the BHA also recognized that large low-income families desperately needed the resource of public housing. Basil Tommy observed that 92 percent of families on the waiting list for large apartments consisted of poor minority households—"a combination of factors that virtually guarantees that they will never find adequate housing in the private sector." "Does the Authority," he wondered, "have a responsibility towards these families?" The consensus seemed to be that the redevelopment ought to accommodate the needs of existing tenants for large units, but that Franklin Field should not be allowed to become a haven for more such families.

Conversely, the Authority was tempted to increase the percentage of one-bedroom units, noting that white families on the waiting list were twice as likely as nonwhites to want small units. By manipulating the unit mix, some contended, it might be possible to encourage racial integration. Others recognized that the mere presence of one-bedroom apartments would not be sufficient to re-attract white tenants to Franklin Field. Instead, having too many one-bedroom apartments would more likely attract an excess of "handicapped, disabled, or displaced" single individuals.[138] In any case, the various meetings cast further doubt on the BHA's initial goals of 400 redeveloped units with pitched roofs, a large community center, and a day-care facility serving 90 children. The conflict between high expectations and clear budget constraints was readily apparent even before the team tried to bring residents on board.

The BHA's redevelopment consultants faced a protracted disagreement over what to do with the 160 units of Franklin Field housing for the elderly. Perennial tensions between the elderly and the young people living in the family development continued to fuel fears about security and isolation. By the early 1980s, the BHA exacerbated these problems by placing nonelderly disabled people, many of whom suffered from disruptive substance abuse problems, into the senior part of the development. CLA-WFEM referred to it as a "ghost town" where "the presence of alcoholics and other disturbed persons makes for a difficult social ambiance." Initially, the design team planned to convert the elderly section into additional housing for families, but eventually outside consultants convinced Spence to retain the housing for seniors. Only in the 1990s did the BHA belatedly begin this conversion. In the meantime, the retention of elderly housing meant that the designers had inadvertently promised residents more family units than they could deliver.[139]

By late September 1981, the BHA realized that every alternative plan the redevelopment team proposed would greatly exceed the construction budget of $24.5 million. BHA calculations, not shared with the design team at the time, estimated that meeting the agreed-upon program requirements could cost nearly $32 million. As the BHA's chief architect, Barbara Manford, lamented in October, "The budget problems at Franklin Field are very real." The BHA suggested many changes to bring down costs. In particular, the Authority objected to the CLA-WFEM proposal for a community center, seen as "far in excess of what is practical or economically feasible." Initial talk of a teen center, balconies, a large day-care facility, and a convenience store slowly succumbed to harsh economic realities. Throughout the last half of 1981, the design team and the BHA struggled to retain the principal aims of the original plan: larger apartments with minimal use of shared entries and direct ground access to a semi-private yard for as many large units as possible, and a site design that emphasized "defined areas equipped for non-conflicting use by various age groups," all part of a design approach that favored "integration with the neighborhood." To save costs and still produce the desired mix of apartments with large rooms, the overall target for units gradually dropped, from 400 to 387 to 375.

In some instances, political necessities outweighed potential cost savings. The architects proposed a more logical construction phasing plan than what the BHA had previously devised, but they had to stick with the BHA plan because tenants had already been notified of their relocation status. Any change would cause "enormous confusion and dissatisfaction" that would "severely damage the Authority's credibility." In November 1981, the design team revised its Design Concept 1 (known as the "'Budget' alternative") to achieve still greater economy but continued to press for its preferred-but-overbudget Design Concept 2 (known as the "'Program' alternative"), because only this plan actually met the terms of the initial redevelopment goals. Ultimately, the designers recognized that they would need to go with the "budget" plan, but they hoped it could be improved enough to "achieve minimal acceptability by residents." On November 23, the design team came to Franklin Field to "explain to residents the kinds of improvements that can be made at the available budget of $24.5 million and solicit their reaction to current plans." Although the design team termed the turnout "particularly good considering the cold weather," only twenty-six residents stayed through the end of the meeting and completed a questionnaire.

The CLA-WFEM team came away from the meeting convinced that residents had expressed "overall approval with the plans." Those present felt strongest about the idea of blocking off courtyards from general public access by providing fences and gates, and vehemently opposed any plan that would give only a handful of large families the privilege of private yards. Echoing the egalitarian sentiment expressed at West Broadway, they wanted "all families in a building" to "commune and create together in the 'building yard.'" In addition to these matters of security and community, the residents cared a great deal about tenant relocation during construction. Although the team had not thought to make a presentation about this aspect of the plan, tenants raised it "many, many times," expressing their dissatisfaction over how relocation was being communicated and handled. The development team observed that this aspect of redevelopment preoccupied tenants to the extent that it "interfered with their ability to focus upon planning issues." With many of the larger redevelopment issues already decided by budget constraints and at meetings where they were not present, however, it should hardly have been surprising that immediate questions of personal displacement should rank rather high as a "planning" priority for tenants. The CLA-WFEM team took note of this "serious problem area," worrying that it could have "potential negative effects for the scheduling of construction."[140]

In December, apparently ignoring tenant input about shared courtyards, the BHA pushed CLA-WFEM to have as many private yards as possible, and the designers responded with a revised "budget" scheme that was closer to the $24.5 million threshold but still would exceed it by a couple of million if the design were to include the private yards and a maximum number of duplexes for large units. Again, the consultants reiterated their opinion that funds must be devoted to community facilities, arguing that "the community facilities aimed at older children and teenagers (especially the gym-multi-purpose space) are a very important component in reducing vandalism in the development." They noted that kids from Franklin Field said they get "attacked" if they try to use existing facilities at either the Lee School or Lena Park (at the site of the former Hecht House).[141]

REDEVELOPMENT PRIORITIES: TENANT DESIGNS

Having already helped residents to hire a tenant organizer, the BHA now paid to have the tenants hire their own architect, someone to help them review and understand the design options being proposed. As 1982 began, the tenants—armed with design consultants from John Sharratt Associates—belatedly sought to influence the priorities of the redevelopment, more than a year after CLA-WFEM had commenced their work. In some cases, these priorities bore little resemblance to the tenant preferences expressed the previous fall. Tenant views, now shaped in consultation with professionals, carried a new stridency.

In mid-January, Harry Spence went to Franklin Field to meet with tenants about the redevelopment. Tenant Task Force Chairperson Peggy Santos left the meeting convinced that Spence had come to understand that "we must have social services delivered through an adequate Community Center Complex, and that the site, building, and unit designs must be based on sound safety and security considerations." In a letter to Spence confirming her interpretation of their meeting, she underscored that *"we do not want any interior public or semi-public stairs leading to apartments."* Santos praised Spence for his "support of desperately needed community space" and affirmed that tenants wanted site, building, and unit designs to be based on a townhouse concept of "private apartment front doors to the outside (street)." She assumed that Spence would "redirect" the design team to make these changes.[142]

On February 4, eleven tenants including Santos met with John Sharratt and two of his associates, joined by the community organizer Phil Horne. Residents complained that Basil Tommy had failed to order the design consultants "to change directions as a result of the community meeting with Spence," and that Tommy did not adequately convey the tenants' insistence on "community space." Sharratt told this small group of tenants (who composed Franklin Field's Redevelopment Design Committee) that their "committee needs to set priorities on where to spend money and then notify BHA and the consultants to prepare plans accordingly." He urged them to resist "accepting the consultants' budget figures as the basis for cuts" and suggested that they "tell the BHA and its consultants to find a way to build the community center by taking monies out of the site budget."[143]

Two weeks later, Santos adopted a more activist stance. In a hand-delivered letter to Spence, copied to a number of BHA and state officials and consultants, she bitterly complained that the Tenant Task Force's input had been ignored, and she stated, "We reject the plan outright until the BHA proceeds to address our concerns." Her three-page letter summarized "the major problems of the plan" as seen by tenants (views clearly influenced by the input of their design consultants). First, she objected to the "excessive site budget," seen as diverting funds from the "priority need for suitable housing and community space." Second, she criticized "inadequate building design," insisting that all units should now have "private exterior entrances" so that "we can eliminate entirely the problems found in the common, shared hallways," which "provide an opportunity for assailants to hide behind the stairs and in blind corners and to attempt break-ins without being seen." Third, she complained that the BHA now proposed only 346 redeveloped apartments, well "short of the minimum we had targeted." Finally, Santos objected to the "lack of sufficient community space," noting that the gym, multipurpose rooms, and teen center had been dropped from the budget.

Beyond these more technical questions of priorities and program, she also raised troubling questions about how the BHA viewed its tenants. Santos questioned whether "enough is being done to change the image of our buildings" and expressed the wish that Franklin Field be transformed to "make a statement of an attractive townhouse development." Even more pointedly, she objected to the BHA's intent to seek a waiver of the state building code that required two means of egress from each apartment. "As public housing residents," Santos argued, "we do not feel that we should be treated as second-class citizens and denied a second means of egress. We will continue to protest this aspect of the plan as unsafe and life-threatening." She concluded by expressing the hope that Spence would "respect our interest in this development enough" to "meet with us immediately about redirecting the consultants in their work."[144] Needless to say, the tenants were not on board.

From Basil Tommy's perspective as the BHA's redevelopment manager, the system of sponsored tenant advocacy—however valuable and necessary—had stymied cooperation. In particular, Tommy blamed the tenants' principal design consultant, Sharon Lee of John Sharratt Associates, for being "always antagonistic" and "never constructive." She took the view that "if you are engaged by the tenants, then they are your clients and the BHA is the enemy. So you always need to demonstrate that the Authority is trying to shortchange you." In reality, Tommy insists, the BHA "genuinely wanted to do right by the community" and, if anything, ran into trouble largely because Harry Spence made more promises to tenants than the BHA's budget could afford to keep. At base, Santos and the other Franklin Field tenants had wanted the new community center, and its "disappearance" left lingering resentment.[145]

Meanwhile, at a time marked by high inflation, the BHA and its consultants grew increasingly apprehensive about new delays prompted by tenant recalcitrance, fearing the loss of precious construction dollars through start-up delays. Eager to reach accommodation with the tenants, Harry Spence's deputy John Stainton replied to the letter from Santos in early March, assuring her that the BHA shared many of her concerns. He evinced hope that many of the tenants' preferences could still be met, although he remained "extremely concerned" about the cost of constructing, maintaining, and operating the proposed community facility. "It will not be in the best interest of either the Authority or the tenants of Franklin Field," Stainton warned, "to build and then not have it possible to maintain the facility." He stated that BHA staff would continue to meet with "interested residents" to "attempt to resolve this issue." He declined to reconsider the new figure of 346 redeveloped units, since "there is only a certain volume within the buildings": in substantially increasing the size of all rooms while retaining the mix of large and small apartments, he concluded, 346 redeveloped units "is what you end up with."[146]

A "Final Development Plan and Program"

A week before Stainton sent his letter to Peggy Santos, the CLA-WFEM team released its *Franklin Field Redevelopment Design Report,* detailing its "Final Development Plan and Program." The plan began by reviewing the history of CLA-WFEM's "intensive community participatory planning program," explaining that the team tried to work with tenants and the BHA to revise the plan to "fit within budget constraints with the least loss of quality of the final result." The designers immediately pointed out that the final plan fell short of meeting "two serious concerns" raised by tenants. First, they acknowledged the "elimination of the broad range of community facilities originally proposed," stating that they hoped some of these could be restored, especially if the tenants could take the lead in obtaining funds. Second, they conceded that it had been "physically and financially infeasible" to meet the tenants' request that all shared interior stairwells be eliminated and that all apartments instead be provided with individual entries directly to the outside.

Despite such shortcomings caused by the "surprising severity" of budget constraints, the design team remained "convinced that a successful turn around at

Franklin Field can be achieved." They affirmed that "most of the elements needed to bring about the transformation . . . have been maintained" and concluded that "this plan will create an environment in which life can be good." The report praised the tenants, noting that many residents "against the odds, have remained positive and ready to live and work together to bring about a better future for themselves and their children."

At the same time, however, the consultants worried about the future of a community dominated by single-parent, jobless households. They called for the BHA to re-tenant Franklin Field with a "greater age balance" and "more two-parent families" (to "provide models for other family types"), adding that "low income does not necessarily mean the poorest of the poor nor need it be restricted to those on Welfare and A.F.D.C." Yet the design team also concurred with the BHA's intention to provide for a high proportion of large families at Franklin Field, acknowledging that "even to rehouse the present population will require this." This commitment to housing many large minority families who had few housing alternatives posed a "central challenge": to "provide an environment which can facilitate the growth and development of these young people, while surviving their energetic use [of the facilities]." "Nearly as important," the designers added, "is to make what will always be a hard life easier for parents and for other older people living on site."

To meet these goals, the design team tried to rethink the project environment at every scale, from apartment interiors to neighborhood relations, with every age group kept in mind (Figs. 3.14–3.16). Room sizes in redeveloped apartments ranged from 20 to 40 percent larger than the current cramped conditions (which failed to meet HUD minimum property standards). The plan provided private entrances and backyards for nearly one-third of the apartments. It maximized the number of duplexes and triplexes with separate entrances for large families, thereby reducing the number of bedrooms per shared entry. Instead of the previous pattern of twelve units per shared stairwell, the new plan called for only three to six, depending on the size of adjacent apartments. The three-units-per-stairwell pattern, the designers noted, mimicked "the most common and successful form of low-income housing in Boston," the triple-decker. The plan balanced the mix of apartment sizes across the site, avoiding any undue concentration of children in any area, building, or hallway.

Outside the buildings, the designers proposed creating shared "building yards" for the eighteen to twenty-four families in each building. They viewed

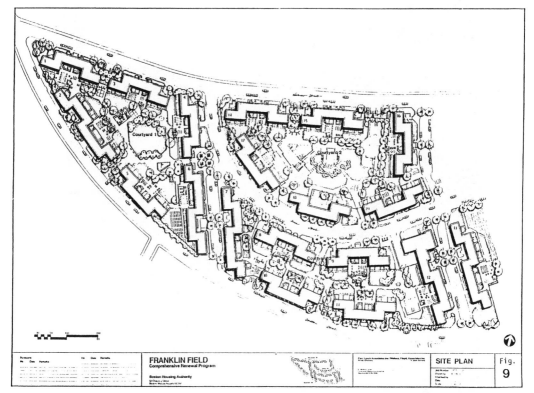

FIGURE 3.14 Site plan for the Franklin Field Comprehensive Renewal Program. The new site plan emphasized the division of the development into three large courtyard areas, with the backs of buildings (including many private yards) facing into the courtyards and the fronts organized along streets.

"spatial identification with buildings" as a means to "increase pride, vigilance, maintenance, and social cohesion." At the same time, provision of private fenced-in backyards for all ground-floor units, triplexes, and duplexes implied a very different social purpose—these would "prevent loitering near buildings and limit the incidence of graffiti at the ground level." More proactively, the backyards would also "furnish large families with play space close to home, as an extension of their interior living areas." As at West Broadway, the larger site plan for Franklin Field envisioned "a hierarchy of outdoor spaces"—private yards, common building yards, and central courtyards with walkways, structured play areas for six- to eleven-year-olds, lawns for picnics and free running play, and adult sitting areas and playgrounds for all residents within courts. These three largest court-

FIGURE 3.15 At play in one of Franklin Field's three large courtyards. Despite landscaping efforts, the large courtyards discouraged supervision and lacked the intimacy of the building yards at West Broadway.

FIGURE 3.16 Private yards and public space. Designers provided families with private yards, but many of these often went unused, often because of concerns about security.

yards, in turn, were also to be fenced and gated, so as to "control the movement of uninvited non-residents through the site." In particular, the designers felt, fencing off spaces between the buildings along Westview Street would "help keep users of Franklin Field Park from entering the housing development to dump trash or relieve themselves." One key "underlying theme" of the entire redevelopment plan, according to the CLA-WFEM team, was to make certain that this public neighborhood would be "viewed by everyone as private territory."

Even while seeking to limit access through the development, the designers reorganized the street pattern to minimize the sense of a superblock, just as their West Broadway counterparts did by reinstituting the South Boston street grid (Fig. 3.17). Franklin Field's redesigners wished all buildings to face onto streets and wanted all apartments to gain street addresses. They sought "to 'normalize' the development and break down institutional isolation" caused partly by nonresidents who "look upon this housing as public property." By channeling the north-south traffic through the development onto two new streets, they also hoped to "stop drivers from forcing their way between buildings and through yard spaces." By introducing on-street parking, they sought to bring cars "within 100 feet and within sight of their owner's apartment," while further contributing to the "normalization" of the project streetscape.

As for nonresidential facilities, the plan provided for a shared maintenance and

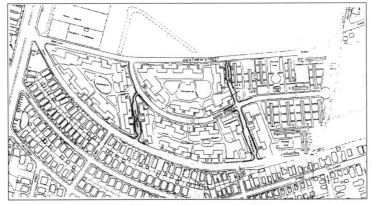

FIGURE 3.17 New street configuration to enhance integration with the neighborhood. The redevelopment plan added new streets to reduce the spatial separation between the project and its neighborhood, and to enable buildings to face streets rather than superblock interiors.

management facility. The design team also argued that "a wide range of community services and facilities would be of great importance to the success of the redevelopment," but they acknowledged that the budget only permitted development of a modest basement day-care facility and allocation of some office space for the Tenant Task Force and social service staff. Without a greater commitment to services, the designers opined, the women of this development would lack the mobility they needed to participate fully in educational and employment opportunities.[147]

More than the physical qualities of the redevelopment, the designers worried about the ability of the residents to sustain it. Only in the past few months, once paid organizers had been hired, had there been much reason for hope. Previously, as the design team assessed it, "the residents received little BHA support and they were in an uphill battle against dashed hopes and expectations from past planning." They suffered from "considerable intergroup bickering and criticism in the past that have undermined the meager possibilities for some successful action and have destroyed good feeling." They praised recent efforts "to overcome resident alienation from involvement in the Task Force and ignorance of its activities." Still, they pointed out that there was not yet a system for "meaningful tenant involvement" in building maintenance, and that communication suffered from the absence of a Spanish speaker on the management staff. Without further organizational initiatives, the redevelopment team doubted that the residents would be able to assist with the "long-term security, maintenance, fundraising, and general administration" needed at Franklin Field: "Only in the presence of a strong tenant group, for example, can the BHA hope to receive assistance in monitoring acts of vandalism. Only through a strong, broadly based organization can resources be gathered that are necessary to carry out successful recreational and day care programs."

A key barrier to successful implementation of the Franklin Field redevelopment, the CLA-WFEM team felt, inhered in the organizational structure of the Tenant Task Force itself, which they felt fostered limited involvement. "The current structure does not provide for broad-based participation or voting by the tenant community on issues," they observed. "All decisionmaking lies with the 4 member elected Task Force. The committee structure is not sufficiently defined to enable groups working on special projects to operate in a semi-autonomous manner. The Task Force Chairperson appears to function as the chairperson of most committees, a job that is too large for any one individual." Taking note of ongoing disagreements within the tenant community, the design consultants phrased the nature of their involvement with residents quite carefully. Since the "Task Force" was so closely identified with a handful of individuals, they noted on the cover of their report that what followed had been prepared "in cooperation with the Franklin Field Tenants and Task Force." At most other developments it would not have been necessary to name two different constituencies.[148]

MOVING TOWARD REDEVELOPMENT: LEADERSHIP IN FLUX

For Franklin Field Redevelopment Director Basil Tommy, the problem of tenant involvement remained a central worry. "We were hard put to scratch together a task force," he noted. In essence, "the task force was a single woman." Moreover, the model of a single woman in charge masked internal dissent over whom that woman should be. Gladys Sanders had presided over the early efforts to obtain pilot funds, followed by Peggy Santos; now, as redevelopment lurched toward commencement, Janie Gibbs took over as the new tenant leader. Because the community went through two Task Force chairpersons as the redevelopment got under way, Tommy observes, "there was a lot of ill feeling, almost a wall between two sides supporting different candidates." Internal "dissension and dissatisfaction" among tenants certainly damaged the consensus-building process: "when the Task Force person who started with the process was dumped, then the whole group that was with her in the whole redevelopment process abandoned the process. And so there was a new Task Force." Michael Jacobs, in charge of overseeing the broader set of BHA redevelopment initiatives, concurs that "Franklin Field was never well organized" and tended to have only "one strong tenant leader" at a time, in contrast to broader-based leadership at West Broadway and elsewhere. In part, the failure to develop tenant organization may have stemmed from a conflict of "style" between tenants and BHA staff, but also, Jacobs contends, "Franklin Field didn't begin to have the [necessary] level of money put into the resident organizing efforts, and I think it shows."[149]

"We genuinely wanted to build up that fragmented and disorganized community," Basil Tommy still insists, but the relationship between tenants and BHA staff remained strained. As much as Tommy and his colleagues wanted to avoid a situation where "we were overwhelming them," he acknowledged that the Task Force consisted of "a group of women who were not very articulate and largely lacking in confidence." Because they were faced with an ongoing barrage of ideas and documents from BHA planners and design consultants, "there was really no way that that group of people could counter anything that we proposed." Desperate to help the tenants feel that their views were significant, Tommy and the attorneys who drew up plans for the forthcoming relocation deliberately offered the tenants a worse deal than they were willing to accept in order to "make them argue why it was that they should get more." The result, he later recalled with pleasure, was that the tenants got "an agreement that they were happy with and that they felt they had beaten us into accepting." This tactic dramatically improved their willingness to make subsequent demands. At the same time, greater confidence also coincided with increased squabbling among hardening factions.[150]

As if the flux in Franklin Field's tenant leadership were not enough, in spring 1982 the project also faced a change of BHA redevelopment stewardship. Basil Tommy returned to South Africa and did not rejoin the Franklin Field effort until 1984; meanwhile, the BHA assigned a white male successor, David C. Gilmore, who had previously never even visited the development. Gilmore found a place where tenant relations were "a little strained," and he wasn't sure why. "My impression was that the tenant organization wasn't terribly strong," he recalls. "There wasn't a long-standing tenant-advocacy group the way there was at D Street. It was one that we at the BHA had to foster and develop the leadership. Because we wanted tenant involvement; we had to have someone to talk to." Mostly, he talked to Janie Gibbs, but he worried that "we had to do whatever we could to encourage her to participate, as opposed to having a self-sufficient force out there." He remembers little participation from the Latino population and cannot recall even a single conversation with anyone from a neighborhood organization. Gilmore, however, has no trouble recalling conversations about the troubled state of Franklin Field's management.

The agency overseeing the use of state funds, by then renamed the Executive Office of Communities and Development (EOCD), wanted Franklin Field to have a strong new manager, and the BHA certainly concurred. When the BHA brought in Franklin Walker, a physically imposing black man, they got not only strength but controversy. To Leslie Newman, Walker was a great addition, "a big fellow with a lot of energy and spirit" who was "quite sophisticated and not threatened by efforts at tenant advocacy." Yet over time "his exuberance was misconstrued and he became a lightning rod." BHA Redevelopment Director Gilmore saw Walker as "very articulate, very capable," with "a lot of skills," a "get-it-done kind of guy." To others, however, Gilmore concedes, Walker was "not a real great team player—though he was pulling in the same direction we were pulling in, he didn't always see the plays in the same way we did." Walker viewed himself as a champion of Franklin Field tenants, and he paid increasingly little attention to the wishes of his bosses at the Authority. Like many BHA managers, Newman observes, he tried to operate quite independently, engaging in various sorts of "covert operations thought necessary to manage that development." Frustrated when workers failed to come out, he would circumvent union rules to try to make repairs. He engaged in various "rent deals" and moved applicants into vacant apartments without going through the official tenant-selection and assignment process. As the BHA began to get serious about redevelopment, the Authority closed the Franklin Field waiting list in order to get some "natural attrition" that would facilitate easier relocation of existing tenants and permit the redeveloped version of Franklin Field to have fewer units, yet still accommodate most current residents. According to Sandra Henriquez, who was the area management director at the time, Walker defied this plan and permitted squatters to take over empty apartments, thereby granting them the right of return to the redeveloped project. When the BHA initially let Walker play by this "different standard," Henriquez chose to leave the Authority.[151]

Meanwhile, the tenant organizer continued to help residents press for new community facilities. Gilmore viewed these "ancillary facilities" as a low priority but observed that "Phil Horne had a youthful contingent of residents for whom a day-care facility was *more* important than housing, and that created some friction between generations." Other tenants viewed community facilities as having "more of a social function—a physical facility for the tenants to use as they wanted for performances or offices or whatever, as opposed to a job training facility." With "little advocacy for social service supports" from neighborhood organizations, the vexed subject of "community space" had lots of definitions and little hope of funding, all of which "led to raised expectations that were dashed." Horne, Gilmore concludes, was a "decent, honest guy, but not terribly effective"; he fell well short of the "more trusted and more capable" tenant organizers at the BHA's other redevelopment initiatives.[152]

In April the BHA formalized relocation agreements with Franklin Field tenants, offering them a choice of on-site or off-site temporary relocation, with a guarantee of a renovated Franklin Field apartment (as long as they did not get evicted for nonpayment of rent or some other cause). They told those who chose either of these temporary relocation options to expect construction to last thirty months, until late 1984. Alternatively, tenants could choose permanent relocation to subsidized housing elsewhere (with no subsequent guarantee or preference for a rehabilitated unit at Franklin Field). To sweeten the deal further, the BHA agreed to pay all reasonable moving costs, and the Task Force and the BHA agreed to a rent-abatement deal that would compensate tenants for "past conditions" and the anticipated disruption to be caused by pending construction. They offered those who owed back rent an abatement of up to 30 percent of their outstanding arrears (up to a limit of $300), and gave those without arrears a credit equal to two months' rent. According to Gilmore, the relocation process was "difficult but not horrible" and "went pretty much according to our schedule." With commitments in place to rehouse all who wished to remain, he recognized that "the only way to be assured of weeding out the bad apples was just to evict them," though he recalls that it was rarely necessary or possible to do so.[153]

By June 1982, the overly optimistic headline of the new *Franklin Field Redevelopment Program Newsletter* read "Progress, Progress, Progress." The newsletter described the plans for the redevelopment, commenting that "tenants will have private and shared yards," and announcing that "there will be a community center with activities for all ages." Both front-page statements incautiously overstated the situation, further raising expectations that went beyond what the plan actually promised. Subsequent articles clarified that fewer than half of all families would get private backyards and that the "new community center" was likely to be no more than a renovation of the existing Elderly Center; they made no reference to the long-coveted gymnasium.[154] Further ambiguity had been introduced into a tense situation.

In August the BHA proposed an innovative solution to the problem of the "missing" community center: a $30,000 state-funded annual contract with the nearby Lee School to provide Franklin Field residents with "exclusive use" of gym and pool facilities during certain regular hours. Because the facilities were to be made available on a predictable schedule, the BHA hoped that its community organizer could successfully develop a program of team sports. The agreement also included a guarantee of at least twenty-five slots in a twenty-five-week after-school tutoring program and twenty slots in a nine-week summer day-camp program. In addition, the plan provided for subsidized use of the Lee School auditorium on twenty-five Saturdays and reduced membership costs, which immediately encouraged one hundred residents to become members. Franklin Field Redevelopment Director Gilmore could not have been more pleased, noting that "these facilities are being made available, of course, without the capital, operating, and administrative costs that would be incurred if the Authority built the same recreation facilities on site as the residents originally wanted." This seemed to be the perfect solution—"they are immediately adjacent to the development—nearly as convenient as on site facilities."[155] Clearly, Gilmore either ignored or was unaware of consistent concern on the part of tenants about any activity that required them to cross Franklin Field Park, a tension that had also been repeatedly voiced by the Carr, Lynch consultants in the months just before Gilmore signed on as redevelopment director.

Communication between Franklin Field tenants and BHA staff continued to suffer. In 1984, still desperate to improve resident involvement, the BHA brought back Basil Tommy as project manager and replaced Phil Horne with a new tenant organizer, David Dance. Tommy concedes that Dance was "more effective in pulling together the community" than his predecessor, but he contends that, like Horne, he too "could never say that the BHA had done a decent job in the end— it was always a confrontational arrangement." Dance arrived at Franklin Field with bitter feelings toward the BHA, having previously served as executive director of the citywide Tenants Policy Council, the organization Harry Spence and Judge Garrity had just disbanded in order to start again with another, better-funded, rival group (the Committee for Boston Public Housing). Even the tenant champion Leslie Newman had an uneasy relationship with Dance, as a result of his "anger and a lack of interest in what went before." At Franklin Field, Dance viewed the tenants' group as having a lot of "unmet potential," and he saw the BHA and the contractors as constant thorns in his side.[156]

With tenant leadership and project management still in perpetual flux, Dance struggled to keep tenants centrally involved. The process continued to suffer from the minimal participation of the development's growing Latino community. Most Latino involvement was channeled through a single person, Elsa Flores, a young resident who had initially been hired as a youth worker by Phil Horne. Flores, who herself became a key participant in the redevelopment effort, was presumed to convey relevant matters to the rest of the Spanish-speaking community. Although the Latino population remained marginalized in terms of power, participation among the development's black population did start to increase once there was clear evidence that change really was taking place; attendance averaged twenty to thirty persons at most meetings in 1984, with occasional large gatherings.[157]

The long redevelopment process, over budget and behind schedule, brought residents a brief flurry of excitement in January 1984, following completion of the first 126 apartments. One hundred and twenty-five people, mostly black women and children, attended an outdoor ceremony. They were welcomed back not only by Harry Spence but also by black Dorchester-Mattapan District City Councilor Charles Yancey, and by Boston's brand new mayor, South Boston's Ray Flynn, who was sworn in only two days before. With television camera crews and distinguished visitors, the mood was upbeat. Frank Walker declared to all who could hear, "I'm telling you, man, things have been happening here!" Janie Gibbs presented Spence with a wooden key to the remodeled units, which the receiver ceremoniously passed on to Flynn. Other tenants remained more circumspect. "Everybody is watching to see what happens," one resident told the assembled audience. "Franklin Field has a new face, but will it last?"[158]

As construction proceeded there was some ground for neighborhood optimism. A short distance from the development, a private firm redeveloped the Paine School and several apartment buildings on Blue Hill Avenue, while other work proceeded on a $400,000 upgrade to facilities on Franklin Field itself, including basketball and volleyball courts. The Franklin Field Corporation community group—formed to lobby for funds to rehabilitate the field—chose to rename it "Harambee Park" (using the Swahili word for "togetherness") so as to avoid "confusion" with both the housing project and nearby Franklin Park.[159] For a brief time, things seemed to be looking up.

Within the development, however, new troubles continued to brew. Manager Walker continued to fight for tenant interests, yet he encountered uphill battles. He was determined that tenants should gain maximum control over the dollars coming into the development, especially in terms of employment opportunities for residents. According to Dance, Walker was "a very, very popular manager," and everyone knew he had been "hand picked by Harry Spence." Yet "ultimately," he observes, "some of his advocacy for Franklin Field tenants was part and parcel of his demise." Spence, too, found Walker initially "terrific," but this view had become more complicated. According to Spence, Walker was committed to "reestablishing the importance of the black male as a powerful figure in the black community," but he came to "so identify with the residents that if he believed something was true, then the whole community was for it. In the process, while modeling himself as hero, he disempowered the tenants a lot. He really wanted to be their savior." Following an altercation with construction staff and rumors of sexual involvement with tenants, the BHA removed Walker in 1984. As the tenants' attorney Newman puts it, "Franklin Field was like a mine field," and eventually he "stepped on a mine." Walker's departure, Dance contends, was "a blow to the tenants and the tenant organization since he'd been so much a part of what we had tried to put together."[160]

RECONSTRUCTING FRANKLIN FIELD: FITS, STARTS, AND STOPPAGES

Problems at Franklin Field continued. Another key advocate for Franklin Field's tenants departed in late 1984 with the end of the BHA receivership. Harry Spence's tenure at the BHA could count many triumphs, but Franklin Field was not yet among them. Spence's successor as BHA administrator was none other than Doris Bunte, the erstwhile state legislator who had played an important role in obtaining Franklin Field's redevelopment funds. Heading out to visit Franklin Field, Bunte was shocked by how little had been accomplished: "they were nowhere near finished; they were barely getting started." To Bunte, the problem was "obvious": "It wasn't important because Harry's gone." Other BHA staff in charge of the redevelopment project just were not as committed to it, at least not compared with their interest in other redevelopment efforts. Franklin Field residents also remained alienated. "Every time I went to a resident meeting at Franklin Field," Bunte recalls, "they began it with a prayer. I didn't want them to pray— I wanted them to get angry!"[161]

As a construction process once estimated to be completed by late 1984 lingered into 1985 and then stalled out completely, many tenants did indeed get upset. Tenant dissatisfaction took two related forms; residents were angry and frustrated by the inability of Wexler-Shah, the contractors, to keep construction moving, and they were equally disappointed by what they found in the completed units. As James M. (Mac) McCreight—the attorney then representing tenants in the lawsuit that had led to BHA receivership—put it, "While families temporarily relocated wait to return, families in newly rehabilitated units have faced rodent infestation, broken thermostats, and poorly laid tile." Franklin Field Task Force member Betty J. Higginbotham, who received a rehabilitated apartment in 1984, observed that "the tenants are very skeptical about anything being done here" and are "disillusioned" by the reality of further unanticipated stays in temporary housing. BHA Director of Communications Bill Wright assured tenants that "the problems that caused the work stoppage and delay have been ironed out," stating that Wexler-Shah was "aiming to" complete work by the end of 1985. A wistful and frustrated Higginbotham was more realistic: "It takes a long time to get things done here."[162]

In November 1986, with Franklin Field still unfinished, a television crew again returned to the project. This time it was not to celebrate a redevelopment milestone but, rather, to bemoan another construction millstone. As WGBH-TV co-anchor Gail Harris phrased it, tenants had been told that "their deteriorating units would be turned into models of urban living. Instead, the tenants say the apartments have become models of disaster." Once again, owing to BHA disputes with Burlington-based Shah Construction, the contractors had virtually suspended all work on the project, "leaving tenants to contend with numerous structural defects and hazardous, unfinished areas." A few weeks before the TV crew descended, the Boston City Council's housing committee held a hearing at the development, at which Franklin Field tenants publicly termed the contractor's work "shoddy," complained that the BHA had failed to provide proper supervision, and called on the Authority to "refuse to accept renovated buildings still containing numerous defects." Tenants now regaled reporter Marcus Jones with tales of ceiling defects, doorbells that didn't work, broken windows, persistent plumbing problems, and unfinished landscaping, walkways, and play areas. Some reported a loss of telephone service for weeks on end. Betty Higginbotham commented: "tenants, when they wash above me—the suds and water come through my toilet and overflow in my bathroom. And sometimes you are sitting on the toilet and you have to jump up." Other tenants criticized a sewage back-up into the basement that had been planned for the day-care center. City Councilor Yancey, who had happily helped preside over the initial reoccupancy ceremony nearly three years earlier, dourly added that "we in the Boston City Council are not at all pleased." Meanwhile, tenants blamed the BHA, and the BHA blamed Shah Construction. Long-term resident Thelma Smith, who would later become Franklin Field Task Force president, put it most succinctly: "It is ridiculous, for the amount of money being spent in Franklin Field, that the place is down like it is."[163]

As the disputes with Shah Construction dragged on into 1987, the BHA attorney Rod Solomon insisted that "construction delays have been largely caused by the contractor." Solomon described Shah Construction's crew system as "unorganized" and blamed the company for "excessive" deficiencies in the resultant buildings. Meanwhile, the contractor sought timely payment for work already completed and wanted assurances that the contract still contained sufficient funds to pay for the remainder of the job. With a tight budget, and a bankrupt major contractor whose departure had left it up to an undercapitalized minority-owned partner firm to complete the job, the process of reconstructing Franklin Field had become as troubled as the conditions that had originally prompted redevelopment. Despite being "generally unsatisfied" with both the pace and the quality of the rehab work, the BHA wanted above all to get the job finished. Tenants and their advocates were placed in the unenviable position of pushing to get the job completed while also trying to monitor its quality. As Tenant Organizer Dance put it, they got into "a situation where white-collar folks sit down with white-collar folks and decide that 'well, we can't do everything that we said we'd do, but we'd both look better if the game continues.'"[164] As the game continued, the disillusioned residents felt like unpaid umpires to whom the players would not listen.

The whole construction process had become a long series of misadventures. Hundreds of windows were improperly manufactured and had to be rejected, yielding costly delays. A basement built with insufficient ceiling height had to have its floor jackhammered away to meet code. There were constant arguments about the failure of contractors to meet their stipulated minority-hiring commitments (especially involving the employment of residents), but the BHA neglected to enforce sanctions. As Dance puts it, "nobody wanted to look." Even the BHA's own published figures confirm that tenant-hiring quotas were not met. Dance, still angry about this years later, estimates that the failure to hire tenants represented more than a million dollars "stolen from Franklin Field residents because of race." The overall result, he says, was "shoddy work" and "unmet promises." At base, Dance claims, the problem was that Franklin Field was seen as a "black project in a black neighborhood," resulting in constant struggles to overcome a "'good enough for Franklin Field' mentality."[165]

By mid-1987, the contractors finally finished the redevelopment of Franklin Field, leaving not just completed buildings but hundreds of frustrated and exhausted people. As Thelma Smith put it, "We was fightin', we was cussin' and everything to get what we got out here. We got it the hard way." Mary Green, who became the Task Force president in the early 1990s, emerged from the redevelopment process with little sense of trust for the BHA. "If you don't watch, they'll screw you up. You can write out the blue print and put it on the paper and turn your back and they'll turn the page and put what they wanted just that fast and you won't know it." When she is pressed for examples, her stories are both prosaic and deeply revealing. "We picked out our floor, we picked out our counters for our kitchens, right? Our cabinets, we picked out the whole works. We asked for yellow and egg-white counters, because them was kitchen colors. We got blue counters. Some was green. Some was yellow. When they got to egg-white, they knocked that out completely. They didn't tell us why or nothin'. Completely out. Off the map." Similarly, Green recounts, "We told them that we want the same tubs that we had taken out of here—we want 'em back in there. They were good; wasn't nothing wrong with 'em. They did not put 'em back in there. They put in smaller tubs. We got a lot of big people here. It's hard on them gettin' in and out of them little tubs." As Thelma Smith sees it, "We told them what we wanted, how we wanted it, and we tried to explain to them as best we could, and it didn't work." Others complained that contractors had put the new kitchen toe-heaters directly in front of sinks, where toes could not only be warmed but dangerously scorched. When asked about this, Smith points out that the BHA eventually "put a cut-off on mine, because I bitched about it and they got tired of my mouth."[166] Tenants felt burned at every turn.

At the same time, those who worked with the tenants saw that many other needs were not being met by the redevelopment, especially since the BHA did not build many of the once-promised recreation and community facilities. Observing the immensity of problems and fearing the further backsliding that would occur as necessary social services continued to be curtailed, David Dance felt ready to move on: "After spending three years of my life at Franklin Field, I know how the people feel who work in Somalia," he commented.[167] Franklin Field's tenants, who had survived the redevelopment process, had nowhere else to go.

THE CRACK-UP

Franklin Field's problems did not cease once the redevelopment stumbled toward completion. By then, a new force had laid siege to the community: crack cocaine. Tenant Organizer Dance recalls no evidence of hard drug selling in Franklin Field during the redevelopment period itself, and no project-based gangs. All that changed with the arrival of crack, which brought a dangerous high-stakes alternative economy to the neighborhood at precisely the time in the late-1980s when various city, state, and federal jobs and services programs were being cut back. By 1990, Mary Green notes, every effort established to assist tenants had been abandoned: "We used to have a community-organizer person in here, used to have someone to help people find jobs and put their kids in day care. We lost *all* that. Now, for everything like that, they got to try to do they own lookin'. There's nobody here to help them." In this context, the drug trade carried considerable appeal: kids "don't want no 5–6 dollars an hour, when they see folks making $1000 a day." Looking back, Dance feels that it was an "impossible task" to "produce a social fabric that could make Franklin Field an island in the midst of an abandoned community." For Harry Spence, who watched his protracted efforts at Franklin Field unravel during the late 1980s and 1990s, "the drug issue was agonizing."[168]

For decades, the citywide and neighborhood press had pretty much chosen to ignore Franklin Field. In part, the inattention was due to the project's physical isolation from any particular neighborhood jurisdiction after it lost its social and cultural links to Blue Hill Avenue's Jewish community; in part, the inattention stemmed from the fact that the most "newsworthy" events in the area all seemed to involve violence located well outside the Franklin Field project. In the late 1980s and early 1990s, all this changed. Franklin Field became the most frequently mentioned public housing development in the Dorchester and Boston papers, and virtually all the press was bad. The fact that upwards of $30 million had been spent to redevelop the place was lost under successive waves of articles that told only of horrific assaults and killings. Franklin Field was back on everyone's map, not because of its redevelopment, but because it had become an epicenter of gang-related and drug-related crime and violence in Boston.

In February 1989, less than two years after the redevelopment had been completed, crews were back in several Franklin Field apartments. This time, however, they were not construction teams but BHA police and Team Police from the city of Boston engaged in a series of drug busts. The raids led to the arrest of nine Franklin Field residents and the seizure of about $25,000 in crack. The *Boston Herald* described the project as the headquarters of "a sophisticated drug ring that used a digital radio scanner to track police operations and investigations in the city." (Whatever the "sophistication," obviously the scanner didn't work too well.) The drug busts focused citywide attention on more than just four apartments with drug traffickers; as the *Herald*'s reporter put it, these were people arrested for "trafficking crack out of a Dorchester housing project." Because the raids occurred in the public neighborhood of a project, the press treated the entire development as guilty by association.[169]

Six weeks later, the *Boston Globe*'s Mike Barnicle used his column to describe the ongoing crack trade "in Franklin Field." He wrote about five young dealers (the oldest of whom was only fifteen) who sold the drug for "a guy named Zeke"; all five "had enough money in their pockets to prove that sales were up and fear was down because when a police cruiser slowly passed, the cops were met with merely a sullen stare." A week earlier, BHA police had caught a thirteen-year-old with twenty-five bags of crack and $250 on the same block of Stratton Street. "The cops got him after watching the boy's father direct customers to his son. The boy's mother was in her apartment and became enraged when informed that he had been picked up before he was able to give crack to her. The 13-year-old's partner was 13 too and he had $1400." For Barnicle, these were stories that would not otherwise have been reported during a week when the tragic Alaskan oil spill of the Exxon *Valdez* dominated the news. Urban "Crack spills," by contrast, were the unreported counterpoints to such environmental disasters, kept out of public view, Barnicle alleged, because the victims were "mostly people of color and their lives are often too violent and thus too upsetting for prime-time viewing." Instead, "the nation chooses to hand the clean-up operation to police, who are given society's simple instructions: 'Keep those blacks away from us.'"[170]

From that point on, coverage of Franklin Field in Boston's newspapers chronicled a rising tide of violence in and around the development. In May 1989, the *Herald* reported the murder of the Franklin Field resident Richard Parris, Jr., providing readers not only with the street address of the crime but also with the fact that the victim lived a block away "in the Franklin Field public housing project." Again, the project name provided not just a useful locational device but also explanatory context, as if to suggest that project residence somehow made the crime understandable or expectable. The same article also noted that Parris had been arrested for crack possession two days earlier, but reported that "it was not immediately known whether the murder was related to street gang activity, which has been known to occur off and on in the project, or to drugs."[171] Whether or not the connection was "known," the confluence of drugs, murder, and Franklin Field had become a triumvirate well worthy of repeated speculation and association.

In mid-1989 the Boston papers briefly paid some positive attention to Franklin

Field, before quickly resuming their usual focus. The *Bay State Banner* printed a photo of Mayor Flynn with the "Finest Hour" music group at Franklin Field's Family/Unity Day, as well as a letter from a "Proud Franklin Field Resident," Janie Gibbs. Gibbs stressed her own success in raising six kids at the development and concluded that "despite the prevailing negative impression some people have of public housing developments, there are families who work to raise our children to become productive individuals. We have success stories, too."[172] An abbreviated version of her appeal appeared in the *Herald,* as well. As at West Broadway, Franklin Field's tenants were clearly mindful and deeply troubled by the way the Boston press constructed their neighborhood. On occasion, the city's papers found more positive things to say, but they cast them as exceptions to the rule. In October, the *Globe* took the time to report the arrival of a Boys and Girls Club of Boston program at Franklin Field, intended to give youths an "alternative to the streets." A month later, the *Herald* chimed in with a report on the same program, noting that this "welcome alternative" could "give direction" to Franklin Field kids, who were "all too familiar with the problems—crack usage, alcohol abuse, drug dealing and violence—that plague so many of this country's public housing communities."[173]

Within the week, news reports placed the problems back at the center: someone fatally stabbed a twenty-two-year-old Dorchester man in a project courtyard off Westview Street, after "an argument over a $10 debt exploded into murder." Once again, the *Globe*'s reporter gave more than a street address for the murder; he also thought it necessary to locate the killing "near the Franklin Field housing development." Two weeks later, the *Herald* reported a story about the recovery of a car believed to belong to the victim of a strangling in Brockton, a small city south of Boston. What made this news, it seemed, was not that the car was found on Ames Street in Dorchester but that it was "recovered at the Franklin Field housing project." Here too, by implication and repeated inference, mere residence at Franklin Field seemed to make tenants somehow complicit as a territorial group.[174]

The worst was yet to come. On Halloween night, 1990, the twenty-six-year-old Franklin Field resident Kimberly Rae Harbour was brutally murdered on Franklin Field, an attack perpetrated by a group of fellow Franklin Field residents, four of them still juveniles. The eight assailants, who had been drinking heavily, had initially set out across the field in search of prostitutes to rob, but instead came upon Harbour and another woman, who managed to escape. Harbour was then robbed, gang-raped, and slaughtered—beaten with a tree branch and a forty-ounce beer bottle, and sliced 132 times with a knife and broken glass. At her funeral, the body was so disfigured that the lid on the coffin was reversed to make the wounds less visible.

BHA officials adopted a defensive posture. Milton Cole, the Authority's superintendent of crime prevention, stated that the grisly crime could have been duplicated anywhere in Boston. "Don't blame housing developments," he said. "It's the neighborhood environment, lack of youth activity programs and education that makes these things happen anywhere." Cole told reporters that "people like to blame housing developments," but that "people themselves are to blame for not doing more to fight crime." He also cast doubt on the guilt of the alleged assailants, noting that "it's very rare that a bunch of kids jump up in a woman's face like that. They may jump up in a guy's face, but the kids I've seen usually treat a woman with respect." He then gave a decidedly improbable counter-explanation for the Harbour murder: "Maybe she attempted to rip them off and they robbed back; and she grabbed one and was beating hell out of him. That's when the rest could have jumped in. It was probably spontaneous."[175] Two years later—after all eight killers had been tried as adults, convicted, and sent to prison—Harbour's name stood as "a benchmark for a kind of virulent strain of '90s violence."[176] At the same time, the tragedy horrifically confirmed the worst possible stereotypes about Franklin Field's young people.

In April 1991, Mayor Flynn went to Franklin Field to announce plans for a new neighborhood gym and recreational facility to serve the development and surrounding areas. Underwritten by the George Robert White Trust Fund, the $4 million facility, Flynn said, would help bring "hope and opportunity directly to our city's youth." The decision, made in the aftermath of the Harbour killing, also followed a study that found that the city's highest concentration of children younger than fourteen—seventeen thousand of them—lived within a one-mile radius of the Franklin Field development, an area with chronic shortages of recreational opportunities. A Boys and Girls Club building designed to serve three hundred neighborhood youths would replace the inadequate facility operating out of a project basement; once again, though, Franklin Field tenants would have to trade away a project-based amenity for a higher-quality alternative nearby.[177]

In the meantime, new crimes plagued the project. In September 1992 police arrested a man in an Ames Street apartment, charging him with stealing bags of mail, which were recovered in a Stratton Street dumpster. Three weeks later, two men were shot "outside the Franklin Field complex" on Ames Street.[178] In October a "wave of violence" rolled through Dorchester, Mattapan, and Roxbury, bringing nine killings in two weeks to places within a short walk of Franklin Field. One murder in particular tore the development apart—the shooting of a thirteen-year-old resident named Dominic Mount, known to all as "Poochie." Gunned down on the corner of Blue Hill Avenue and Floyd Street, just two hundred yards from his Stratton Street apartment, Poochie was a sixth-grader who had been given a "Youth on the Rise" trophy by the BHA. The Boston papers speculated that Mount's twenty-four-year-old companion—another Franklin Field resident, but one who had a criminal record—may have been the intended victim. This was not to excuse the crime but rather to explain it, to place it in the category of gangland activity in the projects, rather than call it what it appeared to be—the unprovoked slaughter of a boy six weeks past elementary school. The *Globe*'s Mike Barnicle—always the self-styled streetwise voice—saw no logic in this particular crime: "He was killed merely because he was there, walking on a city sidewalk about 7:30 in the evening." At the development, residents pleaded with other youths not to avenge the killing—a clear indication that many there believed they knew who had been responsible (although no arrests were made). Many joined in a candlelight walk from Poochie's home to the site of the crime, while some found other ways to mark his memory (Figs. 3.18–3.20). Mount's seventeen-year-old sister told reporters that "the only thing that's making anybody feel any better is spray-painting his name everywhere." Poochie's death brought Franklin Field a new round of unwanted media attention, just as the public memory of the Harbour calamity had begun to recede.[179]

Unfortunately, the association of violent crime with Franklin Field continued. In December, Larry McConnico, Jr.—a former project tenant who had refused to testify against fellow residents accused in the Harbour murder and had been sentenced for contempt of court—was shot on Blue Hill Avenue, just across the field from his former home. Two weeks later, following the arrest of McConnico's alleged assailants, his crack-addicted nineteen-year-old sister, Larricia, was shot dead on Talbot Street, just around the corner from where Larry had been fired upon. The *Globe*'s account of the killing focused on the long-term drug problems of the McConnico family, stressing five years of failed Department of Youth Services and Department of Social Services interventions.[180] Again, the reputation of Franklin Field as a whole suffered from the fate of a single troubled family—one that had not even lived there during the past two years.

FIGURES 3.18–3.20 Memorials to Poochie. With varying degrees of formality and artistry, area youths memorialized Domenic ("Poochie") Mount, whose murder greatly added to the stress and distress of the community. A long mural (above) sets Poochie's killing in the larger context of youth violence and African-American struggles; a spray-paint tag (top right) marks the wall of a Blue Hill Avenue shop just opposite the entrance to Franklin Field; and the words "Poochie R.I.P." even adorned the end of the famous Franklin Field wall—adjacent to a gang reference painted onto the stone bollards (bottom right).

By this point, mere mention of the term *Franklin Field* could conjure up images of myriad dangers. When the *Globe* ran a story about a woman who said she was "abandoned by a taxi driver in the Franklin Field project after midnight," the paper did not have to remind readers why this would be a fear-inducing event. It was enough to identify the project by name and to evoke a sense of entrapment "in" it; there was no need to provide further evidence of danger. Automatically, the story fit perfectly in a broader debate about "whether cabbies should be allowed to turn down fares into highcrime neighborhoods where they feel their safety is threatened." It did not seem to matter that the BHA had just redesigned the development at great expense so that its apartments had entrances facing onto public streets, and that one no longer needed to go "in" to the project in quite the same way.[181]

Meanwhile, according to residents, the vast majority of violent incidents in the development in 1991 and 1992 went completely unreported in the Boston or Dorchester papers, even at a time when "shootings and fights occurred daily." The silence, it seems clear, was a joint product of a community too fearful to file charges and media already too saturated with similar accounts of altercations to bother covering more; only a particularly brutal murder could rise to the level of newsworthiness. To its credit, the *Boston Globe* eventually sent a reporter out to investigate daily project conditions, though even this story, too, was prompted by the discovery "near Franklin Field" of the weapons and vehicle believed to have been used in the "execution-style murder" of a Boston police detective.

The *Globe*'s headline, "Fear a Fact of Life in Neighborhoods," neatly summed up the paper's assessment of Franklin Field in 1993. The story centered on the two public neighborhoods of Franklin Hill and Franklin Field, depicted as effectively and equivalently destroyed by the drug trade. One Franklin Field resident, who feared using her real name because of ongoing threats to her life, described packs of young drug dealers in black sneakers and hoods who hung around the development, talking loud and playing booming music. In seventeen years of residence, she estimated that she had been mugged at gunpoint about a dozen different times. Despite her ordeal, she remained silent: "People around here are scared to talk because they want to live a little longer. I can't blame them. We have children and grandchildren. We have to go to work. We got to live." Another tenant who also preferred anonymity commented: "You know how it is, during the summertime when you want to sit on your front steps and listen to music and talk with your friends? We can't do that here. When the sun starts to go down, we start thinking about getting home. And if you are walking, you definitely want to make sure you can get in your house before dark."

The erstwhile tenant leader Janie Gibbs described one night when she heard "a whole lot of shots" while sitting with her granddaughter near her front window: "The glass started shattering all around us. I pulled the window shade down and ran upstairs to check to see how my other kids were doing." Although her own kids were all right, she returned downstairs to find a bullet-riddled teenager right outside her window: "I could almost reach out and touch him."[182] Needless to say, this was not what Franklin Field's designers had in mind when they planned the new duplexes and private yards.

Frank Hart, an outreach coordinator with the antiviolence program known as Project Free, came to Franklin Field in 1992 and found a bleak environment:

"The very fabric of what makes a neighborhood a neighborhood has broken down," Hart observed. "People have lost faith in each other and city government." Janie Gibbs, then working for Project Impact—a community-based group that provided health care to pregnant women—insisted that self-reliance was the only possible solution. "There are no support systems. No one can help you. Not even the police." Gibbs made clear that the problems of poverty and violence were compounded by an underlying current of racism, a willingness of powerful white-dominated organizations to accept conditions within the black community that would not be tolerated elsewhere. "Sometimes," she said, "I would call the police and tell them names and addresses of people selling drugs and they still wouldn't come out. After a while, I started telling them that a black man was beating a white woman. They'd come out quick then."[183]

The police twice came quickly to Franklin Field in June 1994, but each time they arrived well after another murder had taken place. On June 8, May Flores, a pregnant woman who worked for the group Gang Peace to combat youth violence, was shot to death outside the door of her cousin's apartment. The following day, only a half-block away, a man in a hooded jacket murdered Franklin Field resident Eddie Allen in front of an Ames Street building while he was talking with a group of friends. *Boston Herald* columnist Leonard Greene supplemented the news coverage of the killings with an essay about a prospective tenant—a young mother named Mariabelle Cerino—who was about to move to an apartment near the murder sites. Cerino's problem, Greene opined, was that she "made the mistake of visiting during the day" and therefore failed to understand the way "the picture often changes" at night. After dark, he wrote, it is "as if someone pressed a button and removed the tranquillity." When Cerino visited, she had seen only the rehabilitated buildings and playspaces for children, and was delighted by the news that her transfer from another project had been approved. Despite the news of the murders, she chose to sign her lease since, as Greene put it, "she knows too well that a life in public housing is a life with few choices." "I'm going to give it a try," Cerino said, with a hint of hesitation. "With [the BHA], you never know. I might get put in someplace worse."[184]

THE LIMITS OF REDEVELOPED HOUSING

Tenants who arrived at post-redevelopment Franklin Field between 1987 and 1993 recall strong mixed feelings about their new home. A 1987 arrival said that "it was nice but it didn't last—now we have drug dealers hanging out on corners, people yelling and screaming." Another resident who came in 1988 matter-of-factly reported that "it was nice, quiet, no killing," a clear contrast to events a year or two later. Others who came in 1990 and 1991 complained about "junkies" and "next-door neighbors who ran a crack house." One 1991 arrival recalled "nice people to live around" but "a lot of violence." A block away on Floyd Street, Ruth Botts faced the same fallout: "You used to be able to sit on your stoop in the summertime and talk to your neighbors, but people became fearful and just did what they had to do and then came home immediately and locked themselves up."[185] Ultimately, any self-assessment of the quality of a housing-redevelopment effort entailed a broader reflection on the quality of life that prevailed in an increasingly violent neighborhood.

Interviews conducted with a 10 percent sample of Franklin Field household heads in 1993 confirm that new and long-term residents alike viewed Franklin Field's redevelopment as a mixed blessing at best. In contrast to an 82 percent satisfaction rate reported by tenants at West Broadway, only 42 percent said they were satisfied with the redevelopment results at Franklin Field. Many expressed their dissatisfaction in extreme terms, arguing that the redevelopment had actually made conditions much worse. Two-thirds said they wished to remain no longer than necessary, and only one-third said they would definitely recommend the development to friends looking for a place to live.

Some complaints centered on issues of construction standards: "They shouldn't have touched the interior walls—they were strong—now you hit them and a hole goes through"; "the walls are so thin you have to use thumbtacks—you can't bang things on the wall"; "people are always banging"; "walls are thinner—you hear your neighbors now"; "you hear everything next door—they might as well be talking to me"; "the walls sweat—I can't stand that—I like my heat, but don't blow me outta here"; "they used poor equipment"; "the doors fall off their hinges"; "the first day I moved in, my closet door almost fell on me"; "the smoke detector system don't work—just goes off when it gets good and ready"; "I had two kitchen sinks before, now I only have one"; "the hot water and heat is worse now"; "cold air comes in through the windows and doors"; "You got to sit in the house now in the wintertime like you was goin' outside"; "there are no doors that can be shut on the first floor"; "it's harder on some who have to walk up and down stairs"; "they got a cheap product when they made these houses—leaks, holes in walls, stopped-up toilets, and closet doors that break"; "the water comes in around the baseboards—I have to keep all my clothes away from the walls." A sixty-five-year-old long-term resident commented, "There are a lot of reasons why it's not good enough; it may have to be renovated all over again." Another added simply: "They blew it."

Many residents highlighted personal maintenance problems: "the floors are all white and require too much mopping"; "it gets dusty and there's more to clean"; "the walls are harder to clean"; "I have to snow shovel and clean my yard"; "I got tired of cleaning the hall, and I'm the building captain"; "it's hard for me to wash walls—I just gave up." Two-thirds complained about the BHA's own contribution to maintenance. As one young woman who had lived at Franklin Field for twenty years phrased it, "they respond typically for a project." Another twenty-four-year-old lifelong resident commented that the BHA maintenance staff "need somebody who likes people of all color." She criticized an upstairs neighbor who threw glass in her family's private yard ("I swept it up and put it on her front step"), and suggested that things would improve only if the BHA could be replaced by "somebody with some power like the National Guard."

Almost uniformly, the tenants stressed matters of safety: "I wanted security to improve and it got worse"; "teenagers took over this place"; "I have friends right here on Stratton Street and I won't even go to visit them"; "I don't like outsiders coming in bringing their friends—you can't use the outside"; "for a brief time, the drug problem seemed to be working out, but eventually the same activities creeped in again"; "there's a bigger drug problem and worse attitudes"; "people have changed—no one helps each other"; "they claimed they were going to screen everybody that came in, but they didn't—they can't because of privacy laws"; "I wish we could have more police cars coming around"; "the introduction of crack has been devastating"; "the neighbors have gotten worse—because of drugs, it's like Dodge City"; "it seems like they clean up the streets and bring it all to Franklin Field"; "baseheads will rob you—even if they're shooting at someone else, bullets have no name"; "with the violence and crime between people who visit the area, I wouldn't barbecue or nothing"; "the poor conditions returned after the first two years." A twenty-eight-year-old who had lived at the development since she was a child commented that "it's scary here now—this was home for a long time and now I'm scared. I've made so many work orders to get my door fixed, and they're not doing anything about it." One 1968 arrival wished the redevelopment had never even happened: "Apartments ain't no better; I don't like this apartment, never did, didn't want it." A woman who had lived at the development since 1972 expressed the prevailing sentiment: "I thought it would be much better than this."

Despite the prevalence of such views, a minority of tenants remained both grateful and upbeat. Several praised private entrances, the reduction of shared hallways, better handicapped access, the new appliances and laundry hook-ups, and the overall apartment appearance. A few commented that the redesigned Franklin Field now looked more like a private development, but two-thirds concluded that it "still looks like public housing": "all you see is bricks"; "you know it's public, because everybody lives here"; "it's all bricks and the people make it look like public housing too." Another resident, who had lived in the development for twenty-five years, added, "I've been here so long it all looks the same outside." Someone else commented that it is good that "they put the dumpsters in the back instead of the front of buildings," but why don't public housing residents get their trash picked up from individual barrels, as in other neighborhoods? A visually impaired male tenant complained that he couldn't get the BHA to replace a hall light for two years, adding, "just because you live in the projects doesn't mean you can be treated less than human." Once again, the sight of redesigned buildings proved inseparable from broader questions of social acceptance.

Only a handful of respondents remained wholly effusive: "they did it over good"; "living conditions are better in every way"; "it gave people a sense of pride as opposed to a project"; "I sit back and really enjoy myself here." Sometimes, though, tenants even cast positive judgments in negative terms. One resident praised the redevelopment for sealing off access to rooftops: "it's good they changed roofs or they'd be killing people off them." Another was pleased that there were no shrubs near her apartment, commenting that "I asked them not to put in a lot of trees because the kids would tear them down." Or, as an elderly woman, a resident of Franklin Field since 1976, put it, "In some ways we're better off, but most things are about the same; it's the same people."

Many of the tenant leaders are among those most eager to blame their fellow tenants for many ongoing problems. For the former Task Force president Thelma Smith, success or failure at Franklin Field is a function of parenting: "I hear a lot of politicians getting on TV and saying things about 'the projects.' To *me,* it's not where you bring your kids up, it's the way you start from day one with them, and let that child know what you mean. You got to stick by what you mean and don't let that child try to overpower you when you're trying to bring them up . . . I raised three nieces right here at 100 Stratton. Not one of them have been in jail.

They're not on drugs. I was the mother, I was the aunt, and I was the father to them." For Smith, the rampant joblessness at Franklin Field has little to do with any lack of jobs: "People be talking about how the kids can't get no jobs. We have had jobs fairs here for anybody that want a job; you could raise two of your hands and say how many people at this development got jobs. If you want a job, you can get a job. There are jobs coming in. I post them in the office. Since we have no staff here, I have sent people to jobs. They didn't keep 'em a week. They try it out, make me feel good, but they think they can make mo' money in the streets."[186]

Mary Green says much the same thing: "There are jobs out there! But people around here, they don't want to go out and catch the bus. They want money to go ride there and ride back. They want you to come and pick them up. They don't want to go there and look for jobs. They don't want to sit down and write no resumes and take 'em to 'em. They on the lazy side. I'm sorry to say that. But I always say, they take the welfare from 'em, they'd get off they tail and go off and look for them a job. But they ain't goin' nowhere. You see a welfare check comin' in, you can tell when it come in: drugs come in." Green, a former Girl Scout leader who refers to herself as "one of them good kind," had become the Franklin Field Task Force president, but she served with a weary disillusionment.

By the early 1990s, Green and Thelma Smith could count on little support from others: "We get people elected on the Board, but when it come down to goin' to meetings and have somethin' done, you can't get nobody to do nothin'." As before, tenant leadership at Franklin Field depended on one or two individuals. "You go to two or three meetings every week, you gonna get tired. Every week you got meetings. You want a break too. And ain't nobody ever goin' but you. You tired of that breakin' down." Even worse, for all of her time and trouble, she hears mostly complaints: "you got this other side saying, 'Well, the Board don't ever do nothin'" and 'the Task Force this' and 'the Task Force that.' They don't see what's missing: it ain't what the Task Force's done—it's why didn't *you* help that person get *more* done." To a bitter Mary Green, equally frustrated by the BHA and by her fellow tenants, Franklin Field's redevelopment was no more than the midpoint of a long decline. After the redevelopment, she laments, "It just really went down and all the money they spent was just wasted."[187]

Ongoing Struggles and Hopes

Although the situation has calmed substantially since the early 1990s, Franklin Field is still associated with deliberate acts of brutality. In February 1996 the development made headlines when Leroy [Pete] Dates, a double-amputee in a wheelchair, allegedly opened fire with a shotgun, killing a crack-addicted twenty-eight-year-old intruder accused of trying to rob him; neighbors hailed him as a hero, while police charged him with murder.[188] That killing was an aberration, however, at a time when Boston's gun violence was experiencing a long lull. From mid-1995 until late 1997, the city went twenty-nine months without a single juvenile being murdered, a streak nationally reported as the "Boston Miracle." Unfortunately, when a new killing finally broke that streak, the victim was a Franklin Field resident. Sixteen-year-old Eric Paulding had apparently strayed to the wrong part of Franklin Hill's turf, and Boston's youth wars temporarily re-erupted, the latest round in what the *Boston Globe* called "a rivalry of almost medieval intensity." This time, however, a rapid influx of Dorchester's ministers and a growing presence of youth workers managed to foster calm and derail plans for retribution. A month later, the *Globe* editorialized about "Keeping Peace at Franklin Field," calling the development a "testing ground for Boston's ability to deliver services aimed a reducing youth violence." For the most part, Franklin Field passed the test, but even so the development's residents remained largely isolated from the services and recreational opportunities they sorely needed. As Sergeant Tony Fonseca puts it, "The movie theaters are gone. The delicatessens are gone. The open-air fish markets, meat markets, fruit markets are gone. The bicycle shop is gone. The neighborhood fire station is gone. Pop Warner football is gone. Little League baseball is gone. When people today talk about the 'problem with the youth' in the area, I have to correct them. The youth didn't create this; this was created for them and they were born into it. There's very little here for children now" (Figs. 3.21–3.23). Even with newly constructed Boys and Girls Club facilities nearby on Talbot Avenue and further community facilities at the Lee School, ongoing turf battles have periodically restricted their utility to Franklin Field's youth.[189]

Once again, BHA officials and others called for development residents to make better use of their surrounding community while tenants, now led by the Task Force head Maryann Veale, preferred a more isolationist approach. The one-time Franklin Field manager Sandra Henriquez made her triumphant return to the BHA as its administrator in 1996, becoming the first trained housing professional to hold that post since Harry Spence. Since then, she has paid careful attention to this development that she once found so difficult to control. For Henriquez, despite the downturn in violence at the end of the 1990s, "huge turf issues" remain pressing, as project-based gang members continue their long feud with Franklin Hill. Tenant leaders have responded by trying to find ways to keep kids from going "anywhere off the site for anything," even to facilities on Franklin Field itself. Noting that the Franklin Field team was kicked out of a Boston neighborhood basketball league in 1998 for behavior problems, Henriquez observes: "The more we provide services on site, the more we're reinforcing those turf issues and potentially that bad behavior." For the BHA's leader, the lack of on-site services at Franklin Field, while surely a symptom of larger problems, is not something that the BHA itself can or should address: "It's not appropriate that we should be both the landlord and the full social service provider. We don't do it well, and we are a landlord."

As of late 2000, 147 tenants at the development reported income from full-time jobs, representing about 35 percent of adults aged 18 to 61. While still a dire statistic, this figure marks a dramatic increase in employment over the last two decades. In the aftermath of welfare reform, only about 20 percent of households relied on TANF (Temporary Assistance for Needy Families) grants and 13 percent reported no income at all. An additional 35 percent of households received SSI (Supplemental Security Insurance) payments, reflecting the high rate of disability at the development. Taken overall, more than half of Franklin Field's households reported incomes below $10,000, indicating that widespread poverty is still the norm. The development remains overwhelmingly African-American and Latino, but such categories mask a broad ethnic diversity that includes not just African-Americans, Dominicans, and Puerto Ricans, but also Cape Verdeans, Salvadorans, West Indians, as well as Vietnamese and others. Ninety-five percent of households continue to be headed by single women.[190]

According to Henriquez, however, the main problem at Franklin Field is BHA management, not tenant demographics. After the redevelopment, she fully acknowledges, "We didn't manage it well." Henriquez doubts that she "could look at it today and say that more than $30 million went into that site." She clearly faults her predecessors at the BHA: "We spent all this money as an organization and did no preventive maintenance schedules. We got our shot to manage it but went back to business as usual in terms of management practices. There was no coherent understanding of how you manage real estate and that managing public housing is still managing real estate."[191]

By the end of the 1990s, rates of violent crime in the Franklin Field area had plummeted from the barbarous excesses of a few years earlier, thanks to success-

FIGURES 3.21–3.23 "There's very little for children here now." Harry's Variety Store on Woodrow Avenue (above), so beloved by Tony Fonseca and other area youths during the 1950s and 1960s, now stands boarded up (the Franklin Field development is visible at the left rear, behind the truck). Despite the relative stability of this residential neighborhood south of the development, the area is still pockmarked with vacant lots (top right). Conversely, the large Boys and Girls Club facility on Franklin Field (Harambee Park) has been a great boon to the neighborhood, located just a short walk from the development (seen at rear of photo; bottom right).

ful community policing, valiant efforts by church and community leaders, and a strong economy that brought near-record low unemployment rates to the city. In 2000, however, Boston police and university-based criminologists warned that increased rates of violent crime could return, given the release of many felons imprisoned over the last decade and a sizable demographic "increase in the numbers of male teenagers, the group most prone to commit crimes." In this context, the Boston Police Department regarded Franklin Field as one of the city's eight "hot spots" for crime. As a local fireman put it, "This neighborhood has more activity than any other part of Boston. You still have the most fires, most ambulances—more 'runnings' than anywhere." Undaunted, some homeowners in the neighborhood streets below Franklin Field continued to organize themselves, block by block, to enforce high standards of surveillance and upkeep. The city

FIGURE 3.24 Blue Hill Avenue, 2000. Despite some signs of renewed interest by the city and the advent of new businesses, Blue Hill Avenue remains a shadow of its former self. This photo, taken near the same spot as Fig. 3.6, underscores the loss of vitality since the heyday of streetcars and small shops.

planted new trees along the Blue Hill Avenue median and erected a sign announcing entry into the Neponset River Watershed. The neighborhood itself rejoiced when Councilor Charles Yancey replaced Jimmy Kelly as Boston City Council president in 2001. Yancey's leadership, however, ended after a single-year term.

Meanwhile, a new spate of storefront churches and ethnic restaurants emerged to serve the area's rapidly growing community of Caribbean immigrants (Figs. 3.24–3.26). Mostly, though, there were signs of ambivalence. Some local food establishments happily made deliveries throughout the area but refused to enter the development. A few long-term businessmen along Talbot Avenue and Blue Hill Avenue clung to their hopes for a neighborhood revival, but they continued to complain about their inability to get business-improvement loans. Caterer Paul Brooks, whose function hall is located just a short walk from the development, welcomed the occasional patronage of Franklin Field residents (and agreed to let his neighbors paint the memorial to Poochie on the back wall of his building). At the same time, after more than twenty years in business, he struggled to acquire

FIGURE 3.25 Storefront churches along Blue Hill Avenue. In recent years, many vacant buildings along Blue Hill Avenue have been converted into storefront churches. Diverse and growing immigrant populations have also encouraged new shops and restaurants to open in the area.

FIGURE 3.26 Franklin Field wall. A half-century after public housing arrived at one end of Franklin Field, and thirty years after the neighborhood faced racial upheaval and massive disinvestment, the famous wall along Blue Hill Avenue is a silent reminder of an earlier era.

loans to upgrade his facilities. The city supported the revival of Blue Hill Avenue south from Morton Street to Mattapan Square and north from Talbot Avenue to Grove Hall, but Brooks felt caught "in the middle."[192] In 1999 a Liberian immigrant opened the Kid's Choice day-care center directly across from the Franklin Field development, surely an auspicious sign. Even so, Director Bobby Boone worried about the security of the neighborhood. "When I started seeing syringes and broken beer bottles, I didn't feel safe for the kids anymore, so we don't go over into Franklin Field. If we can't get a van to take us somewhere else, we just take a walk." A murder directly behind the center in November 1999 hardly assuaged such fears. From her vantage point next to the development she could "observe drugs being sold each day." "People are still scared in Franklin Field for their life, and their apartments, and their children. That's all they have."[193] Such a comment neatly encapsulates the ongoing struggles at Franklin Field, where adversity continues to be met with a dizzying oscillation of self-empowerment and self-defeat.

ACCOUNTING FOR FAILURE

Any convincing attempt to come to terms with the collective failure to restore Franklin Field to a desirable living environment must take account of a variety of barriers that, in many cases, were more impenetrable than those faced at West Broadway. Most obviously, the ongoing unrest in the surrounding neighborhood made it impossible to insulate one large piece of public investment from broader pressures.

David C. Gilmore found the whole redevelopment process "really pretty wearing," and as a result he chose to stop working in the public sector.[194] He sees the failure to turn around Franklin Field as the understandable result of a strategy that was still rooted in assumptions of "physical determinism": "Looking back on it—and I think I had some inkling of this at the time—you can't cure people's problems by getting them more decent housing." He points out that "we did actually try to do some job training and tenant advocacy" but acknowledges that "those efforts were much less successful in Franklin Field" than they were at D Street. He blames the adjacent neighborhoods—an "area of rampant drugs, crime, and gangs"—for the development's ongoing difficulties. By contrast, West Broadway's neighborhood had compensating qualities: "South Boston has all kinds of problems, but it's also very insular and contained and has a kind of

'Southie attitude' whether you like it or not. That sort of thing is not there in Dorchester." Franklin Field's tenants suffered from more than public housing redevelopment efforts could cure. "I felt that we were addressing 10 percent of the problems of the people there in Franklin Field," Gilmore laments. "We had a lot of successes, just building this stuff and everything. But when you really get down to it, getting the money and programming and building it is the easy part. When it comes to ongoing management, tenant selection, and the control of the development—especially in the face of these overwhelming problems of drug dependency and unemployment and welfare dependency and all that—the deck's stacked against you." Others also viewed Franklin Field's problems in terms of stacked decks, but saw them as stacked against the tenants, not the BHA.

Basil Tommy views the issue in terms of power. For him, the level of disagreements between tenants and the BHA was no greater at Franklin Field than it was at West Broadway. The key difference was that West Broadway had "lots of clout" and was in a "preferred part of town," so that much of its more positive outcome resulted "not because the BHA made choices but because of the preferences of legislators and their willingness to make additional money available." In addition to such access to opportunities, West Broadway's tenants also benefited from their ability to be much more demanding from the start about what they needed, wanted, and expected from a redevelopment. By contrast, Tommy points out, the redevelopment at Franklin Field had to be driven more by the BHA itself than by the tenants.[195] In all this, Tommy's euphemism about a "preferred part of town" seems not only a code word for racial politics but also a reminder of just how difficult it had been to implement a community-oriented redevelopment in a community that was being torn asunder by violent crime. Others involved with the Franklin Field redevelopment process see additional factors beyond neighborhood unrest, inadequate services, impoverished tenants, and poor management working to limit positive change at this particular place.

For Doris Bunte, it all comes down to race: "public housing is a necessary option for many persons of color," whereas most poor whites manage to avoid even applying for public housing. She emphasizes that nonwhites are far more willing to take public housing in white neighborhoods than whites are to venture into predominantly nonwhite areas. The combination of desperate need, political alienation, and inadequate communication constitutes a triple threat to progress. Reflecting on the story of the toeheaters under the sinks in the new kitchens at Franklin Field, placed where people could easily burn themselves, she comments that "there was no way they could have been listening to residents if they did this." Bunte also blames an inadequate budget for a lot of the problems. Because officials still thought of Franklin Field as the "second" development in terms of state funding, "the dollars weren't comparable and so therefore the redevelopment wasn't comparable." There was no pressure to recognize an inequity, she says, because "the black community didn't know anything about it, neither did the residents at Franklin Field."[196]

Harry Spence is even more forthcoming about the role of race in the struggle to redevelop Franklin Field. He had come to the BHA receiver's post talking about "targets of opportunity." He wanted to target funds and import strong managers to developments with existing effective tenant organizations, especially if they were linked to effective neighborhoods. The experience of working at Franklin Field, however, convinced him of the fundamental naiveté of this view. It quickly dawned on him that "the reason two hundred people turn out at D Street is that they had thirty *years* of reinforcement. If *five* people turn out at D Street they can get a hundred times more money than a hundred people can at Franklin Field." In political terms, "the feedback loop just works much better at D Street, because the power of the South Boston delegation is huge, and the power of the black delegation is tiny. Ultimately, you get symbolic exceptions. 'OK, we'll give Franklin Field as much.' But the message still to other nonwhite developments is that the feedback loop just doesn't work as well." When pressed about the potential of tenant organizing to provide meaningful empowerment, Spence remains unconvinced. Even with the high visibility of the pilot grant and its attendant funds for "community capacity building," Franklin Field's tenants needed to travel too great a distance. "What your asking for is that a year-and-a-half of experience in a small part of their lives, which is their housing, should overcome every bit of experience they've had through all the rest of their lives and everyone else they know who's black has had."[197]

At Franklin Field, despite the best efforts of many tenants and the presence of first-rate design consultants, the experience of redevelopment marked yet another round of dashed expectations and ongoing frustrations. And, in important ways, the project reached its most stigmatized state during the early 1990s *after* redevelopment, rather than beforehand. For Franklin Field's tenants, a half-century of struggle—whether against leaks and rodents, against racism and disinvestment, or against drugs and violence—has left this particular public neighborhood far from reclaimed.

FOUR

Commonwealth: Public Housing and Private Opportunities

IN SHARP CONTRAST to West Broadway and Franklin Field, the Commonwealth development stood distant from the racial battle-grounds that periodically tore the city of Boston apart during the late 1960s and 1970s. Although race permeates the history of this place just as it does all public neighborhoods in Boston, at Commonwealth racial tensions in the neighborhood did not drive the decline of the development to the extent that they did at either West Broadway or Franklin Field. This relative neighborhood peace did not keep the project from suffering a collapse comparable to the others, but it certainly helped to nurture its recovery. At Commonwealth, the BHA tried to manage the problem of race through judicious imposition of quotas and careful negotiation between the development and its surrounding institutions and neighborhood groups.

Geopolitically, Brighton is a separate section of Boston, an annexed municipal peninsula cradling the more affluent town of Brookline (Fig. 4.1). When the BHA built the 648-unit Commonwealth development in 1951, it replaced Brighton's last remaining farm. Not surprisingly, the location exhibited few if any of the negative characteristics often associated with public housing site selection. As at Franklin Field, Commonwealth's local politicians viewed public housing as a neighborhood amenity and were willing to trade off desirable vacant land to obtain it. Commonwealth development (long known colloquially as "Fidelis Way")

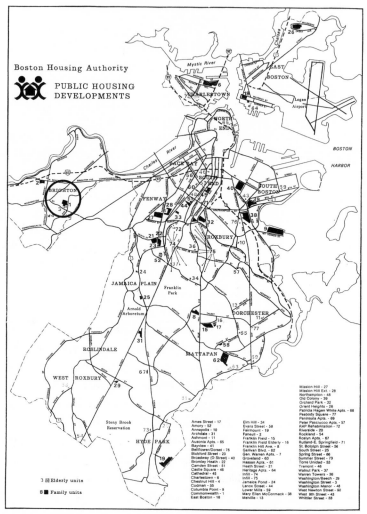

FIGURE 4.1 Brighton's Commonwealth housing development. Opened in 1951, Commonwealth enjoyed a pleasant neighborhood location, but one quite spatially isolated from other parts of Boston. Conversely, the public transit opportunities along Commonwealth Avenue afforded great connectivity.

after the lone street the BHA built to wind through it) was auspiciously located on a high ridge adjacent to its namesake avenue, a major east-west artery through the city that stretches from the Public Garden to the western suburbs. Commonwealth Avenue, initially a key spoke in Boston's streetcar suburb system of the late nineteenth century, still hosts a major public transit line, now mostly bordered by mid-rise brick apartment buildings that extend four miles westward from Boston University to Boston College.

Commonwealth's neighborhood, though predominantly white and Catholic, has demonstrated little of the feisty ethnic self-consciousness of South Boston. It has instead been a mixed-income mélange with large numbers of students and elderly residents, along with a variety of moderate-income families. In contrast to the rapid racial and ethnic turnover that engulfed Franklin Field and led to a period of extended turmoil and massive neighborhood disinvestment, the area of Brighton surrounding Commonwealth changed more slowly than did the composition of the development itself, only gradually becoming more racially and ethnically diverse. At all times, the development has been buffered (or isolated) by large medical and religious institutions that border it on its northeast and northwest sides, and by the wide swath of Commonwealth Avenue and its trolley line, which separated the project from all neighbors to the southeast. Only on the southwest did the development connect to a residential area, but even on this side most of Commonwealth was set several hundred feet back from direct engagement with the Washington Heights neighborhood.

In short, as Commonwealth's decline accelerated during the 1970s through a combination of deferred maintenance and social unrest, the development (and its residents) came to be regarded as the scourge of an otherwise stable neighborhood. By the time of the BHA receivership in 1980, the development was one of the most physically distressed in the entire system. At the same time, however, its residents were becoming highly organized, and, through a series of community planning efforts and reports, the BHA identified Commonwealth as a prime target for redevelopment. In the course of the next five years, tenants and the BHA transformed the development from a state of social and physical devastation to a nationally recognized model for public housing revitalization. The dramatic physical reconfiguration of its low-rise and mid-rise structures and the reprogramming of the site, combined with an innovative privatization of management functions, reclaimed this particular public neighborhood as an immensely valuable public resource.

BOSTON'S "WILD WEST": BRIGHTON BEFORE PUBLIC HOUSING

Through the mid-nineteenth century, Brighton, Massachusetts, remained a small independent town dominated by its cattle market, separated from Boston by the open waters of the Back Bay and by the limitations of public transportation. By the turn of the twentieth century, however, the Back Bay had been filled and the town annexed to Boston. Once a rural outpost informally known as the "Wild West" of Boston, Brighton now welcomed the streetcar-oriented suburban development that characterized other newly annexed districts such as Dorchester.

In the nineteenth century, the hilltop that eventually became home to Brighton's Commonwealth development consisted of farmland and the large Nevins family estate known as Bellvue, yet it was only a short walk from a jumble of fancy hotels, slaughterhouses, cowboy gambling spots, small shops, and middle-income residences. Following construction of a centralized abattoir a mile further to the north in 1870, Brighton housed the largest stockyard in the United States, and the cattle-oriented precincts shifted away from the more southerly residential areas.[1]

Annexation, which formally occurred in 1874, united debt-ridden Brighton and the neighboring Allston district with Boston and provided almost immediate benefits: two new schools, a library, a fire station, and a fivefold increase in the number of local police. As Boston's electric streetcar system expanded in the last decade of the century, the landscape irreversibly changed. Fewer of Brighton's citizens viewed themselves as primarily linked northward across the Charles River to Cambridge and Watertown; now the infrastructure as well as the economy tied residents to Boston. At first the primary spoke of this portion of the emerging streetcar system followed the western extension of Beacon Street, constructed between 1887 and 1892. This avenue, designed by Frederick Law Olmsted, traversed independent Brookline and paralleled Brighton's southern edge, leaving parts of Brighton itself still undeveloped.

Even before land values skyrocketed on and near Beacon Street in anticipation of easy commuter access to the center of Boston, Olmsted's firm developed plans to extend Commonwealth Avenue all the way through Brighton to the Chestnut Hill Reservoir, creating what would become another major east-west electrified spur to residential development. In 1884 Olmsted himself drew up plans for the portion of the road that would one day run past the Commonwealth public housing development, rendering it a 200-foot right-of-way, with bridle paths and some trees near the Washington Street intersection (Fig. 4.2). In 1886 a group of six Boston businessmen championed the Commonwealth Avenue extension, envisioning it as a continuation of the grand tree-lined boulevard that had already sparked development in the Back Bay. Although the proposed street route passed through land apparently owned by only four different businessmen—some of

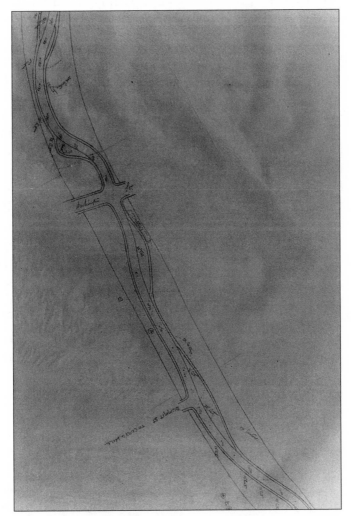

FIGURE 4.2 Designing Commonwealth Avenue. In 1884, Frederick Law Olmsted drew this sketch for the roadway section that would someday pass directly by the Commonwealth public housing development. In altered form, Commonwealth Avenue accommodated a surface trolley line (still operating), but the 200-foot right-of-way substantially isolated one side of the street from the other, a problem exacerbated by dramatic changes in elevation.

whom were even eager to donate the roadway portion in anticipation of fast profits from increased adjacent land values—the city of Boston did not approve the development plan until 1892, just as Brookline's Beacon Street neared completion. Construction delays ensued as a result of swampy terrain and large rock outcroppings, and the Depression of 1893 only compounded these frustrations by reducing the demand for development. Commonwealth Avenue did not reach completion until 1899, so Beacon Street's developers emerged clearly victorious in the ongoing competition.[2]

The city did not plant street trees along the avenue until after the turn of the century, and developers completed only a handful of apartment buildings before 1910. They constructed the brick apartment houses that now constitute Commonwealth development's southeasterly neighbors chiefly between 1910 and 1925, a symptom of the rapid expansion of the entire district (Fig. 4.3). Between 1915 and 1920, the Commonwealth Avenue area grew by 38 percent, the fastest growth rate in the city. Between 1880 and 1915, the population of Allston-Brighton had increased from 6,700 to more than 30,000, and it doubled again during the next fifteen years. By 1930 this district had a higher population density than any other outer-Boston neighborhood.[3] Boston's Wild West had become a streetcar suburb.

Along Commonwealth Avenue and elsewhere in the district, the construction boom coincided with a "Yankee exodus." Most new arrivals were middle-class Irish, although Jews composed about 15 percent of the Commonwealth Avenue section, prompting construction of more than a dozen kosher meat markets and several synagogues. By 1930 the area housed about 5,000 Jews, trailing only Dorchester's Blue Hill Avenue as a center for Jewish life in Boston. By 1950, buttressed in part by the departure of Jews from Roxbury and Dorchester, the Commonwealth Avenue section was nearly half Jewish.[4]

Across the street from Commonwealth Avenue's brick apartment buildings and atop a ridge, the future site of the Commonwealth project remained farmland, now encroached upon by development of woodframe houses to the southwest and new institutions to the north. As testament to the increased presence of Catholics in the area, in 1908 the Passionist Religious Society established St. Gabriel's Monastery as a retreat house and church. The Passionists initially occupied some of the rundown buildings of the old Nevins estate, but they built a new monastery in 1909 and sponsored construction of the present St. Gabriel's Church in 1927. Meanwhile, St. Elizabeth's Hospital opened on eight more acres of the former

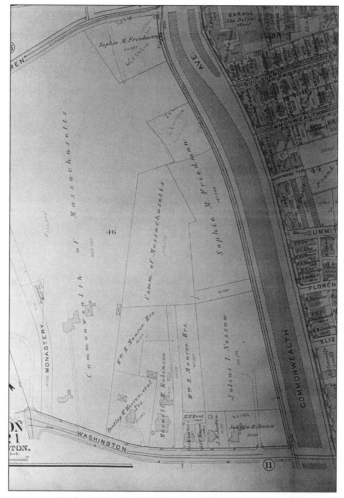

FIGURE 4.3 Brighton's last farm. By 1925 one edge of Commonwealth Avenue had been fully built out with apartment buildings. Across the street—the future site of the Commonwealth housing development—there was still farmland, much of it now owned by the Commonwealth of Massachusetts. With little other government-owned vacant land in the district, this proved a highly desirable site for public housing.

Nevins property in 1914 and became the Catholic institution that has had "the greatest material impact on Allston-Brighton." In 1930, on a nearby parcel of land, the city opened a new Brighton High School, and additional hospitals opened to lend increased credence to the name "Institution Hill."[5]

Encircled by new developments of various forms, the future site of the Commonwealth development remained state-owned farmland, the last piece of open space in an area that had been favored for quail and pheasant hunting when the century began. In 1935 local developers set their eyes on this prize, proposing a plan for an enormous apartment complex at the intersection of Commonwealth Avenue and Washington Street. Expected to contain 1,779 one- to five-room apartment units, the project was to house approximately 5,000 persons. News of the venture, to be supported by subsidies from the federal government in the form of mortgage insurance, sparked outrage from apartment house owners in the area. The Apartment House Owners Association engaged in "vigorous protest," voicing their opposition to Governor James Michael Curley and Mayor Frederick Mansfield, as well as to local and national housing officials. They argued that the project would cause "unnecessary abandonment of hundreds of apartments in the vicinity," yielding an "inevitable flood of foreclosures," lower property values, and decreased municipal tax revenue. By late 1935, however, federal housing officials and Boston neighborhood groups had already nixed a variety of limited-dividend plans to build subsidized housing in South Boston, East Boston, and elsewhere, and this project came to naught as well.

The setback was not permanent. A survey by the Boston City Planning Board in 1946 showed that every outer neighborhood in the city still retained hundreds of acres of developable land—except for Allston-Brighton, which had only 16 1/2 acres left.[6] With the 14 acres of farmland still in state ownership at this time, public housing seemed all but inevitable.

PUBLIC HOUSING ON BRIGHTON'S LAST FARM

In contrast to West Broadway, where the BHA razed the housing project site before the war—and unlike Franklin Field, where the Authority located permanent public housing on a site already developed for temporary veterans' housing—Commonwealth's planning occurred only after the war's conclusion. The BHA commenced site selection for public housing in Brighton even before the Massachusetts legislature had passed the Veterans Housing Program legislation (Chapter 200) in 1948. Initially, the Authority hoped to build near the western edge of Brighton on a site known as the City Yards, but abandoned the effort because extensive ledge outcroppings rendered the quality of the land poor. Instead, by December 1947, city and state officials looked to Institution Hill, since it contained state-owned property adjacent to the hospitals and monastery complex. A local newspaper touted the venture as a "$3,000,000 deluxe veteran's 335-unit apartment house project," and Mayor Curley extolled the site as "one of the better apartment house sections of Brighton and one of the finest the city could procure." In August 1948, with the necessary legislation in place, the State Board of Housing formally approved the project, now expected to contain 648 units and cost more than $6 million, approximately double the original estimates.[7]

The location of the new project seemed ideal. The BHA described the site as "a high point of land on the west side of Commonwealth Avenue at Washington Street" that was "strictly devoted to institutional and residential uses." With "no industry whatsoever in this neighborhood," the housing project was "extremely fortunately situated," abutting St. Gabriel's Passionist monastery and church, Brighton High School, Hahnemann Hospital, and the U.S. Marine Hospital, and adjacent to a small group of neighborhood stores, an apartment building, and a couple of private homes. The BHA could think of "no adverse influences in this neighborhood." Even better, the proximity of Commonwealth Avenue meant that tenants could walk to public transportation—the MTA's Lake Street–Park Street line. The K–6 Baldwin School was only a hundred yards from the site, and two other elementary schools and a middle school were within a ten-minute walk. All had room to serve the children of the new project.[8] By grouping the apartments into seven six-story blocks and six three-story walk-ups, the architect, Saul Moffie, managed to leave more than 75 percent of the site as open space (Figs. 4.4–4.7).

In a neighborhood dominated by large institutions and full of similarly scaled private brick apartment buildings, public housing fit in well. Most everyone welcomed the arrival of well-screened vets to this part of Brighton.[9] The *Boston Globe* (like most everyone at the time) referred to Commonwealth as the "Monastery Veterans' housing project" and described the new development as a "hill-top brick apartment 'village.'" The monastery moniker derived from its location adjacent to St. Gabriel's monastery and church, whose pastor, Reverend Bertrand

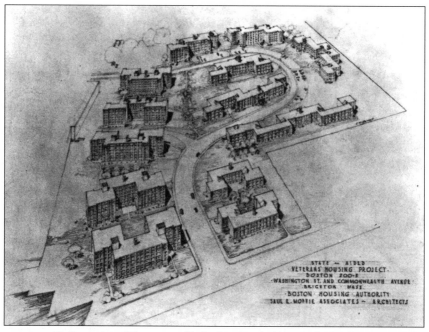

FIGURE 4.4. Bird's-eye view of Commonwealth development. Architect Saul E. Moffie's sketch shows seven mid-rise buildings, six low-rise structures, and lots of room for grass.

McDewell, strongly supported the project. McDewell's enthusiasm dimmed, however, once he discovered that his parishioners might not get a large share of the nearby apartments.

As Father McDewell told a reporter from the *Globe,* "I have asked for only 30 families. I felt that, since the politicians are getting 30 families each, I should get 30 families. I'm not trying to fill the project." The Passionist priest also took his complaint directly to Mayor Hynes, declaring: "It would seem that I, who worked for months to put this project through, should have some rights in this matter." He added that construction of the new St. Gabriel's School (located between the monastery and the project) would save the city of Boston "thousands of dollars" (presumably by siphoning off public school demand), so it was only fair that he be "able to name a few of the people who will occupy that project." McDewell himself took full credit for bringing about "this big project," noting that he had "almost single-handedly" pushed it through, overcoming the objections of some of the same politicians who now asserted claims upon its tenant selection. Now, he complained, BHA officials had "thrown a smokescreen" around the cases he

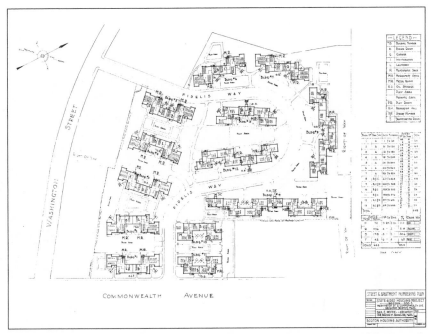

FIGURE 4.5 Plan of Commonwealth development. Moffie's plan shows a single street, Fidelis Way, snaking through the superblock of the new project. Predictably, the project quickly took on the nickname "Fidelis Way."

referred to them and "kicked their applications from pillar to post" in an "abominable" manner. Hynes insisted that "no tenancies should be parcelled out to any politicians or other individuals, and that persons who are given apartments in any project should be eligible without regard to political influence." Even as the mayor took the high road, however, a Brighton city councilor launched an inquiry into the "constant reports that people are paying money to obtain apartments and that applicants must also have a sponsor."

BHA Board Chairman Cornelius Kiley predictably denied all the accusations and insisted that "political considerations" played no part in selecting applicants. "This Authority receives literally thousands of requests from people in public, private and religious life asking for consideration for certain families," Kiley admitted, but "this is only coincidental and not the determining factor in whether the family is housed or not." Kiley and Hynes implicitly condoned the prevailing practice of patronage as a means of bringing particular families to the attention of the Authority, even if they did not publicly choose to acknowledge the extent to

FIGURE 4.6 Commonwealth under construction, 1950.

which such applicants, if otherwise eligible, would be housed. Undaunted by his seemingly low rank on the patronage totem pole, McDewell continued to insist that the families on his list "would make good citizens of this area." The BHA, embarrassed that its tenant-selection practices had been criticized in the head-lines of the city's major newspaper, responded by examining the eligibility of McDewell's cohort on a case-by-case basis. As it turned out, project-wide, fully three-quarters of the original tenants came from outside Allston-Brighton, so, to the extent that patronage played a role, it was far from a purely parochial exer-cise.[10] At Commonwealth, as elsewhere during the early 1950s, admission to pub-lic housing could be considered a reward and a measure of well-connectedness.

As Commonwealth received its first tenants late in 1951, the BHA filled all but one of the initial 281 units with white families. This prompted an outcry from the

FIGURE 4.7 Commonwealth: "Another Veterans Housing Project."

Massachusetts Commission against Discrimination (MCAD) and led to weekly meetings between MCAD Commissioner Elwood McKenney and BHA officials. The MCAD charged that nonwhite families had been "influenced to express preference of the so-called segregated projects" or lacked sufficient information about alternatives. Reinforcing this viewpoint, the NAACP established a coalition of twenty "community relations agencies" to press for further public housing integration. By May, the MCAD had identified twenty-four minority families who wished to live at Commonwealth and were deemed financially eligible to do so. Satisfied with the BHA's willingness to consider such applicants for admission, the commissioner concluded that "there is little doubt that the Boston Housing Authority is at the present time doing all that is being asked of it to cooperate with this Commission, and to see to it that there is neither discrimination nor segregation in the Boston public housing program." The *Boston City Record* reported the process in the best possible light, under the headline "Mayor Hynes Highly Commended for Efforts to End Discrimination in Families Admitted to Housing Projects." The NAACP's coalition also praised Hynes for "fairness" in tenanting Commonwealth on an integrated basis, but pointed out that many older projects remained wholly segregated, that housing authority personnel remained almost exclusively white, and that potential public housing applicants were not adequately informed that new public housing was being made available on a nondiscriminatory basis. In August, the MCAD head McKenney wrote to Hynes again to express his pleasure that eighteen of Commonwealth's apartments had been tenanted by nonwhite families. The MCAD's aggressive action—and the willingness of Mayor Hynes to cooperate—ensured that Commonwealth opened as an integrated development, albeit one that was more than 97 percent white (Fig. 4.8). To a neighborhood that had been 99.7 percent white before the development, however, the black presence at Commonwealth seemed quite noteworthy.[11]

FIGURE 4.8 Multiracial children at play, 1951. The BHA took great pride in the fact that Commonwealth opened as a racially integrated development (even though it was 97 percent white).

Those who first occupied Commonwealth's 648 apartments toiled away at more than a hundred different occupations, though only a dozen of the adult women reported working outside the home. Among the men there were eighty clerks, fifty-nine salesmen, and thirty-eight chauffeurs. The rest worked in all manner of trades, industries, and professions. At Commonwealth in 1952 one could find the homes of thirty-three laborers, but also thirteen engineers, seven accountants, four attorneys, a dentist, and a physician. Tenants with training in various building-maintenance trades (such as electricians, plumbers, carpenters, and painters) greatly outnumbered the on-site BHA staff assigned to deal with such matters. The development as a whole resembled a complete cross-section of the American city, replete with teachers, bakers, butchers, milkmen, barbers, pharmacists, postal workers, jewelers, bartenders, opticians, social workers, and repairmen. If all of their workplaces had been located in the same place, the development would have seemed a wholly self-sufficient enclave. And it would have been the safest place around, given that nearly 10 percent of Commonwealth's original households were headed by a policeman or a fireman.[12] Although no more than a couple of dozen households were headed by men on active duty with the U.S. Navy, Army, or Air Force, this veterans' housing project clearly placed a premium on public service when evaluating and selecting good tenants.

Within a short walk along Commonwealth Avenue, tenants of the early 1950s had access to many of the same amenities enjoyed by their counterparts at West Broadway and Franklin Field (Fig. 4.9). There was the Washington Heights Meat Market, Hirschorn's Food Mart, the Nancy Ann Food Shop, the Fruit Basket, and the Peter Pan Bakery. Residents were also in easy reach of Melvin Pharmacy, Aberdeen Garden Liquors, the Delux Delicatessen and Restaurant, a Chinese laundry, a clothing store, and a dentist, not to mention the range of immediately adjacent hospital facilities.

TENSIONS EMERGE

Almost from the moment of first occupancy, however, tensions began to develop between Commonwealth (already referred to as Fidelis Way) and its neighbors. In particular, disputes arose with Hahnemann Hospital, located just east of the development. In early 1952, faced with complaints that youths from the project made continual disturbances, the BHA erected a 270-foot-long chain-link fence "so that the children residing in the development might be prohibited from entering the grounds of the Hospital." Since the fence was only four feet high, however, it hardly constituted an insurmountable barrier. By October, a Hahnemann of-

FIGURE 4.9 A lot of children, a lot of milk. When Commonwealth opened, Fidelis Way received a lot of traffic from milk delivery trucks.

ficial complained directly to Boston Mayor John B. Hynes. He expressed the "annoyance" of hospital supervisors faced with "boys running over the hospital grounds, damaging trees and shrubbery as well as the sign 'Hahnemann Hospital' that was erected a year ago at considerable expense." "Since the Housing buildings have been occupied," he charged, "there have been eleven (11) windows broken by boys throwing stones, and one day this week a stone was thrown through a third floor window with such force that it went across the room. It is readily apparent that if a patient had been injured, the hospital corporation (and Trustees) would have been involved in Court action." He added that efforts to speak to the boys "in a friendly manner" had been "to little or no avail."

Three days later the mayor sent a note to BHA Chairman James Mahar, asking him to investigate and suggesting that "one of the best ways of controlling this would be to have the manager or someone in authority apprehend one of the boys committing an act of vandalism and then requesting his parents to pay for it. In this way, it might set an example to other boys." Mahar responded immediately to the mayor. He stressed the presence of the new fence but agreed to send out a letter "asking the tenants residing at the development to be more considerate of the patients." In an age of close cooperation between a mayor and his BHA chairman, when public housing still relied on paternalism as well as patronage, it is hardly surprising to see evidence of prompt attention at the highest levels, however ineffectual the action. Even though some journalists still referred to the development as the "Monastery project," its fifteen hundred children hardly viewed themselves as nascent monks.[13]

Local City Councilor Michael J. Ward undertook a more concerted effort to find better play areas for the kids of Fidelis Way. He repeatedly reiterated this "need and urgency" to Chairman Mahar and passed along a petition containing more than five hundred signatures from those "in this district" who supported the idea. He also suggested that "chains be put across the parking entrances, at least from 9:00 A.M. to 5:00 P.M. for the protection of the children playing in that area." Even as the BHA built one chain-link fence to keep kids in, Ward wanted further chains to protect them from the automotive incursions of outsiders. Mahar acknowledged "great concern" and argued that "the very curbing of much of the teen age delinquency which presently exists in some sections of this city and in any other large city, is best checked by children participating in recreational facilities." Unfortunately, he told Councilor Ward, the "interpretation of the law allowing for the construction of housing accommodations for veterans by the State Housing Board has not allowed for the expenditure of any monies for recreational purposes."[14]

As would later become typical of residents at this development, tenants themselves soon championed their own cause. In 1955 one Commonwealth resident took the matter directly to Hynes:

> Dear Mr. Mayor,
> I live in a project and we have no place to play baseball.
>   We would like it if you made an athletic field to play ball in. I'm ten years old and like to play ball. Would you please grant our request. Our neighbors complain because we make too much noise.
>   Yours sincerely,
>   (signed) Leo Sullivan

Hynes passed the matter on to Mahar, who responded not to young Mr. Sullivan but to the mayor, affirming that "local housing authorities have not been allowed to provide any community facilities under the State-aided program," and adding that, in any case, "lack of space" would prevent construction of a baseball field at Commonwealth.[15]

In early 1954 another tenant complained directly to Mayor Hynes about the large number of broken windows at no. 23 Fidelis Way. BHA Board Chairman Owen Gallagher assured the mayor that the "constant maintenance problem due to vandalism" was caused "by children who mostly do not reside at the development." He blamed students at Brighton High School and the Taft Middle School, who "use our Development for short cuts to and from schools." To combat such intrusions, the BHA installed grilles over all basement windows and began locking some outside doors to buildings to limit access to outsiders. As to the matter of broken glass in exterior doors, Gallagher assured the mayor that the problem "is being remedied at the present time by substituting a panel which reduces the number of lights of glass in each door from nine to three."[16] Unable to check the problem through new policies, the BHA resorted instead to mathematics, an innovative if spurious way to eliminate two-thirds of glass breakage.

Other local politicians and residents rose to complain about traffic dangers. The BHA intended superblock construction to increase the separation between cars and pedestrians, but high-speed incursions into the Fidelis Way loop from Commonwealth Avenue posed a continual threat. Accidents occurred throughout the 1950s, and one observer noted that "hardly a day or night passes without the report of screeching brakes from near misses." In September 1958, six-year-old Walter Schroeder died at St. Elizabeth's after falling under the wheels of a slowly moving election sound truck. Schroeder, a first-grader at St. Gabriel's School and the son of one of the project's resident policemen, had been hanging on the back of the placard-festooned truck with other kids. The Boston press blamed public housing policy for the tragedy, noting that "project parents were bitter over the failure of authorities to provide play areas." One parent claimed that five or six children had been struck by cars, yet the BHA insisted on surrounding the only grassy area with chain-link fences. "They told us we'd be evicted if our children played there," another resident remarked. "There are 648 families here, and there must be 3,000 children. The chain-link fences keep the grass green and they keep the children out, but they don't save children's lives." Desperate parents told their children to "play in the project parking areas," even as BHA staff struggled to keep those lots off-limits.[17]

Like their counterparts at other Boston housing projects, tenants at Commonwealth fought three battles simultaneously—external ones against the BHA and against accusatory neighbors, and an internal one between the "good tenants" and the minority of residents and outsiders who initiated continual disruptions.

These battles, which began as infrequent skirmishes in the late 1950s, gradually escalated during the 1960s.

Shortly after John Collins took office as mayor in 1960, an aide prepared a thoroughly scurrilous overview of the Boston Housing Authority personnel he had inherited, pairing character assassination with an account of which politicians each particular manager or official had used to obtain his position. Invariably, these long-term employees were linked to the "wrong" Irish pols—either past mayors or BHA chairmen or, worse still, to State Senator Johnny Powers, whom Collins had just defeated in the 1959 election. Commonwealth's manager, Henry Chambers, was seen as a "harmless guy" but couldn't be trusted because he was the godchild of the outgoing BHA Board chairman, John Carroll. Chambers "rides home evenings" with his godfather, the aide warned, and is "beholden to him and no doubt 'reports' all the time." Assistant Manager Robert Hardy, a Hynes appointment, fared no better, since he was "no doubt Powers a mile a minute." Hardy, a musician who "owns a rest home on the side," was seen as a "limited talent" who was "always 'bitching' about something" and paid little attention to his job: "no strain—no pain—if you know what I mean." It is not clear that Collins paid much attention to these assessments when deciding whom to retain, but they clearly signaled an era when patronage rights at the BHA remained within the mayoral orbit, as long as the mayor could outmaneuver other contending politicians.[18]

Long after Chambers and Hardy had moved on, however, Commonwealth continued to experience problems with its managers. In 1967, senior BHA management officials came to the project to address long-standing problems with Manager Stephen Bowen, who was accused of "extended and unexplained absenteeism and other accounts of misconduct." They told him that his fellow workers had been extremely critical of his performance and blamed the BHA for tolerating it. They warned Bowen that "this was the last, very last chance you would have to protect your position with this Authority." Bowen prevailed, though, and remained at Commonwealth for the rest of the decade.[19]

Gradually, during the course of the 1960s, the variety and severity of complaints about BHA management and maintenance at Commonwealth began to increase. At first the issues were rooted in perennial problem areas such as elevators, insects, and hallway cleaning. Some residents complained about the personality of Manager Bowen, while others chided the BHA for lax maintenance. As one disgruntled woman put it, "If the men that work for the project gave fifty cents worth of labor for every dollar paid, rather than spending time in nearby bar-rooms, maybe the City of Boston could afford to do what should be done." In 1965 the city building commissioner repeatedly cited the BHA for violating state regulations in the operation of its basement daycare; by 1970 others complained that management had failed to stop racial and religious harassment of some black and some Jewish tenants; and in 1971 complaints centered on the continued use of illegal incinerators.[20] In short, Commonwealth's second decade of operation brought increased tension between the development and the housing authority accused of mismanaging it.

Any kind of tension, by its very nature, operates in more than one direction; just as Commonwealth's tenants complained about the BHA, so too the housing authority found continual fault with many of Commonwealth's residents. Throughout the 1960s, BHA officials repeatedly pleaded with tenants to behave more responsibly. Replying to a complaint about hallway conditions at Commonwealth, BHA Chairman Edward Hassan called for "a real and earnest effort on the part of some of the mothers and fathers to control the children responsible for such conditions," adding that "management constantly pleads with tenants to remove baby carriages, bicycles, sleds, etc. in the hallways." He requested that some tenants reduce the "amount of deliberate glass breakage and defacing of walls." "A subsidized public housing program," Hassan noted, "cannot survive financially without the thoughtfulness and consideration of the occupants in helping to keep maintenance and utility costs within reasonable limitation." With adequate cooperation from tenants and neighborhood residents, Hassan noted, public housing could be "a source of pride" to the "general public."

Tenants often engaged their state legislators to complain about various aspects of tenant behavior or inadequate response to maintenance requests. In 1964 Representative Arnold Epstein called upon the BHA to replace all doorbells at Commonwealth. An exasperated Hassan responded by noting that "substantially all" of the doorbells at Commonwealth failed to operate "due to constant tampering by persons unknown over a period of years." Moreover, many tenants requested that the doorbells be disconnected "because of the many pranksters who delighted in placing a pin or some other object into the bell so that the bell would ring constantly during all hours of the evening." The Authority, Hassan claimed, had "conscientiously and devotedly" tried to address these problems, and it would "be futile to attempt to expend thousands of dollars to replace door bells." Meanwhile, with no way for residents to know if they had visitors, at least one tenant suffered because emergency medical personnel "left when no one answered the doorbell." Other tenants registered complaints about abandoned cars in the development as well as malfunctioning elevators. Elevator troubles had periodically plagued the project since the year it was built, but by the late 1960s these problems became increasingly severe, as deferred maintenance combined with deliberate sabotage. Once again, tenants complained to local politicians, who in turn pressured BHA officials to do better. Julius Bernstein, the most tenant-oriented Board chairman of the entire era, felt thoroughly frustrated by the problem, which he claimed was caused by "young vandals who have been undoing the repairs . . . almost as quickly as the repairman leaves the building."[21] With the BHA financially unable to cope with its lack of operating subsidies and physically unable to contain youthful pranks and incursions, residents were left to suffer.

When tenants complained to State Senator Oliver Ames about declining conditions and rooftop mischief at Commonwealth in 1964, Ames suggested that the BHA erect fences or barriers on the roofs of buildings to prevent kids from falling off. Hassan, who viewed himself as in charge of "the moral side of housing" and well as the physical parts, consistently called for greater parental responsibility. The "real answer," Hassan told Ames, "is for the parents to forcefully and specifically warn their children that under no circumstances should they go on to the roofs of the buildings." Unwilling to make rooftop adjustments, Hassan took a more grounded approach, agreeing only to post more "Slow Children" signs along Fidelis Way. At Commonwealth, as elsewhere during the mid-1960s, the BHA struggled between its lingering paternalism and the growing realization that it was losing control of its developments and their residents.[22]

Until civil rights pressures and internal reformers forced the BHA to accept all families regardless of their source of income, seasoned BHA staffers fought a rearguard action on behalf of the traditional nuclear families who once populated the projects. Even in 1964, the tenant-selection chief John Crowley still attempted to keep welfare-dependent tenants out of the "better" developments such as Commonwealth. "In the interest of assuring solvency," Crowley would write to such applicants, it is necessary "for the time being" to assign only tenants "who have incomes calling for rentals in excess of the minimum rental" associated with ADC status. "Also," he reminded such would-be public neighbors, "Veteran status is required."[23] As late as 1970, top BHA officials would provide commendation letters ("to be placed in your file") to individual tenants who exhibited particularly meritorious behavior (such as taking care of common hallway maintenance).[24] Not all Commonwealth residents won merit badges, however, and skirmishes with nearby institutions occurred with increased frequency and rancor.

Battling the Neighborhood

The perennial tensions between the project and its neighboring hospitals continued throughout the 1960s. In 1962, Hahnemann Hospital Board President Parker Converse took the matter to BHA Chairman Hassan and to the Boston police. Converse reminded the BHA of the hospital's long history of problems caused by "the vandalism of the children in the Project" and contended that the situation had "grown considerably worse and dangerous," to the point where it threatened the safety of patients. Converse was even more forthright with Police Chief Edward McNamara. He called Commonwealth's children "generally malicious and destructive," adding that "they ignore 'no trespassing' signs, have repeatedly broken the shrubs, climbed the trees, and done so much damage in this area alone that we have been forced to give up any attempts at keeping the grounds looking presentable. A great deal of hospital money has been really wasted in this endeavor." Converse noted that hospital personnel frequently called the police at the request of doctors, patients, priests, and visitors—whenever the situation went "beyond our control to handle." He counted thirty-six broken or cracked windows, and noted one recent Friday evening when "a good-sized stone was thrown into the dining room on the first floor during a supper period; and at the same time a stone was thrown into a private room almost directly over the dining room," narrowly missing "an elderly, very feeble gentleman." Other stones had been thrown through windows of an operating room, sending glass splinters all through equipment and supplies and necessitating the closing of that room, forcing postponement of surgery. In response, the local police captain called for an eight-foot-high fence to be erected around the entire development "to protect both the Project and the hospital." Undaunted, some youths threw rocks at a neighboring synagogue instead. Commonwealth, still without its baseball facility, had no shortage of would-be pitchers.[25]

By 1967 BHA central management made little effort to suggest that perpetrators of mischief might be nonresidents. The Authority simply chose to apologize for the "annoyance" caused by "children of tenants at our Commonwealth development" and offered to "cooperate in trying to eliminate any disturbance they may cause to your patients and staff."[26]

Commonwealth residents and BHA staff continued to seek alternative recreational outlets for the development's young people. Beginning in 1969, tenant groups at Commonwealth actively sought ways to obtain adjacent land for playground and park use. In 1972 the BHA General Counsel acknowledged the "dire need of recreational facilities at this project" and urged BHA support for a plan to use "surplus" U.S. Public Health Service Hospital land and the right-of-way for an unbuilt street behind the development for this purpose. Eventually, another piece of city-owned land adjacent to Commonwealth was developed into Overlook Park. This probably did divert some unwanted attention away from Commonwealth's hospital neighbors, though the park itself, tucked behind the development, proved difficult to supervise.[27]

BATTLING FELLOW TENANTS

As the battles between Commonwealth tenants and neighboring hospitals persisted, and as tensions continued to develop between residents and BHA management, a third kind of strain emerged, one that pitted tenant against tenant. As problems at the development became more apparent, residents understandably began to blame fellow residents, especially since they perceived the BHA to be increasingly lax about whom they were permitting to reside in the project.

A decade after first occupancy, the development's demographic profile had shifted substantially. Once a place almost exclusively devoted to families with young children—housing fewer than a dozen retirees—it now had a significant and growing population of elderly residents. Increasingly, the presence of Commonwealth's large youth population created tensions not only with neighboring hospitals but with neighbors in the project itself. Even though 75 percent of the original households had moved elsewhere within a decade, many of those families who stayed now had teens instead of toddlers. As one resident complained to Mayor Collins in 1964, "The hallways are a hangout for a wild crowd of teenagers, where they at times even have drinking parties! These youngsters get rather rough, and it is frightening to get by them. When the manager of the project is told about this, he says, 'there is nothing I can do, call the police yourself!'"[28]

As early as 1964, a group of tenants circulated a petition urging the eviction of one particular family for constituting "a constant threat to the peace and contentment of the other neighbors in the building and throughout the neighborhood."[29]

Despite such action, however, through the mid-1960s BHA officials simply could not regard Commonwealth as one of their chief problem spots. In an era of major civil rights challenges to the BHA's entrenched policies of segregation, the Authority had to contend with the travails of "pioneer" families in South Boston and racial turnover in Dorchester. A few stray rocks in Brighton registered much more strongly with the neighbors than it did with the BHA. The Authority paid closer attention to destructive behavior on its own property but, despite repeated complaints of "vandalism and rowdyism," the BHA judged the situation at Commonwealth as less "aggravated" than that prevailing "in many other locations." Rather, the Authority assured its critics, "We have enjoyed very good cooperation with the police, and the officers in this area are in regular contact with our management personnel."[30]

By the late 1960s, Commonwealth tenants frequently complained about loitering that resulted from inadequately locked doors to buildings. One such protest, submitted to the "Tell It to Joe" Action Line (a complaint department that appeared daily in the *Boston Traveler* and on Sundays in the *Herald*), received a particularly poetic response from BHA Director of Management Albert J. Palmer:

> "The whining schoolboy, with satchel, and shining morning face, creeping like snail unwillingly to school" said Shakespeare, except that in this case we substitute a pack of cigarettes for the satchel and the boys now loiter in the hallway, at 29 Fidelis Way, Brighton, smoking cigarettes, before going to school. The rear door has been reopened over the strong objections of tenants. We'll try again.[31]

As problems with tenants deepened, the BHA grew less literary and less flippant. In 1969, Commonwealth's manager, Stephen Bowen, called upon the BHA to provide a full-time social worker to be shared with three other developments, but even this modest request could not be met. Leo Donovan, the BHA's director of management, acknowledged that "the need is certainly well-documented" and stated that "we have pressed and dramatized the urgent need for social services in our State-Aided developments." The problem, he emphasized, lay with the State Board of Housing, which refused to budget for such services. In the meantime, Donovan promised, "we will try to assign a worker on those crisis situations, as you report them."[32]

By the late 1960s, the growing contingent of elderly residents expressed ever greater frustration with the noise of children in their buildings, yielding the first calls to designate some buildings for elderly-only occupancy. Gertrude Weiner, an attorney with the Boston Legal Assistance Project, took up the cause of Commonwealth's seniors in 1968, a time when fully 291 households at the development were headed by an elderly person. Weiner sent letters not only to BHA Chairman Jacob Brier, but also to Brighton's state representative, Norman Weinberg, and to Mayor Kevin White, accompanied by petitions with sixty-six signatures calling for the conversion of one of Commonwealth's mid-rise buildings into elderly-only housing. Such a change, the tenants asserted, would enable them to be nearer to transportation and shopping, would permit dedicated recreation areas, and would free them from "children or noisy families in their buildings."[33]

In 1971 elderly residents at Commonwealth requested dead-bolt locks to frustrate would-be intruders, but these were not authorized until two years later. Other kinds of intruders were already inside the buildings as squatters; the BHA launched investigations into the presence of "unauthorized residents" in Commonwealth's apartments, a violation of Authority policy against subletting apartments. By 1973 concern for the elderly grew more vocal, with a variety of efforts made to secure some community meeting space within the development. Tenant leaders garnered the support of the Allston-Brighton Area Planning Action Council (APAC), which termed the lack of elderly lounge space at Commonwealth "one of the more serious problems we have dealt with over the years." The tenants also worked through Attorney Weiner, who helped with the lobbying of state legislators. Brighton's Weinberg interceded with BHA Administrator Cornelius Connors, commenting that "the Fidelis Way Project is no bed of roses for the residents" and that he ventured there only "with a great deal of trepidation with respect to my personal safety." Weinberg concluded on a personal note: "I feel that we do not at present do an adequate job for these people and frankly I feel quite guilty about it."[34]

Despite the growing concerns of residents and the lingering guilt of local politicians, by most measures Commonwealth remained one of the BHA's more enduring successes during the 1960s. The citywide study of BHA tenants conducted by the Brandeis doctoral candidate Gerald Taube in 1969 found Commonwealth to be one of the few public neighborhoods left that still served upwardly mobile tenants. "They do not reside here because of impoverished circumstances," Taube observed, "rather because it enables them to live an otherwise middle-class existence, while they are preparing to move upward financially." Indicative

FIGURE 4.10 Stephen Brown and John Murphy, best friends in 1971.

of overall tenant satisfaction, an "overwhelming majority" said that they would help their friends or relatives to move into the project. Most Commonwealth respondents described themselves as "middle class," and the development boasted a lower proportion of families receiving AFDC (6 percent) than any other BHA family project. Taube's study acknowledged that many residents complained about slow response to maintenance requests, inadequate recreation facilities, dirty hallways, and carousing teenagers, but contended that "the project is not plagued with serious trouble" (Fig. 4.10). The vast majority of tenants surveyed expressed no fear about living in the development and indicated that any "trouble" came chiefly from the incursions of outsiders. "Aside from the manager's lack of responsiveness," Taube concluded, "these people, at least comparatively, have little to complain about in public housing."[35]

For the first twenty years of its existence Commonwealth generally seems to have received high marks from residents. Lengthy interviews conducted with seventeen Commonwealth residents who first moved into the development before the mid-1970s reveal a place that was quiet and clean with reasonably well-kept grounds. Notwithstanding the sizable collection of sundry complaints from the 1950s and 1960s that have survived in the BHA archives, it seems clear that Commonwealth managed to delay the onset of the tumult that had already confronted both West Broadway and Franklin Field by the late 1960s.

This was no more than a temporary reprieve, however; throughout the 1970s, Commonwealth's problems mounted rapidly.

FIDELIS WAY, SCOURGE OF THE NEIGHBORHOOD

The BHA and the housing developments it managed underwent a prolonged period of decline during the 1970s, marked by institutional corruption, financial distress, physical deterioration of the housing stock, and social disruption among the residents and their neighbors. A combination of factors necessitated the redevelopment effort at Commonwealth. Some factors were specific to this individual housing development, while others were more rooted in broader failures of the public housing system. Although there were certainly aspects of the architectural design that contributed to the problems faced by residents, at its core, Commonwealth suffered from a breakdown in management that exacerbated both physical and social decline.

One measure of the shifting fortunes of Commonwealth can be observed by tracing the evolution of its name. Neighborhood identities are both self-constructed and imposed by others. By the late 1960s, tenants and their advocates consistently referred to the project as Fidelis Way, an obvious extension of the fact that all project apartment addresses also carried this name. For outsiders, too, the name Fidelis Way stuck, especially once the project began to decline and neighbors wished to distinguish this place from the less-tarnished precincts that marked the rest of Commonwealth Avenue. From both perspectives, the name Fidelis Way emphasized uniqueness as well as isolation. Meanwhile, official BHA correspondence continued to use the formal name Commonwealth—and some long-term BHA employees even referred to the place as "Monastery" into the early 1970s. Tenants took on "Commonwealth" in the name of the Tenant Task Force and its successor organization, the Commonwealth Tenants Association, but this seemed due more to legal requirement than to firm conviction. Throughout the 1970s, as the project's reputation declined, it was always "Fidelis" that bore the brunt of criticism.

Between 1969 and 1975, the BHA tried five different managers at Fidelis Way, and none of them had the ability or the funds to stem the deteriorating conditions at the development or to arrest the outflow of long-time tenants. To the extent that Fidelis residents had a choice about where to live in the early 1970s, they increasingly chose to go elsewhere. Ninety families left during the second half of 1975 alone. The manager at the time, Tom Finch, observed that those who departed tended to be "the people who have the incomes—the jobs—to deal in the private market." Abraham Halbfinger, the rabbi of neighboring Congregation Kadimah-Toras Moshe since 1965, watched the change: "When I first moved here, everybody wanted to live in the Commonwealth Development. After the veterans started moving out, it changed from a tight-knit community and became almost like a jungle." In 1975 80 percent of those moving out were white; two-thirds had lived at the development for more than six years; and the majority found private housing in the suburbs of Boston. They fled from an environment of increased crime, which included home invasions as well as an epidemic of purse-snatchings. Some blacks left as well, seeking to evade "barely veiled racism." By 1975, interest in apartments at Commonwealth had shifted from older white families to younger minority families on public assistance. A development that was 92 percent white as late as 1969 now had a minority population of 30 percent. The BHA expected the shift to continue given that Brighton residents no longer considered the development a local resource. In 1970 21 percent of arrivals to Commonwealth had come from Allston-Brighton, but a survey of the waiting list five years later showed that only 11 percent of applicants were residents of this area. Any lingering demand for housing at Fidelis Way among whites was almost entirely for scarce one-bedroom units, whereas demand for two-, three-, or four-bedroom apartments came almost exclusively from nonwhite households.[36]

The racial shift was matched by a parallel socioeconomic change. In 1969, only 28 percent of Fidelis Way's households were headed by a single parent; six years later, that figure had ballooned to 73 percent, bringing the development closer to the citywide BHA average. Similarly, in 1969 fewer than one in ten families at Commonwealth received AFDC (a figure comparable to Allston-Brighton as a whole) but, by 1975, one-third of households were on welfare and 82 percent reported no employed worker. In little more than five years, a housing development that had blended in reasonably well with its neighborhood, both physically and socioeconomically, had become a major neighborhood sore point. As Rabbi Halbfinger puts it, "the neighborhood went downhill and a lot of people blamed it on Commonwealth because it was bringing in people who were not stable."[37]

At the same time, however, the project continued to attract the interest and support of a few well-connected outsiders. With the victory of the BHA tenants in the Perez case in 1975, Judge Paul Garrity appointed Robert Whittlesey as master, charged with transforming the BHA. Whittlesey and his staff made visits to all developments but paid particular attention to a few places where they felt real change could happen. Among these were both D Street and Fidelis Way.

Fidelis Way appealed to Whittlesey for several reasons, not least because it served as an example of a racially integrated development at a time when the rest of Boston was at war over busing. In contrast to D Street, where both blacks and Puerto Ricans had been forced out, and unlike many other developments like Franklin Field that had "tipped" completely from white to black, Fidelis Way struck Whittlesey as a place where "we could achieve integration and improved management." Whittlesey came in with "an orientation toward private management," and he hoped that this advantageous site with its high proportion of older households would offer "a clear possibility" for successful transformation.[38]

Whittlesey's visits to Fidelis Way began in earnest in October 1975 and provided the master with a good sense of the problems and potentials of an increasingly desperate place. His team confirmed that the biggest changes at the development had occurred only since the early 1970s, when it "slipped from being one of the most desirable developments in the BHA system to one exhibiting many characteristics of decline: physical deterioration, boarded windows, vacant units, unkept grounds, accelerating move-outs of 'stable' families, racial transition, conflict between elderly residents and children, [and] deteriorated levels of service." All this sent the project on "a rapidly accelerating downward track," one that could only "be reversed or slowed down by skillful and thorough intervention."[39]

The master's staff observed a highly destructive combination of deferred maintenance and rampant vandalism as well as "a feeling of powerlessness and apathy" among many tenants. During 1975, five of the seven active members of the Tenant Task Force moved away from the development, confirming and deepening the malaise. Police made a dozen arrests for purse-snatching but could never prosecute because witnesses refused to come forward and get involved. The local police tried to organize a meeting with Fidelis juveniles, but no one showed up.[40]

In March 1975, the BHA and the Commonwealth Task Force temporarily shut down "Our House," a basement youth center established in 1972 as an attempt to "bridge any communication gap between the Fidelis community and its Youth," introduce "educational and vocational training and counseling," and yield "off-street social and recreational outlets to an area currently with little or no access to area-wide resources." Instead, the facility suffered from costly vandalism, ineffective supervision, and twenty-five registered complaints from tenants. Although the teen center reopened that June with promises of refurbished space and a grant from the State Department of Mental Health for a part-time worker, this funding soon ran out. Active use of the facility shifted from almost all white youths to a group that was almost entirely black, and by 1976 its coordinator reported that he sometimes had to shut the kids out rather than put up with rowdy behavior.[41] Once again, supervised recreation—seen as the socially productive flipside to vandalism—proved difficult to introduce at Fidelis Way.

Even the development's ongoing modernization program proved to be "more of a problem than a solution," as protracted delays further alienated tenants from BHA staff. At the same time, the master—who preferred to use the official name Commonwealth development—recognized that the project still potentially held long-term appeal owing to its solid construction, desirable neighborhood, convenience to transportation and shopping, and unparalleled views of Boston. Boston's views of Commonwealth, by contrast, continued to deteriorate.[42]

NEIGHBORHOOD REACTION TO COMMONWEALTH'S DECLINE

Community spokespersons complained to Whittlesey's staff that the BHA deliberately sought to place "problem" families at Commonwealth. They perceived the development "as a sinking ship which will soon go under," and foresaw the eventual demolition of the buildings. Instead, they wanted the development to offer "good housing for hard-pressed low-income households living in the Brighton-Allston area," though they asserted that such families would refuse apartments under the current circumstances. Worse, local residents, businesspeople, and community leaders claimed that "crime and vandalism are being exported by Commonwealth to the surrounding neighborhood by the population moving into the development." Manager Finch resisted the idea that his tenants were causing problems elsewhere: "Scattered incidents around the area outside the development have been attributed to some of our tenants, but to no great extent."[43]

Although much of the discussion centered on problems of development maintenance related to repairs and vandalism, at base much of the outcry focused on whether the development could be maintained as a white-majority outpost. Assistant Manager Charles Foley complained about rapid turnover during 1975 and feared that racial change was coming "too fast." Already, he noted, the high number of white seniors masked the fact that the number of "black *family* units exceeds the number of white family units." The exodus continued unabated; during one two-week period, seven families who had been at the development since 1952 all departed, and nearly 30 percent of all apartments turned over in a single year.[44]

Fidelis Way was well distant from the hotbeds of tension over "forced busing," but racial tension simmered across the city. Although nearly half the residents of this part of Brighton were first- or second-generation immigrants and the neighborhood embraced a great deal of ethnic diversity, the area housed few blacks outside of Fidelis itself. The master's report called for "an over-all positive and symbolic change" at Commonwealth so as "to attract stable families and maintain the stable families who presently live there." This carefully coded talk of "stability" in reality meant concerted marketing efforts to reach whites, as well as carefully monitored racial quotas designed to retain the pattern of integration, since a court order on desegregation issued in December 1975 required the BHA to admit a minority family to Commonwealth only after two white families had been selected.

A study of census figures conducted by the master's staff found evidence of "hundreds of white families living in Allston-Brighton who are eligible for and would profit from public housing," and urged the BHA to find a way to get these families to apply. The master called for "all reasonable efforts . . . to slow down the white exodus and get more white families on the waiting list," but he worried that "market demand may be a force beyond the control or influence of any reasonable and workable policy." While management struggled in vain to arrest the drop-off in "white move-ins," internal memos reveal that vacancies mounted in certain three- and four-bedroom apartments marked "awaiting assignment for white families."[45]

The language of the courts framed the issue in racial terms, but the master's staff fully recognized the intertwining of race and class that underpinned the socioeconomic transformation of Commonwealth. As Whittlesey's report put it, "Extended discussions" of Commonwealth's social tensions "lead us to believe that the issue is more that of lifestyle and family composition than race."[46] Once again, the question turned to the slippery issue of "standards," and everyone concerned voiced the opinion that the BHA's own tenant-screening practices and eviction efforts had become entirely ineffective.

Local State Representative Norman Weinberg consistently exhibited a heartfelt interest in the fate of Commonwealth's tenants, even as he sought to prevent their most wayward members from ruining neighboring areas of his district. As Weinberg put it in letters sent to the BHA administrator, the BHA Board, the mayor, Judge Garrity, and the local Brighton police precinct captain in 1976, "I am deeply disturbed concerning present conditions at Fidelis Way and, also, the manner in which Fidelis Way is changing the character of the surrounding neighborhood, and the pattern of life in the Brighton area." Weinberg, like many long-term residents of the project, chiefly blamed lax tenant selection for the internal and external problems: "BHA put the wrong kind of people in there—too many one-parent families."[47]

Manager Finch, in turn, blamed the tenants for the development's problems, complaining that "the Perez case" prevented him from evicting anybody. He lamented the BHA's legal inability to obtain enough information about potentially disruptive tenants in time to keep them from ever getting apartments, and he viewed the situation as worsening. "Most of these boys are from homes that lack two parent families or if two parents are in the household, the families have some sort of problems whether it be alcohol or drugs or they need psychiatric assistance. The crimes that do occur in this development," he opined, "can . . . be connected to residents of the development with very little participation by outsiders." He noted that youths "constantly smashed out" hall windows and had inflicted "extensive damage" on the penthouses throughout the development by stealing their copper flashing, thereby "creating severe leakage to the apartments below." Other project youths had succumbed to the temptations of heroin or alcohol, and 52 percent of kids at the development did not attend school during 1975–76. "It is not uncommon," Finch observed, "to see thirteen- or fourteen-year-old youths parading around drinking to excess, and most other teenagers seem to have access to all the liquor they require. The older group, twenty to twenty-two years of age, start drinking in the early morning and continue all day." Even worse than the loitering, according to Finch, was the more active campaign to disrupt elevator service:

> The vandalism that occurs daily to the high rise building elevators
> is unreal. The Buchanan Elevator Company has to respond to an

average of five or six repair calls a day. There are fourteen elevators in this development and six or seven of them have to be repaired on a daily basis. The elevators are constantly being put out of service by placing such articles as cans, bottles, bolts, rolled up papers between the door and the wall thus causing the door to go out of cycle or burn out the control coils in the elevator control room.

He described another instance in which "kids climbed through the top of an elevator at 33 Fidelis and robbed a man, then took off his pants so he wouldn't chase them." "Security problems," Finch concluded, "are caused not by buildings but rather by the persons residing in the buildings."[48]

Fidelis Way's tenants saw things differently, blaming "weak and floating management" for their problems. As one resident commented, "Now people know that you can't be evicted and that means there are no boundaries on behavior." Another tenant cited the example of a family who was throwing garbage out the window, and complained that Finch refused even to talk to them, adding, "If tenants feel any kind of behavior can be tolerated then there are no boundaries to what behavior goes on." With every passing month, the once-dense network of engaged community members dissipated further. A cycle of disarray and neglect set in, now that "Commonwealth [had] lost its reputation."[49]

In April 1976, Louise Elving of the master's office convened a meeting with a variety of neighborhood civic and religious leaders to discuss the situation at Commonwealth. Despite at least a decade of ongoing efforts to assist residents of the development, service providers now lamented that some "elderly are too frightened to come out of their apartments." Many agreed that the project was "getting an over abundance of multi-problem families when we don't have the social workers to deal with them." Joseph Smith of the Allston Civic Association argued that the tenants needed to stop seeing themselves as separate from the larger community. According to Smith, the citywide Tenants Policy Committee had led Fidelis residents to believe that "the project is the *tenants'* community, but it really belongs to the larger community." Smith worried that the established leadership of the Fidelis community had moved out, leaving a vacuum. He suggested that the BHA capitalize on underutilized resources in the Brighton community, noting that "we too have a vested interest in what happens" at the project. Whittlesey's team also recognized the need for community involvement, but feared that most of the local social services institutions had been "set up to deal with a white working class population" and did not communicate or connect well with the population coming into Commonwealth.[50]

TASKS FOR TENANTS

During 1976, a small corps of new tenant leaders emerged at Fidelis, prompted in part by an effort to develop a "social code" for behavior at the development. Acting on a suggestion from the local police sergeant James Cox, who knew of a similar initiative at a project in Kansas City, tenants formed a committee. Cox called for a code that everyone could vote on and that peer pressure could maintain. He also hoped for a youth recreational program with parental guidance and control and a curfew for older kids, observing that "the police can't do everything." The Tenants Task Force, led by Bart McDonough, Julie Padro, and Susan Touhey, redoubled efforts to enhance maintenance of common hallways, an initiative championed by Representative Weinberg, who argued that those who don't clean should be evicted. Weinberg told the tenants that he wished to convince state legislators to make Commonwealth a pilot project for new modernization money, but he warned them that the Department of Community Affairs wouldn't consider this seriously unless they could demonstrate "an organized group of tenants." By December, the tenants presented the BHA with a "Proposal for Tenant-Run Programs at Fidelis Way" that included a system of thirty-five building captains (one per entrance way, with McDonough as "Resident Patrol Supervisor"), a tenant-orientation committee (to clarify the meaning of the lease), and a code of conduct, which included a set of rules about "cleaning of common areas, vandalism and other types of crime, responsibilities for pets and children, and speed limits." Later that month, the Tenants Task Force, Representative Weinberg, Sergeant Cox, and Manager Finch met with BHA Administrator Samuel Thompson to report on their progress and to press for further efforts to screen tenants and get more applicants from Brighton. They enthusiastically told Thompson about the new code of conduct plan, but he replied with skepticism: "It could be hard to enforce standards which are higher than the lease in a Court on evictions." Thompson also refused to endorse Commonwealth for the DCA pilot program, indicating that he was against the whole concept of the pilot program. Meanwhile, Thompson's would-be overseer—Master Robert Whittlesey—called for immediate action at Commonwealth so as to forestall the need to deal with the development "in much more expensive and much more desperate terms five years from now."[51]

Despite the urgent call, Whittlesey's team had no funds of its own to take such action, and the quality of life at Fidelis Way continued to plummet. Commonwealth participated in the Boston Public Housing Security Program during the mid-1970s but gained little from the effort. In addition to its marked failure to improve conditions at the development, the program suffered from a protracted power struggle between Fidelis residents and their partner, the local Allston-Brighton Area Planning Action Council (APAC). APAC's director concluded that the "Security Program" title was a misnomer since "it was misleading to project the image of a group that could deliver" this goal. Even worse, the Security Program's evaluation team commented, the publicity around the effort "may have worsened the traditionally negative image of the Commonwealth housing development in the surrounding community."[52]

ALL SYSTEMS STOP

The Allston-Brighton Interagency Council, an umbrella group of social service agencies, weighed in about conditions at Commonwealth in March 1978. In a letter to BHA Master Whittlesey, Council Chairman William Margolin decried the "abominable" living conditions, commenting that "vandalism is rampant, and there is now taking hold the slow and steady erosion and deterioration of all that we as human beings hold sacred." The development, Margolin observed, "has become an island unto itself within the Allston-Brighton Community, and it is with a sense of shame and necessity—not pride and desire—that the vast majority of the residents continue to live there." A few months later, a cable repair foreman sent Judge Garrity a memo entitled "Fidelis Way Working Conditions," detailing one basement with no light, steam leaks, and impassable garbage; two buildings where the furnace emitted "so much soot and smoke that it was difficult to breathe"; and two other buildings where the basement sewage pipes had broken, leaving "waste spilled over the floor, with flying bugs and cockroaches everywhere." Two weeks after that, Ann Muenster, the manager of the Allston-Brighton Little City Hall, informed Garrity that supervisors at New England Telephone "are reaching the point where they find it unhealthful to send their men in there and tenants may be left without the telephone service they need and deserve." Even for those who did not fully venture "in there," the situation seemed dire. Sometimes management problems led to acts of desperation or even tragedy. Elderly residents who huddled in front of the stoves they used for heat had to be evacuated to protect them from asphyxiation. Ten-year-old Donald

Mahony went ice skating with friends on the roof of no. 29 Fidelis Way, slipped, and fell to his death. The *Boston Globe* columnist Mike Barnicle disparagingly described the Fidelis landscape as "littered with glass and the debris you always see where troubled people end up in troubled buildings, living in troubled times."[53]

The *Allston-Brighton Citizen-Item* took up the plight of its community's most decrepit institution in a January 1979 editorial entitled "Fidelis Needs Aid." "Time is running out on Fidelis Way," the paper warned, observing that "physical plant breakdowns, vacancies, and crime" were getting worse every month. "Many good people are trying to reverse the deterioration of the project, but it is like building a sand castle at the water's edge when the tide is coming in . . . The specter of Pruitt-Igoe, the massive public housing project in St. Louis which authorities finally gave up on and blew to rubble, lurks in the back of everyone's mind."[54]

Judge Garrity himself went out to Commonwealth in April 1979 to gain evidence firsthand for ordering the recalcitrant BHA into receivership, which he did three months later. At Commonwealth, he described grounds "littered with glass and rubbish," six-foot deep ditches filled with garbage next to play areas, "bombed-out" apartments that had been left unsecured, basements with two inches of stagnant water, broken elevator doors and "dog manure on the stairway," exterior doors ripped from their hinges, hallways that reeked of "excrement and other noxious odors," "filthy walls and ceilings that are flaking and chipping," wide-open access to roofs, plugged roof drains, and broken skylights above stairwells.

The interiors of inhabited areas fared no better. Judge Garrity described his visit to the apartment of an elderly woman who had no hot water for a bath but a kitchen sink where the water could not be shut off. At another apartment he observed plexiglass panels screwed into the inside face of windows as a response to the vandalism that left the glass in jagged shards around the perimeter. In yet another apartment, he commented that the "walls in the vestibule appear to be disintegrating as a result of leaks. I have just entered the bathroom," he further intoned into his tape recorder, "which is literally disgusting. There is an entire section of the wall just in back of the toilet which is totally destroyed." Amid this compendium of horrors—and seemingly without irony—he paused to note that "incidentally the view [from the roof] is superb—this is a beautiful location."[55]

The Massachusetts Department of Public Health also conducted its own assessment of conditions at Commonwealth. The inspector found a panoply of serious violations of the State Sanitary Code's "Minimum Standards of Fitness for

Human Habitation." Although he judged the buildings to be structurally sound, everything else was a shambles. Those windows that remained were not weather-tight; there were "major, multiple water leaks in the plumbing throughout the complex, many located within the walls," while—within the vacant buildings—vandals had "removed the visible copper piping." The heating system was in "a general state of disrepair," prone to chronic breakdown and frozen pipes, with many radiators removed from apartments and sold for scrap value. Kitchens and bathrooms had not been updated since the original installations; the sewage system suffered from "frequent blockages and overflows," exacerbated by the use of individual clothes washers in a system not designed to handle this load, and by vent stacks that were blocked by debris that tenants deposited from the roof. Moreover, the solid waste disposal relied on "illegal and improper incineration," which created "a nuisance condition affecting not only the development but the entire neighborhood." As Garrity put it, "Fidelis Way was a place which people in the neighborhood viewed with fear and loathing. I think 'fear and loathing' is a perfect expression."[56]

It is one thing to read the reports of the various outside inspectors, but quite another to experience the conditions at Fidelis Way as a resident. Interviews with tenants who moved into the project during the dark years of the late 1970s reveal memories dominated by images of decline. The tenants describe the development as "dirty," "dumpy," "ugly," "ragged," "terrible," "horrible," with "many empty burned apartments." One resident likened the place to "a war zone." Socially, several people indicated that "everyone kept to themselves." Many felt ashamed to invite friends over, since visitors would have to cross the development's desecrated landscape and negotiate filthy hallways to reach their apartment. As one resident described it, while "inside my apartment was pretty nice, outside everything had deteriorated: fences were down, the grass was gone, and the trees were broken." Another responded similarly, "My apartment was OK, but outside in the hallway was like hell, with holes in the walls. There was no security in the building—the doors stayed open all the time and anyone could walk in and out." Those who lived on the upper floors of the mid-rise buildings invariably complained that the elevator was "almost always broken."

For some residents, even the inside of the apartments did not remain a haven, given the presence of mice, rats, and cockroaches. Long-time tenant activist Rosetta Robinson recalls the battle over failing refrigerators. This was more than an inconvenience, since it led to spoilage of baby's milk and insulin. Tenants gained new appliances only because "we jammed the BHA [phone] lines." Another resident, Doris Balware, was driven out of Commonwealth following eleven years of residency only after four separate floods in her apartment damaged her furniture and possessions. Until the floods forced her evacuation, she feared even to leave her apartment, trapped in a "filthy building" with "rats and bugs and smelly dog odors" that lacked even "a single safe mailbox."[57]

When Boston public housing was built, all manner of politicians regularly lobbied the BHA to get their constituents into it; in the late 1970s, however, much of the lobbying concerned ways to get their constituents *out* of it. Norman Weinberg intervened directly with the BHA administrator to get one such tenant relocated, noting that "she is a sick woman and is unable to put up with the drinking, drugs, fires, and noise at the rear of the project."[58] As conditions worsened, individual tenants tried to take action, complaining to all relevant public officials. As one Commonwealth resident and her two sons put it in a letter to Senator Edward Kennedy:

> We have lice, mites, and other insects in the whole building. People like me are getting bit . . . [and] the Boston Housing Authority doesn't do anything to solve this problem. They raise the rents and they don't do anything and they don't care for anybody.
>
> We don't have to live like this. We live in America . . . Now it is up to the State to care for its citizens. I am very ashamed of how we have to live in these housing projects.

Kennedy's office intervened with the BHA administrator, who responded that proper extermination was impossible because only about half of the residents were willing to cooperate with the program. Moreover, the BHA had no wish to work closely with this particular tenant since, as a letter from a probation officer at the Brighton Municipal Court attested, she "has demonstrated such hostility and belligerence toward others in the community that her safety, and that of her children is in danger." The officer added that "her appearances in court are too numerous to mention" and her "cooperation is impossible." He acknowledged that "ironically, it would appear that . . . [she] is a victim in many circumstances" but contended that "in fact she is the precipitator of much of the violence."[59]

Not surprisingly, given such physical and social conditions, vacancies at Fidelis Way rapidly escalated. In 1975, tenants still occupied 98 percent of the apartments, but only three years later nearly one-quarter of the units were empty. By late 1979, the vacancy rate had soared to 42 percent, finally peaking at 52 percent at the end of 1980. The high vacancy rate stemmed from the complex interaction of social, managerial, and architectural factors: major plumbing failures necessitated abandonment of some apartments, which were then vandalized beyond repair; elderly residents vacated sixty more units when offered the chance to move a few blocks away to the new Washington-Corey development for seniors (leaving behind apartments that the BHA again failed to secure properly, extending the cycle of vandalism and abandonment); and the BHA continued to keep some apartments vacant while waiting in vain for enough white applicants to meet integration criteria.[60] Clearly, some aspects of the decline at Fidelis Way could be blamed on conditions peculiar to this property, but many other BHA developments faced similar vacancy rates, confirming a systemic breakdown.

Organizing the Tenants

All BHA developments suffered from the collapse of the Authority, but certain places persevered much more than others. As Commonwealth approached its nadir, a core group of tenants continued to fight to save their homes and environment. Tenant organizing at Fidelis Way received a major boost from St. Elizabeth's Hospital in 1978, when the Allston-Brighton Medical Care Coalition launched the Commonwealth Health Improvement Program (CHIP), an on-site health-referral agency aimed at preventive care. Initially funded through the United Way and staffed by Orlando Isaza, a Colombian-born medical social worker, CHIP sought to build multiple bridges for Fidelis Way tenants. Many tenants used the area's plethora of medical facilities on an emergency basis only; emergency room use by Commonwealth residents at St. Elizabeth's soared by 79 percent between 1972 and 1977, for instance. CHIP's promoters foresaw a vast untapped need for preventive medical assistance, estimating that, in the first year of operation alone, 15 percent of Fidelis participants would receive referrals for alcohol- and drug-dependency counseling or treatment, while even greater percentages would get referrals for other needs: emphysema screening and follow-up (35 percent); smoking-cessation assistance (30 percent); hypertension (20 percent); social service assistance, including child protection in cases of suspected child abuse or neglect (75 percent); educational and vocational counseling or assistance (40 percent); recreational-socialization activities (50 percent); legal and related (for example, police) assistance (20 percent); psychological, neurological, learning, and developmental disabilities (15 percent); and primary health care management (75 percent).

Nonetheless, CHIP's initial encounters with the tenants made it clear that the "residents did not consider health, in the strict sense of the word, one of their priorities." To the tenants, CHIP's staff soon realized, "health started with security and safety, personal and community sanitation, adequate housing, financial security, employment, education, recreation, and access to quality services from public and private institutions." Because of this, CHIP rapidly evolved into a much more wide-ranging organization, with information, referral, and advisory activities that attempted not only to solve tenants' healthcare problems but also to attend to their housing, security, employment, education, day-care, legal, and recreational needs.[61]

In the fall of 1979, Izasa agreed to supervise Donald Rapp, then an MSW student at Boston University. When Isaza left Commonwealth in spring 1980 to become special assistant to the receiver, Rapp took over at CHIP, where he remained as executive director until 1984. As the Fidelis Way redevelopment effort gained momentum, CHIP added a second "H" to its acronym, and became known as the Commonwealth Health and Housing Improvement Program (CHHIP). Initially Rapp found a small but dedicated group of about half a dozen tenants, led by Bart McDonough, Cora Rothwell, Rosetta Robinson, and Willis Jette, all still pressing for improvements to their development but perpetually frustrated by the BHA's inability to spend modernization dollars effectively. As Rapp puts it, "This wasn't a group that was really going anywhere fast, but as individuals they were competent and committed to the community and knew everyone. It was just an ideal base from which to build a solid organization." The core group contained both white and black tenants and eventually came to include a couple of key Latino leaders, especially Nereida Otero, who ensured the involvement of the development's chief linguistic minority. In late 1979, the Commonwealth Tenants Task Force—which had been established as part of a citywide initiative a decade earlier—became newly incorporated as the tax-exempt Commonwealth Tenants Association (CTA), a status that enabled the organization to seek foundation grants more actively and directly.[62]

Rapp wanted to help tenants at Fidelis Way to organize and obtain funds for redevelopment and social services, but he struggled mightily to convene meetings during his first couple of months on the job. He couldn't understand the reluctance on the part of some tenants—even key leaders—to attend these evening gatherings. The problem, he finally realized, was that they lived in high-rises above totally abandoned floors, and, as he puts it, "the elevators wouldn't work, and you couldn't get women to climb all the way down the dark stairs from their fifth- or sixth-floor apartments." To compensate, Rapp carried a flashlight in his car; at night he would hike up the stairs to the apartments and then back down again—all to take the tenants to a meeting that was being held in their own development. He remembers thinking that "this is a level of fear that I just can't imagine living with . . . The whole development was dark, and it was a very scary place." One formal assessment of security conditions at Commonwealth, commissioned by the BHA as part of a larger report, found evidence of "high crime, high fear," and what was described as "moderate-high incivility." Although its crime rate was only slightly higher than the citywide average, Commonwealth bore the brunt of its district's assaults and robberies, and therefore stood out as a problem place. Tenants and management concurred that crime was the development's biggest problem, noting that both nonresidents and residents alike were perpetrators.[63]

The decline of the physical environment greatly exacerbated security problems. Inside the buildings there were long and unexplained power outages and a constant smell of urine in the hallways and stairways. Even beyond that, Rapp recalls, "the sewage problem was just monumental. Periodically, every few weeks, something happened and [the system] would back up, and out of people's sink drains and toilets would pump up all the sewage from the development and come out into the house. So I'd come in the morning and know that it happened the night before because everybody's carpets and pieces of furniture would be hanging out on the lawn and being drained." This story, and others like it, confirm what a dehumanizing place this public neighborhood had become. BHA planner Pamela Goodman concurs that, by 1980, the physical conditions at Fidelis Way had become "just horrendous," even worse than those prevailing at West Broadway or Franklin Field. She notes that there was so much ice inside the buildings that "kids used to go sledding down the back stairwells . . . The plumbing situation created problems that no one could address, because you couldn't just keep doing bandaids. You can't imagine living in that condition."[64]

Rating Redevelopment

Amid such conditions at Commonwealth and elsewhere, the BHA's planning department—to its great credit—instituted a complex and multidisciplinary evaluation effort to determine where scarce redevelopment dollars should be spent. The staff evaluated the agency's ten "most distressed" family developments, judged to be those having the highest vacancy rates as of August 1979. Commonwealth, nearly 42 percent vacant at that time, was near the top of this list, but all ten projects considered for large-scale rehabilitation had vacancy rates of at least 27 percent. High vacancy mattered for two reasons: it signaled broader and deeper problems and also, paradoxically, served as a helpful precondition to redevelopment, as it allowed for more flexibility in relocating existing residents during reconstruction.[65]

Members of the planning department sought to determine where investment would have "the greatest impact as well as the greatest likelihood of success." They first analyzed all ten projects in terms of site accessibility, physical design, neighborhood characteristics, and tenant characteristics, since they knew these were important to the potential success of any large-scale rehabilitation effort but were mostly factors that remained beyond the BHA's ability to change or control. The three top-ranked developments according to these initial measures were then subjected to further review of a more qualitative and development-specific nature, one that addressed such issues as "the political aura surrounding a site, ongoing efforts of the Tenant Task Forces, environmental impact concerns, and future neighborhood development plans."

Commonwealth scored very high in the first-stage review for many reasons. Certainly, its rating was aided by its excellent access to public transportation, its reasonable proximity to shopping and recreation, and its adjacency to several hospitals. It scored less well in terms of physical design factors, owing primarily to the presumed intractability of its seven mid-rise structures, its relatively large size (fourth largest among the ten "most distressed"), and its relatively high density (45.6 units per acre), more than double the density of the least dense among the ten projects under consideration. Despite these problems, however, Commonwealth scored high in terms of its plenitude of parking, the clear street-orientation of its buildings, and its safe surroundings.

Other neighborhood characteristics also augured especially well for Commonwealth. Noting that capital investment in a public housing project has a greater likelihood of success in a neighborhood with stable or ascending residential market values, high percentages of owner-occupied units, low concentrations of other subsidized housing, low unemployment rates, and potential for simultaneous publicly or privately sponsored revitalization programs that could reinforce the positive change taking place in public housing, the BHA used data from the Boston Redevelopment Authority to rank all ten projects. Here, Commonwealth's Brighton neighborhood ranked first in terms of low unemployment (6.8

percent, compared with a high of 21.6 percent in the least-employed neighborhood) and third in terms of low neighborhood concentration of subsidized housing (10 percent, compared with a high of 40 percent elsewhere). Although its residential real estate values had not appreciated quite as rapidly as those of several other neighborhoods, Brighton ranked fifth in this dimension and had the fourth highest rate of owner-occupied units—73 percent. In terms of investment potential, the BHA ranked Brighton as average and described Commonwealth as being in a "relatively stable, well-kept residential neighborhood" (though, of course, most of its immediate neighbors were institutions).

The last of the BHA's initial set of criteria focused on tenant characteristics; the Authority believed that it was important to examine a development's tenant population because, "although there is no single profile of the 'problem tenant,' the inter-relationship of a variety of tenant characteristics such as employment, single-parent households and high concentrations of minors [is] often perceived to be correlated with 'troubledness' of a public housing development." By these measures, Commonwealth's tenants at that time could be seen as fairly typical of those in other BHA family developments, with only 14 percent of adult residents employed, half of all tenants under the age of eighteen, and 94 percent of families headed by a female. Not surprisingly, given the wide prevalence of this tenant profile, the BHA did not weigh these factors very highly.

On the basis of these initial criteria, Commonwealth ranked second among ten BHA family developments in terms of "likelihood for successful redevelopment." When evaluated in terms of less quantifiable measures during the second level of study, Commonwealth emerged as a clear redevelopment priority for the BHA. When compared with the other two most highly ranked sites for potential redevelopment (Archdale in Roslindale and Orient Heights in East Boston), the BHA judged Commonwealth to have the "most urgent unmet physical needs" and "much more of a pressing community and political concern."[66]

While few would question the dire physical circumstances of the Fidelis Way project, the matter of "pressing community and political concern" requires further examination. Ultimately, decisions about redevelopment priorities hinge on such highly subjective judgments. It is worth recalling that the BHA also supported the redevelopment effort at Franklin Field, even though that project ranked dead last in the same study that rated Commonwealth first. Because pilot funding provided by the state to Franklin Field paralleled that targeted by Billy Bulger for West Broadway, Franklin Field's redevelopment was already politically irreversible a year before the 1979 study was completed. Clearly, studies by the BHA planning department were neither a necessary nor a sufficient condition for subsequent redevelopment.

Despite all the attention lavished on Commonwealth by the master's office between 1975 and 1978, the organizers of the state's pilot program, caught up in the racial politics of balancing Southie and Dorchester, did not select the development for funding. According to Bernie Stewart, who coordinated that program for the state, Commonwealth survived the snub quite handily. "It's almost like *not* getting funded spurred them in their organization," he noted. "I don't think it's always bad when somebody gets told 'No, not this time.' It spurred them on, and spurred other people on to really do something up there."[67] Fidelis Way did not get one of the large modernization awards, but it did receive a smaller grant from DCA (by then renamed the Executive Office of Communities and Development), which paid for two major studies. The first, produced by Community Planning and Research, Inc., put forth proposals for capital improvements, management reorganization, and expansion of resident services and opportunities, while the second, by Walsh and Associates, Inc., examined Commonwealth's finances and marketability.[68] Because of these studies, by late 1979, when the BHA commenced serious consideration of substantial rehabilitation options for some of its developments, Commonwealth was among the best documented of BHA properties.

The first report (known as the "CPR Study") set out approaches for the physical and social redevelopment of the project, concluding that the development would have to be reduced to no more than 450 apartments if these apartments were to meet the state's occupancy standards, which called for units that were approximately 30 percent larger than what existed.[69] This report also stressed the need for management reforms, including a much greater management role for residents, and emphasized the importance of increased resident training and employment opportunities, together with improved delivery of social service programs.

Marketing Fidelis Way

The second report (known as the "Walsh Report") focused on financial issues, confirming that "the Fidelis Way development, unlike other public housing projects, has excellent real estate redevelopment potential by virtue of its hilltop location, its surrounding middle class residential/institutional community, and its proximity to transit." Beyond its locational assets, the report took note of Commonwealth's ample parking opportunities, the relatively trouble-free racial and ethnic integration of the development, the continued strength of real estate values in the area immediately adjacent to the project, and "the high degree of desire to improve the project coming from the tenants themselves." This report explored many different financing options for a redevelopment effort and helped to introduce into the discussion some of the mechanisms that did come to be used. First was the idea of "federalization," in which federal HUD funds could be used to reduce the mortgage on a state-owned public housing development, and the state money then being used for debt payments could be used instead for rehabilitation. Under this federalization arrangement (an option that no longer exists), the development could also receive operating subsidies from both the state and the federal governments.[70]

The Walsh Report also gave impetus to a second development strategy: use of a turnkey approach to redevelopment. Under this process, the emptied buildings of the project would be turned over to a private developer, who would execute the rehabilitation according to a detailed agreement and then sell the revitalized development back to the BHA. By temporarily removing the development from the public sector, the turnkey process allowed the housing authority to use advantageous construction financing terms available from the Massachusetts Housing Finance Agency (MHFA), as well as to bypass the expense of the public bidding process and union regulations. Although the BHA had developed more than 2,500 units of housing under the turnkey process between 1970 and 1981, most of these were in scattered site housing and elderly housing. Commonwealth was to become the single largest effort of this kind.[71]

The Walsh Report harshly criticized BHA management practices, and this helped initiate discussion of private management for Commonwealth in addition to turnkey redevelopment itself. The project offered unusual challenges to the BHA, since it would be "financially feasible" to let a private developer transform the place into market-rate housing, and the Authority received "a certain amount of pressure . . . to sell the property." Thus, much discussion revolved around how to obtain federal funds and private-sector involvement while preserving the housing for "low and moderate income" tenants.

The Walsh study also tackled the matter of race, a central aspect of the development's political marketability in Brighton. The authors observed that "although the community perceives Fidelis Way in a racial context, the project has been basically free of racial incidents." That said, the report decried the "predicament of minority families," who have been "moved in on an accelerated basis before any real thought was given to what their special social and cultural needs might be in a new environment, or whether the community could successfully absorb them in such concentration." Nonwhite residents were left "stranded" and "alienated," "unable to get out" and find other homes in a neighborhood that resented the scale of their influx. This led to "stagnation," which "unless dissolved implies long-term guardianship [of such families] for the BHA." In response, the Walsh team called upon the BHA to admit fewer nonwhites to the project, according to a ratio that more closely matched "the minority evolution taking place in the neighborhood." The team claimed that "the benefits of a limited minority ratio moving through the project and into the community, as opposed to a resident matrix of permanently poor going nowhere, are obvious." Fortunately, the report concluded, the racial tensions and physical decline of Fidelis did not yet seem to have damaged real estate values in the adjacent area: "The project has not fouled its own nest beyond the need to repair its immediate perimeter."[72] Hardly just an apolitical analysis of real estate, the Walsh Report typified the desperate effort of the BHA and its allies to entice upwardly mobile whites back into Boston public housing.

Despite suggesting various redevelopment strategies and policies, involving the creative reallocation of funds from other state and federal housing programs, the Walsh Report was not sanguine about the possibility of finding the estimated $20–25 million needed to rehabilitate the development. According to the report, a funding mechanism to provide adequate levels of dollars for capital improvements and subsidies "does not presently exist."[73]

An Uphill Search for Funding

One major attempt to find some of these redevelopment funds emerged only a month after the Walsh team completed its report, through the efforts of a Planning Task Force established in June 1979 to discuss development options for the larger area surrounding Fidelis Way, still known as Monastery Hill. In order to grapple with the implications of a decision by the Passionist Fathers to sell off fourteen acres of hilltop land containing St. Gabriel's Church and associated outbuildings, the Boston Redevelopment Authority established the Monastery Hill Planning Task Force (MHPTF). The task force was formed to help the BRA coordinate all planning and development activities on that site and adjacent parcels, including Fidelis Way. Although it ultimately did not get to plan the future of

Monastery Hill as a whole, the MHPTF did serve as a major catalyst for the Commonwealth redevelopment.

Planning for Monastery Hill did not begin as a public housing redevelopment effort. Rather, it commenced as a pitched battle with outraged homeowners in the adjacent Washington Heights neighborhood, who were now as furious with the Church as they were with the housing project. According to David Trietsch, who served as the BRA's area planner for Allston-Brighton, the large Italian community across Washington Street was "bowled over" by the announcement that St. Gabriel's was to be put up for sale, especially since the announcement came from real estate people from the Passionists' New York office. Some members of the Washington Heights Civic Association regarded St. Gabriel's as their parish, although it was not a parish church. As Don Rapp put it, "They felt like they were being abandoned by their priest." They were furious with the Passionist fathers and felt that the church owed it to them to stay put. Once the BRA got involved and started talking about including the housing project in a broader development plan, the Washington Heights people "went even more nuts." Not only did they have to "acknowledge that the property was going to be sold"; it now appeared that "their 'sacred land' was going to be linked with this 'sewer with black people in it.'" In their minds, the land was going to "turn into one gigantic housing project." In Trietsch's analysis, "They had so much hostility around the issue of the Church coming out and doing this, but were so unable to express it toward the Church that it came at the city, and the BHA."

Every step of the way, Rapp recalls, whenever rehabilitation of the development came up at meetings of the Monastery Hill Planning Task Force, community members would "stand up and shout horrible racial stuff in front of the tenants. Even though *we* knew that barely a third of the people there were black, it was regarded by the community as the place where all of the black people lived, the slum. It took on that racist tone." Trietsch, who became the de facto co-chair of the task force (as the BRA's representative), describes the scene at an early task force meeting held at St. Elizabeth's: the people from the Civic Association would "start talking about 'those people' in very derogatory terms. 'Those people' were responsible for what the place looked like, and the crime and all that. And 'those people' were in the room, and totally silent. At the end of the meeting, I remember sitting down with them and saying, 'I don't understand. How could you let them say that about you when you and I know that it's not true?' And what they said to me was that they didn't feel that they had the right to stand up and say anything because why would anybody listen to them." For Trietsch, the message of this nonexchange came through loud and clear:

> When you're talking about redevelopment and making changes that have to do with people who have lived in low economic situations—you've got to start *way back*. They had to learn how to interact at a meeting and to interact with one another, to know what you could say. The only way that interactions really work is if there's a relatively level playing field. In order to level that field, there's a lot of organizing to be done, there's a lot of personal self-esteem work that has to be done. Not until you've done some of that work can you expect to then bring people together and have them interact over complicated and difficult issues and come up with a reasonable outcome.

Gradually, once-silent tenant leaders such as Bart McDonough gained the confidence to speak out, exhibiting "incredible personal growth." As Trietsch observed, "We found that there were people at Fidelis who had opportunities to live elsewhere but stayed there because that was their home. That was *their* community, it was going to get better, and they were going to see it through. Hidden under all this stuff was this spark, this pride, this hope. There's an element of courage there that's unbelievable." Even as Isaza and Rapp nurtured tenant empowerment, however, others in the neighborhood still hoped that the half-empty Fidelis Way project could be torn down and replaced with a large park. "Open space in Allston-Brighton" became the popular catch phrase. As Trietsch recalls, the Washington Heights Civic Association representatives "would come to our meetings, say, 'I have a statement to make,' read a prepared statement, and then leave—either physically or mentally."[74] By contrast, the Fidelis Way residents held their ground.

As Trietsch comments, "the people at Fidelis Way became outcasts in the Allston-Brighton community." Even though Allston-Brighton had long been much more ethnically and racially mixed than most other Boston neighborhoods, owing to its student population and its tradition of housing diverse immigrants, "it wasn't necessarily more progressive." Many Commonwealth residents internalized this neighborhood disdain. Kids coming home from school on the MBTA would get off two stops before Fidelis "because they didn't want people to know that's where they lived." Bart McDonough remembers hearing a cop yell out to a group of Fidelis youths on Washington Street, "Hey monkeys, back in your cage," and thinking that Commonwealth *"was* like a cage." In turn, the neighbors were only too pleased to let physical and socioeconomic isolation of the development become an excuse to ignore Fidelis residents when it came to any broader neighborhood issues. As Trietsch observed, prior to the Monastery Hill Planning Task Force, "if you had meetings in that community of the various civic associations and neighborhoods, Fidelis was never included."[75]

The new task force changed all this. Its diverse membership brought together representatives from all of the city and state planning, funding, and regulatory agencies alongside a broad array of neighborhood agencies and groups—including representatives from both the CTA and CHIP. It thereby provided a highly public platform for discussing the needs of the development and its residents, a forum unparalleled and unprecedented in the city. In the often acrimonious debate over the future of the St. Gabriel's site, it soon became clear that any agreement hinged on some resolution about the future of Fidelis Way.

The MHPTF issued its report in October 1979 and, drawing heavily on the Walsh and CPR studies, advocated limited private housing development on the St. Gabriel's site sufficient to leverage $4 million in federal Urban Development Action Grant (UDAG) funds for the rehabilitation of Fidelis Way. The UDAG program, administered by HUD, was intended to encourage and facilitate public-private partnerships for urban development in places where federal money could leverage significant amounts of private dollars to revitalize the local economic base or reclaim neighborhoods experiencing excessive housing abandonment or deterioration, and task force leaders touted this as the most promising vehicle for filling some of the gap in funding for the Fidelis redevelopment. At about the same time, the local press reported that the three developers in the running for St. Gabriel's were "more interested in the Fidelis Way possibilities than in any extensive work at the Monastery; they are largely concerned about St. Gabriel's as a way to get to work on Fidelis" (Fig. 4.11).[76]

Almost before the ink was dry on the MHPTF report, however, the central feature of its recommendations—the linkage between St. Gabriel's and Fidelis Way—was rendered irrelevant. On October 24, 1979, the Passionists agreed to sell the St. Gabriel's site to neighboring St. Elizabeth's Hospital, which, in turn, claimed to have no immediate plans to develop it further. With this abrupt and unexpected conclusion to the debate over the St. Gabriel's site, the task force did not fold up and disappear. Instead, working through its Housing and Health and

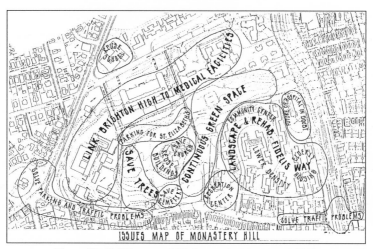

FIGURE 4.11 "Issues Map" of Monastery Hill. In 1979 the Monastery Hill Planning Task Force grappled with a variety of issues: how to link the various area institutions together, how to preserve and extend green space, how to solve traffic and parking problems, and—above all, perhaps—how to redevelop the Fidelis Way project.

Human Services subcommittees, it refocused its energy even more directly on Fidelis Way. As the MHPTF report had already stated, "The Task Force and the community have taken the position that no matter what the future holds for St. Gabriel's, Fidelis Way must be rehabilitated."[77]

Redevelopment proponents lost the possibility for federal dollars through the UDAG program since St. Elizabeth's Hospital was not a private developer interested in such a plan, but the MHPTF brought tremendous long-term gain. By giving the plight of the project and its residents high visibility in city and state government, by integrating well-organized tenants into a major coalition of powerful figures, and by incorporating the views of neighborhood residents without letting abutters gain the capacity to control the whole process, the task force laid a great deal of the groundwork for a successful redevelopment effort. As Don Rapp observed, "From an organizing standpoint," the MHPTF "was crucial for me. It was the place that the Commonwealth Tenants Association really began to come together. They began to feel not only the possibility of having something big happen and what it means to get access to resources beyond themselves, but also for the first time they felt that they had stood up and confronted some of the racism and hatred that surrounded them; it was important growth time for the group."[78]

By the end of 1979, the local Brighton press could rightly claim that Fidelis

Way was receiving "more attention" than any other housing development in the city. Because of the Monastery Hill report, BHA Planning Director William Karg acknowledged that the BHA felt "an urgency to improve the project." Orlando Isaza and other MHPTF members even wrote a bill for the Massachusetts legislature—sponsored by the state representatives John Melia and William Galvin—calling for new redevelopment funds for "severely distressed" public housing, a thinly veiled effort to fund Fidelis. Fidelis Way's tenants also benefited greatly from a well-cultivated relationship with the area's neighborhood newspaper, the *Allston-Brighton Citizen-Item*. In stark contrast to the frequent hostility toward D Street expressed in the South Boston papers and the near-total absence of press reports about Franklin Field in Dorchester, Fidelis Way received almost uniformly good press. Rapp regarded the local reporter Jayne Seebold as "a friend" who was "really ideologically committed to our cause." She cast her stories to showcase "an opportunity to do something decent for poor families." By contrast, the Washington Heights people "lacked a real voice in the media. They didn't have the access we did." Rapp and the CTA expended a lot of energy claiming that the redevelopment effort would benefit from its "supportive neighbors," but this was largely a strategy to attract funding. As Rapp recalls, "It was always a lie. There was hostility only. And those who were not hostile were students who were not involved in the process." To preserve the illusion of community support, Rapp would "periodically trot out" some of his friends in the neighborhood to "show that there was all this liberal-minded political support for poor people," even though these outsiders were "totally irrelevant to what was going on."[79]

RIGGING HARRY SPENCE'S FLAGSHIP

With so much background work already completed, the arrival of Harry Spence and the commencement of the BHA receivership in February 1980 brought the possibility for a funding mechanism. When the newly appointed receiver made his first official visit to Fidelis Way to meet with tenants and view a video documenting the horrendous conditions in the development, he came away "incredibly excited." "People are getting angry again," Spence commented. "Therefore there is more hope for Fidelis Way." In Seebold's analysis, Spence's enthusiasm was all but inevitable: "Because of the joint efforts of the community and tenants, which have never been so closely allied before, the receiver was hard put not to recognize Fidelis Way and the opportunity there." As Spence later recalled, "We picked Commonwealth precisely because it seemed like it had the greatest potential to be the most successful turnaround effort." At a time when many in the Kevin White administration promulgated the view that public housing was a "doomed program," Spence and his colleagues "had to convince people that this was worth investing in. Therefore we needed a flagship project that would begin to show what it could be at its best." Spence sought to "get people to listen to why what was bad was bad, instead of just writing it off as all a problem."

Spence saw Fidelis Way as a "target of opportunity." Fidelis, he recalls, "was interesting right away because it had a pretty good tenants organization already and they had some relationship with agencies in the surrounding neighborhood." He noted that, because of ongoing interest in the development by state representatives and by State Senator George Bachrach, tenants "were already dealing with the legislature" and felt "psychologically empowered." As a result of the MHPTF and the outreach of CHIP, Spence found a development with a "much more permeable boundary" than most others in the BHA system. Architecturally, too, he observed a building complex that already "fit nicely into the scale of the neighborhood." He also discovered a place that "seemed to work reasonably well as a racially mixed development in a neighborhood that was more amenable to racial integration than much of Boston in 1980." Spence understood that "there were people in the neighborhood who were absolutely opposed to the reconstruction" of the project, but "at least there was engagement. Most of the projects were just totally isolated." In contrast to the firebombings and shootings that tore other developments apart, a few racist outbursts at community planning meetings at Fidelis seemed the very embodiment of peaceful coexistence. In short, "structurally, politically, institutionally, and racially" Fidelis Way "seemed to hold more promise than any [other developments]." Alerted by angry residents and buttressed by voluminous reports, Spence "decided to move very quickly."[80]

Spence directed a tremendous amount of energy and discretionary budget allocations toward the realization of this redevelopment effort. Ultimately, $20 million of the funding for the redevelopment came from unexpended HUD development funds already committed to the BHA, augmented by $6.2 million more from HUD and $5.3 million from the Commonwealth of Massachusetts.[81]

REDEVELOPMENT PARTNERSHIP: A THREE-WAY STREET

The $31.5 million transformation of the Fidelis Way housing project into Commonwealth Development is a story of a strong corps of residents, activated with the assistance of a hired community organizer, and backed by a strong network of neighborhood, city, and state organizations. Tenants jointly worked with the BHA and a private development company to negotiate the physical and social goals for the redevelopment, as well as the means by which the redevelopment effort could be managed and sustained. At base, theirs is a story about the process of building mutual trust and respect among parties that had previously been perpetual adversaries. Residents, working with skilled architects, landscape architects, planners, and urban designers, agreed on the priorities for the physical redevelopment and helped negotiate a 223-page Management Plan that established a binding agreement covering a wide variety of community rules and procedures and set methods for addressing any violations of these norms. The design goals drew on the CPR study and considerable input from BHA staff. They called for a reduction in the number of apartments, an increase in their spatial standards, and a variety of measures to make the buildings more compatible with the specific needs of all segments of the public housing population. In short, the redevelopment effort involved a drastic overhaul of the physical character of the site combined with a wide-ranging and serious attempt to introduce and enforce a management and maintenance plan that could sustain the development as a secure and attractive community.

Revitalizing the Tenants

Throughout the redevelopment process, the residents of Fidelis Way remained at the core of the attempt to revitalize the physical environment and management practices. Engagement by the residents and with the residents preceded both design and management reforms, and ultimately helped to shape them in significant ways. Redevelopment was not something that simply happened to these people; rather, many of them actively fought to attain it. Although it may seem, in retrospect, almost inevitable that Harry Spence would have been drawn to Commonwealth as a priority, this seems so only because so many different forces converged to support revitalization. Without tenants clamoring for redevelopment, attention and money could well have gone elsewhere. From the real estate development discussions of the MHPTF, Fidelis Way residents learned that their home had great value in the eyes of others. Initially, this realization caused some to fear that the development could be sold out from under them, but it also served to build their confidence. Tenants who once sat silent while neighborhood residents berated them as just another obstacle to more "open space" became animated participants in community meetings. Fancy-titled and politically connected persons came to regard tenant needs as central to multimillion dollar deals.

FIDELIS WAY SPEAKS

By the time Harry Spence came aboard to captain his flagship, Fidelis tenants and their advocates had already done a lot of the rigging. The residents, still angered and frustrated by a decade of BHA malfeasance, had at least two productive channels for action—CHIP and the CTA—and were ready for more. In 1980 the CTA began publishing a bilingual monthly newsletter, *Fidelis Way Speaks . . . /Fidelis Way Hablas . . .*, which not only provided updates on redevelopment progress but served as a forum for concerned residents to discuss openly the kinds of high standards for resident behavior that ought to accompany future architectural and managerial changes. By this time "Fidelis Way" as a place and a phrase held highly negative connotations in the community, but residents still sought ways to demonstrate its more positive qualities and rehabilitate the name. *Fidelis Way Speaks* gave voice to "the decent people of the project," those who cared about "the place that we want to call our homes" and were willing to "start reporting the ones that are destroying" it. Resident Donna Fantuzzi observed that fellow tenants undermined efforts by the BHA to keep the roofs repaired: "Oh boy! Did we ever complain about those roofs when they were leaking. But now that they have been repaired, you'd think we would take care of them by staying off them, but I guess some tenants will never learn. Instead they use the roofs for dog runs, letting their animals use the roofs as toilets, while others string up clothes lines and are up there almost daily hanging clothes (you know who you are—and we do too)." Fantuzzi and others like her sought to send a strong message—"Violators will no longer be tolerated in Fidelis Way." A group of five Fidelis youths (aged eight to twelve) wrote in to urge the BHA to "fix up the projects quicker," and they offered several suggestions: "First fix the doors so that we can keep people out of hallways. Signs say people can be evicted and they don't do anything. They should fix up the park. They should have a little league team. We have nothing to do so kids break windows. They should fix empty buildings so people don't get hurt. Windows should be fixed." An adult resident, writing anonymously, explained the consequences of misconduct, singling out those who "throw garbage off the roofs and out their windows":

> Now we know who the people are that just don't care. You people
> are not showing a good example to our youths by just throwing

[bottles] on the ground when there is a dumpster ten or twenty feet away. All you have to do is just walk over and deposit it there. Just think of the exercise you will get!! That way our youths will not be throwing them up against the wall where they can lose their eyesight by glass bouncing back at them. Also they wouldn't be throwing them in the parking lot so we can avoid flat tires. Just think it can take five or more maintenance men to clean up after you people that like to throw trash all around. They could be doing other things to make this place liveable.

Much of the high moral tone of *Fidelis Way Speaks* was set by the elderly black CTA Board member Willis P. Jette, who contributed a monthly column as well as selections of his own poetry. Jette called upon fellow tenants to "start taking care of the halls and stairs again" and to stop "the playing of TVs and loud music at 3 o'clock in the morning" (since "there are some people that have to work and need their rest"). He blamed the BHA for lax maintenance, noting that the Authority emptied dumpsters only once a week instead of three times, as they did when the development was first built. He hoped he could "make them mad enough [so] we will get some service." Most of all, Jette urged the BHA to markedly upgrade its tenant-screening process instead of worrying so much about racial quotas: "I want everyone to remember that when we were fighting for everything in Fidelis Way it was all races fighting together." He therefore called for tenant selection to be on "an equal basis"; "I don't care who they are as long as they have been well screened." Without such screening, he feared that "a few people will come in after it has been redeveloped and destroy" the development's "new frame."[82] Fortunately for Fidelis Way, other people simply refused to let this happen.

The CTA, under the leadership of resident Bart McDonough, brought together a group of tenants willing to make the redevelopment of their neighborhood a central focus of their lives for years on end. As a result, resident voices could be heard at all key decision points of the redevelopment process, whether regarding design or management. As residents gained confidence that the redevelopment would indeed take place, their leaders enthusiastically supported reviving its official name, Commonwealth. Don Rapp countered that dropping the name Fidelis Way implicitly devalued the community that had struggled to survive during the darkest days. He felt that the change "somehow simplistically labeled that Fidelis Way community 'bad' and the new Commonwealth community 'good,' when really the only thing that made Fidelis Way bad was the BHA's failure to manage the property to the level of quality tenants deserved." Overriding Rapp's objections, the tenants went with the name Commonwealth Development.[83] That decision, like many others, confirmed the importance of tenant contributions. At Commonwealth, the BHA anticipated and legally guaranteed the importance of tenant input.

Revitalizing the Apartments, the Buildings, and the Site

The BHA's careful, thorough, and ambitious "Developer's Kit" for Commonwealth, issued in June 1981, set the parameters for the resultant redevelopment effort. The plan required at least 390 units of housing divided into a carefully articulated unit mix of elderly housing and family housing in apartments of various sizes based, in large part, on the bedroom requirements of the existing population. It proposed consolidation of housing for the elderly into two adjacent mid-rise buildings with a community building connecting them. It called for the transformation of low-rise buildings into duplexed or triplexed townhouse-like apartments with individual entrances and private yards, and the reconfiguration of the lower two floors of other mid-rise buildings into similar duplexes for large families. It proposed reducing density through selective demolition of a mid-rise building and its replacement with a community center and management building, and it insisted on the articulation of "defensible space" in public areas. In addition to these and other basic design and programming matters, the Developer's Kit contained a wide variety of lengthy appendixes, including a very detailed set of "Planning and Design Criteria." These included recommendations for grade changes in the landscape to permit all private entrances to be accessed from ground level (to make for "a residential feel and clear delineation between semi-private and public space"). The Kit called for parking to be located in small lots where cars could be viewed from owners' apartments, and it mandated that "every portion of the site must be dealt with and programmed."

The BHA clearly wanted potential designers and developers to "avoid an institutional and repetitive design." To accomplish this, the Kit proposed that each building and apartment have "a definite front and back." Fronts should be "typically associated with the street, where cars are parked, and where units are entered. Back doors should also be provided for individual units not only for convenience but also to help establish private territory at the back of the buildings. The goal is to define as much of the building edges as possible as private territory associated with a particular unit in order to discourage loitering in these areas.

Buildings should be paired so fronts face fronts and backs face backs." The effort should be, in short, "to convert the low-rise walk-up buildings to row house type structures."[84]

Six teams submitted bids. The selection team (which included residents as well as BHA personnel) chose the proposal by developer-contractor John M. Corcoran and Company and architect Tise Associates. They concurred that the Corcoran-Tise submission not only offered a competitive price and the fine reputation of its team members, but also excelled in a number of the most important design criteria articulated in the Kit:

> All common areas are eliminated in the low rise buildings, which will contain most of the large families. Individual access also is provided for a number of large family units on the first two floors of the mid-rises, and results in the lowest number of elevator-accessed family units proposed. These aspects substantially will bolster security and the livability of both the individually accessed apartments and the elevator apartments. The relationship of buildings to site also is particularly strong. Pedestrian pathways are clear and safe, parking spaces are both convenient to and visible from units and open space is well programmed for maximum tenant identification and responsibility. Security and maintenance problems should be reduced as a result. The proposed design is not fancy or elaborate, but rather a straightforward application of housing development design fundamentals.[85]

As one part of the thoroughly commendable selection process involving wide community consultation and careful scrutiny of proposals by the BHA and various Massachusetts state agencies, the CTA hired a consulting architect, David Lee, who spent thirty hours ensuring that residents would be "fully informed as to the content, significance and implication of the technical aspects of the six proposals."[86] As part of what tenants called a "painstaking review" of each proposal's drawings, the architect constructed scale-model pieces of furniture to help tenants envisage life in the redeveloped apartments. This independent review by the CTA Board and other interested residents concentrated on design and programming issues. Tenants extolled the Corcoran proposal as "the overwhelming favorite," marking it three grades higher than the next highest-ranked submission.

The winning scheme followed closely the demands of the Developer's Kit, but

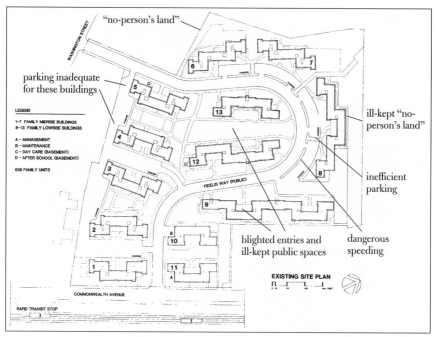

"no-person's land"

parking inadequate
for these buildings

ill-kept "no-
person's land"

inefficient
parking

blighted entries and
ill-kept public spaces

dangerous
speeding

LEGEND

1-7 FAMILY MIDRISE BUILDINGS
8-13 FAMILY LOWRISE BUILDINGS

A - MANAGEMENT
B - MAINTENANCE
C - DAY CARE (BASEMENT)
D - AFTER SCHOOL (BASEMENT)

638 FAMILY UNITS

WASHINGTON STREET

FIDELIS WAY (PUBLIC)

COMMONWEALTH AVENUE

RAPID TRANSIT STOP

EXISTING SITE PLAN

FIGURE 4.12 Commonwealth before redevelopment. Designers found many faults with the existing site plan of Fidelis Way.

the Corcoran-Tise team made significant advances in terms of programming and design. Before redevelopment, two-thirds of the apartments were in six-story buildings, with thirty families sharing an entrance and a single elevator. The redevelopment plan proposed demolishing two of these seven mid-rises to reduce the actual and perceived density of the site, replacing them with a low-rise day-care facility and a management and community building. Corcoran-Tise transformed the single street looping through the development into two parts, one a more direct route through the development that served as a public way and ran past the new community buildings, and the other a private loop intended for the use of residents and their visitors (Figs. 4.12–4.16).

The Corcoran-Tise team addressed the perceived mismatch between families and elevator-dependent buildings in a couple of different ways. As proposed by the Developer's Kit, the designers agreed to reconfigure two of the mid-rises to accommodate elderly residents in small apartments, connecting these buildings

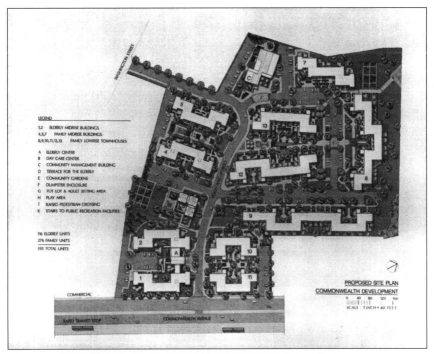

LEGEND

1,2   ELDERLY MIDRISE BUILDINGS
4,5,7 FAMILY MIDRISE BUILDINGS
8,9,10,11,12,13   FAMILY LOWRISE TOWNHOUSES

A   ELDERLY CENTER
B   DAY CARE CENTER
C   COMMUNITY MANAGEMENT BUILDING
D   TERRACE FOR THE ELDERLY
E   COMMUNITY GARDENS
F   DUMPSTER ENCLOSURE
G   TOT LOT & ADULT SITTING AREA
H   PLAY AREA
I   RAISED PEDESTRIAN CROSSING
K   STAIRS TO PUBLIC RECREATION FACILITIES

116 ELDERLY UNITS
276 FAMILY UNITS
392 TOTAL UNITS

PROPOSED SITE PLAN
COMMONWEALTH DEVELOPMENT
0   40   80   120   160
SCALE : 1 INCH = 40 FEET

COMMERCIAL

RAPID TRANSIT STOP   COMMONWEALTH AVENUE

FIGURE 4.13 Commonwealth, proposed site plan. The new site plan, fully realized, envisioned a second street through the development, demolition of two mid-rise buildings, and construction of new community facilities.

at the ground floor with a new structure housing community facilities for these households. Following another suggestion in the Developer's Kit, Corcoran-Tise retrofitted rowhouses into the base of other mid-rises, thereby reducing the number of families relying on elevators and increasing the number able to have private back gardens. Similarly, they reconfigured the three-story walk-up buildings that made up the rest of the site into two-story and three-story rowhouses with private entrances and gardens.

As at West Broadway and Franklin Field, the designers of Commonwealth tried to adapt Oscar Newman's principles of defensible space. Owing to its hilly topography, Commonwealth offered both greater challenges and greater opportunities for developing new zones of privacy and control. The architect Stephen Tise and the landscape architect Kathy Schreiber used the landscape in particularly innovative ways, regrading parts of the site by as much as nine feet to foster

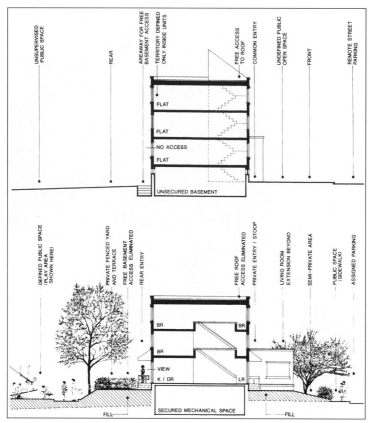

FIGURE 4.14 Commonwealth's buildings: before and after. Before redevelopment, Commonwealth's low-rise buildings contained stair-accessed apartments and had little connection to the outdoor realm, which remained wholly public and alien. After redevelopment, many buildings featured triplex apartments and carefully considered interrelation with adjacent yards, terraces, and walkways.

different levels of privacy by creating a variety of traversable, semi-traversable, and non-traversable barriers (Figs. 4.17–4.18). The design transformed a series of apartment blocks with common entries eight steps (five feet) above grade into 176 duplexes and triplexes, each with a private entrance at grade, insulated from the sidewalk by a gentle slope of grass-covered fill. This thoughtful regrading created a clear zone of semi-private space that visually "belonged" to the townhouse behind it. At the rear, in many cases, the change of grade also allowed the private backyard/patio to be on a different level from the semi-private and semi-public

FIGURE 4.15 Rooftop view of Commonwealth after redevelopment. This photograph, taken from the same spot as Figure 4.9, shows the effect of the redevelopment: the new street, the landscaping, and the reduced building density. Also, there are no milk trucks.

play areas that were defined beyond it. Consistent use of curbing in other, more public, areas created barriers that most people would not violate, even in pursuit of a shortcut. In addition to the small and subtle cues offered by landscaping, at a larger scale the site plan contributed to the definition of spatial hierarchies through the management of traffic and parking.

The site plan also carefully delineated play areas for children of different ages, replacing the ubiquitous and useless "open space" that characterized the design of the original project. The plan emphasized dispersion, diversification, and safety; it juxtaposed play facilities with residences and with each other to meet the requirements for surveillance by both parents and older children. Moreover, the designers recognized that children inevitably wish to play in areas other than those built especially for them by architects. Rather than fight this tendency, they accommodated it, with extra-wide sidewalks and the provision of a variety of both

FIGURE 4.16 Tenant leader Bart McDonough, 1987.

FIGURE 4.17 Semi-private space, Commonwealth. The new duplex apartments with private entrances built into the bases of mid-rise structures permitted residents to lay claim to semi-private outdoor space in front of their apartments.

FIGURE 4.18 Lush landscaping. The careful regrading of the site and intensive planting efforts made the once-empty spaces between buildings completely unrecognizable.

hard and soft surfaces. From parking lots to tot lots, the planners of Commonwealth followed the BHA directive to regard every square foot as having a potential use and a potential user. Beyond such technical matters, however, attention to landscape also helped to rebuild trust between residents and management. Immediately after taking over Commonwealth, Corcoran planted flowers in the public areas of the development. As Bart McDonough recalls, "I was shocked. Flowers. It only cost them a couple of hundred dollars, but no one had thought to do it before."[87] Two decades later, at a place where flowers continue to be planted and carefully maintained, this first simple act seems to be lodged in the memories of residents and housing authority officials as a symbol of a new kind of respect.

Throughout the redevelopment process, tenant decisionmaking remained continual, well-informed, and legitimately influential. At the groundbreaking ceremony, held in September 1982, residents held center stage, with McDonough as the master of ceremonies. "We waited five years for this to happen," he proclaimed. "Finally, it's coming about because of the efforts of the CTA." He also stressed the importance of the Brighton community and commended all tenants for being strong enough to "go out, grab the neighborhood and bring it in." BHA

Receiver Spence stressed his "special personal relationship" with Commonwealth's tenants: "When I come to Fidelis Way today, it feels like family . . . Today's occasion should be to celebrate our family. This is a family reunion." Brighton State Representative Tom Gallagher admitted that he once thought the development "would be sold off to people who could afford this view," but he now evinced high hopes for its future as public housing. City Councilor Mike McCormack, who had grown up at the development twenty years earlier, commented from personal experience: "I hope that Fidelis Way will return to what it was, when people were proud to say they lived in Fidelis Way." Willis Jette inaugurated the reconstruction by breaking a champagne bottle against an empty building (probably the only time he condoned broken glass at the development). Jette, who suffered from a terminal illness, would not live to see the rest of Commonwealth's dramatic rebirth. Instead, fellow tenants memorialized him by naming the development's redesigned street "Jette Court."[88]

Revitalizing the Management

When the BHA and the CTA undertook to rebuild Commonwealth, they did so not only with a private developer but also with an additional commitment to privatize the management. Although the BHA under Spence first raised the notion of private management, tenants wholeheartedly endorsed the concept. Spence began the receivership with the idea of getting a development or two under private management, viewing this as "a kind of competitive standard and a threat to mobilize others, a burr under the saddle." As Don Rapp recalls, Spence looked for tenant support and certainly got it: "The tenants also had no confidence the BHA would manage the place well. It was not controversial." Beyond any shift to private management, the tenants wanted to play a substantial role in management themselves—though they expressed little interest in taking on responsibility for day-to-day operations. MHPTF Co-Chair Trietsch shared this commitment to enhancing the clout of the tenants: "We knew that unless the tenants had a significant role in the management of the project, it wasn't going to succeed. We weren't going to get the tenants to buy in to the work they were going to need to do to see the thing through."[89]

In 1982, after a separate bidding process, the CTA entered into a legally binding agreement for a Management Plan with the BHA and a private firm, the Corcoran Management Company (CMC), an affiliate of John Corcoran's development company. Don Rapp warned Commonwealth's tenants that they had better "really insist" on work-order turnaround time, since this remained one of the BHA's chief failings. Rapp had helped Greater Boston Legal Services write new performance guidelines for Judge Garrity to impose on the BHA, so he was very familiar with the standard measures. He approached a meeting with CMC armed with "all these things that I thought were incredible demands"—and was totally startled by what transpired: "The Corcoran folks came in that night and said they wanted to propose the same thing they use in their other [private-sector] developments, which is 24 hours after a call comes in, they'll come out and either have fixed it or give you an estimate as to when it will be if there's a part that needed to be ordered. This was far beyond anything I would have asked for."[90]

The resultant agreement set standards for management and maintenance that greatly exceeded the BHA's own capacities, and even allowed the tenants to fire the management with thirty days' notice. The Management Plan addressed a broad range of issues, and, nearly two decades later, it remains a reference point for considerations of tenant selection, rent and utility allowances, charges associated with damage to apartments and repairs, community rules, eviction policy, maintenance (including a detailed account of CMC's preventive maintenance program, corrective maintenance procedures, and standards for janitorial and grounds maintenance), resident services, tenant orientation, security, personnel policy regarding the hiring of residents, the budget, and the lease. Of utmost importance, the Management Plan instilled a sense of co-responsibility for the quality of upkeep and behavior in the development. Since residents had themselves helped to formulate the rules, and since CMC was willing and able to enforce them, any departure from the high standards that both management and residents had set could be met with widely supported sanctions.[91]

TENANTING THE NEW COMMONWEALTH

CMC took over the management of Commonwealth in the middle of the redevelopment process; it did not simply come in to run facilities that were already refurbished. This meant that the management team had time to build up a level of trust with tenants and to articulate the new standards well before the new buildings were actually ready. The first time the managers planted flowers, no one was quite sure whether the large floral "C" stood for Corcoran or for Commonwealth. Soon it would be clear that it stood for both. Don Rapp recalls watching two members of the Corcoran maintenance staff—one of whom was a tenant the team had hired—carefully employ scrapers and brushes to clean out the tiny little tile in the entryways. "They were scrubbing out the grit. And I remember just thinking, if this isn't symbolic of something brand new. The BHA would never do this; they would print notices warning people they would be evicted if they don't start cleaning their hallway." For CMC President Bob Pickette, this was all part of the challenge to get the tenants to "believe that we would do what we said we would do. They had gone around and looked at our other jobs, talked to our tenants, and could still never believe that what we were saying was going to happen."[92]

Despite flowers and scrubbed tile, gaining the trust of tenants took considerable effort. Tenant organizer Rapp and BHA planner Pam Goodman remained strong and reassuring forces, but the residents needed further convincing. Even after much of the fear that the development might be sold off had subsided, tenants and their advocates grappled with the terms of a rehousing agreement. Initially, Don Rapp recalls, the BHA proposed that no tenant who owed back rent (and 95 percent of them did) would be permitted to return to a new apartment after redevelopment. The CTA worked closely with their legal adviser, Leslie Newman, and—after "an extremely contentious and nasty struggle"—eventually negotiated a comprehensive Rehousing Agreement that maximized the chances that existing tenants would be able to move into the redeveloped units, even if they had substantial rent arrearages. Under the agreement, the BHA unconditionally waived a set percentage of everyone's arrearages, set individual plans to repay the rest in small monthly installments, and actually gave the twenty or so families that were current in their rent a credit against future rent. Rapp terms this "the single most important battle waged and won by tenants" during the entire redevelopment period; without it, "hundreds of families would have been displaced over the four-year construction and rehousing process." As another part of the rehousing plan, the BHA offered tenants a one-time payment and a Section 8 voucher usable to subsidize their rent elsewhere. Most of the well-known troublemakers chose to take advantage of this opportunity. Some seniors also elected a one-time chance to move into a housing development for the elderly. Those who wished to remain and be a part of the "new" Commonwealth had to agree to the terms of a new orientation (which not only explained all the new appliances in the apartments but emphasized that rules of conduct would be enforced, including the prohibition against pets). In addition, all who wished to return had to have their furniture fumigated (to reduce the possibility of further insect infestations), and—most onerously for many—had to commit to a repayment plan for rent arrears that in a great many cases was quite considerable. Taken overall, 58 percent of the families residing at Commonwealth in 1981 returned to the redeveloped site. As the site manager Mary O'Connor put it in 1985, "Not all former residents will be rehoused. The BHA, prior to Corcoran's taking over, did a real clean-out of the development. They went after the people who had records of committing crimes on the property or in Brighton. Essentially, we were left with the cream of the crop." The net result of all this was a post-redevelopment population that was cleansed of many of its most problematic families without resort to a high number of evictions.[93]

The BHA also persisted in its long-standing efforts to manage the racial balance of the development. In July 1983 Judge Garrity approved a tenant-selection plan for Commonwealth that proposed a 60 percent white (non-Latino) majority for the 277 reconstructed family units and 75 percent white occupancy for the 115 units designed to serve the elderly, yielding a place that would be almost two-thirds white-occupied overall. The BHA termed these goals "consistent with integration in the surrounding neighborhoods" and "sustainable over the long term." Since Commonwealth's actual tenant composition had become close to majority nonwhite, the BHA recognized that "the return of previous Commonwealth tenants at first will constrain achievement of the racial mix goals" and that "marketing to attract whites may be necessary." For CMC Manager O'Connor, this marketing effort made good political sense: "We are targeting our advertising in Brighton in the hope that people in the area who need subsidized housing will apply. Through that process, we hope to get the development back into the Brighton community and not have it isolated the way it was before."[94]

Just as the BHA hoped that tenant turnover would slowly enable Commonwealth to recapture its once-substantial white majority, so too the agency wanted to target one-fourth of apartments to families with employed household heads at the upper end of income eligibility for public housing. The income-mixing plan, however, soon met with objections from the new mayor, Raymond Flynn, as well as from HUD. Even this modest effort to restructure occupancy toward families of higher income (far less extreme than the plans that became commonplace across the country by the late 1990s) proved impossible to implement. Similarly, the BHA failed to return Commonwealth to two-thirds white occupancy, though white occupancy did actually increase slightly during the course of the 1980s and the development did not house a clear nonwhite majority until the early 1990s. Whatever the actual results, the policy intent itself seems significant: to protect its investment in Commonwealth and to ensure the hard-won goodwill of the Brigh-

FIGURE 4.19 A well-managed landscape. Corcoran Management Company has paid careful attention to the appearance of Commonwealth's environment for two decades. The management and community building can be seen at the rear of this photo, with St. Gabriel's Church rising behind it.

ton neighborhood, the BHA felt it necessary to house public neighbors who were more white, more elderly, and more wealthy than those who generally sought to gain entrance to Boston public housing.[95]

DEDICATION AND PRAISE

Taking note of Commonwealth's formal rededication in June 1985, the *Boston Herald* described the development as located "on the site of the former Fidelis Way project." This choice of language affirmed the totality of the transformation that had just taken place. Both Corcoran Management and the BHA sought to capitalize on the change by insisting that the property now be referred to as Commonwealth Development (Fig. 4.19). Over the next several years, Commonwealth received multiple awards for design and development, including an Urban Design Award from the Boston Society of Architects in 1985, a Governor's Design Award in 1986, a merit award for landscaping for multifamily housing from the Boston Society of Landscape Architects, a citation for multi-family housing design from the Boston Society of Architects in 1987, and an Award for Excellence from the Urban Land Institute in the category of Rehabilitation Development in 1989.[96]

Notwithstanding all the awards, however, the redevelopment process suffered delays and cost overruns, and all parties concede that John M. Corcoran and Company did not gain financially from the undertaking. Corcoran Management Company President Pickette puts it most bluntly: the development side of Corcoran's business "lost their shirts." Essentially, he points out, "John [Corcoran] gave them the job." Everyone involved emphasizes the wholehearted commitment that Corcoran's leader felt toward this venture. "I won't say it became an obsession," Pickette notes, but "he wanted to leave his mark. If they were going to do the job, they were going to do it right." This meant spending much more money on the unusually elaborate community and management building than the Boston Housing Authority was expecting to pay. When Doris Bunte came on as the BHA administrator following the end of Harry Spence's receivership in 1984, she found Corcoran "holding the last two buildings hostage." According to Bunte, "the developer claimed they were due money we were withholding; we claimed they hadn't done some things." The eventual accord left everyone disgruntled but allowed the revitalized Commonwealth to open, about a year behind schedule. Compared with the protracted impasses at West Broadway and the construction fiascoes at Franklin Field, however, the whole development process at Commonwealth stands out as a model of goodwill and cooperation (Fig. 4.20).[97]

Commonwealth achieved 100 percent occupancy in 1986, a major milestone for a place that had been a half-empty hellhole when the decade began. The startling transformation continued to garner good press (even though the press still used the old name), with headlines such as "Fidelis Way: A New Chapter Begins," "Pride Replaces Despair at Fidelis Way: Architects and Attitudes Produce a Public Housing Showpiece," and "A Model of Success: Integration Works at Fidelis Way." The journalist Jane Holtz Kay described the "$30 million reincarnation" as resembling "one of those calm suburban developments where lawn care heads the list of worries." Another *Globe* writer put it more glibly: "The residents went from the outhouse to the town-house," adding that "buildings once littered with condoms today look like graffiti-free condos." The Dorchester-based *Bay State Banner* ran a profile of Barbara Jeffress, a black woman who succeeded O'Connor as Commonwealth's site manager. Its reporter described the development as "a townhouse community, trimmed with well-kept lawns and embellished with children's jungle gyms and outdoor sculptures," a far cry from the former "dreary, monolithic" project, "rundown and largely vacant, its hallways used

FIGURE 4.20 Commonwealth youths with BHA Administrator Doris Bunte, 1985.

for drug deals and gang fights." Paul Creighton, the head of Allston-Brighton APAC, lauded a new tenant spirit: "They think they've died and gone to heaven."[98]

ASSESSING "SUCCESS"

Not everyone sees Commonwealth as subsidized Elysium, but when asked to evaluate its success, a wide range of individuals associated with the redevelopment give the impression that the transformation has succeeded in many different ways. Though some tenants, particularly teens, voice some concern that the stricter enforcement of community rules has been too draconian, nearly everyone else praises what has happened here.

Surveys of residents carried out in 1979—near the nadir of the pre-redevelopment conditions—and again in 1993, after nearly a decade of reoccupancy, offer some indication of the magnitude of change that occurred.[99] In 1979, nearly 80 percent of adult tenants surveyed concurred that Fidelis Way was not "a good place to raise kids"; after redevelopment, the results were totally reversed: nearly 80 percent praised the place for just this reason. Similarly, in 1979 only 19 percent of respondents thought there were "good places for children of all ages to play" at the project; after redevelopment, this figure had ballooned to fully 90 percent, a clear endorsement of the landscaping efforts, the private yards, and the rehabilitation of Overlook Park, which adjoins the development (Figs. 4.21–4.23). Another important measure of the redevelopment's success is the clear indication that residents now feel far safer than they did in 1979. Even with the dramatic acceleration in drug activity and drug-related violence that has devastated so many low-income communities since the mid-1980s, the survey results from 1993 showed a marked increase in security after redevelopment. In 1979, when respondents were asked "How safe do you feel" at Fidelis Way, only 11 percent indicated that they felt "very safe." Nearly two-thirds said they felt "somewhat unsafe" or "very unsafe." In complete contrast, the 1993 survey results—incorporating both daytime and night-time assessments—found that fully 73 percent of respondents reported feeling "very safe," an additional 22 percent said they felt "somewhat safe," and only 5 percent say they felt "somewhat unsafe" or "very unsafe."

In terms of management and maintenance issues, the contrast between pre-redevelopment and post-redevelopment is equally stark. In 1979, three-quarters of the respondents complained about the inability of maintenance staff to address problems in their apartments; in 1993—after a decade with CMC—only 10 percent indicated that they had experienced any problems with maintenance.

Interviews with residents confirm the ways in which stringent management expectations markedly improved their quality of life: "There's now more respect for the property. The children do not destroy the surroundings, and they don't write on the walls"; "The development is watched over more. Management watches, so it doesn't get damaged"; "It's not like other projects where there is no one keeping a watchful eye"; "Living here is full of pride and family-like"; "I can go out at whatever hour at night, I'm not afraid"; "The elevators seem to work more often, and it's made it a lot easier for elderly people to get around"; "We're better off because there are more restrictions." Most residents particularly appreciate the privacy made possible by townhouses: "It is like a little house in a development; it's like having a home, having a yard"; "I like best that I'm the only one who comes through my front door. There's no public hallway"; "I like the yard because I

FIGURES 4.21–4.22 Resident-initiated personalization of outdoor space. Following redevelopment, most tenants at Commonwealth made frequent and sometimes elaborate use of their new rear yards.

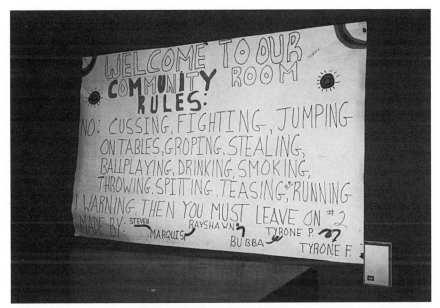

FIGURE 4.23 Everyone helps establish community rules. Adult tenants, working through the Commonwealth Tenants Association, helped devise community standards for the development, but this poster suggests that Commonwealth's young people had standards of their own for use of the community room.

consider it mine"; "It's private space—you have your own door, walkway, and yard"; "There's no adjoining windows and people can't look in your house—everything is closed."

Some respondents did point to shortcomings: "These super-huge apartments takes you a whole day to clean"; the white floors need to be "mopped all the time"; "The walls are much thinner—you can put your hand through them"; "The walls are thin and you can hear everything"; "Everyone knows your business—there's no privacy"; "Everyone is on top of each other." One life-long resident expressed resentment at the loss of earlier freedoms: "It went under private management and feels like a prison." Others complained that suburban commuters now used Commonwealth as a convenient place to park their cars before boarding the MBTA, forcing residents to park elsewhere. Although the parking crunch proved an inconvenience, it surely served as a marker of just how far the development's reputation had changed in a few years.

That reputation did face some challenges, however. In July 1986 a Commonwealth resident murdered two fellow elderly tenants, setting off a brief and understandable panic. At first, many tenants talked about leaving the development, fearing that they could be the next victim. After a tenants meeting to "dispel myths," the situation eased. As Cora Rothwell, who resided in the building where the murders occurred, put it, "Once there was knowledge that it was an inside job, I think a lot of people felt better. People who were saying, 'I'm getting out of here' aren't saying it now." For Jack Mills, the CTA's executive director at the time, the main issue became how to prevent negative publicity in the surrounding community, since "it seemed as though the television stations wanted to blame [the murders] on a public housing development." As CTA Board Member Peggy Mackin observed, "If it happened somewhere else they wouldn't have talked about it for two days." Still, Mackin more optimistically opined, the post-redevelopment "public image" of Commonwealth had not been irreparably damaged: "You talk to people around here or on Washington St. or Commonwealth Avenue, or you go to the Stop 'n' Shop and people still treat you the same. This place has really changed since it was done over—people know crime is not a problem here."[100]

The new Commonwealth survived a double murder and, four months later, an apartment fire, but it could not fully escape the nationwide scourge of drugs. Drugs became a serious problem at Commonwealth, especially during the crack epidemic of the late 1980s and early 1990s. In 1989, as the culmination of a full week of drug-education programs, a hundred adults and children took part in a candlelight march through the development, chanting "Take your drugs and go." As one resident put it, "We want people to know that we don't want people dealing drugs here anymore. We never singled out anyone while we were marching, but we slowed down when we walked past certain homes." Local police pointed out that drug-related violence (averaging about one incident a month) was well below that prevailing in other public housing developments across the city, yet Commonwealth's residents did not find this particularly reassuring. As CTA Co-Chair Cora Rothwell observed, "We're doing good so far," but "if there are drugs and guns, we're going to go right back to where we were."[101] Commonwealth's ever-wary tenants consistently guarded against any signs that the development would falter. Much of this wariness centered on the caliber and character of their newest fellow tenants.

Between 1984 and 1988, immediately following redevelopment, Commonwealth had its own waiting list, and it drew new tenants from this rather than from a citywide list. In this way, CMC and the CTA could exercise considerable control over who was admitted, including extensive background checks and home visits. In 1988, however, the BHA entered into a Voluntary Compliance Agreement with HUD that prohibited such separate lists on the grounds that they could be used to foster racial segregation. Since then, Commonwealth (despite being perhaps the most racially and ethnically diverse development in the city) has had to accept tenants from the citywide waiting list, and has had no more than an advisory role in keeping out those deemed undesirable. As one former manager of Commonwealth comments, "They say in the [BHA] Occupancy Department that everybody wants to live at Commonwealth. We end up getting a lot of the 'trash,' if you will, from across the city. It's really unfair to long-term residents there who came in under a different standard." Moreover, in part because of its reputation as a safe and well-managed place, Commonwealth began to receive a disproportionate share of internal citywide emergency transfers, persons whose lives were thought to be in danger in other public housing. Often, CMC staff claimed, new problems accompany such people: "When you have these internal transfers out front on the steps drinking beer or throwing their trash out the window from the sixth floor, the people at Commonwealth want [the site manager] to get these people out *now*."[102] Having worked hard to achieve the redevelopment, Commonwealth residents had come to expect a higher standard of behavior.

Commonwealth's more-established residents, admitted or re-admitted under this higher standard, almost uniformly call for greater scrutiny of would-be public neighbors: "It's not fair that we can't choose who we want to live here. BHA sends losers to us. Send us more responsible people here, not just those on BHA's list"; "Some have waited five years, and BHA took the undesirable ones"; "People are causing trouble who move in here"; "In order to keep the place in good condition you need to get out the bad seed"; "Having people come here from other developments is like buying a used car and getting someone else's headaches"; "When people come from other developments they bring trouble with them"; "Most of the people they're sending in now either have some problems like drugs or thugs in the family, and they drove them off on us, and that's not fair"; "Tenants who come here from other BHA developments are problem tenants."[103]

The BHA tenant-selection chief John Murphy—who held the post from 1973 until 2000—understood the frustrations of Commonwealth's tenants, but he firmly believed that the BHA, as a public agency, should be prepared to welcome all eligible applicants. "The public housing system," he points out, "is based on rejections, not selections. We don't really select who we want to live in our units

. . . If we *can't* find a reason *not* to allow you to move in, then you've got to be housed. Even though you might not have all of the characteristics that a private management company would consider an ideal tenant." By contrast, subsidized private landlords such as Corcoran would prefer to "look at five families and say, 'Well, this one has a minor problem there and that one has a minor problem there, so we'll select number 4.' Private management has always had a way of being able to exclude people for reasons that are not entirely legitimate."[104] After 1988, HUD and BHA rules largely reined in this discretion.

In addition to the struggles over tenancy and drugs, Commonwealth suffered from budget cuts to social programs. State funds supported a wide array of programs through the CTA during the late 1980s—including a family day-care program and an employment and training outreach worker—but budget cuts forced staff layoffs and program cancellations after 1989. Despite the intermittently successful fund-raising efforts of the CTA and others, any kind of substantial and sustained investment in education and job training is still absent. As one newspaper article put it in late 1993, "Commonwealth's social-service safety net is hanging on by a thread." Since then, despite intermittent success at grantsmanship, a long-standing tutoring program staffed by Boston College students, and some funding from the BHA, the CTA has struggled to fund social and economic programs for needy tenants.[105] For the most part, Commonwealth stayed well outside newspaper headlines during the 1990s, a testament both to its relatively smooth operation and to the greater turbulence occurring at other housing projects in the city. It probably also helped that Commonwealth now housed about 75 percent fewer children than it did when fully occupied in the 1950s.

Corcoran did suffer one newsworthy embarrassment in 1995, however, when its manager attempted to evict Beatrice Todd, an eighty-year-old gadfly, alleging that she owed $7 in back rent. Todd learned that the discrepancy had been caused by a minor fluctuation in her income linked to a shift in interest rates following a bank merger, and so she decided to fight back. "When I got the court order about the $7," she recalls, "I went to City Hall and I talked to [City Councilor] Charles Yancey." Yancey called a reporter at the *Boston Globe,* and the media floodgates opened to include not only an article with a photograph in the *Globe,* but also stories on television, in the *Boston Herald,* and on the AP wire. Needless to say, Corcoran quickly backed off and issued a public apology, calling the eviction notice "an error in judgment." Other tenants raised complaints about inadequate security and faltering elevators.[106] Activists in the CTA continually sought ways to remind the BHA that Commonwealth should not be forgotten. In 1998, scheming tenants called for the city's inspectional services department to cite the development for violations. Sympathetic BHA Administrator Sandra Henriquez called this a "nice idea but bad strategy," since it would only be a "one-shot fix." Instead, she told tenants, "let's figure out what you really need, how systemic is it, and let us work together."[107]

Throughout the 1990s, CMC managers insisted that the BHA was underfunding the long-term maintenance needs of Commonwealth's apartments, and that CMC was being asked to manage Commonwealth with about half of the BHA's average per-unit allocation of funds. In 1993 BHA Deputy Administrator Bill McGonagle countered such claims by asking: "Should a development that's had a $38 million facelift receive as much of the operating budget as a development of similar size and age that hasn't received the same amount of capital improvements?" While there is, of course, considerable validity to the BHA position, both tenants and management voiced fears that chronic underfunding could permit conditions at Commonwealth to decline. Meanwhile, CMC continued to collect nearly 100 percent of rents due, while generating about $20,000 per month in excess rents over expenses (beyond their management fee). Under the terms of their management agreement, they had to return this money to the BHA, rather than reinvest it in Commonwealth. In 1999 the BHA approved $3 million to address systemic problems in the development's parapets, lintels, and brickwork that had not been adequately solved during the reconstruction process fifteen years earlier. Although tenants continued to complain that the housing authority was slow in implementing repairs, the BHA did respond to this crucial need.[108]

After fifteen years at the helm of the BHA's flagship, CMC continued to manage Commonwealth and to enjoy widespread tenant support for its efforts. In 1997 BHA officials finally remembered to rebid the management contract (which had been allowed to continue indefinitely since 1983). Ten private management firms expressed interest but remained suspicious that the contract was wired for Corcoran. BHA staff (with CTA concurrence) did indeed rehire CMC, this time for a three-year period, to permit tenants to consider the possibility of moving toward tenant management. In 2001 the BHA rebid the Commonwealth contract and again chose CMC. Tenants continued to discuss the possibility of greater self-management and accepted CMC's view that "the CTA and CMC [should] become business partners, working together to satisfy the short and long-term needs of the residents."

Even as most tenants praised Corcoran, they sought new ways to guarantee still higher standards for management and maintenance; they clamored for increased legal rights as a "third party signatory" on the management contract; and they remained inveterately suspicious of anything to do with the BHA and its "good faith" agreements. Alex Rosin, a CTA Board member who is a paraplegic, observed that, in contrast to long-term tenants, the BHA staff has a high turnover rate and a short memory. "I will live here my whole life," Rosin commented, "and the majority of us are here for decades." Eventually, the CTA, BHA, and CMC signed a new "Memorandum of Understanding" affirming their mutual commitment to "meaningful tenant participation" and "full and effective monitoring" of Commonwealth's management and operation.[109] In 2000, as in 1980, the Commonwealth Tenants Association continued to produce leaders to fight for the fu-

FIGURE 4.24 View of the development and of Boston from a Commonwealth apartment. Tenants at Commonwealth look out on a well-maintained development and enjoy broad vistas of the entire city beyond.

FIGURE 4.25 Commonwealth Avenue: transit and amenities. Commonwealth Avenue, with its trolley line and its shops, is a good neighbor to the Commonwealth development (seen at left center). The brick apartment buildings on the other side of the avenue are also in keeping with the scale and materials of the public housing development.

ture of their homes. As Commonwealth's first half century came to a close, its fortunes had come full circle, and the struggle continued.

As the twenty-first century began, Commonwealth's residents continued to benefit from the stability of their broader neighborhood, even though real estate prices and high rents kept them from moving into it (Figs. 4.24–4.25). Interviews conducted with a variety of local business owners confirmed that the "scourge" of Fidelis Way has largely disappeared. Most praise the quality of the redevelopment maintenance and management and credit the transformation for a distinct increase in neighborhood safety. The owner of Reliable Medical Supply, located across Commonwealth Avenue from the development, comments that "compared to what it used to be, it's a gem right now." Even though he still considers Commonwealth a "welfare dump," he acknowledges a peaceful coexistence. A local realtor notes the improvements to "Fidelis Way" but contends that the rising economy of the 1990s—which attracted those who could afford higher rents—is more responsible than redevelopment for the change. Many new businesses opened, frequently run by Russian or Chinese immigrants. Within a half-block of Commonwealth development, residents could walk to four drug stores, multiple medical facilities, an optician, a family dentist, a hair salon, a variety of eating places, a new bank, a dry cleaners, and a supermarket. Despite all that had transpired in fifty years, this neighborhood remained a desirable place to live.[110]

Accounting for Success

In the end, there is little consensus about which aspect of Commonwealth's redevelopment mattered most or whose role was most central. Local business owners stress the relative economic health of the surrounding neighborhood. Planners point to the Monastery Hill planning process as the crucial catalyst, emphasizing the need to build a coalition of powerful players before large-scale redevelopment dollars for a low-income community could be obtained. Designers believe in the paramount value of their own contributions. They extol the reduction of density on the site, the reconfiguration of buildings and outdoor spaces to reduce the number of hallways, the increase in apartment sizes, the increase in the number of private entrances and private yards, the redistribution of elderly residents and young families into units and building types better suited to their needs, the regrading of the site, the creation of multiple age-specific play areas, and the programming of new community facilities.

Many of those involved in the management of Commonwealth, however, suggest that the place could have been just as successful with a lower investment in design costs, particularly for amenities such as the elaborate community facility. John Corcoran himself comments that "we could have done it with one-third the money and got the same effect" (a view that seems to represent rueful reconsideration of his actual cost overruns). Others recognize ways that management tasks have been eased by design changes (such as the reduction in the number of unsupervised hallways and in the number of young children living in elevator buildings with no place for play), but note that the overriding issue is the quality of the management. Some claim that management quality is closely tied to the ability of the private sector to circumvent the rules that bog down government bureaucracies. By hiring on-site maintenance personnel who are skilled at many trades, without having to work through a central housing authority that is operating under union regulations, they argue, it is much easier to establish and maintain a responsive maintenance system. When the removal of political minefields such as union-hiring is combined with the added capacity to have service personnel closely tied to the Commonwealth community (either because they are themselves residents or because they have come to know the residents well through sustained involvement), the relative advantage of private management is further enhanced. A sometimes heated debate remains over how much credit should go to this privatization effort. There seems to be little or no criticism of the performance or cost-effectiveness of Corcoran Management Company, but many are reluctant to see their qualities as too closely bound up with the fact that they are a for-profit real estate company rather than a public agency. Good management, these critics argue, means the same thing, whether it is accomplished by government or the private sector.[111]

In assessing the success of the Commonwealth redevelopment, all parties concur that the Commonwealth Tenants Association, together with the community organizer who assisted the group, was also central. Most tellingly, the tenants who lived through the redevelopment effort themselves believe this. When twenty of them were asked, "Who played the most important role in the redevelopment efforts?" most credited "tenant leaders" or "all residents." A few mentioned architects, one person credited everyone equally, but nobody singled out either the Boston Housing Authority or the private developer as the key player. Commonwealth also remains a triumph of racial and ethnic integration: as of 2000, its residents were 38 percent black, 29 percent non-Latino white (many of them Russian émigrés), 24 percent Latino, and 9 percent Asian. Similarly, its tenant leadership is still commendably diverse.[112]

If one measure of success in American public housing is the rate at which its residents become economically able to leave it, Commonwealth's success is more limited. Post-redevelopment Commonwealth, like the devastated Fidelis Way that preceded it, remains largely the province of households dependent on public assistance of various kinds, most often disability payments or social security. As of late 2000, only eighty-three Commonwealth residents reported full-time employment—approximately 20 percent of those aged eighteen to sixty-one. And even for this minority of tenants with stable jobs, there are few affordable market-rate housing alternatives in the area. In Allston-Brighton, sixteen thousand students occupy more than one-quarter of the entire private housing stock, with thousands more in university dormitories. Exacerbated by the end of Boston's rent control in the late 1990s, the presence of so many students increased demand for housing, placing upward pressure on rents.[113] Not surprisingly, turnover at Commonwealth remains very low—no more than a dozen or two apartments each year.

Fully 42 percent of those who moved into redeveloped apartments still lived in them fifteen years later.

For many, the development remains a safe haven rather than a launching pad for other opportunities. Sometimes, though, it is both. Harry Spence tells the story of one tenant he knew at Commonwealth during the mid-1990s, a black woman with three children born out of wedlock (starting when she was sixteen) who lived at the development for many years before abruptly moving to New Hampshire to manage a McDonalds. Spence notes that "she's not going to show up on your employment statistics for Commonwealth," but he stresses that her move owed as much to the stabilizing influence of the Commonwealth environment as it did to the harsh push of welfare reform in Massachusetts. Such moves, he proposes, are easier to make from a place like Commonwealth than they would be from more troubled projects: "If she'd been living in Franklin Field for the last fifteen years, her courage in moving to New Hampshire would probably be a lot less."[114] It is unclear how commonplace such examples of upward mobility from Commonwealth may be, but they serve as a reminder that public housing can still productively act as a waystation for some households.

Commonwealth also warrants praise for what it delivers to those who choose to stay put. Surely some component of success in public housing redevelopment should be measured by the enhancement of an attractive, safe, and stable community where even many of those who can afford to leave will choose to stay. Moreover, because Commonwealth's success in these terms was achieved through tenant activism, responsive design, and effective management—*without* resort to the income-mixing so often touted as necessary to revitalize public housing—it raises important questions about current policy trends. Despite the ongoing problems with inadequate operating funds, tenant selection, drug activity, and lack of economic incentives and opportunities for residents, no other redevelopment effort in Boston (and few, if any, elsewhere in the United States) was able to match or sustain the range of successes found at Commonwealth. It is a track record that HUD's HOPE VI program will be hard-pressed to match.

Commonwealth (like its parallel and successor initiatives) still has its critics. Some denounce the enormous public investment necessary to reclaim the project. Others condemn the Commonwealth redevelopment effort because it entailed a net loss of about 40 percent of the original units. In the context of long (and growing) waiting lists for public housing and an overall shortage of affordable housing, strategies that reduce density without providing low-income replacement housing may be seen as ultimately shortsighted, since replacement housing remains very difficult to find or build. Beyond these issues, the nature of Commonwealth's management experiment created tensions within the BHA over the usurpation of their management role by a private firm, though such privatization became the rule for most HOPE VI experiments, and many urban public housing authorities are devolving management responsibilities for other projects as well. Here, too, decisions that were controversial in the early 1980s have become conventional wisdom two decades later.

As high-quality private management companies gain a broader foothold in public housing across the country, one hopes that more public housing authorities will learn from their methods and match their ability to treat public housing tenants like everyone else. In essence this means developing a consistent set of expectations for behavior in return for a consistent and reliable provision of services. As John Corcoran puts it, "It's mutual respect. We listen to the tenants—we have to, because they can fire us if they're not happy with us. At the same time, we plant those flowers, and not one pansy gets stepped on." Or, as one former Commonwealth manager puts it, "The word 'project' is out of our dictionary."[115] In the American context, where public housing serves only a small minority of citizens and where public housing residents and advocates must constantly struggle to overcome the stigma associated with life in "the projects," revitalizing and normalizing public housing communities is never easy. Achieving success in the multiple dimensions described is arduous and expensive, but the story of Boston's Commonwealth Development shows that it is indeed possible.

FIVE

Reclaiming Housing, Recovering Communities:
A Comparison of Neighborhood Struggles

THE THREE PUBLIC neighborhoods of West Broadway, Franklin Field, and Commonwealth still stand after half a century, but they stand for very different things. It is clear that all three projects endured the institutional collapse of the Boston Housing Authority, and that all three suffered from the broader stigmatization of American public housing. Yet somehow the policies and procedures of a highly troubled public agency affected each group of residents in rather divergent ways. Faced with the accelerating demise of the BHA, the residents of each place, their supporters, and their detractors responded quite differently. The three public neighborhoods—located in distant corners of a single city—all struggled with the racial politics of Boston and the nation, but the struggles took different forms, with different consequences for the viability of each community. Each project found itself an isolated outpost, resisted by outsiders. At the same time, the residents of each place recognized their embeddedness in a larger evolving neighborhood that was experiencing social and economic changes that went well beyond the capacity of residents or the BHA to control. Ultimately, these are stories of collective coping mechanisms, some of which seemed to have worked much better than others.

TRAJECTORIES OF COLLAPSE

All three public neighborhoods collapsed as communities by the end of the 1970s, but they did not collapse in identical ways. Superficially, each place looked physically similar: a half-vacant wasteland of brick and crushed glass, pock-marked with boarded-up windows that failed to stem ongoing vandalism. They also shared socioeconomic similarities. Each place housed residents who were largely dependent on public assistance, experienced widespread depression, and had few on-site recreational outlets. At each place residents were angry, alienated, and frustrated. Seen collectively, however, these three Boston projects defied the national stereotypes about distressed public housing. Only Franklin Field was occupied primarily by minority households; by contrast, D Street was all white and Fidelis Way highly integrated, both racially and ethnically. In Boston, it seems, public housing collapsed on an equal-opportunity basis (Fig. 5.1).

The racial occupancy patterns, observed over the course of fifty years, reveal three very different types of neighborhood experience (Figs. 5.2–5.3). All three projects began with an overwhelmingly white population. At West Broadway, de-spite desperate efforts to achieve modest integration with "pioneer" families, the project remained a white stronghold until the 1990s. This defensive struggle en-tailed severe and ongoing consequences for the lives of all those who lived in or near the development. D Street did not just happen to remain all-white for most of two generations; its whiteness was guaranteed only by all manner of actions—sometimes subtle, sometimes egregious—that increased racial and ethnic ten-sions for decades. By contrast, Franklin Field experienced racial change suddenly and wrenchingly. When the housing development—and its larger neighbor-hood—tipped from Jewish to black, it faced not simply racial and ethnic change but also socioeconomic upheaval. The public housing project gained a new co-hort of tenants, but the broader neighborhood continued to lose its established institutions and economic vitality. Commonwealth's tenants gained comparative ground simply because they did not have to cope with the stress of either of these two extremes. Despite racial tensions, Fidelis residents of all races were well re-moved from the frontlines of Boston's busing battles. Some neighbors in the Washington Heights section expressed racial hostility to be sure, but this stopped well short of the violence that exploded in South Boston. Similarly, because the

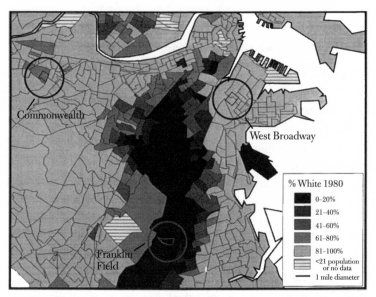

FIGURE 5.1 Three pre-redevelopment racial contexts. In 1980, as redevelopment efforts commenced at the three public neighborhoods, each faced a very different racial climate. West Broadway's planners contended with all-white South Boston and with the subsequent challenge of helping to re-integrate it; Franklin Field's team wrestled with the challenges of a minority community with much disinvestment and little political clout; while Commonwealth's supporters struggled to preserve an integrated housing development in a somewhat less integrated community.

broader Brighton neighborhood changed slowly—and changed in the direction of ever-greater ethnic and racial diversity—Commonwealth's tenants could continue to regard their surroundings as an abundant resource for daily needs. When Franklin Field residents left their development, they saw signs of further neighborhood decay and disinvestment. The landscape sent a consistent and contiguous message of abandonment. By contrast, Fidelis Way residents—however stigmatized as the scourge of their neighborhood—needed only to cross the street to see signs of reassuring stability in both the buildings and the local economy.

NEIGHBORHOOD DETACHMENT

From the time the BHA first built and tenanted the three public neighborhoods, they experienced a distinct separation from their surroundings. Some of this separation was architectural and urbanistic—the project superblocks stood out from nearby streetscapes of woodframe houses—but some of it was social. Few resi-

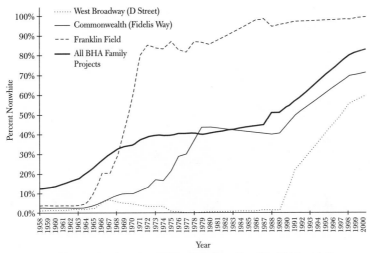

FIGURE 5.2 The racial trajectories of West Broadway, Franklin Field, and Commonwealth. In contrast to the gradual shift in Boston family public housing toward greater minority occupancy (see thick black line), each of the three public neighborhoods behaved rather differently. West Broadway remained a white stronghold until 1989, then shifted dramatically; Franklin Field shifted suddenly from nearly all-white to nearly all-black and Latino; and Commonwealth remained closest to the overall BHA pattern, owing to efforts to keep racial quotas in place during the 1980s.

dents came from the wards nearest the project, despite the broad promises of local politicians that bringing public housing to each ward would serve local people (Fig. 5.4). At West Broadway and Commonwealth, approximately 80 percent of the first tenants came from outside South Boston and Allston-Brighton, respectively. Only Franklin Field drew somewhat more from the neighboring Dorchester wards, yet even there about 60 percent of tenants came from somewhere else.[1]

This neighborhood disconnection meant that project residents were often newcomers to the area, yet this was counterbalanced by another tendency: the BHA, its supporters, and their constituents used early Boston public housing as a self-selecting vehicle for consolidating neighborhood nationalities. In the 1950s, for example, Irish politicians and housing authority personnel gladly placed Irish applicants into the projects of South Boston (such as West Broadway), just as Italians went happily to East Boston. Similarly, BHA marketing materials touted the proximity of synagogues and a Jewish community center to Franklin Field, and this place—located in the heart of the city's largest Jewish neighborhood—

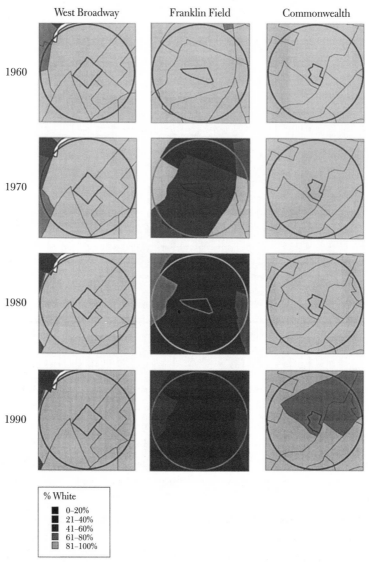

FIGURE 5.3 Neighborhood racial change, 1960–1990. Between 1960 and 1990, the racial change in the three developments (or lack thereof) mostly paralleled the racial changes in the neighborhoods within a half-mile radius of each place.

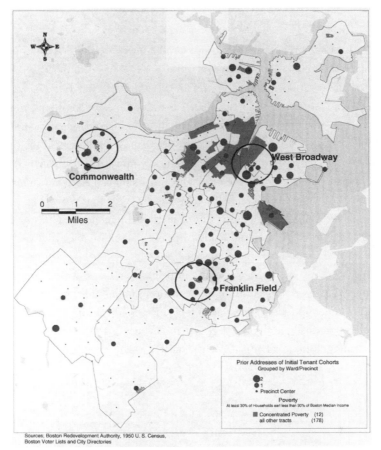

FIGURE 5.4 Location of prior residences of initial tenant cohorts. The first tenants to occupy the three projects came from all over the city, with relatively few hailing from
nearby neighborhoods, and even fewer coming from areas of highly concentrated
poverty.

became predominantly occupied by Jews. The relatively higher neighborhood
draw of Franklin Field, compared with West Broadway and Commonwealth, may
therefore be attributable to its appeal to Boston's lower-income Jews, who were
disproportionately concentrated in the wards near the project. In short, neighborhoods were "served" not by providing housing for their least advantaged residents but by importing more upwardly mobile residents who conformed to the
dominant ethnic make-up of the district, even if this meant that those desirable
persons came from diverse areas of the city.

ARRIVALS AND DEPARTURES

At Franklin Field, West Broadway, and Commonwealth, the first tenants came from many different places, and most did not stay for very long. Each project, sited in white neighborhoods, housed chiefly white male war veterans and their families—who had successfully negotiated an arduous selection process designed to ensure that only the most "deserving" and best connected of low-income families could gain an apartment. In these early years, most families used the projects well and wisely, moving onward and economically upward as soon as their wages and savings rose. On average, the original residents moved elsewhere after about six years; in each development, half were gone after only four years (Fig. 5.5). Efforts to track the subsequent addresses of the initial tenants at each project suggest that as many as half used public housing as a waystation to leave Boston completely, headed for suburbs or other cities. Among those who stayed in Boston, few chose to move into private housing in neighborhoods near the project, and fewer than 10 percent moved on to other Boston public housing.[2]

Despite initial optimism and considerable local political support, public housing projects gradually took on a stigma that has been extremely difficult to overcome. Demographic changes at each project accelerated during the 1960s, as

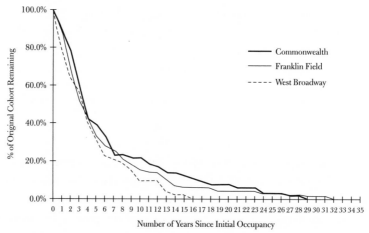

FIGURE 5.5 Residential mobility of initial tenants. Tenants at each place stayed an average of six years, and most were gone after only four. A small percentage of tenants at each place stayed on for a decade or more.

Boston's white working class increasingly resisted application to most BHA developments. Simultaneously, civil rights groups successfully challenged housing authority efforts to keep out single-parent families and forced the BHA to start to pay serious attention to matters of racial integration. As the waiting lists for housing increasingly came to contain more single-parent and nonwhite applicants, the BHA gradually accommodated itself to the needs of those economically strapped families seeking entry.

Those entering into Boston public housing in 1970 came during an intense period of social engineering. Pressured by lawsuits filed by the NAACP and CORE and prodded by a reform-minded administrator during the 1960s, the BHA sought to redress racial and ethnic imbalances in the city—as well as to overcome outright segregation in many projects—by encouraging applicants to go to projects where their race was in the minority. Moreover, the BHA's stated policies gave increasingly little leeway to applicants to choose a particular project. Instead of neighborhood-based and project-based waiting lists, the BHA claimed to operate from a single citywide list, according to which applicants would be assigned to one of the three projects citywide that had the most vacancies.

That said, site-based project managers and many staffers in the tenant-selection bureaucracy worked against "official" policy by assigning most applicants outside the "1-2-3" system based on vacancy. Franklin Field, Commonwealth, and West Broadway were not among the developments with the highest vacancy rates in 1970, yet these three projects gained a combined total of 399 new arrivals in that year alone, thereby indicating considerable flexibility in tenant assignments, as well as high turnover. This all suggests that applicants and individual housing authority officials exercised more discretion over tenant placement than the official policy was supposed to permit, yet the increasingly centralized selection and assignment system still worked against the ability of projects to serve neighborhood residents. For the most part, the projects served not neighbors but increasingly desperate families from across the city.

By 1970 the neighborhood origins of public housing residents at the three projects seemed less tied to ethnicity than to race and poverty. More residents came from high-poverty areas of the city than was the case in the 1950s, and, closely related to this, more came from the city's nonwhite neighborhoods (Fig. 5.6). Indicative of how neighborhood-specific public housing appeal tends to be, Franklin Field drew 38 percent of new residents from its neighborhood, nearly

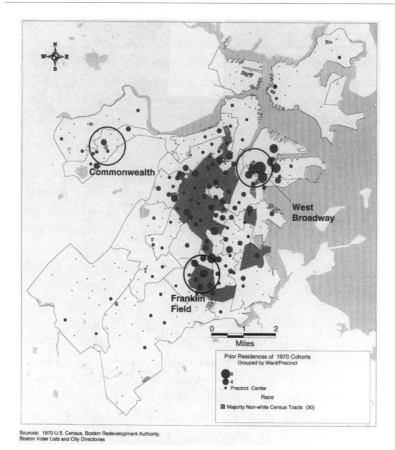

FIGURE 5.6 Location of prior residences of tenants arriving in 1970. A substantial number of tenants newly entering West Broadway, Franklin Field, and Commonwealth in 1970 came from the city's majority-nonwhite neighborhoods, though South Boston continued to feed some whites into West Broadway.

twice the rate of Commonwealth (21 percent). In all three cases, however, the vast majority of 1970 arrivals continued to come from disparate areas of the city, just as they had in the 1950s.

Even though many old-timers in the tenant-selection department favored more traditional family patterns, reform-minded bureaucrats in the agency's Tenant and Community Relations division consistently pushed the system toward accepting those deemed needy. Frequently, neediness resulted from the absence, death, or departure of a male wage-earner. An extreme example of this occurred at Franklin Field; when the development opened in 1954, nearly all its families contained two spouses, compared with only 28 percent of the 124 households that gained entry in 1970. Similarly, at West Broadway in 1950, 96 percent of the original households arrived with a spousal pair, compared with only 32 percent of arrivals two decades later. At Commonwealth, the trend was the same, though somewhat slower to develop—nearly all members of the original cohort were married couples, but only half fit this pattern by 1970.[3]

In keeping with the shift away from the initial pattern of young two-parent households, the 1970 arrivals were markedly older and less likely to have small children. The original tenant families, on average, were headed by thirty-year-old couples, whereas by 1970 the entering families were headed, on average, by persons who were one or even two *decades* older. The aging of the entry population, while consistent across all three projects, was markedly more extreme at Commonwealth—where the average age at entry in 1970 was fifty-two—another reminder that so much about public housing demographic trends remains project-specific. Commonwealth, even as early as 1970, attracted a sizable elderly population whereas more of the older residents at the other two projects consisted of those who had arrived young and stayed for many years.

Surprisingly, perhaps, those who arrived in 1970 were no more likely to linger on in public housing than were the initial tenants. As in the 1950s, new arrivals stayed on average slightly less than six years. When the overall patterns of longevity at the three projects are plotted together and both time cohorts are compared, an even more striking finding emerges. Despite the radically different socioeconomic profiles of the original tenants and those who arrived in 1970, the pattern of length of residence appears almost indistinguishable (Fig. 5.7). In the 1970s, as in the 1950s, half of the tenants left their projects within four years of arrival, and the rest left more gradually in what looks to be a remarkably similar distribution. Similarly, when they left, 80 percent of the 1970 cohort found new housing well beyond the neighborhoods of the projects.

While graphically compelling, this finding is also quite misleading. However much one might be tempted to conclude that patterns of mobility out of public housing in the 1970s mirrored those of the 1950s, the numbers and charts tell only part of a highly complex story, and they mask as much as they reveal. At base, the issue is that movement out of a public housing project—like movement into one—

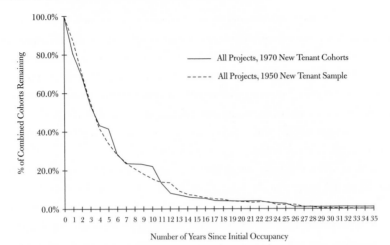

FIGURE 5.7 Comparison of resident mobility, 1950s versus 1970s. Tenants arriving at West Broadway, Franklin Field, and Commonwealth in 1970 tended to stay no longer than the initial resident cohorts did during the 1950s. However, the act of entering and leaving public housing in the 1970s had changed dramatically, so the apparent similarity of tenure trajectories in this chart masks many important discontinuities.

can mean many different things. As the three neighborhood sagas presented here attest, leaving public housing in 1975 was a fundamentally different socioeconomic act than it was in 1955.

The Boston public neighborhoods of the 1970s were not always economic dead ends, but those who entered into and left the three projects in the 1970s were much less likely to move on to the suburbs and somewhat less likely to move on to more suburban areas of Boston itself than were the earlier arrivals. For nearly one-quarter of those who moved into West Broadway, Franklin Field, and Commonwealth during 1970, life in one project became merely a waystation to life in another one. In other words, leaving *a* project—in many cases—did not entail leaving *the projects.* Moreover, the BHA completed a large number of housing developments designed for the elderly during the 1970s, and many older residents of family public housing projects successfully sought transfer to the elderly-centered facilities (often located in more affluent areas than the family projects). Also, unlike the young group of original residents, many among the older 1970 cohort left public housing because of death or extreme disability, another factor that skewed the average length of residence downward.

Moreover, it should be remembered that departure from one of these three projects—even if the move also signaled a final transition out of public housing and into the private market—did not necessarily mean that West Broadway, Commonwealth, and Franklin Field constituted a tenant's *first* experience with public housing residence. Many, in fact, transferred into one of these projects from other Boston public housing. Among the original public housing residents, only 4 percent had moved to one of the three projects from another Boston public housing development, yet fully 11 percent of the 1970 arrivals had done so. In short, the 1970 arrivals were three times as likely to have come from a project as their 1950s counterparts and were nearly three times as likely to move on to another project when they left.

FEAR, FRUSTRATION, AND FLIGHT

Only by examining the community stories unique to each specific public neighborhood is it possible to understand what it meant to move into or out of public housing during the 1970s. At D Street, dozens of Puerto Rican and black families (as well as some whites) left not because they could afford to relinquish public housing but because they feared for their lives. In some cases, they did not even survive long enough to leave alive. At Franklin Field, distraught tenants of all races fled a neighborhood where wholesale racial, ethnic, and economic change occurred with terrifying rapidity and unforeseeable consequences. At Fidelis Way, the racial animus was less lethal and the neighborhood somewhat less hostile, but the physical devastation of the project compelled exit.

Residents of all three developments faced a full onslaught of problems—racial and ethnic upheaval, crumbling infrastructure, widespread management failure, and accelerating vacancy, vandalism, and violence. Tenants at the three places experienced each of these challenges in varying degrees of severity, and in slightly differing chronology, but the cumulative suffering was extreme in every case and surely contributed to early departure for those who could afford to leave. In contrast to life in the newly completed, well-maintained, and politically valued projects of the 1950s, the residents of public housing in the 1970s faced ravaged environments besieged by internal conflicts and broad public hostility. Thus, the fact that newly arriving public housing residents stayed in these developments for almost identical lengths of time in the 1950s and in the 1970s does not indicate consistency of experience but rather masks the true extent of differences in the social, biological, environmental, and economic forces that compelled some to move on and others to stay put.

The struggles of individual families in D Street, Franklin Field, and Fidelis Way were matched by pressures faced within the BHA itself and were greatly exacerbated by these larger troubles. Caught between declining rent receipts and inflationary pressures, the Authority struggled through the 1970s in a state of near financial collapse, and so chose to defer maintenance needs at most developments. West Broadway, Commonwealth, and Franklin Field, like other BHA family projects, suffered through an accelerating period of extreme decline during the 1970s characterized by physical decay, managerial corruption, and social disorder. By 1980, the three projects had vacancy rates of between 30 and 50 percent, and Judge Garrity placed the BHA itself into receivership—a last-ditch attempt to reverse its mismanagement and restore its ability to provide tenants with decent housing.

In the 1980s West Broadway, Commonwealth, and Franklin Field were among the biggest beneficiaries of changes at the BHA. Each place gained from major reinvestment initiatives—comprehensive redevelopment efforts intended to rebuild them into physically attractive and socially stable communities. Yet, because of the ways they had declined, and because of the kind of communities they had become, the three places were not equally well placed to benefit from the redevelopment largesse.

TRAJECTORIES OF REDEVELOPMENT

Close examination of the redevelopment efforts at West Broadway, Franklin Field, and Commonwealth suggests some characteristics that seem to contribute to success in these ventures as well as some features that seem to stymie most efforts to implement positive change.[4] How and why did redevelopment work out better for residents of Commonwealth than it did for those at Franklin Field or West Broadway?

Table 5.1 shows a few of the many ways that one might compare the three places, revealing many similarities as well as potentially significant variations. Franklin Field, West Broadway, and Commonwealth may have been built in the same era and redeveloped during the same period, but there are differences among the projects in racial and ethnic make-up, in size, in building type, and in the form of post-redevelopment management. Beyond such easily labeled measures, each place has its own history and aura; it exists in its own highly individual neighborhood context and has its own internal dynamic. In interpreting the

TABLE 5.1   THREE BOSTON PUBLIC NEIGHBORHOODS

	FRANKLIN FIELD	WEST BROADWAY	COMMONWEALTH
Year constructed	1954	1949	1951
Dates of redevelopment	1977–1987	1977–1991, 2000–	1979–1985
Size (as built)	504 units	972 units	648 units
No. apts. occupied (1990s)	~348	~649	~392
Building type	3-story walk-up	3-story walk-up	3-story walk-up, 6-story mid-rises
Racial/ethnic makeup (1950s)	~99% white	~99% white	~98% white
Racial/ethnic makeup (2000)	49% black 47% Latino 3% Asian 1% white 1% American Indian	40% white 29% Latino 17% black 12% Asian	38% black 29% white 24% Latino 9% Asian
Form of management (2000)	BHA	BHA	Private

trajectories of redevelopment, all these factors matter. Often, they matter in ways that are all too predictable, but sometimes the significance is counterintuitive.

Just before the receivership began, the BHA's Planning Department internally circulated its report entitled *Site Selection Criteria for Substantial Rehabilitation.* The study compared the "ten most distressed" BHA family developments (including Commonwealth, West Broadway, and Franklin Field) in terms of site accessibility, physical design, neighborhood characteristics, and tenant characteristics It then assessed BHA redevelopment priorities and prospects in relation to the research findings contained in HUD's national study of "troubled" public housing. In terms of site accessibility, the BHA planners hypothesized that redevelopment would be more likely to succeed in cases where the site was well served by transportation, shopping, recreation, and health-care facilities. In terms of design, they felt more confident in the ability to effect a turnaround in cases where a development was small, lacked high-rise units, had ample parking, featured buildings with identifiable fronts and backs, was of relatively low density, and was amenable to greater territorial control by residents. As far as neighborhood characteristics were concerned, they stressed the hypothetical advantages of rising residential market values, a high percentage of owner-occupied units, a low percentage of subsidized units, low unemployment rates, and high ongoing public and private neighborhood investment. Finally, in terms of tenant characteristics, they hypothesized that redevelopment success would be best ensured in places with a low percentage of female-headed households, a high percentage of working adults, and a low percentage of minors, relative to other developments. Despite some effort to include aspects of "neighborhood characteristics," the BHA chose not to pass judgment on the racial or ethnic composition of a development, though everyone must have recognized that redevelopment prospects depended in large part on the quality of the racial climate.[5] Table 5.2 summarizes the Boston Housing Authority's assessment of the pre-redevelopment situation at Commonwealth, West Broadway, and Franklin Field, relative to BHA averages, for all of the above categories.

Table 5.2 reveals no clear pattern. No one development jumps out as either consistently below BHA average or consistently above it, if one looks across all four broad categories. Equally striking, the table suggests that each of the three developments had its distinctive strengths and weaknesses relative to the other two; out of eighteen different categories of assessment, there is not one where all three developments are in the same place relative to the BHA average. That said, if one were to give equal weight to all eighteen categories, the composite scores showed that Commonwealth (+4) had a better-than-average ranking, West Broadway was about average (−1), while Franklin Field (−4) lagged behind BHA averages, a score brought down by the intensity of its residents' poverty and by the perceived limitations of its neighborhood.[6] Reflecting this, the BHA's own weighted point scores for the ten developments based on these eighteen categories ranked Commonwealth at the top, West Broadway in the middle, and Franklin Field dead last. The hypothesis was clear: Commonwealth was the place where comprehensive redevelopment would "have the greatest impact as well as the greatest likelihood of success."[7]

BHA planners did not define success, however, and their aggregate development scores thoroughly conflated the factors that might condition it. Moreover, as they realized at the time, many of the most crucial aspects of comparative advantage and disadvantage at individual developments were highly subjective and interlinked and did not lend themselves easily to quantitative assessment. In addition to the eighteen categories mentioned above, the BHA recognized other mitigating factors such as the presence of a strong tenant organization, the evidence of influential outside neighborhood support, the track record of previous or ongoing revitalization efforts, the relative availability of state (versus federal) funds for

TABLE 5.2   PRE-REDEVELOPMENT CHARACTERISTICS
RELATIVE TO BHA AVERAGE

Characteristics	Franklin Field	West Broadway	Commonwealth
SITE ACCESSIBILITY			
Transportation	−	+	+
Shopping	−	+	0
Recreation	0	+	0
Health care	0	0	+
PHYSICAL DESIGN			
Total no. of units	0	−	0
High-rise vs. low-rise units	0	0	−
Parking	+	−	+
Fronts and backs	+	0	0
Low density	+	0	0
Defensible edges	0	−	+
NEIGHBORHOOD CHARACTERISTICS			
Increase in residential market values	−	0	0
High percentage of owner-occupied units	+	0	+
Low percentage of subsidized units	0	−	0
Low unemployment rate	−	0	+
Public and private investment	−	−	0
TENANT CHARACTERISTICS			
Female-headed households	−	0	−
Adults working	−	0	0
Low percentage of minors	−	+	0
TOTAL (if given equal weight)	−4	−1	+4

Note: + denotes that the development ranks well ahead of the Authority-wide average.
− denotes that the development ranks well behind the Authority-wide average.
0 denotes that the development approximates the Authority-wide average.
Source: Adapted from BHA, 1979.

certain developments, the limitations imposed by HUD regulations on renovating certain building types, and the relative urgency of a development's physical needs. As the community histories of each development make clear, West Broadway, Franklin Field, and Commonwealth differed substantially in all of these qualitative sorts of ways. To a very great extent, it is these less quantifiable factors that seem most essential in explaining what actually happened.

Although it is quite possible that Commonwealth residents felt less stigmatized by their surroundings before redevelopment than did tenants at the other two developments, in large part because of the neighborhood context in which they lived, it must be remembered that the physical conditions at Commonwealth at its nadir were arguably even worse that those prevailing at the other places. Thus it seems logical to credit the redevelopment effort with fostering improvement in how residents viewed their environment, especially given the amplifications and explanations offered by residents during the interviews.

SEVEN KINDS OF SUCCESS

Success in reclaiming public housing may be measured in many ways and may be an indication of many different things. It is not only that individuals and groups involved in these struggles may use widely differing criteria for evaluation; it is also that these criteria and goals for redevelopment efforts rarely seem to be set out explicitly. As a consequence, even when there is general agreement that a redevelopment effort has been a success or a failure there is often less consensus about how or why this is so. The number of definitions of success is accompanied by an equally large number of attempts to explain it. Interviews with a wide range of individuals associated with each of these redevelopment efforts, including tenants, managers, designers, housing authority officials, service providers, and community organizers, suggest at least seven different kinds of success:

1. Smooth implementation
2. Recognized design quality
3. Improved tenant-organization capacity
4. Enhanced maintenance and management performance
5. Improved security
6. Progress on socioeconomic development
7. Resident satisfaction

Certainly, some individuals measure success according to many of these measures rather than only one, yet personal and professional identities often dictate the lens through which the redevelopment is seen. Moreover, the reasons that individuals give to explain success according to one or more of these measures are closely linked to such personal stakes and institutional affiliations. Each of these measures exists as a continuum, and evidence of progress—in almost every case—is rarely collected or assessed. In the end, however, true institutional learning—the capacity to fix problems in midstream and to do better next time—depends on such reflective assessment and requires a consolidated and holistic view of success. Each of these forms of success matters.

What follows is an articulation of the seven measures of success, as applied to the efforts to reclaim West Broadway, Franklin Field, and Commonwealth. All seven forms of success may be seen as contingent on the community dynamics and neighborhood characteristics unique to the history of each place.

Smooth Implementation

For many housing authority officials, particularly those in a construction-management division, the overriding challenge is to "get it done," and the key measure of success is adherence to contract dollars and timetables. Success means coping with strict budgetary constraints and managing the complex processes of construction and resident relocation. As the three accounts discussed here make painfully clear, all three redevelopment efforts experienced costly delays and were compromised by the limitations of their budgets.

At West Broadway, the BHA carried out the redevelopment in distinct phases. From the beginning, the Authority knew that the initial funding would be insufficient to implement a comprehensive redevelopment of the whole 972-unit project. Rather than scale back the degree of intervention by eliminating the dramatic reconfiguration of the buildings, the BHA chose to work intensively on limited areas of the project at a time. Predictably, perhaps, it has taken twenty years to get the funding to complete the last phase of the redevelopment, yielding a lingering eyesore and festering inequities. Clearly, this long delay has compromised the plan's success. Commonwealth, too, experienced delays and cost overruns, and all parties concede that its developer lost money. Even so, this redevelopment effort still proceeded much more smoothly. In fact, all the key players seem to regard it as a high point in their professional careers. By contrast, the redevelopment effort at Franklin Field suffered the greatest number of setbacks, most significantly involving the bankruptcy of the major contractor. There were major tensions over the budget from the beginning, and tenants continually complained about dashed expectations and shoddy construction. Fifteen years after completion of the job, bitterness persists. Tenants lament the low level of resident influence, while redevelopment planners continue to debate what went wrong; no one defends either the process or the end product.

Those who played principal roles offer diverse explanations for the wide variation of quality in the three redevelopment processes. Some stress the relative strength of political connections, which clearly favored West Broadway and Commonwealth. Powerful neighborhood politicians in South Boston championed West Broadway as a candidate for redevelopment, just as they had influenced early decisions to site a disproportionate share of Boston's highly coveted public housing in their neighborhood. Moreover, the court-appointed master Robert Whittlesey went out of his way to tout the redevelopment potential of West Broadway (as well as Commonwealth), and the West Broadway tenants' association actively engaged the support of excellent outside community development and design consultants, who initially worked on a *pro bono* basis. Armed with an arsenal of connections and a clearly demonstrable need, West Broadway garnered a coveted pilot modernization grant from the state's housing agency, and tens of millions more followed from the state legislature. Franklin Field, by contrast, received its own pilot grant and subsequent redevelopment funding not because its residents and their elected representatives had clamored for attention and funding but because the state legislature—having been pressured by a Southie-based Senate president to award funds to all-white West Broadway—had to save political face by also awarding redevelopment funding to a black-majority spot. Thus, even in its moment of greatest financial triumph, Franklin Field's entry into the redevelopment sweepstakes hardly signaled political strength. As BHA Administrator Sandra Henriquez comments, "The things that infuriate me about Southie—all the constituency services stuff because it's Southie—it's the very thing that I wish that Roxbury and Dorchester and Mattapan had, because that would add balance to the politics of the city. West Broadway had the president of the Senate as its patron; it had everything going for it, plus lots of people interact with that community all of the time."[8]

Commonwealth's relative political clout came about less because of state house connections (although these were ample) than because of its location on a highly desirable parcel of land. Prior to the BHA's decision to seek substantial funding for its redevelopment, Commonwealth had not only Whittlesey's attention and blessing but also reams of documentation attesting to its promise. As a result, by the time the BHA was ready to commence its large redevelopment efforts, Commonwealth had emerged as a clear priority, especially since—in stark contrast to Franklin Field—it ranked as "most likely to succeed" in the BHA's own internal judgment.

Many, including some in the BHA itself, attribute much of Commonwealth's success to the presence of an outside private developer who, under the turnkey process, bypassed some constraints associated with the usual public bidding process. What seems particularly commendable, however, is not only the fact that the BHA hired a good private developer but also that the Authority, through the extremely fine detail included in its *Developer's Kit* and through the careful process by which it scrutinized and evaluated six creditable proposals from developers, served as a highly active player throughout the process. Delegation to the private sector did not entail abrogation of responsibility.

Local political influence surely seems central to getting redevelopment projects launched. Similarly, Commonwealth clearly gained a lot from its private developer. Yet some key players in the redevelopment efforts attribute Commonwealth's relative success to less tangible factors. Several participants in the Commonwealth redevelopment spoke of the effort as a kind of confluence of personalities, one that was not matched elsewhere. It is not fully clear how to interpret this, since the confluence may well be a symptom of other successful aspects of the process, rather than the cause. At the very least, the relative quality of the relationship among the various parties during the process does seem to be a key indicator of problems. During the course of the Franklin Field redevelopment, especially, participants openly quarreled about how to proceed. All suffered from an undesirably large number of turnovers in on-site management, tenant organizers, BHA redevelopment staff, and resident leaders. Part of this "confluence of personalities" explanation also seems rooted in the presence of specific strong leaders, whether tenants, consultants, or housing authority personnel; the Commonwealth redevelopment process seems to have been cast with stars for every role.

The relative difficulty of the redevelopment processes clearly depended on deeply rooted community and neighborhood factors, inseparable from the broader racial politics of the city. As BRA planner David Trietsch observes, "You can't treat a project in isolation. Projects are part of neighborhoods, and you've got to deal with neighborhood-wide issues, the dynamics between neighbors and residents, as well as the land-use issues. You really have to see it as part of a system, because it is." Although each tenant group clearly distrusted the BHA when the redevelopment processes began, the negotiations at West Broadway and Commonwealth benefited from the vocal presence of local politicians and nearby institutions determined to transform a neighborhood scourge, whereas Franklin Field experienced no such outside agitation. "Commonwealth," Trietsch points out, "was able to get a lot of support from the Allston-Brighton community, and that gave it a lot of credibility in city government and [helped attract] other funders. Whenever there were letters needed for foundation support, [they] were able to produce a wide variety of groups that would say, 'this place is part of our neighborhood,' 'this is an important thing not just for this project, but for this surrounding neighborhood.'"[9] By contrast, the lack of clear neighborhood identification further marginalized Franklin Field's tenants; they were regarded as simply "out there" somewhere amid the rest of the disinvestment along Blue Hill Avenue. Further, since BHA staff knew that Franklin Field had been preranked as having a very low probability of successful redevelopment, it remained hard to avoid a self-fulfilling prophecy.

Clearly, successful project management during planning and construction is one kind of success, and may well be a good predictor of others. Yet, while it does serve to expedite completion, this form of success does not necessarily lead to sustainable positive change.

Recognized Design Quality

In addition to the central concerns about the time and money involved in a redevelopment process, almost everyone in a housing authority cares about the quality of the resultant product—the redeveloped housing. Designers (and those who work in design, development, and planning sections of housing authorities) often measure this quality by the number and kind of awards that professional societies confer upon these ventures. In this regard, both Commonwealth and West Broadway each won multiple regional and national design and planning awards, while Franklin Field won none.

More immediately, design quality is measured on a daily basis by residents. Several years after completion of the redevelopment efforts, eighty-one long-term residents of West Broadway, Commonwealth, and Franklin Field who had witnessed the processes were asked to discuss the "most important" physical changes that had occurred. In each case, more tenants stressed changes that had taken place *within their apartments* than any other kind of change. Residents of each development most frequently mentioned such things as larger rooms, more convenient layouts, better kitchen facilities, second bathrooms in larger apartments, and the addition of laundry hook-ups. They also valued transformation at the scale of individual buildings, involving such matters as private entrances, private yards, reduction or elimination of common hallways, elimination of flat roofs (at West Broadway), and better overall appearance. Many residents—especially at Commonwealth—also mentioned site-level improvements such as landscaping, improved parking areas, children's play areas, and new community buildings, but they commented more frequently on changes closer to individual apartments. Taken together, residents clearly favored all changes that made apartment buildings resemble townhouses—the most expensive sort of rehabilitation.

Design quality may be measured in ways other than overtly voiced resident priorities. Design interventions also work to improve the image of public housing in the eyes of residents, neighbors, and the general public, whose political representatives ultimately decide on future funding. Design awards, usually conferred not long after occupancy (if not before it) rarely take into account the social effects of public housing design, which ultimately form its most enduring legacy. To measure such effects, respondents from the three developments were asked whether they believed that the development where they lived looked like public housing. Strikingly, only about one-quarter of respondents from post-redevelopment Commonwealth said that their housing still had the stigmatized "look"—markedly smaller than the comparable figures for West Broadway and Franklin Field. This seems especially noteworthy given that only Commonwealth has mid-rise elevator buildings, a design element long associated with the negative image of public housing. At Commonwealth, however, the nearby presence of other large brick buildings had helped to contextualize public housing architecture right from the beginning; once again, the specifics of neighborhood development colored both the perceptions of outsiders and the self-perceptions of residents.[10]

At West Broadway, despite some elaborate attempts to deinstitutionalize the development's appearance, the image transformation ranked less well than Commonwealth's—40 percent of respondents still said the redeveloped parts looked like public housing. And at Franklin Field, although designers reconfigured the buildings in ways similar to the other places, fully two-thirds of respondents said the result still looked like public housing. The extreme variation of responses underscores the fact that design issues are always interwoven with social concerns.

Successful architecture and urban design entail tackling the social implications of design processes. Elaborate rehabilitation of buildings necessitates resident relocation, which in turn provides an opportunity for restructuring occupancy before the redeveloped apartments are re-rented. More directly, the success of design projects may be measured by their ability to incorporate resident input in significant ways. When offered the chance, residents did far more than choose the colors of kitchen counters; at times, they exercised important influence over fundamental design decisions. At West Broadway, most dramatically, residents succeeded in reversing the BHA plan to begin the phased redevelopment in the most publicly visible place. Instead, they convincingly argued, it should be sequenced beginning at the rear, so that the eyesore of the front would remain as a testament to the continuing need for new funds to complete subsequent phases. Design, in this sense, is tenant organizing carried out by other means.

IMPROVED TENANT-ORGANIZATION CAPACITY

For community organizers and for many tenants, helping the residents become active and influential decisionmakers in their developments while building their capacity to attract additional resources is a key dimension of success in public housing redevelopment. In each of the three cases, housing officials recognized from the outset that such transformations could not simply be imposed on residents but must emerge through negotiation. In two places—West Broadway and Commonwealth—years of tenant organizing preceded the redesign efforts. Only at Franklin Field, where the redevelopment effort ultimately proved to be far less successful in most other dimensions as well, was resident involvement limited and belated.

At both West Broadway and Commonwealth, tenants played the central role and—equally important—knew that they had done so. At these two places, more than 80 percent of respondents asserted that tenants had been most important to the redevelopment process. At Franklin Field, however, only 39 percent gave credit to the tenants, and the majority credited (or blamed) either the on-site management or the BHA for the redevelopment. Moreover, all those at Franklin Field who did credit the tenants credited only "tenant leaders," whereas respondents from Commonwealth and West Broadway often credited a broader variety of resident participation. Clearly, something went right at Commonwealth and West Broadway that did not happen at Franklin Field. As David C. Gilmore—one of the BHA staff members responsible for coordinating the Franklin Field redevelopment—puts it, at Franklin Field "it was more of a top-down situation, as opposed to the other two, which were much more bottom-up, people saying, 'we want to be redeveloped,' and pushing themselves to the forefront . . . I don't think there was ever a neighborhood that said, 'we want to be in that housing.' I just don't think people saw it as a resource." Or, as Bob Whittlesey phrases it, "It was never their deal. It was always somebody telling them something." Some tenants at Franklin Field surely saw themselves as key players in the redevelopment, but it seems significant that many at the BHA persistently struggled to engage residents.[11]

BHA Receiver Spence insists that there was never any intent to give Franklin Field short shrift. "I spent loads of time at Franklin Field," he recalls, "trying to get the tenant organization off the ground. I think we gave equal organizational effort to all three." Still, Spence is quick to admit, "I'd have to say that I had a personal commitment to Fidelis, and a relationship there that was warmer than anywhere else. I just felt hopeful about it, in a way that I found it harder to feel hopeful about any of the others." His successor, Doris Bunte, who took over the reins of the post-receivership BHA, acknowledges Spence's good intentions but remains convinced that the treatment was unequal. Commonwealth represented "the Authority's view of what an alternative could be, followed by D Street. Franklin Field, without question, was at the bottom of the redevelopments at that time." Still, Bunte concedes, "if Harry and the folks under him hadn't cared, it would never have been redeveloped. And they did care about it."[12]

At Commonwealth and West Broadway the redevelopment process sustained a striking degree of tenant involvement at all levels of decisionmaking. As with most tenant organizations, a relatively small number of committed individuals led the efforts, but many meetings attracted dozens, if not hundreds, of participants. More than mere numbers, what mattered was that the BHA conducted the redevelopment efforts at these two places as true partnerships with the tenant associations. Rather than simply receive the wisdom of professionals, for instance, the residents hired their own architectural consultants to clarify, defend, and advance tenant interests.

This kind of initiative went beyond design issues as well. At Commonwealth, the CTA entered into a binding agreement with the housing authority and its private management partner. This agreement in updated form continues to govern the post-redevelopment management of Commonwealth and allows the tenants to fire the management with thirty days' notice. The BHA spent the vast majority of the money in these redevelopment efforts on physical improvements, but it spent a great deal of the time on improving the climate of negotiation.

Here, too, neighborhood politics mattered. Commonwealth's tenants gained immeasurably because their redevelopment fight could be conceptualized as part of a broader strategy for Monastery Hill, which confirmed the desirability of their land in the eyes of others. Similarly, West Broadway's tenants cleverly withheld support for developing the most visible side of their property first so as to force neighborhood commuters to recognize the ongoing need for further redevelopment funding. By contrast, Franklin Field's tenants regarded BHA efforts to substitute use of neighborhood recreational facilities for an on-site community center as a key sticking point in negotiations. In short, the more successful redevelopment efforts used tenant organizing to manipulate neighborhood suspicions as a means to advance development prospects, whereas at Franklin Field, residents simply regarded the neighborhood as a liability to be minimized. In turn, such negative experiences with tenant organizing and project management did little to lessen the social costs of distant and top-down management.

Enhanced Maintenance and Management Performance

For many people working in housing authorities and other development organizations, the key measure of success in public housing is always management. Measuring the success of management is, in part, a matter of tracking the performance of "official" maintenance and management scores, such things as work-order turnaround times. But it is also a matter of assessing the relationship that is built (or rebuilt) between the representatives of management and their tenants. Here, taking account of both quantifiable assessments and more intangible accounts about tenant-management relationships, interviews with residents clearly suggest that privately managed Commonwealth has fared best. In interviews conducted several years after the redevelopment efforts, respondents were asked whether they had experienced problems with the response time of maintenance: only 10 percent of those at Commonwealth reported problems with Corcoran Management Company, compared with more than 33 percent at West Broadway, and nearly 66 percent at Franklin Field, both of which are still managed by the BHA. Although CMC still has its critics, the BHA's own ability to turnaround completed work orders at its family developments cannot yet come close to matching Corcoran's track record.

When residents were asked about the maintenance of the development as a whole, a similar pattern prevailed. Respondents were asked to rank maintenance in terms of several components: grass, trees, and flowers; dumpster areas; parking areas; and overall cleanliness. Ninety percent of those from Commonwealth reported that maintenance of the development's public areas was either very good or good. At West Broadway (despite the fact that the redevelopment there remained incomplete), 57 percent of respondents voiced similarly positive views about development maintenance. Once again, Franklin Field lagged behind: most respondents rated project maintenance as fair or poor.[13]

The statistics attest to the superior performance of management and maintenance at Commonwealth but fall short of explaining why this should be the case. Many at the BHA are personally and institutionally reluctant to say that the Corcoran Management Company succeeds at Commonwealth because it is a private and for-profit organization. As the former BHA redevelopment coordinator Pam Goodman comments, "I hate to admit it but [private management] was critical. They respond to the tenants: they cut the lawn; they repair the toilets when the work order comes in; they shovel the snow. I want to believe that a public housing authority can do the same thing, and in my mind there's no reason they shouldn't be able to. But it has not worked in Boston. If you compare D Street with Fidelis (I'm not even sure you can compare Franklin Field because I think there were always problems) at Commonwealth they're just better managers, they have a better handle on the situation." Kevin Young, Corcoran's former site manager for Commonwealth, adds: "When you talk to West Broadway and Franklin Field tenants about Commonwealth, they are very much shocked by the structure of the organization and its operation, because of the consistencies that happen on a day-to-day basis between the tenants' association, the management company, and the residents. You don't see the same consistency of expectations at some of the other jobs that received just as much money."

In 1996 Sandra Henriquez returned to head the BHA after a career in private housing management, and she vowed to do better. She told all managers that she wanted every development to "operate and look like you would be proud to have your parents or grandparents or your favorite aunt live there," adding that "if that's not the standard, then you've got lots of work to do."[14] As of 2000, despite some clear progress at many places, the BHA still indeed had lots of work to do. There is clear consensus that much of the management success at Commonwealth comes from setting and enforcing very high private-sector standards and from having maintenance carried out by on-site staff trained in multiple trades, rather than—as with the BHA—by centrally administered specialists who work according to union regulations.

At base, Corcoran Management Company succeeds because Commonwealth's residents helped negotiate the terms of the 223-page Management Plan that remains a reference point for an enormous range of matters. Tenants at Commonwealth get not just a lease but a set of community rules formulated by their fellow tenants and a commitment by the management to undertake a detailed preventive maintenance program, with written standards for corrective maintenance procedures, janitorial service, and grounds maintenance. At the same time, the Management Plan describes eviction procedures and spells out charges associated with costs incurred by damage to apartments. Interviews suggest that the private managers and most Commonwealth residents have accepted a sense of co-responsibility for the quality of upkeep and behavior in the development; after nearly two decades of partnership between residents and management, both groups seem committed to maintaining and enforcing high standards. Even when Commonwealth tenants considered alternatives to Corcoran—the BHA re-bid the contract in 1997 and 2000—tenants continually sought the manager that offered them the highest possible standards of upkeep. At the same time, by encouraging them to expect the standards found in condominium complexes in the neighborhood and elsewhere, the private management contract gave Commonwealth's tenants another important link to the world beyond their development.

IMPROVED SECURITY

Some who participated in the redevelopment efforts argue that, beyond issues of management and maintenance, any determination of redevelopment success must be measured against the security problems that have plagued much of the nation's inner-city public housing stock for many years. In this sense, success has to do with the ability of residents and management to cope not only with problems internal to a development but also with external forces (such as gangs) whose incursions thwart its manageability. More broadly, this view of success asks that one take into account the specific socioeconomic context of each redevelopment when attempting comparisons. Socioeconomic trends in surrounding neighborhoods may either help residents of a public housing development change in positive ways or hinder such growth. In this regard, many involved with the redevelopment efforts in Boston emphasize that Commonwealth is located in a relatively stable and economically diverse neighborhood with excellent public transportation access, whereas the pre-redevelopment Franklin Field was one distressed piece of a broader distressed neighborhood and remains part of an area that has experienced sustained impoverishment and relatively little new investment since the completion of the redevelopment effort.

A decade after the redevelopment efforts began, residents at each place were asked whether they believed that most people in the surrounding neighborhoods were "better off, worse off, or about the same" than they were ten years before. All twenty-three of the long-term Commonwealth residents who responded to the question indicated that they believed neighborhood residents were better off or about the same; only 46 percent of Franklin Field respondents were so sanguine. Household heads from each place were also asked to rank their own sense of security as "very safe, somewhat safe, somewhat unsafe, or very unsafe" in a wide variety of settings in and around the development, ranging outward from the interior of their apartments. Two-thirds of respondents from Franklin Field said that they felt somewhat unsafe or very unsafe going into the surrounding neighborhoods at night, whereas only 10 percent of Commonwealth respondents and about one-third of West Broadway respondents felt that way. Even during the day, only 14 percent of Franklin Field respondents said that they felt very safe traveling to neighborhoods immediately outside the development. By contrast, the majority of respondents from both Commonwealth and West Broadway did report feeling very safe in their neighborhoods during the day.

Perceptions of insecurity also varied inside the developments themselves. Even during daylight hours, at Franklin Field only 20 percent of respondents reported feeling very safe in their development, compared with 61 percent of those at West Broadway and 80 percent of those at Commonwealth. Only 3 percent of respondents from Franklin Field reported feeling very safe at night in the development as a whole, and fully 41 percent said they felt very unsafe. At West Broadway, too, perceptions of nighttime safety dipped—only 28 percent reported feeling very safe. Only at Commonwealth did a majority of respondents (66 percent) indicate that they felt very safe in their development after dark, though at least a narrow majority at each place did say they felt very safe *within their own apartments* at night.

Residents almost invariably blamed drug trafficking for the insecurity both inside and outside their developments, since they closely associated drugs with gang activity and violence. Even at Commonwealth, despite its many successes, nearly two-thirds of respondents described drugs as a "major problem" in the development during the early 1990s; at the other developments, distress about drugs was even more prevalent. Although the crack epidemic has eased since these interviews were conducted and Boston closed the 1990s with a dramatic drop in youth-related crime, there is good reason to think that the basic differentials in security at the three developments remain salient. The rate of violent crime near Franklin Field may have dropped, for instance, but the Boston Police Department still regarded the area as one of the city's eight worst "hot spots" in 2000.

By contrast, at Commonwealth, a markedly lower crime rate contributed to a much stronger project-neighborhood relationship. Or, more to the point, perhaps, because neighborhood groups perceived neighborhood crime as concentrated in the project itself, they were able to regard redevelopment (seen as leading to the forced departure of troublemakers) as a great boon to neighborhood peace. Brighton-based community organizations grew more involved in the development, which enjoyed a carefully cultivated relationship with the local media. This component of a "neighborhood-effects" explanation—regardless of whether the neighborhood functions as a help or as a hindrance—makes clear that some measures of redevelopment success have little to do with the bricks-and-mortar investment that absorbed the vast majority of the money.

One might wish to conclude from all this that violent neighborhoods are a fact of life around most public housing, that matters of insecurity and drug trafficking tend to overwhelm efforts at redevelopment, and that some redevelopment programs—such as the one at Commonwealth—are fortunate not to have to cope with problems that are quite so severe as elsewhere. All of that may be true, but there also seems to be some evidence that redevelopment efforts can enhance security.

Proponents of defensible space initiatives contend that design changes enhance the perception of security and reduce the reality of crime. A comparison of resident perceptions of safety in the West Broadway development between those who lived in its carefully programmed and zoned redeveloped parts with those residing in the vast undefined expanse of the old part points clearly to important gains in security from the redevelopment effort. Whether they were talking about their apartments, the area outside their front doors, or the shared courtyards, respondents from the redeveloped part of the project consistently reported feeling safer than did those who still lived in the old parts. Conversely, those in the non-redeveloped part reported much higher instances of fear about gangs and fear of people from outside the development, while the largest number of respondents from the new part of the development reported that they feared "nobody." Residents frequently voiced and demonstrated pleasure at the control over outdoor space that was possible in the new parts of the development—especially apparent in the heavily used shared courtyards and the many well-tended private gardens. Many tenants praised the subdivided outdoor space, the elimination of the ability to cut through buildings, and the shared commitment to keeping doors locked, noting that "undesirables" tended to enter the development through the old part (where resident surveillance had little architectural reinforcement).

However promising, defensible space measures in themselves are only a part of a broader effort that is needed to improve security in public housing and in the depressed neighborhoods that so often surround it. When residents were asked about measures that could be taken to improve security, most stressed the need for enhanced community policing, private security firms, and stricter management practices. The central importance of security to residents of public housing cannot be over-emphasized, and the ability of development-based or neighborhood-based violence and illegal activities to disrupt the course of a redevelopment effort and limit its sustainability remains a key factor in any assessment of success.

Progress on Socioeconomic Development

Success in public housing redevelopment may also be measured in broader public policy terms. Redevelopment can be seen not only as a measure to fix up a housing project but also as an opportunity to address the root causes of the poverty that led residents to need public housing in the first place. Sometimes initiatives (such as job training programs) are targeted only to residents within a particular public housing development; other cases entail development of common facilities to be shared with residents of surrounding neighborhoods. In other instances, city officials have proposed economic-development policy initiatives directed at large areas that border and include public housing developments. Here, concern for the economic well-being of public housing residents may be expressed indirectly at best—the main goal usually entails the deconcentration of poverty by attracting high-income residents. Beginning in the 1990s under HUD's HOPE VI program, many housing authorities centered redevelopment initiatives on such public policy goals, most frequently on efforts at achieving an "economic mix" and on efforts to develop consolidated and coordinated social service facilities in the name of improving "family self-sufficiency."

The public housing redevelopment efforts at West Broadway, Franklin Field, and Commonwealth—which commenced fifteen years before HOPE VI—also stressed the provision of new community facilities and the need to increase employment among residents, but they did not make education and job training a priority of redevelopment, nor did they do much to link these redevelopment efforts to other initiatives in the surrounding communities.[15] Despite active efforts on the part of tenant organizations to raise outside funds for starting or sustaining programs, service provision has remained wholly inadequate even in the most successful of funding cycles. In short, the innovative approaches to physical redesign have not been matched by systematic commitments to exploring new strategies for socioeconomic redevelopment. Despite the physical improvements that were implemented at Commonwealth, West Broadway, and Franklin Field, it is hard to sustain any claim that the redevelopment efforts have done much to improve the economic circumstances of residents.

The heavily subsidized public housing rent (which also covers utilities) remains tenants' obvious and centrally important economic benefit. At least at Commonwealth and West Broadway, redevelopment has meant that income devoted to paying rent is money well spent—clearly not the case in 1980. Lifted by the booming local economy that closed the 1990s and prodded by welfare-reform legislation, more Boston public housing tenants reported income from work, but the BHA saw no noticeable increase in overall rent receipts, suggesting that incomes remained at near-subsistence levels for most residents. Moreover, as of late 2000, only a small minority of adults between the ages of eighteen and sixty-one reported that their principal source of income came from employment: 35 percent at Franklin Field, 29 percent at West Broadway, and, surprisingly perhaps, just 20 percent at Commonwealth. Counterbalancing this, though, Commonwealth residents were enrolled as full-time college students at twice the rate found at West Broadway and three times the rate at Franklin Field.[16]

Perhaps the continued presence of a well-managed and well-maintained environment at Commonwealth can have far-reaching effects that are not easily measured by the customary economic terms of jobs and current annual income. If redevelopment, tenant activism, and private management have contributed to a significant increase in domestic tranquility, perhaps this may enhance the prospects of socioeconomic mobility for the next generation. Commonwealth benefits greatly from a long-standing program of volunteer tutors from Boston College, which may well encourage more of Commonwealth's teens to continue their education. The widely discussed efforts in Chicago to relocate some public housing families to the suburbs have been praised for enhancing the school performance and job prospects of the relocated youth; is it possible that well-managed public housing in the city also can help foster these same kinds of improvements?[17]

The restoration of a peaceful domestic environment is certainly an important starting point, but it is surely not a complete substitute for the need to enact long-promised improvements in the quality of the city's public schools. At the same time, demonstration of the social and economic value of learning and earning—and the means for moving in these directions—could be demonstrated more tangibly to jobless residents by enhanced efforts to attract greater numbers of employed residents to public housing. For the time being, however, it seems fair to say that while the BHA still likes to regard Commonwealth as a showpiece, the redevelopment effort has attained this status mostly for reasons other than its success at reducing rates of economic dependence among residents.

RESIDENT SATISFACTION

If one potential public policy goal of public housing redevelopment is to foster an economic environment that enables families to afford to leave that housing, then even Commonwealth's success is limited. If, by contrast, success in public housing redevelopment is measured by the enhancement of an attractive, safe, and stable community where even many of those who can afford to leave will choose to stay, then the effort at Commonwealth—and, to a great extent, the effort at West Broadway—warrants the highest praise. Despite lingering high rates of joblessness, the long-term residents of Commonwealth and West Broadway who were interviewed for this book overwhelmingly agreed that they were better off than they were before redevelopment had commenced.

Tenants from Franklin Field did not concur. Their responses resembled those from other interviews conducted at housing developments that have not undergone a major redevelopment effort, where a majority reported that their circumstances are, at best, unchanged. In the interviews with Franklin Field residents, many tenants actually said that they believed their apartments were better before redevelopment than after, chiefly because of more solid original construction, though it seems that they could not fully separate out such design issues from the broader feeling of insecurity that continued to pervade the development.

Similarly, when asked to rate their level of satisfaction with their public housing development, 90 percent of Commonwealth respondents and 82 percent of West Broadway respondents reported feeling very satisfied or satisfied with the development, whereas only 42 percent of Franklin Field residents said they felt this way, and nearly a quarter reported feeling very dissatisfied.[18] Despite their overall praise, residents of West Broadway and Commonwealth were far more divided over whether, if they were to move elsewhere, they would want to move to a similar place: at each development, about half said yes and half said no. As for respondents from Franklin Field, fully 87 percent indicated that they had no desire to move to a similar place. The message seems to be that although redeveloped public housing can be a more acceptable and desirable form of public housing, it still falls short of other kinds of living environments.

When asked, "How long do you want to live in this development?" two-thirds of respondents from Commonwealth and West Broadway indicated that they wished to stay "as long as possible" or "for a while," whereas two-thirds of the Franklin Field respondents made it clear that they wished to remain "no longer than necessary." Only one-third of Franklin Field respondents said they "definitely would" recommend the development to friends looking for a place to live. By contrast, two-thirds of West Broadway respondents and three-quarters of those from Commonwealth indicated that they definitely would do so. Similarly, only 42 percent of Franklin Field respondents agreed that the development was "a good place for raising kids," whereas 69 percent of respondents from West Broadway and 82 percent of respondents from Commonwealth found favor with the childrearing environment in those places.

In the end, this notion of "resident satisfaction" is a kind of meta-criterion for success. It is, at least in part, an indirect measure of the successes achieved in the other six dimensions. Yet it also may prove to be a deceptive barometer; even high scores may mean little more than temporary stability in high-pressure lives. Alternatively, for some who care about public housing but do not live in it, high rates of resident satisfaction may even be seen as a liability, if these imply that tenants will make less of an effort to leave public housing. Ultimately, the questions may be more about which kinds of people are most satisfied and about whether these are the kinds of people who are contributing to community stability. Arguably, the most successful public housing communities will be those where many of the tenants most able to leave will choose not to. Yet this community-centered definition of success is in conflict with a more individual-centered and family-centered model of success that is predicated on the development of education, skills, and sustainable employment as a means to exit from public housing and from other sources of government subsidy. Moreover, a community-centered success criterion directly contradicts any lingering belief that public housing developments should be reserved exclusively for the most disadvantaged members of society.

EXPANDING AND APPLYING THE MEASURES OF SUCCESS

The stories presented here suggest that public housing redevelopments can, in the best cases, improve residents' satisfaction with their living environments but that some redevelopment efforts will improve resident satisfaction much more than others. Moreover, even where high levels of satisfaction are achieved, redevelopment may do little to ensure that this satisfaction translates to increased residential or economic mobility. Individually and collectively, public housing tenants have a lot of problems to overcome. Those who attempt to reclaim public housing must recognize that they are wrestling not just with failed buildings but with several decades of cumulative human mistrust. In all three public neighborhoods, this mistrust emerged from year upon year of failed promises and falsely raised hopes. Redevelopment came only after a decade of formal litigation and tens of thousands of smaller informal confrontations that simply passed for daily life at each project. At Franklin Field, moreover, mistrust also carried a special kind of racial undertone.

Racial politics surely permeates the community history at D Street and, to a lesser extent, at Fidelis Way, but only at Franklin Field did tenants have to approach redevelopment while firmly identified as a minority community. As Harry Spence observes, "The sense of disempowerment is much deeper in the black public housing communities in many ways. It's harder to organize black and Hispanic projects because the power structure isn't them; it's not their power structure." In addition to its political isolation, he adds, Franklin Field suffered from its geographic separation: "It doesn't feel at all part of any real neighborhood," Spence comments. "Who wanted to live there? Franklin Field was always a less desirable development, and more desperate people went there."[19] Even if Franklin Field wasn't "always" a less desirable place, the inability of its tenants to take ownership of the redevelopment initiative seems inseparable from the broader history of neighborhood abandonment and racial strife that had decimated Blue Hill Avenue since the 1960s.

Local history also mattered in the white precinct of D Street. Here, it was not just the history of powerful Southie politicians coming to bail out their constituents in the projects. There was also a darker side, a unique kind of despair felt by poor whites. As Spence puts it, "In the black community it's possible to say to yourself, 'I'm here because of discrimination.' In the white community, there's more taking in a sense of guilt about failure, often a greater sense of failure." Even as D Street gained an upper hand from its well-placed pols, its residents still faced the cumulative stigma of life in the Lower End.

Spared either extreme of racially encoded class isolation, the mixed-race community of Commonwealth could more readily blossom. During the late 1970s, the BHA (not to mention its Brighton neighbors) desperately wished to prevent the development from tipping to predominantly nonwhite occupancy, and they kept the project majority-white through the 1980s. Such racial quotas, ostensibly in service of broader neighborhood stability, constituted a highly questionable form of community management at a time when nonwhite households increasingly dominated BHA waiting lists. It is not surprising that HUD forced the housing authority to abandon Commonwealth's site-based waiting list in 1988, on grounds of discrimination. In the meantime, however, the long period of racial integration brought substantial gains to the community. As the tenants' attorney Leslie Newman puts it, "The crucial difference for Commonwealth was that it was an integrated development. They had a sense of pride that black and white could live together."[20]

The BHA of the receivership era found Commonwealth appealing precisely because of its integrated character; it offered an alternative to the usual politics of program balance, in which a benefit accorded to a white public neighborhood needed to be matched by some perk accorded to a minority one. Yet Harry Spence's personal fascination with Commonwealth's racial integration went well beyond its useful symbolism in a torn city. He genuinely believed that its strength as a community inhered in its multiracial and multiethnic character. "Fidelis always stands for me for the difficulty—but also the enormous rewards—of managing diversity," Spence comments. "It's hard to do that, but out of it a far more sophisticated capacity to deal with the world emerges. As you learn to manage differences in a tightly knit group, while that takes a lot of energy and would seem to be distracting, in fact out of successfully resolving them, people learn mastery of a set of things that are immensely valuable in the world. Therefore, that resident group just had more purchase on the world than the other two, because it was a racially mixed group. I believe that very deeply. I couldn't prove it, but I think it's true."[21] As Spence contends, Commonwealth's lack of homogeneity contributed significantly to its relative strength as a community organization.

Tenants fought for the redevelopment of Fidelis Way not as victimized whites or as victimized blacks, but as victimized low-income Americans.

The racial and ethnic dynamics of West Broadway, Franklin Field, and Commonwealth illustrate a vitally important way that public neighborhoods can differ. Public housing communities may all be dominated by households with very low incomes, but each has its own collective personality, forged by the circumstances of its birth and by the forces of its upbringing. The complexity of each public neighborhood's history, in turn, makes community redevelopment efforts all too easy to derail. They can be stymied by implementation impasses and cost overruns, by design miscalculations, by the absence of tenant support, by the inability to manage and maintain the changes, by unchecked crime and violence from surrounding impoverished neighborhoods, and by the inability to propose, implement, and sustain commitments to programs that can improve the socioeconomic prospects of residents. Redevelopment efforts can fall short because of a failure in any one of these seven areas, and a failure in one area in turn exacerbates the problems in all others.

Taken together, the three redevelopment efforts discussed here confirm the promise of well-conceived attempts by well-organized communities to implement well-designed redevelopment plans, but they also highlight the ways that equally well-intentioned plans—especially if they lack a solid base of community support, fall victim to implementation snafus, and take place in extremely disadvantaged neighborhoods—may do relatively little to improve the lives of public housing residents. Although there is considerable evidence to suggest that the physical redevelopment of Franklin Field itself was problematic, it is clear that many of the major problems at that development have been driven by an inability to stem the crime that continues to plague the community, and by an inability on the part of management to work cooperatively with residents. At the other extreme, when comprehensive physical redevelopment is accompanied by adequate security provisions, careful maintenance, and strict rule enforcement, the results seem to justify the substantial second round of public investment entrusted to such places.

Fifteen years after its redevelopment was completed, Commonwealth has sustained its successes in nearly every way. So too, West Broadway—in spite of the long delay in completing its last phase, and in spite of the added challenges of introducing racial integration—receives high marks on many measures. Even though the BHA focused these redevelopment efforts on bricks-and-mortar initiatives and de-emphasized their role as economic development ventures, these design changes seem to have generated a cooperative climate for future resident initiatives. Creating safe and attractive apartments, buildings, and community facilities may be seen as a crucial first step in rebuilding communities and may serve as a vital haven for individuals struggling to cope with the debilitating psychological and social effects of persistent poverty. The most disheartening thing about this book, however, is that there are not *three* redevelopment success stories to report. It is readily apparent that success does not come cheap, but it is also once again all too clear that money, in itself, does not guarantee success. Just as the BHA Planning Department had hypothesized in 1979, Commonwealth's redevelopment proved most successful, West Broadway achieved many partial successes, and Franklin Field lagged behind.

At a time when federal funding for public housing remains under attack, what does it mean that the place that had the most perceived advantages when the redevelopment process began also turned out to be the most successful? If it is indeed possible to anticipate success, what does this suggest for cases where success in any or all of the seven measures outlined here seems highly unlikely right from the start? Was it a mistake to make such a large public investment at Franklin Field? Is it good public policy to focus only on the projects that can be seen as having the greatest chance of success?

Clearly, every housing authority contemplating large-scale redevelopment would like to replicate the range of successes achieved at Commonwealth, while avoiding the failures of Franklin Field. The core problem here is that all housing developments are not equally promising sites for redevelopment, and a good redevelopment process can only go so far to salvage the most troubled cases. For housing authorities with several properties that would qualify as severely distressed by almost anyone's measure, this would seem to entail choosing for redevelopment only the most salvageable from among the most distressed places, even though this means failing to help those residents who need assistance most.

Yet if one does wish to focus scarce dollars on the "least-disadvantaged" of highly disadvantaged places, what does that choice imply for the places that are most in decline? The key to an equitable and morally acceptable strategy may be for housing authorities to acknowledge frankly that there are some places where—owing to the density of impoverished families housed together in a devastated neighborhood—the problems are beyond repair through any existing redevelopment program. In these places, untransformable even through the unprecedented generosity of the Boston experiments or the federal HOPE VI program, and unlikely to be able to attract a wider mix of incomes, the best solution may be to rehouse residents elsewhere through voucher programs and, as this is accomplished, to demolish the projects. Indeed, HUD's own "viability" threshold now makes such calculated decisions mandatory.

The three examples presented here, when taken together, suggest that this kind of triage should, however, be seen as a last resort. Withholding public housing redevelopment dollars from the most distressed neighborhoods would represent yet another blow to the prospects for reinvestment in such places. The story of Franklin Field, for all its problems—before, during, and after its redevelopment—is not necessarily a tale of woe that was either inevitable or irreversible. Before giving up on places like Franklin Field that seem to be at the margins of salvageability, whether in Boston or elsewhere, it seems worth trying more of the techniques that worked so well at Commonwealth.

The redevelopment effort at Franklin Field suffered for reasons that went well beyond the problems of its neighborhood and the poverty of its residents. At the heart of the failure was, and is, a level of animosity between tenants and management that works against the formation of the kind of partnerships that were the hallmark of the Commonwealth redevelopment effort. One can only speculate whether use of a first-rate private developer and private management team could bring about Commonwealth-type results at places like Franklin Field, but such measures seem well worth trying, especially in combination with enhanced efforts to recruit and retain a resident population with mixed incomes.

If privatization is to proliferate, however, it is important to scrutinize the spirit and the structure of the Commonwealth redevelopment process. The public sector has no monopoly on lousy landlords. Commonwealth's success entailed a carefully considered and scrupulously monitored process of finding not only an available private-sector alternative, but the best possible one from among many to meet a variety of goals and to work in partnership with a variety of constituencies. It is not merely that a public agency devolved its responsibilities onto the private sector; it is that a highly intelligent group of thoughtful and motivated housing authority officials, working with a core group of committed and well-advised tenants, jointly developed a vision for a tenant-monitored system of private development and private management. It is not the act of privatization itself, but the hundreds of hours that went into reaching consensus on the thousands of details that went into both the Developer's Kit and the Management Plan that laid the groundwork for Commonwealth's sustained successes.

RECOVERING COMMUNITIES

One resident of Franklin Field summed up the problems and potential of her development in a single sentence: "We are part of the recovering community," Fronnie Watkins told those who attended a tenant meeting in November 1992, "but there is still a community out there that is lost."[22] Her concept of the *recovering community* seems a useful way to characterize and give direction to certain sorts of positive change that can occur through attempts to reclaim public housing. Building on this evocative phrase, it becomes possible to develop a conceptual filter that lets through and gathers together a wide variety of efforts that share a communitarian commitment to rethinking the purpose of public housing.

The broad term *communitarian* emerged from debates in political theory during the 1980s and is associated with the critiques of liberalism put forth by such figures as Michael Sandel, Alisdair MacIntyre, Charles Taylor, and Michael Walzer. These critiques turn on the wish to see greater constraints placed upon the rights of an individual when these rights come into conflict with the values and commitments of the community in which he or she is a member. To communitarians, individuals have *responsibilities* as well as rights, and this enhanced behavioral expectation forms a key underpinning of high-quality communities. In the 1990s, communitarian theories found application in diverse areas of social policy, most prominently in the work of Amitai Etzioni and the diverse cosigners of his "Responsive Communitarian Platform," yet the term had faded from public discourse by the end of the decade.[23] The underlying ideals, however, have continued to gain momentum. My intention here is to outline some of the ingredients of a communitarian approach to the recovery of public neighborhoods. Reclaiming public housing ultimately entails more than redeveloping buildings; it requires recovering communities.

Toward Communitarian Recovery

The stories of West Broadway, Franklin Field, and Commonwealth demonstrate how individual public neighborhoods have borne the brunt of efforts to concentrate the poor in poorly designed and poorly managed places. Similarly, the three

trajectories of redevelopment make clear that recovery from such destructive policies and attitudes is also always community-centered. Still, after decades of struggle to "fix" public housing, pursuit of communitarian objectives is met with profound ambivalence. The most important unresolved dilemma divides those who
would like public housing developments to function as temporary domestic
waystations and those who prefer to see these places as stable and semi-perma-
nent residential communities, in which even some of the more economically successful tenants would find good social reasons to remain. Most successful city
neighborhoods manage to achieve both objectives. For public neighborhoods—
artificially assembled through the mechanisms of public housing project-based
subsidies—this dual role is harder to sustain. Policymakers have all too often emphasized one or the other extreme. Waystationists seek to enhance avenues for
emigration, whereas communitarians wish to rebuild public housing environments into attractive places that are saturated with the kinds of social support services that dense concentrations of people with very low incomes require, while
also seeking to "stabilize" the community by skewing occupancy to admit increasingly greater percentages of families whose principal source of income
comes from employment, and enforcing much stricter expectations for tenant behavior.

There is much to commend both the Waystationist and the Communitarian
positions, but they imply very different sorts of communities. One suggests a development comprised of incubating individualists; the other is premised on sustaining and enhancing social networks. The challenge is to do both of these well,
without letting one undermine the aims of the other. Promising policies that appear to move in opposite directions need to coalesce rather than cancel each
other out.

The search for stable communities in public housing contains a revealing para-
dox. The term *stable* implies both a sense of stasis and a modicum of social control, and is rightly associated with a variety of anticrime and antiviolence measures. Yet, in the end, communities achieve and sustain stability not through
negation but through infusions of economic dynamism. In the late 1990s, as evi-
denced by the nationwide HOPE VI initiative, policymakers concluded that public housing needed a drastic influx of employed households to serve as socioeconomic role models. They contended that communities consisting wholly of the
sorts of families who currently reside in public housing and who dominate the
waiting lists to get into it lack social viability.

Ignoring the countervailing evidence from Commonwealth, policymakers instead touted the model of Boston's Harbor Point. Here, during the same era as the other three major redevelopment efforts, the BHA sold off the severely distressed Columbia Point project, located on what had become prime oceanfront real estate, to a private developer. Harbor Point was reborn as market-rate housing in return for an agreement that approximately one-third of the redeveloped units would be reserved in perpetuity for low-income residents, including those from the former public housing project.[24] Other approaches that interpreted income-mixing in a much narrower range also gained favor. At Chicago's Lake Parc Place, for instance, the Chicago Housing Authority rehabilitated two high-rise buildings with the stipulation that half of the units would be reserved for low-income working families (earning between 50 and 80 percent of the local median), while half remained for previous residents with very low incomes. Most HOPE VI initiatives of the late 1990s—including those in Boston at Mission Main and Orchard Gardens—also embraced a strategy that replaced some public housing units with a broad range of subsidized and market-rate townhouses and apartments. Meanwhile, the federal public housing reform legislation (more formally and tellingly known as the Quality Housing and Work Responsibility Act of 1998) sought to rein in the proportion of public housing units that would serve those with very low incomes.

Precisely because three-quarters of the country's existing public housing population earned less than 30 percent of the median income, the 1998 legislation permitted housing authorities to reserve up to 70 percent of openings in public housing projects for those earning *more* than this amount, thereby allowing a substantial proportion of apartments to go to those earning between 50 and 80 percent of median. In Boston, this meant that a family of four earning more than $50,000 would be eligible, though few such families were clamoring to apply to any but the places just renovated under HOPE VI.[25] In other words, current policy aims to accommodate as many as possible of those at the upper end of income eligibility, even though waiting lists for public housing in big cities are dominated by those with the very lowest incomes.

In the increasingly ascendant view, the future of public housing—if it is to have a future at all—must be as mixed-income communities. The goal is to create places where public investment is used to leverage private capital sufficient to attract a higher-income clientele, especially in the case of those housing developments where gentrifying neighborhoods already support such a trend. Even as tenant leaders complain about displacement of low-income people to make way for the less needy, housing officials throughout the country frequently concur that public housing can no longer afford to serve only those who are among the least well off. In supporting this argument, congressional critics point backward to the origins of American public housing, stressing that the projects were intended to be temporary waystations for stable families with stable jobs—not subsidized housing for the long-term unemployed.

Clearly the current stock of public housing cannot absorb all people with very low incomes who have the need and the desire to enter into it, but neither can the nation's overall system of subsidized housing abandon its commitment to serve the neediest. Deconcentrating poverty in public housing, in the absence of attempts to house the most impoverished somewhere else where there is also a mixture of incomes, is at best a partial solution.

Policymakers may tout the importation of higher-income people as a means to enhance the social capital of the low-income tenants they join, but a true communitarian approach to income-mixing would recognize the ways that mere co-presence of employed and unemployed families is just a first step toward recovering communities. This measure must be accompanied by an attempt to make public housing environments attractive to working families—not because federal policy favors those with higher forms of low-income, but because the community maintains standards that working-class families expect. The problems of public housing lie not only with the tenants but with how they are treated. The addition of a few (or even a majority) of tenants who are slightly better off but still low income will not magically transform the lives of the rest of the residents in the absence of other mutually supportive interventions in the realms of design, management, and service provision.

Enhancing social capital in public housing is central to a communitarian approach to reform, but it cannot be seen as an alternative to sustained recovery efforts in other dimensions.[26] It may be true that the presence of role models is vital to the process of reducing "labor-market estrangement" among the jobless, but the barriers to jobs are manifold. Role models who have jobs and know how to get them are not necessarily also teachers, counselors, carpool drivers, and childcare providers.

The restructuring of occupancy to enhance the production and circulation of social capital depends on a broader restructuring of community life. It is not just that occupancy changes can bring broad community gains; it is also that broader community changes are necessary to attract a less-troubled tenant population. To attract more working families to public housing—families who may well have other options in the private market—requires sustained commitment to rebuilding environments that do not look like, or feel like, places of last resort. In a communitarian context, extensive redesign of public housing apartments, buildings, and landscapes is not only a physical intervention but an investment in self-respect, one that benefits existing residents and attracts an economically diverse constituency. For highly stigmatized places whose reputations have been systematically constructed (and usually destroyed) by a variety of outsiders, the restoration of self-respect is never easy. If the goal is recovering communities, then attracting economic role models, dispersing some impoverished individuals who want to move, and developing the capacity of those who remain are three approaches that must be considered together. Homeownership initiatives, income-mixing, housing vouchers, large-scale redesign efforts, scaled-up service provision, and management reforms should be seen not as alternative policies to be tried out in separate pilot programs but as part of a mutually reinforcive strategy for recovering communities. Each piece should be encouraged, implemented, and evaluated for its ability to advance a communitarian agenda.

Housing Individuals, Hampering Communities

A communitarian approach to public housing redevelopment means that certain individual rights may need to be tempered by the greater goal of community safety and stability. The challenge, from the start, is to reverse the trend in public housing policy that has consistently favored the needs of individuals over the needs of communities. In the recent past, for instance, public housing communities have suffered from federal policies that allowed the elderly and the nonelderly mentally ill to be housed together. Only after many violent confrontations did policies that favored community well-being find favor. During the 1990s, the tension between the rights of individuals and the rights of communities came to a head most dramatically in the legal confrontations over drug "sweeps" in public housing (in Chicago and elsewhere), and in discussions about the possibility of banning guns in public housing. Organizations ranging from the American Civil Liberties Union to the National Rifle Association stepped forward to decry the infringement of individual rights, but many residents argued for their own rights to live in a safe community, and for the responsibility of their landlords to do all they can to protect them.[27]

A similar situation arose over evictions related to behavior infringements, such as illegal drug activity. In many cities, even the seemingly most straightforward of cases took years to resolve, given the prowess and tenacity of legal-aid attorneys, while the law-abiding majority of the public housing community was left to suffer. In 1996 President Bill Clinton issued an executive order dubbed "One Strike and You're Out," aimed at evicting public housing tenants charged with a felony even before they had been found guilty by a court. Clinton also called for renewed efforts to keep those previously convicted of felonies from ever getting into public housing in the first place. In a similar vein, the Quality Housing and Work Responsibility Act of 1998 closed a loophole in the definition of "persons with disabilities" that had previously given preferred eligibility for public housing to some persons "solely on the basis of drug or alcohol dependence." Moreover, the new legislation permitted housing authorities to prohibit admission to any households believed to include illegal drug-users or alcohol-abusers, and to insist on access to criminal records, sex-offender registries, and records from drug-abuse treatment facilities during the tenant-screening process. Conversely, the Act allowed housing authorities to rent apartments to police officers (who would not otherwise be income-eligible), as part of efforts to increase security.[28] Some of these measures (particularly the "One Strike" law) have created unwarranted difficulties for the families of those accused of transgressions and clearly raise legal and ethical questions about an individual's right to a fair hearing in a court of law. Still, the broader intent of a communitarian approach to caring about public housing residents gives useful focus and representation to group-based claims.

REDEVELOPMENT AS RECOVERY

The neighborhood histories of West Broadway, Franklin Field, and Commonwealth show that there are viable vestiges of communities in public housing developments, despite the daily toll of poverty and the frequent incursions of drugs, gangs, and guns. These three communities, and those like them throughout the nation, warrant full assistance in their own concerted efforts to preserve and enhance their living environment. If reclaiming public housing is conceptualized as a process of community recovery, it seems clear that various participants—whether residents, managers, designers, or service providers—will see the process differently. One hopes that these multiple lenses can all be focused on a shared positive vision.

The notion of *recovery* operates as both adjective and verb: that is, a recovering community connotes a type of community as well as an active process of change. As the three redevelopment histories make clear, community recovery is not a gift from enlightened bureaucrats. It is instead a kind of ongoing descriptor of moral and social progress. A recovering community means a community that is engaged in constant self-monitoring, charting progress but recognizing that there is no final point at which a community is said to have "recovered" fully. Ultimately, the recovery of community must take place in three mutually reinforcive dimensions: the emergence of a more cooperative and participatory attitude toward management and public safety, the social effects of design and symbolism, and the creation of new social networks that promote personal growth and economic opportunity.

MANAGING, DESIGNING, AND SERVICING COMMUNITY RECOVERY

Communities recover in a managerial sense when places once lost as manageable entities are stabilized and restored. The Commonwealth model—transferring standards and procedures used by successful private-management companies to public housing—is one promising approach. Much of this process simply entails stricter enforcement of existing public housing rules (something that seems to be favored by most residents). As the Commonwealth story indicates, a program of rule-setting and strict rule enforcement works best when implemented in full collaboration with tenants. As Harry Spence sees it, much of Commonwealth's success has to do with the high expectations that CMC sets for tenant behavior. "Public housing got infected with the notion that to be compassionate was to have inordinately low expectations," he comments, but Corcoran's management team refused to give into this. Corcoran executive Ed Marchant used to give Spence a "lecture" on this subject, averring that as "a good white working-class kid" he understood what Spence didn't because of his more affluent upbringing. Marchant's message was "goddamn it, you just needed to ask more of these folks," whereas Spence was "filled with the liberal guilt of the privileged." Spence acknowledges "some truth" to this, adding that "there's something to be said for people standing up and saying higher expectations are essential here. Corcoran's done that. And what's good about Corcoran is that it's done that in a way that's genuinely not racist. They do have high expectations, but that's not an excuse to beat up on black people, which it can often be."[29]

As the Commonwealth experience illustrates, a redevelopment process should entail exiting a development and re-entering it through a different threshold—not just a new door to an apartment but a new threshold of expectations for the behavior of oneself and others. Residents, through their elected tenant-association representatives, are claiming and being given more say in the decisions that affect their domestic well-being. In exchange, they expect a greater degree of responsiveness from housing authorities and a higher standard of responsibility from one another. For public neighborhoods that have suffered from a half century of unchecked incursions by youths from both inside and outside the projects, renewed emphasis on the high behavioral expectations that once characterized these places when they were first tenanted seems central to community recovery.

Recovering communities can also refer to the process of altering the appearance of an environment in order to revitalize it, much as an interior decorator might recover tattered furniture thought to be structurally sound. Public housing is not a chair, but residents clearly believe that improving the physical appearance of their homes contributes substantially to their own well-being. Design changes affect more than those few residents who may have helped frame an architectural plan for redevelopment. More broadly, design is about restoring their collective public face as well as securing their private realm. Design is a social process as well as an aesthetic one. It is about clarifying needs, making demands, gaining influence, and understanding productive compromise. Design entails not just new buildings but also a reimaged reputation.

Finally, and most controversially, perhaps, a social service–oriented interpretation of *community recovery* connotes a community that is "in recovery," in the sense of the ongoing and never-ending processes associated with overcoming major life traumas. At least since the late 1960s large public housing authorities have accepted the notion that public housing is always about more than housing; it also entails job training, day care, and social support for very poor people with very serious financial, physical, and mental health problems. Despite such problems, to say that a public housing community is "in recovery" is not meant to imply that all (or even most) public housing residents suffer from severe substance-abuse problems and the like. What seems undeniable is that they, like others in low-income areas of America's inner cities, suffer disproportionately from the effects of broader societal patterns of drug abuse, and from the violence associated with the drug economy that undergirds it. They are recovering not only from the problems of their members but from the incursions of outsiders—neighbors who use public housing for illicit activities and policymakers who saddle public housing communities with the nation's most disadvantaged persons but fail to provide the resources necessary to cope with their predicaments.

These three components of recovery—housing management, design and development, and service delivery—though seen from the provider's point of view as separate things, are part of the same phenomenon when seen from the consumer's perspective. Taken together, they can provide the basis for enhanced self-esteem, which is central to the social capital that can lead to economic capital and break the cycle of poverty.

A communitarian approach to public housing recovery resists the abandonment and dispersal of communities. Instead, it involves the enhancement of such communities, to such an extent that many of those residents who are most upwardly mobile—who have stable jobs with adequate incomes—will choose to stay, at least for a while.

As the twenty-first century begins, policymakers across the United States seek ways to transform large urban public housing projects, places judged to have become disastrously concentrated pockets of poverty and unemployment. The HOPE VI program has encouraged housing authorities not only to "think outside the box" but to destroy the boxes completely. Compared with the strictures of the 1980s, HUD and Congress now give housing authorities undertaking redevelopment projects far greater freedoms: they no longer have to rebuild on the old footprints of previous structures, and they no longer have to replace "lost" public housing units on a one-for-one basis. Instead, they are encouraged to leverage outside funding and to find other redevelopment partners—and they are expected to get beyond the reality and the image of public housing as housing of last resort.

Signs of Life?

At a time when most of those in Congress seek to abandon—or at least to alter dramatically—any remaining commitment to low-income public housing, the Boston redevelopment efforts suggest that it is possible to salvage some places even when a system is in shambles. The "failure" of public housing in America has been highly differentiated according to local conditions: despite all the dire headlines, it has not faltered everywhere equally. Whatever systemic problems public housing may have as a concept and as an institution, it is also responsive to the countervailing actions of individuals and groups. Despite its broad problems, a public housing development lives or dies as a piece of a neighborhood, and its successes or failures are felt most acutely by its residents. Because neighborhoods and residents matter, some public housing communities can retain or regain a "decent, safe, and sanitary" living environment, while others seem destined to perpetuate the stereotype of an irredeemable federal bureaucracy warehousing a doomed underclass. The latter category of places demands radical new approaches, while the former suggests that—with proper planning and innovative partnerships—it is possible to reclaim the public housing that already exists. Government subsidies for low-income families will perhaps always carry a stigma—or at least the burden of some sort of implied moral reciprocity—but the stories of Boston's efforts to salvage severely distressed public housing show that it is sometimes possible to recover communities all too often dismissed as nonviable.

Beyond Public Neighborhoods

Ultimately, this book carries a dual message—first, *neighborhoods matter* and, second, the *quality of planning, design, development, and management* of such neighborhoods significantly impacts their ability to recover. It is not public housing that has failed; what has failed are *public neighborhoods.* These neighborhoods failed because shifting public policies forced ill-equipped housing authorities to admit and retain the nation's public neighbors, without providing a financial system that could pay for the building maintenance and social service infrastructure required to support such a needy clientele. At the same time, public neighborhoods failed because their design did so little to support basic human needs for privacy, security, and community. Socially and physically, every inch of these single-function public neighborhoods appeared open to free entry, and therefore dangerous.

Housing policymakers and researchers have debated the shortcomings of housing projects for more than four decades. There is now a widely shared repertoire of design techniques that promise safer and more desirable environments—strategies pioneered by Oscar Newman, instituted in Boston, and subsequently applied throughout the country. Similarly, there is now a parallel consensus that urban public housing projects should not be asked to solve the nation's public-neighbor problem. It is less clear, however, how these two inclinations should be reconciled. Must expensive redesign of public housing always entail wholesale socioeconomic transformation of the community expected to reside in it? Is redeveloped public housing really "too good for poor people"?

The central challenge, for housing policymakers and for tenants, is to reclaim public housing in ways that maximize its contribution to the well-being of low-income urban-dwellers. The understandable impulse to deconcentrate poverty should not be used as an excuse to backtrack from a commitment to provide housing units that are affordable to low-income households. No one wants to see public housing redevelopment used to reinvent stigmatized public ghettoes, but it is equally unconscionable to use the "reform" of public housing as an excuse to eliminate it. The successes at Commonwealth and West Broadway suggest that, once tenants sign on as key participants in the negotiations, public housing communities can be productively restructured in a multitude of subtle ways without abandoning a central commitment to the needs of extremely low income households. Sometimes this is best nurtured through involvement by private managers, but the Commonwealth example also shows that tenants and housing authorities still must be regarded as necessary parts of the solution, not simply obstacles to overcome.

As public housing residents themselves clearly realize, the vast majority of their fellow public neighbors are not "problem people" whose presence is detrimental to community stability. Most public housing residents interviewed for this book simply ask for tighter tenant screening and careful enforcement of high behavioral expectations in their communities. Tellingly, at a public hearing convened in September 2000 to discuss a BHA proposal to provide a "new preference for non-emergency households with incomes between 31 and 80% of median income," current tenants voiced consistent vociferous objection. As one resident put it, "We do not have room in my community for a man who's making $50,000." Another asked, "Why open it up to those with higher incomes, ahead of those that's really hurting?" The message came through loud and clear: "keep low-income housing for low-income people."[30] Instead of an influx of higher-income "role models," these tenants preferred policies that would permit more of a scarce housing resource to go to the least-advantaged. Such a policy makes sense, however, only if it yields safe and desirable communities. The story of Commonwealth clearly demonstrates that it is possible to reclaim public housing for the neediest; it does so by showing that high standards and low-income people are not incompatible.

We have much to learn from this place and its people. Commonwealth's community no longer functions in isolation. It feels like a place with some physical and institutional connections that extend beyond its own borders. Commonwealth no longer looks or acts like a ghetto under public management, where fewer and different rules apply. Yet successful public housing redevelopment must be about more than handing a lot of public money to the private sector. It must also be about the power of the public sector to nurture a three-way partnership that empowers community-based nonprofit organizations (such as tenant associations) and private firms. It is possible that future public housing authorities may no longer play the lead role in either public housing development or public housing management. Rather, the public sector's greatest contribution may be as a facilitator and team-builder charged with ensuring that all public housing redevelopment yields communities that are both viable and equitable.

In some cases, such as Commonwealth, a community can be viably and equitably salvaged without looking beyond the ranks of the current public housing applicants, nearly all of whom have low or very low incomes. Every effort ought to be made to maximize the possibility of Commonwealth-like results in other places, through nurturing respectful relationships with tenants, engaging neighborhood organizations, implementing fundamental design transformations, and learning from the best practices of public and private managers.

A key purpose of public oversight is to maximize the presence of rental housing that is affordable to low and very low income households. This does not entail opposition to mixed-income strategies; it simply suggests that an equitable approach will advocate such places only as part of a broader strategy to increase the overall number of housing units that serve those with the lowest incomes. Sometimes, public funds may be best deployed to support a low-income tier in a mixed-income community, but it is not enough to convert existing low-income housing projects into mixed-income communities. To sustain progress in the production of affordable housing entails parallel efforts to include low-income units in new multifamily developments that would otherwise have contained entirely market-rate dwellings. Reclaiming public housing entails both a project-by-project transformation of individual public neighborhoods and a deeper public commitment to assist the society's poorest residents elsewhere, including increased provision of homeless shelters and single-room-occupancy dwellings, as well as increased availability of housing vouchers. Reclaiming public housing requires the elimination of publicly sponsored ghettoes, not the elimination of low-rent dwellings.

NOTE ON LITERATURE AND METHODS

Public Housing: Histories and Policies

THE CURRENT EFFORTS to reclaim public housing projects date back at least as far as Jane Jacobs's pioneering book *The Death and Life of Great American Cities,* which helped launch a rich outpouring of commentaries and case studies. During the 1960s and 1970s, scholars voluminously documented the decline and fall of Pruitt-Igoe in St. Louis in studies that included Lee Rainwater's harrowing and revealing ethnography. Clare Cooper provided a richly sensitive account of life at Easter Hill Village in California.[1] From a more theoretical perspective, there are three other seminal works. The first, Serge Chermayeff and Christopher Alexander's *Community and Privacy,* was published in 1963 and proposed ways to design urban housing that could reconcile the two key concepts of its title; the other two works, by Oscar Newman, extended and adapted this concern to the crime-ridden environments of public housing.

Chermayeff and Alexander argued that "to develop both privacy *and* the true advantages of living in a community, an entirely new anatomy of urbanism is needed. Such an urban anatomy must provide special domains for all degrees of privacy and all degrees of community living, ranging from the most intimately private to the most intensely communal. To separate these domains, and yet allow their interaction, entirely new physical elements must be inserted between them."[2] Whereas Jacobs placed her emphasis on the security that would result only from the promulgation of fully public streetscapes, Chermayeff and Alexander sought ways to guarantee privacy in dense urban housing settings, so as to reassure those who might be willing to seek alternatives to the alleged social inadequacies of the suburbs.

These joint concerns for a layered urbanism that could deliver both public surveillance and private sanctuary were, in turn, more thoroughly developed and applied to public housing in Oscar Newman's landmark volume *Defensible Space* (1972).[3] Through encouraging residents to view parts of their housing project as a continuation of their own living quarters and through encouraging all residents to view the project as a whole as a private community, Newman argued that it was possible to advocate a sense of pride and belonging instead of a sense of stigmatized alienation. Although Newman's work was criticized for overstating the capacity of architecture and urban design to determine behavior, his work must be seen as part of a well-established tradition of attempts to link the qualities of the built environment to the beliefs and actions of those who live in it, dating back at least to the slum-reformers of the nineteenth century. Newman's work was different not only because it proposed a theoretical framework based on human predilections for territoriality, but also because it was accompanied by a wide array of empirical data to support his contentions that many of the most egregious failures of public housing environments could be ameliorated by more sensitive design. Despite an initial barrage of criticisms, Newman's approach to public housing design and redesign gradually caught on, to the point where "defensible space" became a part of the working vocabulary and stated strategy of HUD and public housing authorities across the country.

Community of Interest, Newman's less discussed sequel to *Defensible Space,* is in many ways a more far-reaching proposition. Published in 1980, this book went well beyond discussion of the ways that the physical form of housing projects could be altered to improve security; indeed, it expanded these arguments to a much broader array of residential environments, and its focus shifted toward positive conceptions of desirable communities rather than negatively defined efforts to "defend" neighborhoods against crime. While still acknowledging that "people's experience of crime and their fear of crime remain the critical factors affecting the creation and stability of urban communities in America today," Newman shifted his emphasis to the interaction between physical design settings and socioeconomic conditions. Following on early work by Melvin Webber and others

that has articulated the ways that communities are increasingly structured by perceived commonality of interest rather than by mere propinquity, Newman's housing proposals stressed ways to structure communities according to age and life-
style, in the hope that this approach could transcend otherwise intractable
schisms based on income and race.

Newman's book is an extended argument for the psychological means to
achieve urban integration on the basis of three principles: "1) the grouping of similar age and life-style groups in housing environments designed to carefully fit
their life-style needs; 2) a mix of income groups that will allow the values and lifestyles of the upper-income group to dominate; and 3) [a] percentage of low-income and/or black families that is determined by the community and strictly ad-
hered to." It is, of course, the latter two principles that raised the most hackles,
since they implied that "low-income values and lifestyles" were inherently inferior and could be tolerated only in small numbers, which were to be set in accor-
dance with government-mandated "strictly maintained . . . quotas on the level of
economic and racial integration to be achieved."[4] Newman's invocation of the
"Q-word," coming soon after the highly controversial outcome of the Allan Bakke
medical school admission case (1979), proved especially untimely.

As the backlash against government-sponsored efforts to promote affirmative
action continues, the language and tactics of integrationists have become more
subtle than Newman's blatant defense of quotas, but here too, the underlying
ideas of Newman seem to be gaining renewed currency. Since the mid-1990s,
pushed by the HOPE VI program and by the 1998 public housing reform legislation, public housing authorities across the country have sought ways to reduce
the economic isolation of public housing communities. Often, the attempt to ex-
punge the negative impressions of projects has entailed enhanced efforts to restructure occupancy to include a greater economic mix of residents. Although
such efforts have thus far made little headway except where championed in
HOPE VI redevelopment initiatives, they do affirm the fact that any viable attempt to destigmatize public housing must have social as well as physical dimensions.

Bridging Literatures and Methods

In addition to the books that explicitly concern themselves with the role of design
in achieving social change in public housing, literally thousands of other books,
theses, reports, and articles address the meaning of American public housing

from different perspectives. As a subject, public housing has engaged scholars from a wide variety of disciplines, including history, law, economics, public administration, and sociology. Taken together, these accounts provide a thorough documentation of the contentious legislative history, financial folly, and bureaucratic deficiencies of public housing's institutions.[5] Most historical research on public housing, including several major monographs about public housing in large American cities, tends to abandon the story in the 1960s or 1970s, leaving the reader to ponder the disheartening "decline and fall of the projects" in one troubled urban context or another.[6] Other recent work has remained much more focused on the present, detailing single policy initiatives or alternatives, such as tenant management, drug-fighting strategies, service provision, housing vouchers, or metropolitan deconcentration of poverty. Still other studies take on single housing projects as case studies, grounding their accounts in rich ethnographic detail.[7]

In this book, I have pursued a confluence of methodological approaches. A great deal of research on public housing is either narrowly quantitative and aspatial or anecdotally qualitative and divorced from larger socioeconomic forces, yet the interdisciplinarity of this subject requires new ways to link disparate forms of data. This book relies on extensive archival research (mostly conducted at the Boston Housing Authority archives and in the abundant papers of Mayor John F. Collins, the first Boston mayor to leave such a complete paper trail). It also has depended on photographs, maps, systematic field observation over a period of fifteen years, geographic information systems, city directories, voter-registration records, census data, and resident-generated cognitive maps.

Boston has two seemingly reliable data sets that enable researchers to track the movements of households within the city over time. The first is the Boston City Directory, an annual listing of household heads by address that is found in many large cities. City directories have been used by historians for many different purposes for many years. The second data set is more unusual: it is a resource long known in Boston as the "Police Lists," an annual house-to-house census of voting-age adults conducted by the Boston Police Department every year from 1918 until the late 1950s, when it was folded into less labor intensive methods associated with voter-registration lists. The two sources, which provide slightly different—but substantially overlapping—sets of information, allow for a cross-check of all data points, and a reasonably high level of certainty about when and where families have moved. The police list–voter-registration data have the added advantage of including a listing for prior addresses as well, so that it becomes possible to identify where new arrivals to public housing lived during the year immediately preceding their entry into public housing.

At its heart, this book draws on more than three hundred interviews with public housing residents, BHA employees, architects, landscape architects, planners, service providers, and neighborhood businesspeople. The interview process with tenants deserves some further comment. Tenants helped shape the sorts of questions that were asked of their fellow residents, and they encouraged the author to find ways to raise issues that were important to them. Public housing residents were then hired, trained, and paid to do the actual interviewing of their fellow tenants. Two hundred and sixty-seven hour-long taped interviews—conducted in four languages—uncovered a broad range of tenant opinion at each development, reaching well beyond the realm of the usual activists and spokespersons. Interviews were conducted with a 10 percent sample of adult household heads at five developments—the three places featured in this book in addition to two other places (Bromley-Heath and Orchard Park) that had not yet undergone massive redevelopment (and could therefore serve as a kind of control group for assessing the impact of design changes elsewhere).

This multimethod, historically grounded approach poses challenges to what is often called "postoccupancy evaluation" by emphasizing the mutability of places after they have been occupied (or reoccupied). There is no magic moment at which "success" can be assessed or assured; longitudinal follow-up is always necessary. Understanding complex social and architectural environments requires what may best be termed *transoccupancy evaluation*. Only then can we fully investigate the sustainability of environmental change.

NOTES

1. Introduction

1. U.S. Department of Housing and Urban Development, "About Hope VI," www.hud.gov/offices/pih/programs/ph/hope6/about/index.cfm. HUD authorized razing 115,000 units during FYs 1993–2001. A study by the Johns Hopkins University School of Public Health found that public housing implosions may pose serious health hazards to the lungs of those who gather to watch or who live downwind of the blasts. Given the popularity of this new "sport," the medical researchers suggested new rules for partaking in the spectacle; see "Building Implosions Not a Spectator Sport," press release, Johns Hopkins School of Public Health, January 31, 2001.

2. HOPE VI, an acronym for Home Ownership and Opportunity for People Everywhere, takes its name from a series of policies developed in the late 1980s and early 1990s, centered on increasing homeownership among low-income households. HOPE VI, originally called the Urban Revitalization Demonstration (URD) Program, began in 1993. Over the next decade, Congress appropriated approximately $5 billion to revitalize or demolish "severely distressed" public housing nationwide.

3. There are many possible ways to calculate the number of housing units being lost to extremely low income (ELI) families (those earning less than 30 percent of the area median income) as a result of HOPE VI. Given the absence of clear demographic data from HUD about who is living in redeveloped public housing, housing researcher Wayne Sherwood has provided the author with the following calculation, employing some reasonable assumptions.

In press releases issued in 1999 concerning the HOPE VI grant awards of that year, HUD announced that approximately 11,000 public housing units would be demolished with that year's HOPE VI money ($571 million), including grants awarded for demolition only. Assuming that these apartments had a 90 percent overall occupancy rate, and that 90 percent of the occupied units were occupied by extremely low income families, then the "pre-HOPE VI ELI baseline" would be 8,910 public housing units occupied by ELI families (11,000 × 0.9 × 0.9).

In exchange for the demolished public housing units, HOPE VI redevelopment plans for that same year proposed building 3,720 public housing units for rent; 2,358 units of new, privately owned affordable and market-rate rental housing; and 3,233 units to be sold for homeownership by public housing residents and by market-rate buyers. As proposed by local housing authorities, then, this represents 9,311 units of total replacement housing.

Of this total, however, ELI families are likely to be able to afford only those 3,720 units created as public housing for rent. Moreover, it seems unlikely that housing authorities would choose to fill all those units with ELI families, given HUD's intent to create a "broad range of incomes" in these new HOPE VI developments (including their public housing components), with a special emphasis on attracting higher-income families who are working and have steady incomes. Thus, it seems reasonable to estimate that no more than half of the replacement "public housing units for rent" will be reoccupied by ELI families. This leaves only 1,860 out of the 8,910 units originally occupied by ELI families—a net loss of about 7,000 units annually.

It is also true that, without HOPE VI, many of these units would have been lost anyway as a result of continuing deterioration and obsolescence. The intent of this calculation is only to show the number of such units occupied or occupiable by ELI families that appear to be lost in each year of the HOPE VI program.

4. This book traces the history of individual neighborhoods; for the broader argument about societal ambivalence see a companion volume, *From the Puritans to the Projects: Public Housing and Public Neighbors* (Cambridge, Mass.: Harvard University Press, 2000).

5. Catherine Bauer, "The Dreary Deadlock of Public Housing," *Architectural Forum,* 106, no. 5 (1957), p. 140.

6. Organizations such as the Council of Large Public Housing Authorities (CLPHA), the National Association of Housing and Redevelopment Officials (NAHRO), the Public Housing Authority Directors Association (PHADA), and the National Housing Law Project repeatedly point out that the negative images associated with public housing are largely based on the worst cases of the most troubled large cities and do not reflect the conditions that prevail in the majority of the nation's public housing stock. For example, fully three-quarters of the local housing authorities manage fewer than 250 units.

7. John F. Bauman, "Public Housing: The Dreadful Saga of a Durable Policy," *Journal of Planning Literature,* vol. 8, no. 4 (1994), pp. 347–361. Other recent work has

been much more forthcoming about documenting struggles and victories. See El-len-J. Pader and Myrna Margulies Breitbart, "Transforming Public Housing: Conflicting Visions for Harbor Point," *Places,* vol. 8., no. 4 (1993); Myrna Margulies Breitbart and Ellen-J. Pader, "Establishing Ground: Representing Gender and Race in a Mixed Housing Development," *Gender, Place and Culture,* vol. 2, no. 1 (1995); Jacqueline Leavitt and Anastasia Loukaitou-Sideris, "'A Decent Home and a Suitable Environment': Dilemmas of Public Housing Residents in Los Angeles," *Journal of Architectural and Planning Research,* 12, no. 3 (Autumn 1995); Lawrence J. Vale, "Public Housing Redevelopment: Seven Kinds of Success," *Housing Policy Debate,* 7, 3 (1996); Vale, "Transforming Public Housing: The Social and Physical Redevelopment of Boston's West Broadway Development," *Journal of Architectural and Planning Research,* vol. 12, no. 3 (Autumn 1995); Vale, "Destigmatizing Public Housing," in Dennis Crow, ed., *Geography and Identity: Exploring and Living the Geopolitics of Identity* (Washington, D.C.: Institute for Advanced Cultural Studies/ Maisonneuve Press, 1996); Roberta Feldman and Susan Stall, "The Politics of Space Appropriation: A Case Study of Women's Struggles for Homeplace in Chicago Public Housing," in Irwin Altman and Arza Churchman, eds., *Women and the Environment* (New York: Plenum, 1994); Mary M. Lassen, *Community-Based Family Support in Public Housing* (Cambridge, Mass.: Harvard Family Research Project, 1995); Jane Roessner, *A Decent Place to Live: From Columbia Point to Harbor Point, a Community History* (Boston: Northeastern University Press, 2000).

8. NCSDPH, 1992. For a critique of the National Commission's definition and measurement of "severely distressed public housing," see Lawrence J. Vale, "Beyond the Problem Projects Paradigm: Defining and Revitalizing 'Severely Distressed' Public Housing," *Housing Policy Debate,* 4, 2 (1993), pp. 147–174.

9. Michael H. Schill, "Distressed Public Housing: Where Do We Go From Here?" *University of Chicago Law Review,* 60 (1993), p. 517.

10. United States Federal Public Housing Authority, *Public Housing Design: A Review of Experience in Low-Rent Housing* (Washington, D.C.: Government Printing Office, June 1946), pp. 28–31; United States Federal Public Housing Authority, *Minimum Physical Standards and Criteria for the Planning and Design of FPHA-Aided Urban Low-Rent Housing* (Washington, D.C.: United States Federal Public Housing Authority, November 1945). For an overview of site planning changes, see Karen A. Franck and Michael Mostoller, "From Courts to Open Space to Streets: Changes in the Site Design of U.S. Public Housing," *Journal of Architectural and Planning Research,* 12, 3 (Autumn 1995), pp. 186–220.

11. Gerald Suttles, *The Social Construction of Communities* (Chicago: University of Chicago Press, 1972), p. 52.

12. Ibid., pp. 52–54.

13. Robert D. Putnam, *Bowling Alone: The Collapse and Revival of American Community* (New York: Simon and Schuster, 2000). See also Lewis H. Spence, "Rethinking the Social Role of Public Housing," *Housing Policy Debate*, 4, no. 3 (1993), pp. 355-368.

14. Jerome Bruner, *Acts of Meaning* (Cambridge, Mass.: Harvard University Press, 1990), pp. 11, 16.

15. Erving Goffman, *Stigma: Notes on the Management of Spoiled Identity* (Englewood Cliffs, N.J.: Prentice-Hall, 1963).

16. Stephen C. Ainlay, Gaylene Becker, and Lerita Coleman, eds., *The Dilemma of Difference: A Multidisciplinary View of Stigma* (New York: Plenum, 1986), p. 3.

17. Lee Rainwater, "Fear and the House-as-Haven in the Lower Class," *Journal of the American Institute of Planners*, 32 (1963), pp. 29-30.

18. This history is traced in Vale, *From the Puritans to the Projects*.

19. The term *public neighbor* is meant to be a neutral and descriptive one; indeed, neither "public" nor "neighbor" immediately lends itself to either a derogatory or a celebratory cast, though certainly such persons have been subject to past and present stigma. In assessments of poverty, however, all too often terms intended to be merely descriptive become used as pejorative labels. The dangers of this are discussed in Herbert J. Gans, *The War against the Poor: The Underclass and Anti-Poverty Policy* (New York: Basic Books, 1995), pp. 18-26, 126.

20. This neighborhood appeal of elderly housing was undermined in many places by subsequent federal decisions to include the nonelderly disabled (including the mentally ill) among those eligible for "elderly" housing, a situation that caused frequent disruptions. In some cities, the nonelderly disabled applicants became an absolute majority. For an overview of this issue, see Daniel Wuenschel, "Statement on Behalf of Council of Large Public Housing Authorities to the Senate Committee on Banking, Housing and Urban Affairs Subcommittee on Housing and Urban Affairs," during a "Symposium on Mixed Populations," March 27, 1992.

21. See Congressional Budget Office, *The Challenges Facing Federal Rental Assistance Programs* (December 1994), pp. 4-5; Michael H. Schill, "Privatizing Federal Low Income Assistance: The Case of Public Housing," *Cornell Law Review*, 75, no. 4 (May 1990); Schill, "Distressed Public Housing," pp. 497-554; Bernard J. Frieden, "Housing Allowances: An Experiment That Worked," *The Public Interest*, 59 (Spring 1980), pp. 15-23; Raymond J. Burby and William M. Rohe, "Deconcentration of Public Housing: Effects on Residents' Satisfaction with Their Living Environments and Their Fear of Crime," *Urban Affairs Quarterly*, 25, no. 2 (1989), pp. 117-141; Mary Lou Gallagher, "HUD's Geography of Opportunity," *Planning*, 60, no. 7 (July 1994), pp. 12-13. For an early critique of the voucher idea, see Chester Hartman, "Housing Allowances: A Bad Idea Whose Time Has Come,"

reprinted in J. Paul Mitchell, ed., *Federal Housing Policy and Programs: Past and Present* (New Brunswick, N.J.: Center for Urban Policy Research, 1985), pp. 383–389.

22. See, for example, William Peterman, "Public Housing Resident Management: A Good Idea Gone Wrong?" *Shelterforce* (November/December 1993); William M. Rohe, "Assisting Residents of Public Housing Achieve Self Sufficiency: An Evaluation of Charlotte's Gateway Families Program," *Journal of Architectural and Planning Research*, 12, no. 3 (Autumn 1995), pp. 259–277; Sandra Newman and Ann Schnare, *Subsidizing Shelter: The Relationship between Welfare and Housing Assistance* (Washington, D.C.: The Urban Institute, 1988).

23. Jane Jacobs, *The Death and Life of Great American Cities* (New York: Vintage, 1961), pp. 394–395, 398.

24. Oscar Newman, *Defensible Space* (New York: Macmillan, 1972); Henry Cisneros, *Defensible Space: Deterring Crime and Building Community* (Washington, D.C.: HUD, January 1995). For a fuller description of literature on public housing and its transformation, see the "Note on Literature and Methods" at the end of this book.

25. Cited in May B. Hipshman, *Public Housing at the Crossroads: The Boston Housing Authority* (Boston: Massachusetts Committee on Discrimination in Housing, Commission on Housing [Metropolitan Boston Association, United Church of Christ], and Citizens' Housing and Planning Association of Metropolitan Boston, August 1967), p. 27. A much fuller history of public housing in Boston is provided in Vale, *From the Puritans to the Projects*, chapters 3–5.

26. Barry Bluestone and Mary Huff Stevenson, *The Boston Renaissance: Race, Space, and Economic Change in an American Metropolis* (New York: Russell Sage Foundation, 2000), pp. 1–22.

27. Northeastern University Center for Urban and Regional Policy, *A New Paradigm for Housing in Greater Boston* (Boston: CURP, February 2001 [rev. ed.]), pp. 1–4, 65–68; John Avault, Chief Economist, Boston Redevelopment Authority, personal communication with the author, May 2001; interview with Sandra Henriquez, January 2000.

28. The full saga of the Columbia Point to Harbor Point transformation is well told in Roessner, *A Decent Place to Live.*

2. West Broadway

1. Thomas O'Connor, *South Boston: My Home Town* (Boston: Quinlan Press, 1988), pp. 2–5.

2. Eric Hobsbawm and Terrence Ranger, eds., *The Invention of Tradition* (New York: Cambridge University Press, 1983); O'Connor, *South Boston*, pp. 12–13, 106.

3. O'Connor, *South Boston*, pp. 16–17.

4. The story of the migration of Boston's almshouses to progressively more peripheral locations is narrated in Lawrence J. Vale, *From the Puritans to the Projects: Public Housing and Public Neighbors*, Chapter 1.

5. City of Boston, *South Boston Memorial*, City Document no. 18 (Boston: Boston Common Council, April 22, 1847), pp. 1–29. See also Peter C. Holloran, *Boston's Wayward Children: Social Services for Homeless Children, 1830–1930* (Boston: Northeastern University Press, 1994), p. 29; O'Connor, *South Boston*, p. 31.

6. O'Connor, *South Boston*, pp. 31–32.

7. Ibid., *South Boston*, pp. 36–38, 46.

8. Boston Common Council, *South Boston Memorial*, p. 11; Holloran, *Boston's Wayward Children*, p. 141.

9. O'Connor, *South Boston*, pp. 64–65, 86–87, 120–121.

10. Ibid., pp. 94–95; Thomas O'Connor, *The Boston Irish: A Political History* (Boston: Little, Brown, 1995), pp. 128–133; 161–163.

11. O'Connor, *South Boston*, pp. 127, 180.

12. Eleanor Woods, "South Boston," in Albert J. Kennedy and Robert A. Woods, *The Zone of Emergence*, abridged and edited by Sam B. Warner, Jr. (Cambridge, Mass.: MIT Press, 1962), pp. 40, 130–133.

13. Woods, "South Boston," pp. 133–137.

14. Ibid., pp. 134–135; Albert J. Kennedy, "Roxbury, Ward 17," in Kennedy and Woods, *The Zone of Emergence*, p. 99.

15. O'Connor, *South Boston*, pp. 197–198.

16. These figures are in 1933 dollars and refer to accounting for that particular year. State Board of Housing (Massachusetts), *Annual Report of the State Board of Housing, for the Year Ending November 30, 1936* (Boston, Mass.: Department of Public Welfare, 1937), p. 12.

17. "Social Agencies Back Report: Residents of Various Sections, However, Bitter at Alleged Slurs," *Boston Traveler*, April 2, 1934, pp. 1, 8; "Teachers Declare Boston 'Slums Still Produce Leaders of Tomorrow,'" *Boston Traveler*, April 3, 1934, pp. 1, 17.

18. The long battle to build the Old Harbor Village and Old Colony projects is detailed in Vale, *From the Puritans to the Projects*, chapter 3.

19. Greater Boston Community Council, *What Do You Know about South Boston and Its Neighborhoods: Andrew Square, City Point, Old Harbor Village, Telegraph Hill, West Broadway?* (Boston: Community Studies Research Bureau, November 1944), pp. 11, 14, 16, 20, 26. It should be noted that the number of court appearances is a less-than-satisfactory measure of juvenile delinquency, especially since multiple appearances by a single individual were counted separately; courts exercised highly

variable patterns of "out-of-court" arrangements that did not necessitate recorded appearance; and police practices varied. Still, the pattern is striking enough to suggest that the Lower End would have certainly been saddled with a reputation for markedly higher juvenile crime than other parts of South Boston.

20. "Business Men Back Plan for New Low Rental Project Here," *South Boston Gazette,* May 19, 1939, p. 1; "Editorial: Intown Writer Boosts District," *South Boston Gazette,* May 19, 1939, p. 1.

21. "Business Men Back Plan," p. 1.

22. Boston City Directories and Police Lists (an annual house-to-house census used primarily for voter-registration purposes), 1939 and 1942. The data on applications for project residency from displaced families are reported in Anna L. Kenney, "The Boston Housing Authority," unpublished Master of Arts thesis (Economics), Boston University Graduate School, 1941. The BHA archives do not contain any tenant-application records, so it is impossible to corroborate Kenney's data, which she obtained directly from the BHA at the time.

   Three of the four early slum-clearance projects (Charlestown, Lenox Street, and Mission Hill) had rehousing rates of between 8 and 12 percent. The unusually low figure of 2 percent rehousing occurred in the case of the Old Colony project, and seems largely due to the fact that this project was commandeered by the U.S. government for housing war workers before it could be tenanted by the BHA. The early tenancy of these projects is discussed in Vale, *From the Puritans to the Projects,* chapter 3.

23. "Housing Project for Lower End," *South Boston Gazette,* January 19, 1940, pp. 1, 8; "Housing Projects Discussion Subject during Past Week," *South Boston Gazette,* February 7, 1941.

24. "Housing Project in Lower End Announced by Mayor This Week," *South Boston Tribune,* February 7, 1941, p. 1.

25. The Critic, "Critic Calls upon Housing Committee for Fairness in Taking Property in Latest Housing Area," *South Boston Gazette,* February 21, 1941, p. 1.

26. "Merchants Object to New Housing Project Taking Store Sites," *South Boston Tribune,* February 21, 1941.

27. "Residents Express Indignation at Tactics of Housing Probers," *South Boston Tribune,* April 4, 1941, p. 1.

28. "Ward 6 Housing Site Taken by Court Order: Defense Workers and Families of Enlisted Men Get Preference," *South Boston Tribune,* December 12, 1941, p. 1.

29. Cited in O'Connor, *South Boston,* p. 199; interview with the proprietor of Kay's Laundromat, South Boston, June 2000.

30. Gerald Taube, "A Family Album: The Many Faces of Public Housing," unpub-

lished manuscript, Boston University School of Law, Law and Poverty Program, 1969; Boston City Directory and Police Lists, 1941.

31. Letter from Laura Dapkiewicz to John F. Collins, September 12, 1962; John F. Collins Papers, box 303.

32. Reverend Albert J. Contons, "D Street Project: A New Beginning," Letter to the Editor, *South Boston Tribune,* April 2, 1981.

33. "Councillor Scannell Wants Housing Project Started," *South Boston Gazette,* August 17, 1945, p. 1.

34. "Linehan Paving Way for Housing Project in South Boston and South End," *South Boston Gazette,* July 26, 1946, p. 1.

35. "Letter from State Representative John B. Wenzler to President Harry S. Truman," reprinted in "Seeks Presidential Aid in Getting Action on Housing Project," *South Boston Gazette,* October 17, 1947.

36. "Residents Are Shouting for Housing Project," *South Boston Gazette,* December 26, 1947, p. 1. Others pointed to conflicts between Boston Housing Authority Board members and leaders of the Massachusetts Emergency Housing Authority. See "Councillor Wenzler Continues Campaign for Housing," *South Boston Gazette,* January 9, 1948, p. 1.

37. The legal arguments are discussed in detail in a letter from Philip Nichols, Esq., to John Carroll, BHA Chairman, May 21, 1947.

38. "John Wenzler States South Boston Project Will Be First," *South Boston Gazette,* August 6, 1948, p. 1; "Housing Project Here Now Seems a Certainty," *South Boston Gazette,* August 6, 1948, p. 1; "Housing Project Will Take Eighteen Months," *South Boston Gazette,* October 1, 1948, p. 1; "Much Rejoicing over O.K. for Housing Project," *South Boston Gazette,* October 29, 1948, p. 1; "Housing Project to Have Ramps to Aid Disabled Veterans," *South Boston Gazette,* October 29, 1948, p. 1.

39. James P. Aylward, "More Up-to-Date Homes Should Be Erected in District," *South Boston Gazette,* December 27, 1940.

40. "Veterans Roar over Housing Project Rents," *South Boston Gazette,* August 12, 1949; Joe Alecks, "Veterans Protest High Rent Schedule in Housing Project," *South Boston Gazette,* August 19, 1949, pp. 1, 8.

41. "South Boston Improving in Various Directions," *South Boston Gazette,* September 2, 1949, p. 1.

42. Contons, *South Boston Tribune,* April 2, 1981.

43. "New Names for Project Streets," *South Boston Gazette,* June 24, 1949; "Project Recreation Area Named after Father Flaherty," *South Boston Gazette,* September 16, 1949.

44. The median project household sizes were only slightly larger than those in surrounding areas, so this should not skew the comparison very much. It is, however, worth noting that project rents included most utility costs, whereas most private-sector rentals did not, so the actual gap between project and nonproject rents is not quite so large as it seems, though still quite extreme. These data come from the 1950 U.S. Census, in which the West Broadway project appears as its own tract.

45. Boston City Directory and Police List, 1950. Data on (self-reported) occupations come from a 10 percent sample of both male (n = 100) and female (n = 100) adults. The categorization of occupations in terms of skill level has been adopted from Stephan Thernstrom, *The Other Bostonians: Poverty and Progress in the American Metropolis, 1880–1970* (Cambridge, Mass.: Harvard University Press, 1973), Appendix B, pp. 290–292.

46. U.S. Census, 1950. Police list data (which also list citizenship information for each adult) suggest that the few cases of residency by noncitizens usually consisted of cases where the household head was a citizen who lived with an elderly noncitizen parent.

47. U.S. Census, Police Lists, and Boston City Directories, 1950.

48. J. L. McCarthy, "New Housing Project Seems to Lack Recreational Facilities," *South Boston Gazette,* April 1, 1949; interviews with long-time residents conducted in 1993 and 2000; "South Boston's Face Lifting Would Surprise Ex-Residents," *South Boston Gazette,* October 21, 1949.

49. Interview, September 2000; 1950, 1960, and 1970 U.S. Census. The figures for longevity in the project come from following a 10 percent sample of the initial residents until they departed from the project, using data supplied from Boston City Directories and Police Lists. In the cases where a household moved within the project before departing from it, the length of residency was calculated on the basis of the final move-out, not the internal transfer.

50. U.S. Census, 1960; "A Social Survey of the West Broadway Housing Development," conducted by the South Boston Neighborhood House in 1965, as interpreted in Robert B. Whittlesey, "Report of the Master in the Case of *Perez v. Boston Housing Authority*," July 1976, p. B-VII-9.

51. The presentations were staged downtown rather than at the project, however, and held weeks before the tournament actually began, suggesting clear limits to the solicitude of the highest officials.

52. "D St. Development to Mark Public Housing Week in May," *South Boston Tribune,* April 30, 1964, p. 10; "Housing Week Program Begins Sunday at D St. Development," *South Boston Tribune,* May 14, 1964, p. 4; "Athletic Tourney at D St. Project Will Start on Saturday Morning," *South Boston Tribune,* June 3, 1965, p. 1.

53. "Inter-Agency Meeting Takes Place in West Broadway Development," *South Boston Tribune,* January 19, 1967, p. 5.

54. Letters to Mayor Collins from D Street residents, 1961–1962; John F. Collins Papers, boxes 303, 226.

55. Alan Lupo et al., "Urban Renewal Is Dead," *Boston Globe,* July 12, 1967; Thomas O'Connor, *Building a New Boston: Politics and Urban Renewal, 1950–1970* (Boston: Northeastern University Press, 1993), pp. 214–216.

56. The story of this desegregation effort is discussed in detail in Vale, *From the Puritans to the Projects,* chapter 4.

57. In 1967, the BHA produced a list of the black households that were resident at West Broadway. This list was cross-referenced with Boston City Directory and Police List records to determine the household composition and employment type of black adults in the project.

58. Alan Lupo et al., "South Boston: From Yachts to Rubble," *Boston Globe,* July 12, 1967.

59. Cited in O'Connor, *South Boston,* p. 200.

60. Ibid.

61. Gerald Taube, "A Family Album."

62. "West Broadway Multi-Service Center Funding Request," n.d., p. 6 [1968?].

63. Sister Louise Kearns, interview, November 1993.

64. O'Connor, *South Boston,* p. 200.

65. Ellis Ash reported to the BHA Advisory Committee that, as the attempt to recruit nonwhites proceeded, public housing units would be held open in South Boston ("Advisory Committee, Minutes of Meeting," November 15, 1965). In 1970, only 31 percent of new arrivals to D Street came from South Boston.

66. "Racial Friction in South Boston," memo from Thomas B. Francis, Intergroup Relations Officer, to Richard S. Scobie, April 25, 1967; Roland Peters, "Problem Family Data," March 1967. This is a file folder in the BHA archives containing accounts of the individual interviews.

67. "Recommendations and Comments RE Interracial Situation in South Boston," memo from Roland Peters, Tenant Relations Aide, to Thomas B. Francis, Intergroup Relations Officer, April 25, 1967; interview with Ellis Ash, May 1997.

68. "Racial Friction in South Boston," memo from T. B. Francis, Intergroup Relations Officer, to R. S. Scobie, Director, Department of Tenant and Community Relations, April 25, 1967.

69. John F. Collins Papers, boxes 63, 214, 269.

70. "Recommendations and Comments RE Interracial Situation in South Boston," memo from Roland Peters, Tenant Relations Aide, to Thomas B. Francis, Inter-

group Relations Officer, April 25, 1967; "Racial Friction in South Boston," memo from T. B. Francis, Intergroup Relations Officer, to R. S. Scobie, Director, Department of Tenant and Community Relations, April 25, 1967.

71. "Interracial Disturbances in South Boston," memo from Richard S. Scobie, Director, Department of Tenant and Community Relations, to Ellis Ash, BHA Administrator, April 26, 1967.

72. "Recommendations and Comments RE Interracial Situation in South Boston," memo from Roland Peters, Tenant Relations Aide, to Thomas B. Francis, Intergroup Relations Officer, April 25, 1967.

73. "Interracial Disturbances in South Boston," memo from Richard S. Scobie, Director, Department of Tenant and Community Relations, to Ellis Ash, BHA Administrator, April 26, 1967.

74. Jonathon Morris Pynoos, "Breaking the Rules: The Failure to Select and Assign Public Housing Tenants Equitably," Ph.D. thesis (Urban Planning), Harvard University, 1974, p. 26.

75. Letter from Ellis Ash, BHA Administrator, to Joseph Duggan, President, South Boston APAC, May 17, 1967.

76. Letter from James W. Dolan, Boston Legal Assistance Project Attorney, and Nicholas R. Avitabile, Director, South Boston Action Center, to Ellis Ash, BHA Administrator, July 11, 1968.

77. "Inter-Racial Incident—D Street," memo from T. B. Francis, Intergroup Relations Officer, to Leo J. Donovan, Director of Management, October 8, 1969.

78. Deborah Blumin, *Victims: A Study of Crime in a Boston Housing Project* (Boston: Mayor's Safe Streets Act Advisory Committee, 1973), pp. 45, 47, 109.

79. Ibid., pp. 80, 91, 109, 119.

80. Ibid., p. 117; "Two Ex-Marines Held in Sniper Slaying," *Boston Herald American,* June 7, 1973.

81. The decision to place priests in the project is discussed in Rev. A. Paul White, "The D Street Project and South Boston," *The Pilot,* June 8, 1973, p. 9. One of the accused killers was acquitted in a 1979 trial, while the other fled to Puerto Rico after posting bail and was not captured until 1993 (Doris Sue Wong, "Accused Who Fled 1973 Charges in S. Boston Death Is Arrested," *Boston Globe,* March 5, 1993, pp. 21, 27).

82. "Life on D Street—Daily Diet of Tension," *Boston Globe,* March 25, 1973, p. 1; Bob Sales, "Rowdy Gang Takes Pride in Being Tough," *Boston Globe,* March 25, 1973, pp. 1, 27; Anne Kirchheimer, "Puerto Ricans Are Prisoners in Apartments," *Boston Globe,* March 25, 1973, pp. 1, 26.

83. Joe Klein, "Race War in South Boston," *Real Paper,* October 17, 1973, p. 4. This is

the same Joe Klein, it may be noted, who gained great notoriety in 1996 as the "Anonymous" author of the best-selling political novel *Primary Colors*. In that instance, Klein capitalized on the intense press speculation over the concealed identity of the author, fueled by months of his own vehement denials. Twenty-three years earlier in South Boston, Klein displayed a more immediately confrontational style and an equal appetite for courting controversy.

84. Robert L. Turner, "Two Held in Slaying of D Street Teenager," *Boston Globe,* June 7, 1973; Alan H. Sheehan, "Victim's Sister Testifies in Pratt Case," *Boston Globe,* October 17, 1973; George Buss, "Two South Boston Youths Guilty of Manslaughter," *Sunday Herald Advertiser,* October 21, 1973; Joe Klein, "Another Death at the D Street Project," *Real Paper,* June 13, 1973; Mike Barnicle, "Blacks Aren't Liked on D St."; "Two Ex-Marines Held in Sniper Slaying"; Richard O'Donnell, "Slain Youth Eulogized as Race Struggle Hero," *Boston Globe,* June 10, 1973; Ken O. Hartnett, "Life and Death Ambush in a Tight Little Universe," *Boston Globe,* June 7, 1973; Robert L. Turner, "Two Held in Slaying of D Street Teenager," *Boston Globe,* June 7, 1973; Joe Klein, "Pratt Murder Trial: The Case of the Runaway Witness," *Real Paper,* October 24, 1973, p. 4; Joe Klein, "Revenge Is Sour on D Street," *Real Paper,* October 31, 1973, p. 10.

85. "Letters from South Boston," *Real Paper,* November 12, 1973, pp. 13–14.

86. "Urgent Plea to Move Pratts Didn't Seem Urgent Enough to BHA," *Boston Globe,* June 10, 1973; *West Broadway Bulletin,* vol. I, no. 3 (June 1967); Klein, "Another Death at the D Street Project"; Ken O. Hartnett and Robert L. Turner, "George Didn't Live to See Family Leave D Street," *Boston Globe,* June 6, 1973; Ken O. Hartnett, "She Had Doubts," *Boston Globe,* October 26, 1973.

87. "Parents Ready to Do Battle on 'School Busing' Issue," *South Boston Tribune,* January 6, 1972.

88. O'Connor, *South Boston,* pp. 210–216; Alan Lupo, *Liberty's Chosen Home* (Boston: Beacon Press, 1977); Ione Malloy, *Southie Won't Go: A Teacher's Diary of the Desegregation of South Boston High School* (Urbana, Ill.: University of Illinois Press, 1986); J. Anthony Lukas, *Common Ground: A Turbulent Decade in the Lives of Three American Families* (New York: Vintage, 1986); Jon Hillson, *The Battle of Boston* (New York: Pathfinder Press, 1977); J. Michael Ross and William M. Berg, *"I Respectfully Disagree with the Judge's Order": The Boston School Desegregation Controversy* (Washington, D.C.: University Press of America, 1981); George W. Higgins, *Style versus Substance: Boston, Kevin White, and the Politics of Illusion* (New York: Macmillan, 1984); Ronald P. Formisano, *Boston against Busing: Race, Class, and Ethnicity in the 1960s and 1970s* (Chapel Hill, N.C.: University of North Carolina

Press, 1991); and William M. Bulger, *While the Music Lasts: My Life in Politics* (Boston: Houghton Mifflin, 1996).

89. William Bulger, Michael Flaherty, and Louise Day Hicks, "A Declaration of Clarification," reprinted in full in the *South Boston Tribune,* September 19, 1974, pp. 1, 4. Crime statistics for the first seven months of 1974, supplied to the *South Boston Tribune* by the Boston police commissioner, showed that, compared with South Boston, Roxbury recorded twice as many murders, six times as many aggravated assaults, eight times as many rapes, and nineteen times as many armed robberies (*South Boston Tribune,* September 19, 1974, p. 4).

90. Bulger, *While the Music Lasts,* pp. 116, 119.

91. The School Information Center at City Hall had been established as the official distribution mechanism for reports to both the public and the press regarding all developments in the Boston schools, and South Boston politicians quickly charged that it gave a "distorted downplay" of conditions, leading to the creation of the alternative information system. "Flynn Charges Facts Being Withheld on What Is Taking Place in Schools," *South Boston Tribune,* September 26, 1974, p. 1; "South Boston to Open Information Center," *South Boston Tribune,* October 3, 1974; "South Boston Information Center News," *South Boston Tribune,* February 20, 1975, p. 3; Dan Yotts, "South Boston Information Center News," *South Boston Tribune,* April 24, 1975, p. 1; Dan Yotts, "South Boston Information Center News," *South Boston Tribune,* May 8, 1975, p. 5.

92. Bulger, *While the Music Lasts,* p. 151.

93. Cited in O'Connor, *South Boston,* pp. 224–226.

94. Ibid., p. 230; "Investigation of Outsiders Being Sought," *South Boston Tribune,* August 7, 1975, p. 1. One local civic organization, the South Boston Residents' Group, even "fully investigated" the possibility of South Boston's secession from the city. They dredged up all the old controversies surrounding the original annexation, concluding that "as part of the core city, we have watched the quality of life deteriorate seriously in the past few years and are now seeking an alternative" ("Residents' Group Studies Secession from Boston," *South Boston Tribune,* September 26, 1974).

95. Jean Dietz and Viola Osgood, "Little City Halls—8: Housing Big Issue in So. Boston," *Boston Globe,* November 25, 1969, p. 3.

96. Dan Yotts, "South Boston Information Center News," *South Boston Tribune,* September 25, 1975, p. 3; John Ciccone, South Boston Information Center, *South Boston Tribune,* May 11, 1978, p. 3.

97. "D Street Community Development Program Minority Survey," September 5, 1975.

98. Taube, "A Family Album."

99. Ibid.; 1970 U.S. Census.

100. Robert Whittlesey, "Report of the Master," p. B-VII-11.

101. Taube, "A Family Album."

102. Cited in Blumin, *Victims,* p. 10. The statistic refers to 1969.

103. Blumin, *Victims,* pp. 28–33.

104. Ken O. Hartnett, "Neglect Is Showing Again at D Street," *Boston Globe,* August 11, 1973; Bob Sales and Ken Hartnett, "D Street Whitewashed Look Wears Thin," *Boston Globe,* October 28, 1973, p. A-2.

105. William Buchanan, "Adults Live in Terror of Project Hoodlums," *Boston Globe,* May 21, 1967, pp. 1, 80.

106. *West Broadway Bulletin,* vol. I, no. 3 (June 1967).

107. Lupo et al., "South Boston from Yachts to Rubble."

108. *West Broadway Bulletin,* vol. I, no. 4 (July 1967).

109. "West Broadway Hi-Lites," *South Boston Tribune,* January 2, 1969, p. 7.

110. "We're Watching" [Editorial], *South Boston Tribune,* July 26, 1973, p. 4.

111. Interview conducted outside the South Boston Health Clinic, June 2000; Michael Patrick MacDonald, *All Souls: A Family Story from Southie* (Boston: Beacon Press, 1999), pp. 2, 3, 58.

112. "Life on D Street—Daily Diet of Tension," *Boston Globe,* March 25, 1973, p. 1; Bob Sales, "Rowdy Gang Takes Pride in Being Tough," *Boston Globe,* March 25, 1973, pp. 1, 27; Anne Kirchheimer, "Puerto Ricans Are Prisoners in Apartments," *Boston Globe,* March 25, 1973, pp. 1, 26.

113. Cited in "Activist Club Makes Reply to *Globe* Article," *South Boston Tribune,* April 19, 1973, p. 6.

114. Mike Barnicle, "Blacks Aren't Liked on D St., but Pratts Couldn't Get Out," *Boston Globe,* June 6, 1973; Ken O. Hartnett, "Life and Death Ambush in a Tight Little Universe," *Boston Globe,* June 7, 1973; Joe Klein, "Pratt Murder Trial: The Case of the Runaway Witness," *Real Paper,* October 24, 1973, p. 4; Rev. A. Paul White, "The D Street Project and South Boston," *The Pilot,* June 8, 1973, p. 9.

115. "The Life of an Adequate Person in D St. Project," *South Boston Tribune,* October 23, 1975.

116. D Street Resident, "Letter to the Editor," *South Boston Tribune,* October 30, 1975, p. 6.

117. *West Broadway Bulletin,* vol. I, issue 1 (April 1967).

118. Letter from Anne Marie Neas, Publication Supervisor, *West Broadway Bulletin,* to Jacob Brier, BHA Board Chairman, April 13, 1967.

119. *West Broadway Bulletin,* vol. 1., issues 4, 7, and 8 (July, October, and November 1967).

120. *West Broadway Bulletin,* vol. I, nos. 6 and 7 (October and November 1967).

121. *West Broadway Bulletin,* vol. I, no. 3 (June 1967).

122. "Plans Outlined for a Multi-Service Center in D Street Housing Project," *South Boston Tribune,* January 16, 1969, pp. 1, 3.

123. "West Broadway Hi-Lites," *South Boston Tribune,* April 3, 1969, p. 7.

124. Cited in Taube, "A Family Album."

125. "West Broadway Task Force Planning Open Public Meeting This Evening," *South Boston Tribune,* February 5, 1970, pp. 1, 10.

126. Letter from Herman W. Hemingway, BHA Acting Administrator, to Paul Tierney, Chairman, Boston School Committee, November 2, 1971.

127. "Status Report on Police and Security," memo from Leo J. Gulinello, Director of Security, to Herman Hemingway, Acting Administrator, March 31, 1971.

128. *West Broadway Task Force, Inc., & Others vs. Commissioner of the Department of Community Affairs & Others,* 363 Mass. 745; "West Broadway Task Force vs. Leon Charkoudian and Boston Housing Authority," memo from Brian P. Shillue, Assistant Counsel to Paul F. Liston, BHA General Counsel, January 28, 1972.

129. "West Broadway Task Force Raps Veto of Mental Health Bill," *South Boston Tribune,* December 20, 1973, p. 6.

130. Letter from Rose Hayes, WBTF President, to Samuel Thompson, BHA Administrator, June 12, 1976.

131. *Master's Report,* Chapter VII, pp. 1, 24–26, 33–34.

132. Ibid., pp. 14, 16; "Analysis of Social and Environmental Problems at West Broadway Development," memo from Joseph F. McNamara, Housing Manager, to Robert Whittlesey, Central Office, October 20, 1975; Louise Elving, interview with Joseph McNamara, January 27, 1976.

133. *Master's Report,* Appendix, Chapter IX, pp. 2–3; "Analysis of Market Demand for D-Street," memo to Langley Keyes from Alden Drake, April 15, 1976.

134. Cited in *Master's Report,* A-IX-1, pp. 1–11.

135. MacDonald, *All Souls,* pp. 60–61.

136. *Master's Report,* B-VII, pp. 7, 9.

137. Interview with Robert Whittlesey, Court-Appointed Master, April 1996. Whittlesey also credits interest in the fate of D Street to the black social worker Joanne Ross, his unofficial "co-master," who knew the community well from her previous work there.

138. "West Broadway: BHA Contract with Boston Urban Observatory for DCA Pilot

Project Technical Assistance," memo from Brendan Garaghty, Assistant Administrator of Planning, Development, and Modernization, to Kevin P. Feeley, Acting Administrator, January 6, 1978.

139. Michael Flaherty, cited in the *South Boston Tribune*, February 17, 1977, p. 3.

140. "'D' St. Development Receives State Study Funding," *South Boston Tribune*, November 3, 1977, pp. 1, 4; "D. St. Project Gets $6.5M State Aid," *South Boston Tribune*, July 13, 1978, p. 1.

141. Interview with Elaine Werby, Boston Urban Observatory, November 1995.

142. Interview with Elaine Werby, Boston Urban Observatory, November 1995; Boston Urban Observatory, *Feasibility Study for the Private Management of the West Broadway Development*, prepared for the Boston Housing Authority and the West Broadway Task Force, Inc., March 1980. The BHA subsequently adopted many of this report's suggestions in the redevelopment effort at Commonwealth, where tenants were more receptive.

143. Boston Urban Observatory, *A Comprehensive Plan for the Renewal of the West Broadway Development*, submitted to the Boston Housing Authority and West Broadway Task Force, Inc., July 1979. The project was directed by Francine Price, working with Joe Slavet and Elaine Werby at the BUO, as well as a design team headed by Tunney Lee at MIT.

144. West Broadway Task Force, *West Broadway Multi-Service Center Newsletter*, Fall 1980.

145. Interviews with West Broadway residents, 1993.

146. Interview with Lewis H. (Harry) Spence, BHA Receiver, September 1995.

147. "Tenant Selection and Assignment to Your Development," memo from Kevin P. Feeley, Acting Administrator, to All Residents of Mary Ellen McCormack, Old Colony, Broadway, February 22, 1978.

148. "South Boston Information Center," *South Boston Tribune*, April 6, 1978, p. 4; "South Boston Information Center," *South Boston Tribune*, April 20, 1978, p. 3. The SBIC finally settled on a South Boston flag design only in late 1984; John Ciccone, "South Boston Information Center," *South Boston Tribune*, October 18, 1984.

149. John Ciccone, "South Boston Information Center," *South Boston Tribune*, April 27, 1978, p. 3; May 4, 1978, p. 3; June 1, 1978, p. 3; June 8, 1978, p. 3; June 15, 1978, p. 3; December 14, 1978, p. 3.

150. "HUD Official Details Housing Plan," Letter to the Editor, *South Boston Tribune*, June 1, 1978, pp. 1,3.

151. John Ciccone, "South Boston Information Center," *South Boston Tribune*, June 15, 1978, p. 3; August 17, 1978, p. 3; November 22, 1978, p. 3.

152. Letter from Edward T. Pollack, Area Office Director, U.S. Department of Housing and Urban Development, to Bradley Biggs, Chairman, BHA Standing City-Wide Committee on Troublesome Areas, June 14, 1978.

153. "Guarded Black Integrates Southie Project," *Boston Herald American*, November 17, 1978; Jerry Taylor, "Black Moves into Project in S. Boston, *Boston Globe*, November 17, 1978, p. 25; John Ciccone, "South Boston Information Center," *South Boston Tribune*, November 22, 1978, p. 3.

154. Timothy Dwyer, "S. Boston Residents Protest BHA Policy," *Boston Globe*, November 22, 1978; "We Accuse . . ." [Petition], *South Boston Tribune*, November 22, 1978, p. 8. Kelly and the South Boston Information Center followed through on such threats, sending letters to HUD's regional director of the "Office of Fair Housing and Equal Opportunity" and to the Massachusetts Attorney General. HUD subsequently insisted to the Attorney General that the Boston plan was "appropriate" and "within the principles" of the recently adjudicated Bakke case. See letter from Joseph S. Vera, Director, HUD Regional Office of Fair Housing and Equal Opportunity, to Francis X. Bellotti, Massachusetts Attorney General, February 14, 1979. In later years, the SBIC encouraged white South Boston residents who were on BHA waiting lists to register their names with the Information Center, so as to chart BHA resistance to housing South Boston families in South Boston projects; John Ciccone, "South Boston Information Center," *South Boston Tribune*, October 18, 1984.

155. "Unit Mix at West Broadway," memo from Gayle Epp, Design Specialist, to Mike Jacobs, Redevelopment Director, December 12, 1980.

156. "Demand for Smaller Units at West Broadway," memo from Gayle Epp, Design Specialist to Mike Jacobs, Redevelopment Director, April 6, 1981.

157. Interview with Don Gillis, D Street Community Organizer, and WBTF Executive Director, March 1994.

158. Interview with Michael Jacobs, February 1994; interview with Don Gillis, March 1994.

159. Interview with Don Gillis, March 1994.

160. "Phase 3 Recommendations," memo from Helen Young, WBTF President, to Michael Jacobs, Redevelopment Director, September 28, 1981.

161. "Phase 3 Recommendations," memo from Helen Young, WBTF President, to Michael Jacobs, Redevelopment Director, September 28, 1981; "WBTF Recommendations on the Phase 3 Report West Broadway Comprehensive Renewal Program," memo from Helen Young, WBTF President, to Boston Housing Authority, September 28, 1981; "West Broadway: Revised Recommendations," memo from Michael Jacobs, Redevelopment Director, to West Broadway Team, West Broadway Task

Force, Executive Office of Communities and Development, October 14, 1981; "West Broadway Task Force Holds Annual Meeting," *South Boston Tribune,* October 29, 1981, pp. 1, 7; "WBTF Recommendations on Schematic Design (Phase V) Submission," memo from Helen Young, WBTF President, to Michael Jacobs, BHA Redevelopment Director, January 14, 1982; "West Broadway Comprehensive Program Renewal: Design Development Approval," memo from Mike Jacobs, Redevelopment Director, to West Broadway Team, April 29, 1982; Andrea Blaugrund, "The Renaissance of a Housing Project: D Street and Its People," unpublished senior honors essay, Harvard College, March 1984, pp. 94–97.

162. Interview with Michael Jacobs, BHA Redevelopment Director, February 1994.

163. Interviews with West Broadway residents, 1993.

164. This figure comes from a 1984 survey of sixty-three non-elderly adult residents. See YCF Associates, *West Broadway Public Housing Development: A Survey of Tenant Needs,* Report Prepared for the Boston Housing Authority Planning and Redevelopment Department, December 1984, p. 87.

165. Interview with Michael Jacobs, BHA Redevelopment Director, February 1994.

166. "Recommendations on the Report on Phase 3: Design Options, West Broadway Comprehensive Renewal Program," memo from Mike Jacobs, Redevelopment Director, to West Broadway Task Force and Executive Office of Communities and Development, September 11, 1981.

167. Interview with Donna Hunt, Architect, Lane, Frenchman and Associates, Inc., April 1993.

168. Lane, Frenchman and Associates, Inc., and Goody, Clancy and Associates, Inc., *West Broadway Comprehensive Renewal Program: Report on Phases 1 and 2,* May 27, 1981.

169. Michael Jacobs, quoted in Elizabeth March, "Money Makes It Easier: Turning around Large Troubled Housing Projects" (unpublished MCP Thesis, MIT, 1983), pp. 30–31.

170. Interview with Gordon King, March 1986.

171. Gayle Epp, Seminar Presentation, Harvard Graduate School of Design, April 1986.

172. Interview with Dennis Frenchman, October 1986.

173. Pamela Goodman, Seminar Presentation, Harvard Graduate School of Design, April 1986.

174. These interviews are discussed in greater detail in Lawrence J. Vale, "Transforming Public Housing: The Social and Physical Redevelopment of Boston's West Broadway Development," *Journal of Architectural and Planning Research,* 12 (3), Autumn 1995, pp. 278–305, from which some of the following discussion is drawn. Interviews, undertaken in English, Spanish, Vietnamese, and Chinese, were conducted

in 1993, and included approximately 10 percent of households living at West Broadway at that time. While not a random sample, those interviewed would seem to be highly representative of the adult development population as a whole, in terms of race, ethnicity, age, sex of household head, length of residence, location of residence within the development, and degree of participation in tenant-association activities.

175. John Ciccone, "South Boston Information Center," *South Boston Tribune,* April 10, 1986; April 24, 1986; Jim Kelly, cited in Ric Kahn, "Turf's Up in Southie: Preparing to Fight 'Forced Housing,'" *Boston Phoenix,* May 20, 1986, pp. 1ff.

176. Alex Rodriguez, cited in Kahn, "Turf's Up in Southie," pp. 12-13.

177. "City Council Public Hearing: Tenants Come, B.H.A. Stays Away," *South Boston Tribune,* September 21, 1978, p. 9; "'H.U.D. Policies A Failure'—Flynn," *South Boston Tribune,* November 30, 1978, pp. 1-2.

178. O'Connor, *South Boston,* p. 242.

179. Ibid., pp. 243-245; Peter S. Canellos, "Legacy of Racial, Neighborhood Progress," *Boston Globe,* March 18, 1993.

180. Interview with Barbara Mellan, WBTF President, June 1992.

181. Interview with Sister Margaret Lanen, Integration Coordinator, July 1992.

182. Interviews with residents, 1993.

183. Ibid.; Kahn, "Turf's Up in Southie," p. 8.

184. Interview with Sally McAward, West Broadway Development Manager, February 1993.

185. Interview with Sally McAward, February 1993.

186. Indira A. R. Lakshmanan, "Blacks, Whites Arrested at Same Rate in S. Boston," *Boston Globe,* October 30, 1994, pp. 1, 20.

187. Kevin Cullen, "Police Stats Show Crime Decrease in S. Boston," *Boston Globe,* May 12, 1993, pp. 1, 6.

188. Dean K. Wong, "4 Arraigned in Fight at S. Boston Project," *Boston Globe,* June 30, 1993, p. 23.

189. Interview with Sister Louise Kearns, Director, Julie's Family Learning Center, November 1993.

190. Cited in Kevin Cullen, "South Boston Labors to Come to Terms with Crime in the 90s," *Boston Globe,* May 24, 1993, p. 17.

191. Charles A. Radin, "BHA's Eviction Statistics Rebut Critics," *Boston Globe,* January 27, 1998, pp. B1, B8; BHA statistics, 2000; Ric Kahn, "Suspect Charged in Racial Attack at South Boston Project," *Boston Globe,* February 21, 1997, p. B2; Geeta Anand, "Alarmed Tenants Appeal for Help," *Boston Globe,* February 25, 1997; Mike Barnicle, "About Racism at Old Colony," *Boston Globe,* May 3, 1994, p. B1; Zachary Dowdy and Ric Kahn, "Youth Pleads Not Guilty in Stabbings," *Boston Globe,* Janu-

ary 3, 1996; Stephanie McLaughlin, "South Boston Woman's Windows Vandalized," *Boston Globe,* February 17, 1995, p. 28; Irene Sege, "Two Women of Southie," *Boston Globe,* September 22, 1994, pp. 57, 60; BHA statistics for Family Developments, March 2000. BHA figures do not identify the race of "Hispanic" residents.

192. BHA tenant demographics, special printout, October 25, 2000; "Suicide Prevention in Southie," Editorial, *Boston Globe,* August 9, 1997; Mike Barnicle, "Heroin Menaces South Boston," *Boston Globe,* February 13, 1997; Barnicle, "Dateline: South Boston," *Boston Globe,* March 27, 1997; Brian MacQuarrie, "Legal Aide Faults BHA Handling of Racial Case," *Boston Globe,* June 3, 1997; J. M. Lawrence, "Down and Out on D Street," *Boston Herald,* March 23, 1997; Brian McQuarrie, "On the Silver Screen, Southie Sees Itself," *Boston Globe,* December 27, 1997, pp. A1, A6; MacDonald, *All Souls,* p. 260.

193. Interviews with South Boston businesspeople, June–August 2000. As one white resident put it to the black interviewer George Samuels, "No offense, but you wouldn't be able to interview me right now if this was still the 1980s. There was some serious racial tension here." "U.S. Report Praises Turnaround in Boston Housing Authority," *Chicago Tribune,* November 24, 2000.

194. "Southie: When Buying or Renting in One of Boston's Hottest Neighborhoods, Know the Rules," *Boston Sunday Globe,* August 10, 1997, pp. F1, F7; Stephanie Ebbert and Steven Wilmsen, "Waterfront Meeting to Test Old Southie," *Boston Globe,* June 13, 2000, pp. B1, B6.

195. Stephen Kurkjian and Stephanie Ebbert, "$65m Deal for South Boston," *Boston Globe,* May 24, 2000, pp. A1, A26.

196. Kurkjian and Ebbert, "$65m Deal for South Boston," pp. A1, A26; "The South Boston Betterment Trust," *Boston Globe,* June 8, 2000, p. B8; Stephanie Ebbert and Stephen Kurkjian, "Kelly Willing to Reopen Pact on Fees," *Boston Globe,* May 26, 2000, pp. A1, A23; Stephanie Ebbert and Stephen Kurkjian, "South Boston Leaders Resist Reworked Deal," *Boston Globe,* May 31, 2000, pp. A1, A14; Stephanie Ebbert and Stephen Kurkjian, "Mayor Says Trust Can't Deal on Own," *Boston Globe,* June 2, 2000, pp. A1, B4; Stephanie Ebbert, "Kelly Blasts Councilors over Linkage," *Boston Globe,* June 15, 2000, pp. A1, B7; "A Better Trust for South Boston," Editorial, *Boston Globe,* June 2, 2000; "Residents Outraged . . . Community Meeting Planned," Advertisement, *South Boston Tribune,* June 1, 2000; "Kelly's Tirade: A Blast at Minority Development," *Boston Globe,* pp. B1, B7; Stephanie Ebbert, "Menino Settles Linkage Lawsuit: S. Boston Deal Called 'Bad Idea,'" *Boston Globe,* November 17, 2000, pp. B1, B11.

197. "Southie: When Buying or Renting in One of Boston's Hottest Neighborhoods, Know the Rules," pp. F1, F7; Stephanie Ebbert and Steven Wilmsen, "Waterfront

Meeting to Test Old Southie," *Boston Globe,* June 13, 2000, pp. B1, B6; "More Housing for South Boston," Editorial, *Boston Globe,* April 30, 2000; "A Look at South Boston," *Boston Globe,* June 13, 2000, p. B6.

198. MacDonald, *All Souls,* p. 256.

199. Interviews conducted June–August 2000.

200. Bonz/REA, *West Broadway Development: Market Study and Feasibility Analysis,* prepared for the Boston Housing Authority, February 1998, pp. 1, 6, 69, 75, 78; interview with Sandra Henriquez, January 2000. The $1,760 figure is in 1998 dollars.

201. Interviews conducted June–August 2000.

202. Thomas Grillo, "Affordable Housing Advocates Demand More," *Boston Globe,* March 11, 2000; interviews with Nancy Ludwig, ICON architecture; Hank Keating, BHA; Jim Edwards, Holmes and Edwards; and Barbara Mellan, West Broadway Task Force, October 2000; BHA, "West Broadway—Sources and Uses," draft income mix, November 6, 2000.

203. Interviews with Sandra Henriquez, August 1998, January 2000.

204. Interviews conducted June–August 2000.

205. MacDonald, *All Souls,* p. 257.

3. Franklin Field

1. Cynthia Zaitzevsky, *Frederick Law Olmsted and the Boston Park System* (Cambridge, Mass.: Harvard University Press, 1982), p. 78; Geoffrey Blodgett, "Frederick Law Olmsted: Landscape Architecture as Conservative Reform," *Journal of American History,* 62 (4), March 1976, p. 886; letter from George Clarke, Boston Park Commission Secretary, to Frederick Law Olmsted, n.d. [1892], Olmsted Archives Project 917, Library of Congress; Job 917 Plans and Drawings, Olmsted Archives, Brookline, Mass.

2. Sanborn insurance maps for Dorchester, 1888, 1899, 1908, 1931.

3. Sam Bass Warner, Jr., *Streetcar Suburbs: The Process of Growth in Boston, 1870–1900* (Cambridge, Mass.: Harvard University Press, 1962), p. 158.

4. Gerald Gamm, *Urban Exodus: Why the Jews Left Boston and the Catholics Stayed* (Cambridge, Mass.: Harvard University Press, 1999), pp. 70, 77, 79.

5. Ibid., pp. 11, 196; Wallace Stegner, "Who Persecutes Boston?" *Atlantic Monthly* (July 1944), p. 45.

6. Gamm, *Urban Exodus,* pp. 184–221.

7. Ibid., pp. 187, 213–215, 229–237.

8. Hillel Levine and Lawrence Harmon, *The Death of an American Jewish Community: A Tragedy of Good Intentions* (New York: Free Press, 1992), pp. 65, 71.

9. Gamm, *Urban Exodus,* pp. 27, 30, 37, 186, 199.

10. Ibid., p. 19.

11. Ibid., pp. 21, 207–208, 221.

12. "Mayor Curley Rushing Temporary Housing Programs for G.I. Families," *Dorchester Beacon,* August 16, 1949, p. 1.

13. U.S. Census, 1950, housing—block statistics.

14. Despite Ansel's evident clout in these early years of public housing for veterans, in retrospect it is easy to see that Ward 14's power was soon to dissipate. In 1949, an amendment to the city charter shifted the Boston City Council from twenty-two ward-based representatives to a nine-member council elected at-large. No longer guaranteed a seat to represent Ward 14, Ansel "switched his sights to state office." For a district seeking to gain state-funded public housing, having Ansel in the Massachusetts legislature was quite opportune. At the same time, however, the city charter revision and Ansel's exit from the council signaled a distinct political loss for Ward 14. When Ansel, as the area's principal political force, died of a heart attack in 1965, his part of Dorchester never regained its earlier political clout; Levine and Harmon, *The Death of an American Jewish Community,* pp. 23, 103.

15. Massachusetts State Housing Board, "Application for Financial Assistance, Franklin Field Development, Dorchester," March 27, 1950, pp. 5–6, Commonwealth of Massachusetts, State Housing Board archives, folder 200-11.

16. "Permanent Housing Project on Franklin Field," and "Franklin Field Housing Development," Proceedings of the Boston City Council, *Boston City Record,* March 6, 1950, p. 244; June 4, 1951, p. 639; Boston City Council order, August 27, 1951.

17. Frank R. Kelley, Chairman, Boston Park Department, letter to James J. Mahar, Chairman, Boston Housing Authority, December 7, 1951, box 13, BHA, Massachusetts State Archives.

18. William C. Geary, Chairman, Massachusetts State Housing Board, letter to Boston Housing Authority, June 26, 1951; miscellaneous correspondence, box 13, BHA Project Files, Massachusetts State Archives.

19. Boston City Directory and Police Lists, 1955.

20. Interview with John Murphy, BHA Director of Occupancy, November 1995.

21. "Franklin Field, Dorchester, Boston 200–11, Application for Financial Assistance," April 5, 1950, Massachusetts State Archives; U.S. Census, 1950; Owen A. Gallagher, letter to Daniel Tyler, Chairman, Massachusetts State Board of Housing, November 24, 1953. As the project neared completion, the BHA revised the rent schedule to anticipate an average gross rent of $59.10 per unit, but this included a utility charge of approximately $14 a month; Harland A. McPhetres, Director of Management, Massachusetts State Housing Board, letter to Owen A. Gallagher, December 22, 1953, box 13, BHA, Massachusetts State Archives.

22. Boston Police Lists, 1955; U.S. Census, 1950.

23. Interview with Sergeant Tony Fonseca, December 1999. Since 1977, Fonseca has been a police officer serving his childhood neighborhood.

24. Albert L. O'Neil, Corrective Maintenance, Massachusetts State Housing Board, letter to Owen Gallagher, BHA Chairman, July 7, 1959; "Ruling Sought on Leaks at Housing Project," *Boston Herald,* May 16, 1959; "Seepage Studied at Housing Project," *Christian Science Monitor,* May 18, 1959; miscellaneous correspondence and records, box 13, BHA Project Files, Massachusetts State Archives.

25. Letter from Edward D. Hassan, BHA Chairman, to City of Boston, Administrative Complaints Division, November 1, 1960.

26. "Proposed Repairs to Exterior Building Walls, Project 200-11, Franklin Field," letter from Edward Hassan, BHA Chairman, to Leo F. Benoit, Chairman, State Housing Board, September 8, 1961, BHA Project Files, Massachusetts State Archives; Albert J. Palmer, letter to Norma Wales, Fair Housing, Inc., June 22, 1967; miscellaneous repair requests, 1960-1964, boxes 13-14, BHA Project Files, Massachusetts State Archives.

27. Interview with Tony Fonseca, February 2000.

28. BHA Tenant Status Review, figures for Franklin Field, 1956-1958; Boston City Directories and Police Lists; U.S. Census, 1960.

29. State Housing Board, "It's Spring Cleaning Week," April 23, 1958; "Housing Project Managers Make Appeals to Tenants," *Roxbury Gazette and South End Advertiser,* July 17, 1958, p. 1; *Dorchester Beacon,* July 17, 1958, pp. 1, 4.

30. "Request for Chain Link Fencing at Franklin Field, Boston 200-11," letter from F. A. Cronin, Chairman, BHA, to State Housing Board," June 16, 1958.

31. Interview with John Murphy, December 1995; "More Housing for Elderly Slated at Franklin Field," *Jewish Advocate,* August 2, 1962; letter from Melnea Cass to John F. Collins, February 26, 1962, JFC papers, box 120; interview with Ellis Ash, May 1997; "Franklin Field Elderly Project Wins Attention," *Boston City Record,* March 14, 1964, p. 212; [Confidential] memo to Mayor, with copies to Ellis Ash and BHA Board from Robert Drinan and the Advisory Committee on Minority Housing, March 5, 1964; JFC papers, box 244; letter from James Crowley to Mrs. Alfonso Russo, August 18, 1964.

32. Mark Mirsky, "The G & G on Blue Hill Ave.," *Boston Sunday Globe,* March 7, 1971, p. A-3.

33. Levine and Harmon, *The Death of an American Jewish Community,* p. 20.

34. Staff, minutes of meeting, Boston YMHA–Hecht House, January 15, 1960, box 23, Hecht Neighborhood House Papers, American Jewish Historical Society; quoted in Gamm, *Urban Exodus,* p. 247.

35. Levine and Harmon, *The Death of an American Jewish Community*, pp. 24–25.

36. Mirsky, "The G & G on Blue Hill Ave.," pp. A-3, A-8.

37. Stegner, "Who Persecutes Boston," pp. 45–46.

38. Gamm, *Urban Exodus*, p. 274.

39. U.S. Census data, cited in Boston Redevelopment Authority, *Franklin Field: District Profile and Proposed 1978–1980 Neighborhood Improvement Program*, Summer 1977, p. 4; Gamm, *Urban Exodus*, pp. 37, 39.

40. Gamm, *Urban Exodus*, pp. 241, 255, 353–354, note 38. Gamm's calculations of Jewish population numbers seem to have been more carefully derived than those estimated by other sources.

41. Quoted in Gamm, *Urban Exodus*, pp. 255, 257.

42. Gerald H. Gamm, "Facts vs. Myth about Boston's Jewish Exodus," *Jewish Advocate*, May 1–7, 1992, p. 9; interview with Ruth Botts, December 1999; interview with Wilhelmina Hardy, October 1999.

43. Kevin White, press release, May 13, 1968, p. 1.

44. "Competition in Real Estate and Mortgage Lending—Part 1," Hearings before the Subcommittee on Antitrust and Monopoly of the Committee on the Judiciary, U.S. Senate, 92nd Congress, Second Session," September 13, 14, and 17, 1971, p. 12. An estimated 10–15 percent of BBURG sales went to whites, although many of these may have been to nonresident speculators.

45. Joseph H. Bacheller, Jr., "Memorandum to All Members of the Boston Banks Urban Renewal Group," summary of meeting held on November 17, 1968, November 27, 1968.

46. Boston Banks Urban Renewal Group, "Want to Own Your Own Home?" (Boston: BBURG, n.d.).

47. Susan Blanche Soutner, "The Boston Banks Urban Renewal Group Homeownership Program: A Study of Racial Discrimination in an Urban Housing Market," unpublished paper, Department of City and Regional Planning, Harvard University, November 1980, p. 32.

48. The Civil Rights Act of 1968 defined blockbusting as "for profit, to induce or attempt to induce any person to sell or rent any dwelling by representations regarding the entry or prospective entry into the neighborhood of a person or persons of a particular race, color, religion, or national origin." While Levine and Harmon stress the centrality of blockbusting in Jewish areas, Gamm argues that blockbusters operated in non-Jewish areas as well; his key point is that they were more successful in Jewish neighborhoods than in Catholic ones because the Jewish areas "were especially vulnerable to such tactics"; Gamm, *Urban Exodus*, pp. 41–42; Soutner, "The Boston Banks Urban Renewal Group Homeownership Program," pp. 11–12;

Thomas Oliphant and Janet Riddell, "FBI Probing FHA Official's Hub Dealings," and "A Closer Look at the Issue of Speculators," *Boston Globe,* June 3, 1971, pp. 1, 18, 44; "Judge Assesses Appraiser $348,511 in Conflict Case," *Boston Globe,* April 8, 1980. The most egregious abuses of the BBURG program were curtailed after the Association for Better Housing (ABH) took over the processing of BBURG loans in 1969, but the homebuyers continued to receive inadequate counseling; Anthony J. Yudis, "Unique Group Helps Guide Blacks to Home Ownership," *Boston Globe,* May 23, 1971; interview with Rachel Bratt, March 1996.

49. Rachel G. Bratt, *A Home Ownership Survey,* a report on the Boston Banks Urban Renewal Group, prepared for the Boston Model City Administration, January 1972, pp. 35–38.

50. "B-BURG: Red Lines and Blue Lines," *CPS* no. 3, October 1971, p. 8; Hearings, pp. 8–9. See also Ken Hartnett, "How Men in Power Let Mattapan Area Be Victimized: Crisis in Mattapan—1," *Boston Globe,* April 4, 1972, pp. 1, 16.

51. Hearings, pp. 257, 263. Maps, however, had been prepared as early as July 1968, depicting BBURG as encompassing "the Boston Urban Renewal areas and certain areas adjacent thereto"; Joseph Bacheller ("Joe. B"), letter to Hale Champion, Administrator, Boston Redevelopment Authority, July 2, 1968, reprinted in Hearings, pp. 446–447.

52. Hearings, pp. 255, 265.

53. Quoted in "Boston Banks Back Ghetto Housing" (n.d., early 1969), reprinted in Hearings, pp. 563–564.

54. Soutner, "The Boston Banks Urban Renewal Group Homeownership Program," pp. 14–15, 56, note 50.

55. Levine and Harmon, *The Death of an American Jewish Community,* p. 297; Martin Healy, Philip E. Murray, Jr., and Thomas F. Murray, "You Can Trust the Bankers (to Be Bankers)," unpublished paper, Boston College, May 1972, pp. 22–24.

56. Soutner, "The Boston Banks Urban Renewal Group Homeownership Program," p. 33.

57. Hearings, pp. 284–285.

58. Lawrence Harmon and Hillel Levine, "A Response to Gerald Gamm," *Jewish Advocate,* April 10–16, 1992, p. 11.

59. Levine and Harmon, *The Death of an American Jewish Community,* p. 213.

60. Hillel Levine and Lawrence Harmon, "Profits and Prophets: Overcoming Civil Rights in Boston," *Tikkun* 3 (July/August 1988), pp. 45–48, quoted in Gamm, *Boston Exodus,* p. 42; Levine and Harmon, *The Death of an American Jewish Community,* p. 176.

61. Gamm, *Boston Exodus,* pp. 43–50; Gerald H. Gamm, "Exploding Myths Sur-

rounding Exodus of Boston Jewry," *Jewish Advocate,* March 27–April 2, 1992, p. 11. This article prompted a scathing but largely unconvincing reply by Harmon and Levine, as well as Gamm's own retort; Lawrence Harmon and Hillel Levine, "A Response to Gerald Gamm," *Jewish Advocate,* April 10–16, 1992, p. 11; Gamm, "Facts vs. Myth," p. 9. Gamm's arguments about pre-1968 problems are supported by testimony in the Senate Hearings, pp. 45, 72–73, 92, 99.

62. The list of addresses for BBURG-financed purchases, used in creating Fig. 3.12, was found in the files of Professor Rachel Bratt, and used with her permission. At the time of the Senate Hearings in 1971, Frederick Paulsen (Assistant Administrator, Boston Model City Agency) was asked to produce a map showing the pattern of the BBURG purchases. His response: "We did have at one time a map that was prepared, and I cannot locate it"; Hearings, pp. 147, 155.

63. Levine and Harmon, *The Death of an American Jewish Community,* p. 179.

64. Gamm, *Urban Exodus,* pp. 51, 53.

65. Advisory Committee on Minority Housing, Minutes of Meeting, November 15, 1965, BHA Administrative Files; BHA occupancy data; 1970 Voter Registration Lists.

66. Gerald Taube, "A Family Album: The Many Faces of Public Housing," unpublished manuscript, 1969, pp. 136–142.

67. Ibid., pp. 136–142.

68. Letter (with petition) from Mrs. Carrie Philbrick to John F. Collins, March 1966, JFC Papers, box 62; Robert J. Sales, "Prime Complaint of Elderly Citizens at Housing Projects: No Policemen," *Boston Globe,* November 21, 1969, p. 3; Chris Wallace, "They Live in Fear at Franklin Field," *Boston Globe,* November 21, 1969, p. 3.

69. Robert L. Hassett, "City Housing Project Crime Soars: Tenants Live in Terror," *Boston Herald Traveler,* December 14, 1970, pp. 1, 3; Ryan, quoted in Wallace, "They Live in Fear at Franklin Field," p. 3; security screens, discussed in Boston Housing Authority, "State of the Development Report 1979: Franklin Field, 200–11," September 21, 1979.

70. SLED Protective Inc., memo to BHA Director of Security, November 5, 1970; BHA Central Housing Project Files, box 14, Massachusetts State Archives.

71. Quoted in Hassett, "City Housing Project Crime Soars," p. 3.

72. Interview with John Murphy, November 1995.

73. Leo J. Donovan, memorandum to Daniel J. Finn, BHA Administrator, "Emergency Requisition for Dead-Bolt Locks at Franklin Field," November 17, 1970; Daniel Finn, BHA Administrator, letter to Joseph C. Kelly, General Manager, MBTA, November 18, 1970; J. C. Kelly, letter to Daniel Finn, December 4, 1970; J. C. Kelly, letter to Thomas Francis, BHA, December 28, 1970; Stephen Morse, Jewish Commu-

nity Council of Metropolitan Boston, letter to Mr. Guy Rosmarin, Special Assistant to the Governor for Urban Affairs, February 26, 1971; box 14, BHA Project Files.

74. Serlin, quoted in Leo Shapiro, "Terror, Despair Grip Aged Mattapan Jews," *Boston Globe,* November 25, 1969; Edward Serlin, "Calls for Community Help for Boston Jews," Letter to the Editor, *Jewish Advocate,* July 10, 1969, p. 2.

75. Hassett, "City Housing Project Crime Soars," p. 3.

76. Gamm, *Urban Exodus,* pp. 272–273.

77. Levine and Harmon, *The Death of an American Jewish Community,* p. 217.

78. Ronald P. Formisano, *Boston against Busing: Race, Class, and Ethnicity in the 1960s and 1970s* (Chapel Hill: University of North Carolina Press, 1991), pp. 49–52.

79. "Kudos for Our Community"; "Think of the Children"; "A Gross Exaggeration," editorials, *Bay State Banner,* September 19, 1974, p. 4; September 11, 1975, p. 4; February 5, 1976, p. 4.

80. Hearings, p. 56.

81. Levine and Harmon, *The Death of an American Jewish Community,* pp. 18–19.

82. See Ibid., pp. 228–245, 267–269; "Attack [on] Mattapan Rabbi in Home," *Jewish Advocate,* July 8, 1969, pp. 1, 11, 15.

83. Gamm, *Urban Exodus,* p. 39; *Boston Globe,* May 28, 1970.

84. Levine and Harmon, *The Death of an American Jewish Community,* pp. 316–317.

85. Danice Bordett, "Mattapan Tension Grows: Patrol Organized," and "Mattapan" [Editorial], *Bay State Banner,* December 4, 1969, pp. 1, 4, 8.

86. "Mattapan Survey," quoted in Gamm, *Urban Exodus,* p. 274; Ken Hartnett, "An Uneasy Peace of Mind Prevails . . . Synagogue, Churches, Reflect Change: Crisis in Mattapan—4," *Boston Globe,* April 6, 1972, p. 37.

87. "Madness in Mattapan," Editorial, *Bay State Banner,* July 26, 1973, p. 4; interview with Mort Kane, December 1999.

88. Boston Redevelopment Authority, *The Boston Plan* (August 1977), p. I-2.

89. Hearings, p. 84.

90. Quoted in Levine and Harmon, *The Death of an American Jewish Community,* p. 316.

91. Stephen Curwood, "Mattapan Residents File Zoning Petition," *Bay State Banner,* September 7, 1972, p. 1; Boston Redevelopment Authority, "Blue Hill Avenue—Mattapan Square: Problems and Potentials," Discussion Paper (April 1972), pp. 1–4.

92. BRA, *Franklin Field: District Profile and Proposed 1978–1980 Neighborhood Improvement Program,* p. 18.

93. Levine and Harmon, *The Death of an American Jewish Community,* p. 332; David Rogers, "Foreclosures: Banks Hold the Cards," *Boston Globe,* September 2, 1974, pp. 15–17.

94. Levine and Harmon, *The Death of an American Jewish Community,* p. 276;

Soutner, "The Boston Banks Urban Renewal Group Homeownership Program," p. 30; Hearings, pp. 298, 445, 608–644.

95. Soutner, "The Boston Banks Urban Renewal Group Homeownership Program," p. 31.

96. Boston Redevelopment Authority, *Franklin Field: District Profile and Proposed 1979–1981 Neighborhood Improvement Program* (Boston: BRA Neighborhood Planning Program, 1979), pp. 4–7, 21.

97. Anne Whiston Spirn has documented the relationship between buried floodplains, subsidence, and subsequent housing abandonment in several cities, including Boston, though this issue has yet to be comprehensively examined.

98. Boston City Directory statistics, cited in Owiso Makuku, "Extending the Physical and Cultural Boundaries of Affordable Housing," master's thesis, MIT, 1999, p. 61; BRA, *Franklin Field: District Profile,* pp. 8–9, 12–13, 22; City of Boston, "Neighborhood Revitalization Strategy, Franklin Field Neighborhood Strategy Area," 1980–1981 CDBG application, pp. 102–106; Yona Ginsberg, *Jews in a Changing Neighborhood: The Study of Mattapan* (New York: Free Press, 1975), p. 38.

99. Boston Housing Authority, "Scope of Consultant Services for Pilot Program: Franklin Field (200–11)," November 7, 1978; Boston Housing Authority, "State of the Development Report," 1975, BHA Master's Files.

100. Nieda Spigner, "Franklin Field Tenants Complain," *Bay State Banner,* December 5, 1974, pp. 1, 22.

101. Bradley Biggs, BHA Administrator, letter to Lawrence DiCara, Boston City Council, June 2, 1978.

102. Boston Redevelopment Authority, *Franklin Field: Background Information, Planning Issues, and Preliminary Neighborhood Improvement Strategies* (Boston: BRA District Planning Program, June 1975, draft.

103. Boston Housing Authority, "State of the Development Report," 1975; BHA Master's Files.

104. Marion Cunningham, "The Allocation of Maintenance Resources," memo to Wanda Henton-Calhoun, BHA Director of Civil Rights, April 1982; BHA Receiver's Files.

105. Boston Housing Authority, "State of the Development Report 1979: Franklin Field, 200–11," September 21, 1979.

106. "Vacancies at Franklin Field," memo from Rupert Garvin, Housing Manager, to Paul D. Merrill, BHA Assistant Administrator, October 14, 1977, Master's Files.

107. Boston Housing Authority, "Scope of Consultant Services for Pilot Program: Franklin Field (200–11)," November 7, 1978; Finance Committee report, November 1975; Louise Elving, memo to Bob Whittlesey, December 30, 1975, BHA Master's Files.

108. Charles Moseby, Senior Engineer, memo to Rupert Garvin, Manager, "Roof Leaks, Franklin Field, Boston 200-11," February 9, 1979; Charles Moseby, Senior Engineer, memo to Rupert Garvin, Manager, "Roof Inspection at 200-11, 667-1, and 667-2, Franklin Field Development," December 28, 1979, BHA Central Project Files.

109. Gladys Sanders, Franklin Field Task Force Chairperson, letter to John Murphy, BHA Tenant Transfer Department, October 1977, BHA Master's Files.

110. Interviews conducted in 1993 with a 10 percent sample of Franklin Field's household heads; interview with Ruth Botts, December 1999; Janie Gibbs, "Proud Franklin Field Resident," Letter to the Editor, *Bay State Banner*, July 20, 1989.

111. Tenant interviews, 1993.

112. Carr, Lynch Associates Inc., and Wallace, Floyd, Associates Inc., *Franklin Field Redevelopment: Design Report, Final Development Plan and Program,* prepared for the Boston Housing Authority with the Franklin Field Tenants and Task Force, February 22, 1982, pp. 5–8.

113. Michael Fields, "T Starts Rolling Again for Franklin Field Rte.," *Bay State Banner,* February 1, 1979, pp. 1, 12.

114. Carr, Lynch, and Wallace, Floyd, *Franklin Field Redevelopment,* pp. 5–8.

115. BRA, *Franklin Field: District Profile and Proposed 1979–1981 Neighborhood Improvement Program,* p. 17.

116. Carr, Lynch, and Wallace, Floyd, *Franklin Field Redevelopment;* interview with Sandra Henriquez, January 2000.

117. Boston Housing Authority, "Occupancy Analysis by Development Classification," January 31, 1979, BHA Receiver's Files; interview with Sandra Henriquez, January 2000.

118. Gershon M. Ratner and Bruce Mohl, letter to Governor Michael Dukakis, June 8, 1978, pp. 2–4; interview with Harry Spence, September 1995; interview with Bernie Stewart, March 1996.

119. Interview with Doris Bunte, December 1995.

120. Interview with Harry Spence, September 1995.

121. Ibid.; Boston Housing Authority Planning Department, "Site Selection Criteria for Substantial Rehabilitation," December 1979; interview with Bernie Stewart, March 1996.

122. BHA-DCA correspondence, January 1978, BHA Central Project Files, box 14; interview with Basil Tommy, February 1994.

123. Interviews with Harry Spence, September 1995; Bernie Stewart, March 1996.

124. Interview with Harry Spence, September 1995; Spence quoted in Elizabeth March, "Money Makes It Easier: Turning Around Large Troubled Housing Projects," unpublished Master in City Planning thesis, MIT, 1983, p. 14.

125. Quoted in March, "Money Makes It Easier," p. 30.

126. Interview with Leslie Newman, October 2000.

127. "General Obligation—Federally Assisted Housing Bond Debt Service Fund" (Chapter 490, Section 10 of the Acts of 1980); "Semi-Annual Evaluation, Boston 200-11, Franklin Field Pilot Program, January 1–June 30, 1980," BHA Central Project Files, box 14; Harry Spence, letter to Amy Anthony, Secretary of EOCD, "RE: Franklin Field Financing: Potential Uses for Residual Funds," January 1983.

128. Interview with Sandra Henriquez, August 1998.

129. Wasserman Associates, Inc., *Security in Public Housing*, report prepared for the BHA, December 1980, pp. 191–192.

130. Interview with Tony Fonseca, December 1999.

131. Stephen Carr and David D. Wallace, letter to Basil Tommy, with accompanying proposal for services, December 19, 1980.

132. Interview with Basil Tommy, February 1994; interview with Gayle Epp, April 1994.

133. Carr, Lynch, Associates, Inc., and Wallace, Floyd, Ellenzweig, Moore, Inc., "Franklin Field Family Housing Development," June 16, 1981; CLA-WFEM, "Franklin Field Draft Redevelopment Plan and Program," September 27, 1981; Basil Tommy, "Review of Franklin Field Draft Redevelopment Plan and Program," memo to Dave Wallace and Steve Carr, October 9, 1981; Barbara Manford, "Redevelopment Cost Comparisons," memo to Basil Tommy, October 21, 1981; CLA-WFEM, "Revised Design Concept Alternatives for the Substantial Rehabilitation of Franklin Field Housing," November 10, 1981.

134. Imani Kazana, letter to Franklin Field residents and "Resident Fact Sheet," June 15, 1981.

135. John Stainton, Assistant Administrator, letter to Byron Matthews, Secretary, EOCD, July 22, 1981; Basil Tommy, letter to Peggy Santos, August 24, 1981.

136. Interview with Basil Tommy, February 1994.

137. Ibid.

138. Basil Tommy, "Unit Mix Considerations for Franklin Field," September 17, 1981.

139. Interview with Basil Tommy, February 1994; Carr, Lynch, and Wallace, Floyd, *Franklin Field Redevelopment*, p. 5; interview with John Murphy, December 1995.

140. Imani Kazana and CLA-WFEM team, "Franklin Field Plan Review Meeting," memo to Basil Tommy, November 27, 1981.

141. Stephen Carr and David Wallace, "Franklin Field Priorities," memo to Basil Tommy, John Stainton, Harry Spence, et al., December 7, 1981; Basil Tommy, "Proposed Franklin Field Redevelopment Program," memo to Franklin Field Program Review Group, December 7, 1981.

142. Peggy Santos, letter to Lewis H. Spence, January 28, 1982.

143. Sharon Lee, John Sharratt Associates, "Minutes of Committee Meeting, February 4, 1982," February 9, 1982.

144. Peggy Santos, letter to Lewis H. Spence, February 22, 1982.

145. Interview with Basil Tommy, February 1994.

146. John Stainton, BHA Assistant Administrator for Planning and Development, letter to Peggy Santos, Franklin Field Task Force Chairperson, March 3, 1982.

147. Carr, Lynch, and Wallace, Floyd, *Franklin Field Redevelopment,* pp. 1–83.

148. Ibid., pp. 12, 78–79.

149. Interview with Basil Tommy, February 1994; interview with David Dance, April 1994; interview with Michael Jacobs, February 1994.

150. Interview with Basil Tommy, February 1994.

151. Interviews with David C. Gilmore, February 1994; Leslie Newman, October 2000; Sandra Henriquez, August 1998.

152. Interview with David C. Gilmore, February 1994.

153. Rod Solomon, BHA Legal Department, "Franklin Field Relocation Documents," April 2, 1982; "BHA-FFTF Franklin Field Rent Abatement Agreement," April 29, 1982; interview with David C. Gilmore, February 1994.

154. *Franklin Field Redevelopment Program Newsletter* #2 (June 1982), pp. 1–4.

155. David C. Gilmore, Redevelopment Director, "Contract with Joseph Lee School for Services to Residents of Franklin Field," memo to Rod Solomon, BHA Special Counsel, August 6, 1982.

156. Interviews with Basil Tommy, February 1994; Leslie Newman, October 2000; and David Dance, April 1994.

157. Interview with David Dance, April 1994.

158. Kenneth J. Cooper, "Politicians, Bureaucrats, Media Flock to 'New' Franklin Field," *Boston Globe,* January 5, 1984, p. 26.

159. Franklin Field Corporation, *Franklin Field: Our People, Our Park, Our Festival,* 1984, pp. 1, 25.

160. Interviews Basil Tommy, February 1994; Harry Spence, September 1995; David Dance, April 1994; and Leslie Newman, October 2000.

161. Interview with Doris Bunte, December 1995.

162. Chris Lovett, "Tenants Dissatisfied with Rehab Progress at Franklin Field Units," *Dorchester Argus-Citizen,* November 21, 1985, pp. 1, 3.

163. "WGBH-TV (PBS) Ten O'clock News Transcript," November 3, 1986; Mark Pickering, "Agreement Reached over Franklin Field Rehab; Contractor Returns to Job," *Dorchester Community News,* February 24, 1987.

164. Pickering, "Agreement Reached over Franklin Field Rehab"; interview with David Dance, April 1994.

165. Interview with David Dance, April 1994; "Redevelopment Activity—Franklin Field," *BHA Management Report,* December 31, 1986, p. Q7-4.

166. Interview with Mary Green, July 1992; interview with Thelma Smith, July 1992.

167. Interview with Thelma Smith, July 1992; interview with David Dance, April 1994.

168. Interview with Mary Green, July 1992; interview with David Dance, April 1994; interview with Harry Spence, September 1995.

169. L. Kim Tan, "Drug Bust Suspects Tied to Local Rings," *Boston Herald,* February 27, 1989.

170. Mike Barnicle, "Blotting Out 'Crack Spills,'" *Boston Globe,* April 9, 1989.

171. L. Kim Tan, "One Dead, One Injured in Separate Stabbings," *Boston Herald,* May 26, 1989.

172. Janie Gibbs, "Proud Franklin Field Resident," and "Finest Hour" photo, *Bay State Banner,* July 20, 1989.

173. Sharon Epperson, "Roxbury Club Gives Youths Alternative to Streets," *Boston Globe,* October 2, 1989; Michele Douglas, "A Welcome Alternative: Boys and Girls Club Gives Hub Kids Direction," *Boston Herald,* November 4, 1989.

174. John Ellement, "$10 Debt Led to Fatal Stabbing, Franklin Field Residents Say," *Boston Globe,* November 10, 1989.

175. Doris Sue Wong, "Youth, 17, Pleads Guilty in Killing, Rape of Harbour," *Boston Globe,* June 19, 1992; Peter Gelzinis, "Miles from Franklin Field, the Pain and Suffering Never Leaves," *Boston Herald,* July 7, 1992; Joe Heaney, "Crime Fighter Defends Housing Projects," *Boston Herald,* November 26, 1990.

176. Gelzinis, "Miles from Franklin Field," July 7, 1992.

177. Steve Marantz, "Franklin Field Youth Facility Is Announced," *Boston Globe,* April 9, 1991.

178. Judy Rakowsky, "Dorchester Man Charged in Theft of Bags of Mail," *Boston Globe,* September 1, 1992; "Two Men Shot in Dorchester," *Boston Globe,* September 25, 1992.

179. Cheong Chow, "Roxbury [sic] Boy, 13, Slain by Gunmen," *Boston Globe,* October 18, 1992; Lynda Gorov, "A Call to Grieve, Not Avenge," *Boston Globe,* October 19, 1992; Maurice C. Bernstein and L. Kim Tan, "Psychologists Aid Students Mourning Slain Classmate," *Boston Herald,* October 20, 1992; John Ellement and Efrain Hernandez, Jr., "Shooting Victim Has No Answers: Says He Doesn't Know Why He, Slain 13-Year-Old Were Fired On," *Boston Globe,* October 20, 1992; Mike Barnicle, "A Little Suit for Poochie," *Boston Globe,* October 20, 1992; Lynda Gorov, "'Poochie' Buried with Tears and Vows," *Boston Globe,* October 22, 1992; Ralph Ranalli, "Family, Friends Lay Teen to Rest," *Boston Herald,* October 22, 1992.

180. John Ellement, "Slain Woman 'Wanted to Grow Up So Fast,'" *Boston Globe,* January 12, 1993.

181. Jordana Hart, "Woman: Cabbie Left Me Stranded," *Boston Globe,* January 8, 1993.

182. Quoted in Howard Manly, "Fear a Fact of Life in Neighborhoods," *Boston Globe,* October 10, 1993, pp. 33, 35.

183. Quoted in Ibid.

184. Beverly Ford, "Ex-Boyfriend Held in Slaying: Pregnant Woman Worked for Peace," *Boston Herald,* June 9, 1994, p. 5; Indira A. R. Lakshmanan, "'Caregiver' Gang Peace Employee Slain; Boyfriend Charged," *Boston Globe,* June 9, 1994, p. 35; Indira A. R. Lakshmanan, "Police Vow to Step Up Security after 2nd Killing at Development," *Boston Globe,* June 10, 1994; Beverly Ford, "Police Seek 3 in City's Latest Fatal Shooting," *Boston Herald,* June 10, 1994; Leonard Greene, "Killings Make Young Mother Think Twice about Moving In," *Boston Herald,* June 10, 1994, p. 4.

185. Interviews with Franklin Field residents, 1993; interview with Ruth Botts, December 1999.

186. Interview with Thelma Smith, July 1992.

187. Interview with Mary Green, July 1992.

188. Ric Kahn, "After Killing in His Home, He's Hailed, Prosecuted," *Boston Globe,* date??, pp. 1, 36.

189. Peter S. Canellos, "Street Soldiers' Peaceful Call to Arms," *Boston Globe,* December 16, 1997; interview with Tony Fonseca, November 1999; interview with Allen Platt, November 1999; interview with City Councilor Charles Yancey, November 1999; "Keeping Peace in Franklin Field," Editorial, *Boston Globe,* January 15, 1998; Judy Rakowsky, "Millions in Aid Failing to Reach Franklin Field," *Boston Globe,* January 2, 1998.

190. BHA, special tenant demographics printout, October 2000; Makuku, "Extending the Physical and Cultural Boundaries," p. 70.

191. Interview with Sandra Henriquez, August 1998.

192. John Ellement and Farah Stockman, "Police Eye 'Hot Spots' as Killing Toll Rises," *Boston Globe,* August 18, 2000, pp. B1, B7; Francie Latour, "Cluster Crime," *Boston Globe,* August 27, 2000; interviews with Franklin Field neighborhood businesspeople, October-December 1999.

193. Interview with Bobby Boone, November 1999.

194. Another David Gilmore (not "David C."), who also then worked at the BHA, went on to a distinguished career as a public housing administrator.

195. Interview with Basil Tommy, February 1994.

196. Interview with Doris Bunte, December 1995.

197. Interview with Harry Spence, September 1995.

4. Commonwealth

1. Katie Kenneally, *Brighton,* Boston 200 Neighborhood History Series (Boston: Boston 200 Corporation, 1975), pp. 7–13; William P. Marchione, *The Bull in the Garden: A History of Allston-Brighton* (Boston: Boston Public Library, 1986), pp. 50–55, 64, 69, 73–79.

2. Marchione, *The Bull in the Garden,* pp. 80, 83–89; Olmsted Job no. 944, Olmsted archives (Brookline); Olmsted correspondence files for Job no. 944, National Archives.

3. Marchione, *The Bull in the Garden,* pp. 83, 89.

4. Ibid., pp. 100, 107–109, 124.

5. Ibid., pp. 97–98, 112.

6. Ibid., p. 88; "Voice Opposition to Brighton Apartments," *The Item—Brighton Allston,* November 30, 1935; City of Boston, Annual Report of the City Planning Board for 1946 (1947), cited in Marchione, *The Bull in the Garden,* p. 120.

7. "City to Build $3,000,000 Housing Project in Brighton," *Allston Citizen,* December 11, 1947; "State Board Okays 648 Homes for Vets in Brighton Project," *Brighton Citizen,* August 12, 1948.

8. Boston Housing Authority, "Application for Financial Assistance: Brighton Development No. 1, Washington Street and Commonwealth Avenue," submitted to the Massachusetts State Housing Board, June 1, 1948; BHA Project Files, box 12, folder 200–3.

9. A second Brighton project, known as Faneuil, also moved forward expeditiously. In Brighton's Aberdeen neighborhood, however, public housing construction was stymied. Here, only a half mile away from Commonwealth, residents objected to the BHA's efforts to site the district's third veterans' project. "Panic-stricken" residents of this middle-class neighborhood near affluent Chestnut Hill protested against the project through the Aberdeen Civic and Improvement Association. They charged that the area had inadequate school and recreational facilities to support additional children yet resisted in vain as the city changed the zoning to permit the project. Amid charges that some members of the Zoning Board of Adjustment held a conflict of interest (owing to ongoing business with the BHA), however, Superior Court Judge Vincent Brogna sided with the Aberdeen Association and nullified the rezoning, thereby barring construction; "Commonwealth Contract Awarded—Citizens Protest Aberdeen Project," *Brighton Citizen,* May 11, 1950; "Aberdeen Association Described as 'Infant' Group," *Brighton Citizen,* May 18, 1950; "Mayor Vetoes Council Order as Aberdeen Group Goes to Court," *Brighton Citizen,* June 8, 1950; "Superior Court Nullifies Rezoning: Action Bars Construction of Project," *Brighton Citizen,* June 29, 1950; letter from John Capobiance to John Hynes, May 20, 1950; interview with William Marchione, March 2000.

10. "Priest Raps Housing Board: Charges Politicians Select Brighton Project Tenants," *Boston Globe,* January 4, 1951, pp. 1, 20; "Shanley Ignites Inquiry into Use of 'Influence' for Housing Rentals," *Brighton Citizen,* May 3, 1951; Boston Police Lists, 1952, using previous addresses supplied by a 10 percent random sample of the original Commonwealth households.

11. Letter from Elwood S. McKenney, MCAD Commissioner, to Mayor John B. Hynes, reprinted in *Boston City Record,* May 26, 1951, pp. 533, 535; Isabel Currier, "Presentation to the Honorable John B. Hynes, Mayor of Boston by the Joint Delegation of Public Housing Sponsored by the National Association for the Advancement of Colored People," May 17, 1951; letter from Elwood S. McKenney to John Hynes, August 3, 1951; U.S. Census, 1950.

12. Boston Police Lists, 1952.

13. Letter from Clarence Giddings, Secretary of Hahnemann Hospital, to Hon. John B. Hynes, October 17, 1952; letter from Mayor John B. Hynes to James J. Mahar, Chairman, BHA, October 20, 1952; letter from James J. Mahar, Chairman, to Hon. John B. Hynes, October 23, 1952; BHA Central Project Files, box 12.

14. Letter from Michael J. Ward, Councilor, to James J. Mahar, Chairman, BHA, January 5, 1953; letter from James J. Mahar to Hon. Michael J. Ward, January 21, 1953; BHA Central Project Files, box 12.

15. Letter from Leo Sullivan, 13 Fidelis Way, to Mayor John B. Hynes, September 19, 1955; letter from James J. Mahar, Chairman, to Hon. John B. Hynes regarding the letter from Leo Sullivan of September 19, October 18, 1955.

16. Letter from Owen Gallagher, BHA Chairman, to Mayor John B. Hynes, February 5, 1954.

17. Letter from Peter J. Cloherty, Massachusetts Democratic State Committee, to Timothy O'Connor, Chairman, City of Boston Traffic Commission, March 7, 1958; BHA Project Files; "Lack of Play Area Blamed in Truck Death of Boy, 6," *Boston American,* September 5, 1958.

18. John F. Collins papers, box 315; see also Lawrence Vale, *From the Puritans to the Projects* (Cambridge, Mass.: Harvard University Press, 2000), pp. 291–294.

19. Letter from John J. Kelliher, Assistant Director of Management, to Stephen Bowen, Housing Manager, Commonwealth combination, regarding "Meeting at Commonwealth Development Friday, December 15, 1967 RE Absenteeism—Housing Manager," December 20, 1967; BHA Central Project Files, box 12.

20. Letter from Ruth Weiner to John Collins, September 17, 1964 (JFC papers, box 234); letter from Robert E. York, Building Commissioner, to BHA, regarding safety violations in 9 Fidelis Way, June 11, 1965; letter from Leo J. Donovan, Director of Management, to Michael Donahue, Service Coordinator, Mayor's Neighborhood Service Center, Allston-Brighton Little City Hall, November 5, 1969; correspondence between the Department of Public Health and the BHA, 1971; memo from Herman Hemingway, BHA Deputy Administrator, to Thomas Francis, Intergroup Relations Officer, "Complaints of Harassment," November 9, 1970.

21. Letter from Edward Hassan, BHA Chairman, to Rep. Arnold Epstein, October 28, 1964; BHA Project Files; letter from Ruth Weiner to John Collins, September 17,

1964 (JFC papers, box 234); letter from Jacob Brier, BHA Chairman, to Joseph F. McLaughlin, June 1, 1966; letter from Julius Bernstein, BHA Chairman, to Honorable John E. Kerrigan, January 16, 1970; BHA Project Files, box 12.

22. Letter from Edward Hassan, BHA Chairman, to Richard Sinnott, Mayor's Press Secretary, December 21, 1962; letter from Edward Hassan to John F. Collins, March 12, 1964 (JFC papers, box 244); letter from Edward Hassan to Oliver Ames, October 9, 1964.

23. Letter from James H. Crowley to Donald Fortune, August 6, 1964; JFC papers, box 62.

24. Letter from Herman Hemingway, BHA Deputy Administrator, to Mr. Reid, July 17, 1970; BHA Central Project Files, box 12.

25. Letter from Parker Converse, President of the Board of Trustees of Hahnemann Hospital, to Edward Hassan, BHA Chairman, May 11, 1962; letter from Parker Converse to Edward L. McNamara, Boston Police Commissioner, May 2, 1962; BHA Central Project Files, box 12; interview with long-time neighborhood resident Marvin Levinson, May 2000.

26. Letter from Albert J. Palmer, BHA Director of Management, to Milo O. Blade, M.D., U.S. Public Health Service Hospital, March 28, 1967; BHA Central Project Files, box 12.

27. Letter from Rolland B. Handley, Regional Director, Bureau of Outdoor Recreation, U.S. Department of the Interior, to Mayor Kevin H. White, March 31, 1972; letter from Francis Cedrone, Vice Chairman of Commonwealth Development Task Force, to Cornelius Connons, BHA Administrator, April 5, 1972; memo from Paul Liston, BHA General Counsel, to Cornelius J. Connors, BHA Administrator, regarding "Proposed Playground—Project Boston 200-3 (Monastery)," April 13, 1972.

28. Letter from Ruth Weiner to John Collins, September 17, 1964; JFC Papers, box 234.

29. Quoted in Edward Hassan, BHA Chairman, letter to Richard J. Sinnott, July 24, 1964; BHA Project Files.

30. Letter from Ellis Ash, Acting BHA Administrator, to George E. Berkley, Chairman, Finance Commission of Boston, May 24, 1965; BHA Central Project Files.

31. Letter from Albert J. Palmer to Joseph F. McLaughlin, January 17, 1968.

32. Memorandum from Stephen Bowen to Leo Donovan, September 17, 1969; BHA Central Project Files, box 12.

33. Letter from Gertrude Weiner to Rep. Norman Weinberg, May 28, 1968; BHA Central Project Files, box 12.

34. Letter from Gertrude Weiner, Boston Legal Assistance Project, to Jacob Brier, BHA Chairman, May 28, 1968; memo from Leo Donovan, BHA Director of Management,

to Leo Gulinello, Security Officer, December 3, 1971; BHA Project Files; memo from J. F. Jennette, Chief of Maintenance Engineering, to C. J. Connors, BHA Administrator, regarding 200-3 Commonwealth-Modernization Work, January 6, 1973; memo from Herman Hemingway, BHA Acting Administrator, to Leo Donovan, Director of Management, February 19, 1971; BHA Project Files; letter from Paul F. Creighton, Jr., Acting Director, Allston-Brighton APAC, to Cornelius Connors, BHA Administrator, March 29, 1973; letter from Norman Weinberg to Cornelius Connors, BHA, April 3, 1973; BHA Central Administrative Files.

35. Gerald Taube, "A Family Album: The Many Faces of Public Housing," unpublished study, 1969.

36. Master's Report, A-IX-1, pp. 11-13, 20; Louise Elving, interview with Tom Finch, February 1976 (BHA Master's Files); Boston Housing Authority, *State of the Development Report, 1975;* interview with Abraham Halbfinger, May 2000; Boston Voter Registration List, 1970, which states the previous known address for all fifty-six households that moved into Commonwealth that year.

37. Master's Report, A-IX-1, pp. 11-13; Boston Housing Authority, *State of the Development Report, 1975;* interview with Abraham Halbfinger, May 2000.

38. Interview with Robert Whittlesey, April 1996.

39. Master's Report, B-VII, p. 45.

40. Master's Report, B-VII, pp. 47-48; notes from meeting with Commonwealth Tenants, October 26, 1976; Master's Files.

41. Letter from Commonwealth Development Task Force and Fidelis Way Youth Committee to Cornelius Connors, March 29, 1973; letter from Samuel Thompson, BHA Administrator, to BHA Board, March 20, 1975; BHA Central Administrative Files; Boston Urban Observatory, "Boston Public Housing Security Program—An Assessment/Evaluation," February 1977, pp. 58-59.

42. Notes from meeting with Commonwealth Tenants, October 26, 1976 (Master's Files); Master's Report, B-VII, pp. 47-49, 64.

43. Master's Report, B-VII, p. 62; "Vandalism Report," memo from Thomas J. Finch, Housing Manager, Commonwealth, to Edward Meehan, Operations Officer, BHA, October 14, 1975.

44. Louise Elving, interview with Charles Foley, December 4, 1975 (BHA Master's Files); Tom Finch, at meeting with Commonwealth tenants, August 13, 1976; Master's Files.

45. Master's Report, A-IX-1, pp. 21-22; B-VII, pp. 49, 64; memo on vacancies, November 1976; Master's Files.

46. Master's Report, B-VII, p. 53.

47. Letter from Norman Weinberg to Samuel Thompson, BHA Administrator, June 1,

1976; BHA Master's Files; meeting with Commonwealth tenants, August 13, 1976; Master's Files.

48. "Vandalism Report," memo from Thomas J. Finch, Housing Manager, Commonwealth, to Edward Meehan, Operations Officer, BHA, October 14, 1975; meeting with Commonwealth tenants, August 13, 1976; Master's Files; Louise Elving, interview with Tom Finch, February 1976; Master's Files.

49. Notes on meeting with Commonwealth tenants and service providers; Master's Files, March 30, 1976.

50. Notes from meeting with Brighton civic and religious leaders, April 6, 1976; Master's Files; Master's Report, B-VII, p. 63. The disconnect between Commonwealth residents and local service providers was confirmed by a survey: Community Planning and Research, Inc., *The Commonwealth Report: Proposals for Capital Improvements, Management Reorganization and Expansion of Resident Services and Opportunities,* 1979.

51. Notes on meeting of Commonwealth parties and Samuel Thompson, December 22, 1976; Master's Files; Master's Report, B-VII, p. 64.

52. Boston Urban Observatory, "Boston Public Housing Security Program—An Assessment/Evaluation," February 1977, pp. 60–64.

53. Letter from William Margolin to Robert Whittlesey, March 21, 1979; BHA Master's Files; memo entitled "Fidelis Way Working Conditions," July 3, 1978 (Master's Files); letter from Ann T. Muenster to Paul Garrity, July 17, 1978 (Master's Files); Jane Holtz Kay, "Pride Replaces Despair at Fidelis Way: Architects and Attitudes Produce a Public Housing Showpiece," *Boston Globe,* January 26, 1986; Mike Barnicle, "First Snow Ushers in Season of Misery for City's Poor," *Boston Globe* (n.d., December 1978?).

54. "Fidelis Needs Aid," Editorial, *Allston-Brighton Citizen-Item,* January 18, 1979.

55. Paul Garrity, "Findings of the Massachusetts Superior Court, with Memorandum of Recorded Observations at the Commonwealth Development during the View on April 11, 1979," *Perez* Case, July 25, 1979, p. 102.

56. Letter from Howard S. Wensley, Director, Division of Community Sanitation, Massachusetts Department of Public Health, to Pam Goodman, Redevelopment Director, BHA, May 27, 1981; Garrity quoted in Kay, "Pride Replaces Despair."

57. Interviews with long-term tenants, 1993; interview with Rosetta Robinson, January 1991; letter from Doris Balware to Harry Spence, BHA Administrator, July 7, 1980; BHA Central Files.

58. Letter from Norman S. Weinberg to Bradley Biggs, BHA, August 15, 1978; BHA Central Administrative Files.

59. Letter from David DeLuca, Probation Officer, to Allen Hight, BHA District Direc-

tor, April 4, 1979; letter from Paula Bielski et al. to Edward Kennedy, May 15, 1979; letter from Kevin P. Feeley to Richard Bielski, June 21, 1979; BHA Central Administrative Files.

60. Walsh and Associates, *Refinancing and Marketing the Fidelis Way Housing Project,* 1979, p. 11.

61. Allston-Brighton Medical Care Coalition, "The Commonwealth Health Improvement Program," Application to the Special Hospital Project Grants Program of the United Way of Massachusetts Bay, February 1, 1978; Commonwealth Tenants Association and Commonwealth Health Improvement Project, "Commonwealth Employment Project," a Proposal by the CTA and CHIP, June 5, 1980, pp. 2-3.

62. Interview with Don Rapp, February 1994.

63. Ibid.; Wasserman Associates, Inc., *Security in Public Housing: A Report for the BHA,* December 1980, pp. 185-186.

64. Interview with Don Rapp, February 1994; interview with Pam Goodman, February 1994.

65. Boston Housing Authority Planning Department, "Site Selection Criteria for Substantial Rehabilitation," December 1979.

66. Ibid.

67. Interview with Bernie Stewart, March 1996.

68. Community Planning and Research, Inc., *The Commonwealth Report;* Walsh and Associates, *Refinancing and Marketing the Fidelis Way Housing Project.*

69. The CPR Study was named for the consulting firm that produced it, though the additional connotation of cardio-pulmonary resuscitation certainly seems apposite.

70. Walsh and Associates, *Refinancing and Marketing the Fidelis Way Housing Project,* pp. 5, 25; Jayne Seebold, "Task Force Focus: Fidelis," *Allston-Brighton Citizen-Item,* November 29, 1979.

71. Boston Housing Authority, *Commonwealth Developers Kit,* 1981, p. 1.

72. Walsh and Associates, *Refinancing and Marketing the Fidelis Way Housing Project,* pp. 6, 25, 40.

73. Ibid., p. 68.

74. Interview with Don Rapp, February 1994; interview with David Trietsch, March 1994.

75. Interview with Don Rapp, February 1994; interview with David Trietsch, March 1994; interview with Bart McDonough, January 1991.

76. Wallace, Floyd, Ellenzweig, Moore, Inc., *Recommendations of the Monastery Hill Task Force,* prepared for the Boston Redevelopment Authority, October 1979; Steve Trinward, "Analysis: Task Force Begins to Pull Together," *Allston-Brighton Citizen-Item,* September 27, 1979.

77. Wallace, Floyd, Ellenzweig, Moore, Inc., *Recommendations of the Monastery Hill Task Force;* Boston Housing Authority, *Commonwealth Developers Kit;* Seebold, "Task Force Focus: Fidelis."

78. Interview with Don Rapp, February 1994.

79. Karg quoted in Seebold, "Task Force Focus: Fidelis"; Jayne Seebold, "Task Force Works to Bring Rehab Money to Fidelis," *Allston-Brighton Citizen-Item,* December 28, 1979; Jayne Seebold, "A New Future for Fidelis Way?" *Allston-Brighton Citizen-Item,* November 15, 1979; Jayne Seebold, "Fidelis Way Group Takes Control," *Allston-Brighton Citizen-Item,* March 27, 1980; interview with Don Rapp, February 1994.

80. Jayne Seebold, "BHA Receiver Spence Raises Hopes at Fidelis Way," *Allston-Brighton Citizen-Item,* March 3, 1980; Jayne Seebold, "Analysis: Fidelis Worked Hard to Earn Funds," *Allston-Brighton Citizen-Item,* June 12, 1980; interview with Harry Spence, September 1995. The violence in and around Boston public housing was not limited to South Boston and Dorchester. In mid-1980 Brighton's Faneuil development "exploded" following racially motivated attacks and a shooting. Spence feared that "we were going to lose every black family" in the development.

81. National Commission on Severely Distressed Public Housing, *Case Studies and Site Examination Reports,* "Chapter 4—Commonwealth Development" (Washington, D.C.: GPO, December 1992), pp. 4–36; Lewis H. Spence, "Letter to Marvin Sifflinger, Area Manager, Boston Area Office, US Department of Housing and Urban Development," August 4, 1980.

82. *Fidelis Way Speaks . . . /Fidelis Way Hablas . . . ,* various issues, July 1980–March 1982.

83. Personal communication from Donald Rapp, September 1994.

84. Boston Housing Authority, *Commonwealth Developers Kit.*

85. Boston Housing Authority, "Commonwealth Development: Developer Selection Results," December 10, 1981.

86. Commonwealth Tenants Association, "Tenant Evaluation of Developer's Proposals," memo to Pamela Goodman and the Fidelis Way Redevelopment Selection Committee, October 21, 1981. A thorough and independent real-time account of this selection process, completed as a Master's thesis in 1982, confirms that at the time the process was thought highly successful by all participating groups; Marion Olive Cunningham, "The Evaluation of the Rehabilitation Designs for Fidelis Way" (Master's thesis, Department of Urban Studies and Planning, Massachusetts Institute of Technology, 1982).

87. Teresa M. Hanafin, "Fidelis Way: Private Managers Give New Life to Public Project," *Boston Globe,* January 7, 1989.

88. Ann Malaspina, "Fidelis Way 'Family' Dreams of New Home: Groundbreaking Launches $30m Reconstruction Project," *Allston-Brighton Citizen-Item,* September 16, 1982.

89. Interview with Harry Spence, September 1995; interview with Don Rapp, February 1994; Commonwealth Tenants Association Management Committee, "Memo to Robert Pickette et al., John M. Corcoran Company and Sandy Henriquez et al., BHA on 'Preliminary Management Recommendations for Fidelis Way,'" October 7, 1981; interview with David Trietsch, February 1994.

90. Boston Housing Authority, "Commonwealth: RFP for Private Management Services," April 16, 1982; interview with Don Rapp, February 1994.

91. Commonwealth Tenants Association, Boston Housing Authority, and Corcoran Management Company, *Commonwealth Management Plan: Memorandum of Understanding,* 1983; interviews with forty-one Commonwealth tenants, conducted in 1993.

92. Interview with Don Rapp, February 1994; interview with Bob Pickette, May 1994.

93. National Commission on Severely Distressed Public Housing, *Case Studies and Site Examination Reports,* pp. 4–24; CTA and BHA, "BHA-CTA Commonwealth Rent Abatement Agreement," September 11, 1981; personal communication with Donald Rapp, September 1994; interview with Bob Pickette, May 1994; O'Connor quoted in Christopher Keneally, "Fidelis Way: A New Chapter Begins," *Allston-Brighton Citizen-Item,* February 22, 1985.

94. Boston Housing Authority, "Motion for Approval of Tenant Selection Plan for Commonwealth Development," July 8, 1983, as approved by Judge Paul Garrity, Massachusetts Superior Court, July 21, 1983; O'Connor quoted in Keneally, "Fidelis Way: A New Chapter Begins."

95. BHA, "Motion for Approval of Tenant Selection Plan for Commonwealth Development"; see also Vale, *From the Puritans to the Projects,* pp. 362–365.

96. "Rebuilt Housing Project Dedicated," *Boston Herald,* June 2, 1985.

97. Interview with Bob Pickette, May 1994; interview with John M. Corcoran, Sr., April 1994; interview with Doris Bunte, December 1995.

98. Boston Housing Authority, "Commonwealth Development Achieves 100% Occupancy," press release, December 11, 1986; Keneally, "Fidelis Way: A New Chapter Begins"; Kay, "Pride Replaces Despair at Fidelis Way"; Margaret Burns, "A Model of Success: Integration Works at Fidelis Way," *Allston-Brighton Citizen-Item,* January 29, 1988; Bola Zeitlin, "Dorchester Woman Manages Public Housing Development," *Bay State Banner,* August 7, 1985.

99. The two surveys, conducted in 1979 by Community Planning and Research, Inc., and in 1993 by a team under my own supervision, asked several questions that were

phrased and coded identically, and they seem to be remarkably comparable samples. Both are stratified by race, ethnicity, and sex and accurately reflected the breakdown of those living at the development at the time; both used adult respondents with a broad range of ages and length of residency in the development. The 1979 sample contained eighty respondents, representing about 30 percent of the households then living on site, whereas the 1993 sample contained forty-one respondents, composing about 11 percent of households.

100. Esther Shein, "Fidelis Way Residents, Tenant Group Work to Dispel Post-Homicide Fears," *Allston-Brighton Citizen-Item,* July 25, 1986.

101. Jim MacLaughlin, "Fire Leaves Family out on Street," *Boston Herald,* December 1, 1986; Jane Braverman, "Taking It to the Streets," *Allston-Brighton Citizen-Item,* April 20, 1989; interviews with Commonwealth tenants, 1993.

102. Interview with Kevin Young, May 1994. Despite Commonwealth's notable record of racial and ethnic integration, the development did significantly shift toward non-white occupancy once the development-based waiting list ended in 1988 (see Fig. 5.2).

103. Interviews with Commonwealth tenants, 1993.

104. Interview with John Murphy, November 1995.

105. Jane Braverman, "Tenant Group Loses Funds," *Allston-Brighton Citizen-Item,* June 15, 1989; National Commission on Severely Distressed Public Housing, *Case Studies and Site Examination Reports,* Chapter 4; Ric Kahn, "Brighton Tenants Fear the Bad Old Days," *Boston Globe,* October 10, 1993.

106. Adrian Walker, "Elderly Tenant Threatened with Eviction over $7," *Boston Globe,* May 4, 1995, pp. 29–30; Michele R. McPhee, "Brighton Breakdown Worries Residents," *Boston Globe;* interview with Beatrice Todd, April 2000.

107. Interview with Sandra Henriquez, August 1998.

108. Interview with Bob Pickette, May 1994; McGonagle quoted in Kahn, "Brighton Tenants Fear."

109. Interview with Sandra Henriquez, January 2000; meetings of the Commonwealth Tenants Association, June–July 2000; Corcoran Management Company, *Proposal for Property Management Services for Commonwealth Development and 91–95 Washington Street,* April 12, 2001, section C; Commonwealth Tenants Association, Boston Housing Authority, and Corcoran Management Company, "Memorandum of Understanding," February 11, 2002.

110. Interviews with local businesspeople, April–June 2000.

111. Interview with John Corcoran, April 1994; interview with Don Rapp, February 1994; interviews with various persons connected with the Commonwealth redevelopment effort.

112. Interviews with long-term Commonwealth residents, 1993; BHA, "Family Developments," March 2000.

113. BHA, "Commonwealth Tenant Demographics," October 25, 2000; Geeta Anand, "In Switch, Colleges Asked to Build Dorms," *Boston Sunday Globe,* February 25, 1996, pp. 27, 30.

114. Boston Housing Authority data, special printout showing dates of original leases, November 1998; interview with Harry Spence, September 1995.

115. Corcoran, quoted in Hanafin, "Fidelis Way: Private Managers Give New Life to Public Project"; Jim Reed, Commonwealth Site Manager, presentation to delegation from HUD's Urban Revitalization Demonstration Design Conference, December 1993.

5. Reclaiming Housing, Recovering Communities

1. For each project, the neighboring wards are defined as the two nearest to it, which, taken together, formed a well-understood district; namely, South Boston (Wards 6 and 7), Allston-Brighton (Wards 21 and 22), and Dorchester (Wards 14 and 17).

2. The subsequent addresses of a 10 percent sample from each initial tenant cohort [n = 217] were traced using Boston City Directories and Police Lists with data from their first full year of occupancy—1950 for West Broadway, 1952 for Commonwealth, and 1954 for Franklin Field. It was possible to find specific subsequent addresses for only 53 percent of these households. Since the directories and police lists appear to be remarkably complete, there would seem to be two chief reasons for "losing" some members of the cohort: either they moved beyond the jurisdiction of the directories (that is, they left Boston) or they died (which would presumably affect relatively few persons, given their relative youth). Thus, it seems worth speculating that those whose addresses could not be traced were disproportionately more likely to have moved on to the Boston suburbs or out of the area. This is consistent with the presumed greater economic mobility of these earliest public housing tenants.

3. These figures are drawn from the Boston Police List for a 10 percent sample of households taken from the first full year of project occupancy [n = 217] and from voter registration list data for all new households entering each project in 1970 [n = 399].

4. This section on types of success is an updated and expanded version of the account that previously appeared as "Public Housing Redevelopment: Seven Kinds of Success," *Housing Policy Debate* 7, 3 (1996), and in David Varady, Wolfgang F. E. Preiser, and Francis P. Russell, eds., *New Directions in Urban Public Housing* (New Brunswick, N.J.: Center for Urban Policy Research Press, 1998), pp. 142–178.

5. Boston Housing Authority, *Site Selection Criteria for Substantial Rehabilitation,*

BHA Planning Department, December 1979; Ronald Jones et al., *Problems Affecting Low Rent Public Housing Projects: A Field Study* (Washington, D.C.: U.S. HUD, 1979).

6. The BHA's own point system for assessing these data weighted the categories unevenly, allocating 38 percent of available points to Physical Design scores, 25 percent to Neighborhood Characteristics, 25 percent to Site Accessibility, and 12 percent to Tenant Characteristics. It is worth noting that this weighting worked in favor of Franklin Field (given its relatively high physical-design scores and its relatively low "tenant-characteristics" score), but even under this weighting Franklin Field ranked last, and Commonwealth ranked at the top.

7. BHA, *Site Selection Criteria for Substantial Rehabilitation.*

8. Interview with Sandra Henriquez, January 2000.

9. Interview with David Trietsch, March 1994.

10. Although it is possible that Commonwealth residents felt less stigmatized by their surroundings even before redevelopment, it must be remembered that the physical conditions at Commonwealth at its nadir were arguably even worse that those prevailing at the other places. Thus it seems logical to credit the redevelopment effort with fostering improvement in resident perceptions about the environment, especially given the amplifications and explanations offered by residents during the interviews.

11. Interview with David C. Gilmore, February 1994; interview with Robert Whittlesey, April 1996.

12. Interview with Harry Spence, September 1995; interview with Doris Bunte, December 1995.

13. These figures come from interviews with a 10 percent sample of household heads conducted at each development in 1993. More recent interviews and site observations confirm that the basic differences in management and maintenance performance seem to have persisted.

14. Interview with Pamela Goodman, February 1994; interview with Kevin Young, May 1994; interview with Sandra Henriquez, August 1998.

15. The principal socioeconomic policy initiative of the Boston redevelopment efforts took a different form: the desegregation of public housing in South Boston.

16. BHA Tenant Demographics, October 2000. It is worth noting that all three of these employment figures signal dramatic increases from pre-redevelopment conditions. In 1979, the BHA counted exceedingly few working adults: 14 percent at Commonwealth, 12 percent at West Broadway, and only 3 percent at Franklin Field; BHA, *Site Selection Criteria for Substantial Rehabilitation.*

17. Leonard S. Rubinowitz and James E. Rosenbaum, *Crossing the Class and Color*

Lines: From Public Housing to White Suburbia (Chicago: University of Chicago Press, 2000), pp. 161–172.

18. This level of dissatisfaction is far higher than that reported even at the two non-re-developed places where interviews were also conducted (Orchard Park and Bromley-Heath).

19. Interview with Harry Spence, September 1995.

20. Interview with Leslie Newman, October 2000.

21. Interview with Harry Spence, September 1995.

22. Fronnie Watkins, at a Franklin Field tenant meeting, November 17, 1992.

23. See, for example, Stephen Mulhall and Adam Swift, *Liberals and Communitarians* (Oxford: Blackwell, 1992); Amitai Etzioni, *The Spirit of Community: Rights, Responsibilities, and the Communitarian Agenda* (New York: Crown, 1993).

24. See Jane Roessner, *A Decent Place to Live: From Columbia Point to Harbor Point, a Community History* (Boston: Northeastern University Press, 2000).

25. Quality Housing and Work Responsibility Act (QHWRA) of 1998 (H.R. 4194), sec. 513; Stephanie Ebbert, "Housing Bill Offers New Options for Middle Class," *Boston Globe,* October 12, 1998, pp. B1, B4.

26. See Lewis H. Spence, "Rethinking the Social Role of Public Housing," *Housing Policy Debate* 4, no. 3 (1993), pp. 355–368.

27. National Association of Housing and Redevelopment Officials (NAHRO), *The Many Faces of Public Housing* (Washington, D.C.: NAHRO, 1990); Michael H. Schill, "Distressed Public Housing: Where Do We Go from Here?" *University of Chicago Law Review,* 60 (1993), p. 546; Ben Joravsky, "Don't Sweep on Me: Unheard Voices of the CHA," *The Illinois Brief: A Publication of the American Civil Liberties Union,* 51, 2 (Summer 1994).

28. Schill, "Distressed Public Housing," pp. 517, 544; "'One Strike and You're Out': U.S. Seeks to Banish Felons from Public Housing," *CNN Interactive,* March 28, 1996; QHWRA of 1998 (H.R. 4194), secs. 506, 524, 575–578.

29. Interview with Harry Spence, September 1995.

30. Boston Housing Authority, "Public Hearing for Amendments to the FY 2000 Agency Plan and Other Policy Review and Comment," held at Boston City Hall, September 18, 2000.

Note on Literature and Methods

1. Jane Jacobs, *The Death and Life of Great American Cities* (New York: Vintage, 1961); Lee Rainwater, *Behind Ghetto Walls: Black Families in a Federal Slum* (Chicago: Aldine, 1970); Clare Cooper, *Easter Hill Village: Some Social Implications of Design* (New York: Free Press, 1975). Cooper's multimethod approach of analysis—

involving use of a well-crafted questionnaire in addition to informal interviews (including some with children, whose drawings of the project are included), combined with systematic observation of the built environment and of the behaviors that take place within it—still seems a wonderful model of research design.

2. Serge Chermayeff and Christopher Alexander, *Community and Privacy* (Garden City, N.Y.: Anchor Books, 1965 [1963]), p. 37.

3. Oscar Newman, *Defensible Space* (New York: Macmillan, 1972).

4. Oscar Newman, *Community of Interest* (Garden City, N.Y.: Anchor Press–Doubleday, 1980), pp. 7–8.

5. There are a wide variety of book-length policy histories of public housing that do not focus on particular housing developments or cities. These include Lawrence Friedman, *Government and Slum Housing* (Chicago: Rand McNally, 1968); Leonard Freedman, *Public Housing: The Politics of Poverty* (New York: Holt, Rinehart and Winston, 1969); M. B. Schnapper, ed., *Public Housing in America* (New York: H. W. Wilson, 1939); Harry C. Bredemeier, *The Federal Public Housing Movement* (New York: Arno Press, 1950); Robert Fisher, *Twenty Years of Public Housing* (New York: Harper and Brothers, 1959); Timothy L. McDonnell, *The Wagner Housing Act: A Case Study of the Legislative Process* (Chicago: Loyola University Press, 1957); Nathaniel S. Keith, *Politics and the Housing Crisis since 1930* (New York: Universe Books, 1973); Frank de Leeuw, *Operating Costs in Public Housing: A Financial Crisis* (Washington, D.C.: The Urban Institute, 1970); Tom Forrester Lord, *Decent Housing: A Promise to Keep* (Cambridge: Schenkman, 1977); Harold Wolman, *The Politics of Federal Housing* (New York: Dodd Mead and Co., 1971); Chester W. Hartman, *Housing and Social Policy* (Englewood Cliffs, N.J.: Prentice-Hall, 1975); Raymond Struyk, *A New System for Public Housing: Salvaging a National Resource* (Washington, D.C.: The Urban Institute, 1980); R. Allen Hays, *The Federal Government and Urban Housing* (New York: State University of New York Press, 1985); R. Allen Hays, ed., *Ownership, Control, and the Future of Housing Policy* (Westport, Conn.: Greenwood Press, 1993); J. Paul Mitchell, ed., *Federal Housing Policy and Programs: Past and Present* (New Brunswick, N.J.: Center for Urban Policy Research Press, 1985); and Rachel Bratt, *Rebuilding a Low-Income Housing Policy* (Philadelphia: Temple University Press, 1989). Books that examine conditions in individual places from the residents' perspectives include those by Rainwater and Cooper, as well as Jay McLeod, *Ain't No Makin' It: Leveled Aspirations in a Low-Income Neighborhood* (Boulder, Colo.: Westview Press, 1987); Jane Roessner, *A Decent Place to Live* (Boston: Northeastern University Press, 2000); David T. Whitaker, *Cabrini Green in Words and Pictures* (Chicago: W3, 2000); and Sudhir Alladi Venkatesh, *American Project* (Cambridge, Mass.: Harvard University Press,

2000). Compelling accounts by journalists of "life in the projects" include Alex Kotlowitz, *There Are No Children Here* (New York: Doubleday, 1991); and Daniel Coyle, *Hardball: A Season in the Projects* (New York: Putnam's, 1993).

6. On St. Louis, see Rainwater, *Behind Ghetto Walls;* Eugene Meehan, *Public Housing Policy: Myth versus Reality* (New Brunswick, N.J.: Center for Urban Policy Research, 1975); and Meehan, *The Quality of Federal Policymaking: Programmed Failure in Public Housing* (Columbia: University of Missouri Press, 1979); as well as works by Roger Montgomery and others. Books on Chicago's public housing include Devereux Bowly, *The Poorhouse: Subsidized Housing in Chicago, 1895–1976* (Carbondale: Southern Illinois University Press, 1978); Arnold Hirsch, *Making the Second Ghetto: Race and Housing in Chicago, 1940–1960* (Cambridge: Cambridge University Press, 1983); Martin Meyerson and Edward Banfield, *Politics, Planning, and the Public Interest: The Case of Public Housing in Chicago* (Glencoe, Ill.: The Free Press, 1955); William Moore, *The Vertical Ghetto: Everyday Life in an Urban Project* (New York: Random House, 1969); Gerald Suttles, *The Social Order of the Slum* (Chicago: University of Chicago Press, 1968) [a book that addresses public housing's neighborhood relationships]; Nicholas Lemann, *The Promised Land: The Great Black Migration and How It Changed America* (New York: Knopf, 1991). See also the books by Kotlowitz, Venkatesh, Whitaker, and Coyle. On Philadelphia, see John Bauman's *Public Housing, Race, and Renewal: Urban Planning in Philadelphia, 1920–1974* (Philadelphia: Temple University Press, 1987). On Boston, see Lawrence J. Vale, *From the Puritans to the Projects: Public Housing and Public Neighbors* (Cambridge, Mass.: Harvard University Press, 2000). Peter Marcuse is at work on a history of the New York City Housing Authority and has already published several incisive articles on the subject. Aspects of New York public housing have also been extensively discussed by Richard Plunz, *A History of Housing in New York City: Dwelling Type and Social Change in the American Metropolis* (New York: Columbia University Press, 1990), among many others. See also Mathew A. Thall, "Design Visions and New Missions: The Origins of High-Rise Public Housing in the United States" (unpublished Master in City Planning thesis, Massachusetts Institute of Technology, 1975); and Katherine Bristol, "Beyond the Pruitt-Igoe Myth: The Development of American Highrise Public Housing, 1950–1970" (unpublished Ph.D. dissertation, University of California, Berkeley, 1991). These last two works both deal with several cities.

7. See, for example, William Peterman, "Resident Management and Other Approaches to Tenant Control of Public Housing," in *Ownership, Control, and the Future of Housing Policy,* ed. R. A. Hays (Westport, Conn.: Greenwood, 1993); Langley Keyes, *Strategies and Saints* (Washington, D.C.: The Urban Institute, 1992); Sandra

Newman and Ann Schnare, *Subsidizing Shelter: The Relationship between Welfare and Housing Assistance* (Washington, D.C.: The Urban Institute, 1988); Michael Schill, "Privatizing Federal Low Income Assistance: The Case of Public Housing," *Cornell Law Review,* 75, 4 (May 1990); and Anthony Downs, *New Visions for Metropolitan America* (Washington, D.C.: Brookings Institution, 1994).

CREDITS

Fig. 1.1   U.S. Department of Housing and Urban Development, *A Vision for Change: The Story of HUD's Transformation* (Washington, D.C.: HUD, 2000), p. 89.

Fig. 1.2   U.S. Department of Housing and Urban Development, *A Promise Being Fulfilled: The Transformation of America's Public Housing* (Washington, D.C.: HUD, July 2000), pp. 16–17.

Fig. 1.3   Boston Housing Authority; U.S. Bureau of the Census, *Historical Statistics of the United States, Colonial Times to 1970, Bicentennial Edition, Part 1* (Washington, D.C., 1975), pp. 639–642; and U.S. Bureau of the Census, *Statistical Abstract of the United States: 1989* (Washington, D.C., 1989), p. 699.

Figs. 1.4, 5.2   Compiled from Boston Housing Authority data.

Figs. 1.5, 1.6   Boston Housing Authority; U.S. Census, 1950.

Figs. 1.7, 2.1, 2.5, 2.11, 2.12, 2.14, 3.1, 3.8, 4.1, 4.5, 4.6, 4.7, 4.9, 4.16   Boston Housing Authority.

Fig. 1.8   U.S. Census, 1990.

Fig. 2.2   Henry McIntyre map of 1852. Courtesy of the Norman B. Leventhal Map Collection, Mapping Boston Foundation, Inc.

Figs. 2.3, 2.4   Massachusetts State Board of Housing.

Figs. 2.6, 2.7, 2.8, 2.9, 2.10, 2.15, 2.16   Boston Housing Authority; photographs provided by the Bostonian Society.

Figs. 2.13, 4.4   Boston Housing Authority, 1949 Annual Report.

Fig. 2.17   Derived from U.S. Census data.

Figs. 2.18, 5.5, 5.7   Boston City Directories and Boston Police Lists.

Figs. 2.19, 2.22, 2.24, 2.25, 2.26–2.27, 2.28, 2.29–2.30, 2.33, 3.15, 3.16, 3.18–3.20, 3.21–3.23, 3.24, 3.25, 3.26, 4.15, 4.17, 4.18, 4.19, 4.21–4.22, 4.23, 4.24, 4.25   Author's photographs.

Fig. 2.20   Boston Housing Authority archives.

Figs. 2.21, 4.13, 4.14   Stephen E. Tise, AIA. Reprinted with permission.

Figs. 2.23, 2.34   ICON architecture. Reprinted with permission.

Fig. 2.31   *Boston Herald;* photograph by George Martell. Reprinted with permission of the *Boston Herald.*

Fig. 2.32   *Boston Globe;* photograph by Mark Wilson. Republished with permission of Globe Newspaper Company, Inc., from the May 23, 2000, issue of the *Boston Globe,* © 2000.

Fig. 2.35   Holmes and Edwards, Inc., Architects.

Figs. 3.2, 3.3, 4.2   Olmsted archives. Courtesy of the National Park Service, Frederick Law Olmsted National Historic Site.

Figs. 3.4, 3.11   Gerald Gamm, *Urban Exodus: Why the Jews Left Boston and the Catholics Stayed* (Cambridge, Mass.: Harvard University Press, 1999), map 1, p. 12; map 10, p. 47.

Fig. 3.5   Boston Housing Authority, 1949 Annual Report.

Fig. 3.6   Frank Cheney and Anthony Sammarco, *Boston in Motion;* photograph from the collection of Kevin T. Farrell.

Fig. 3.7   Boston Redevelopment Authority.

Fig. 3.9   Personal files of Rachel Bratt.

Fig. 3.10   *Boston Globe.* Reprinted courtesy of the *Boston Globe.*

Fig. 3.12   Compiled by author.

Fig. 3.13   Boston Redevelopment Authority, *A Demonstration Program to Arrest Housing Abandonment in the Mattapan Section of the City of Boston* (March 1973), map 3.

Fig. 3.14   Carr, Lynch, and Sandell, Inc. Reprinted with permission.

Fig. 3.17   Adapted by Lisa Makuku from Boston Redevelopment Authority map.

Fig. 4.3   Bromley Atlas of Brighton, 1925.

Fig. 4.8   Boston Housing Authority, Halberstadt Photographs.

Fig. 4.10   Josephine Murphy. Reprinted with permission.

Fig. 4.11   Wallace, Floyd, Ellenzweig, Moore, Inc. *Recommendations of the Monastery Hill Task Force.* Prepared for the Boston Redevelopment Authority, October 1979. Reprinted with permission.

Fig. 4.12   Adapted from material supplied by Stephen E. Tise, AIA.

Fig. 4.20   Boston Housing Authority; photograph by Bob Hale.

Fig. 5.1   U.S. Census, 1980.

Fig. 5.3   Assembled from U.S. census data.

Figs. 5.4, 5.6   Boston Redevelopment Authority; U.S. Census, 1950; Boston City Directories and Boston Police Lists.

INDEX